James Hudson Taylor

China's Millions

James Hudson Taylor

China's Millions

ISBN/EAN: 9783743346543

Manufactured in Europe, USA, Canada, Australia, Japa

Cover: Foto ©ninafisch / pixelio.de

Manufactured and distributed by brebook publishing software (www.brebook.com)

James Hudson Taylor

China's Millions

CHINA INLAND MISSION.

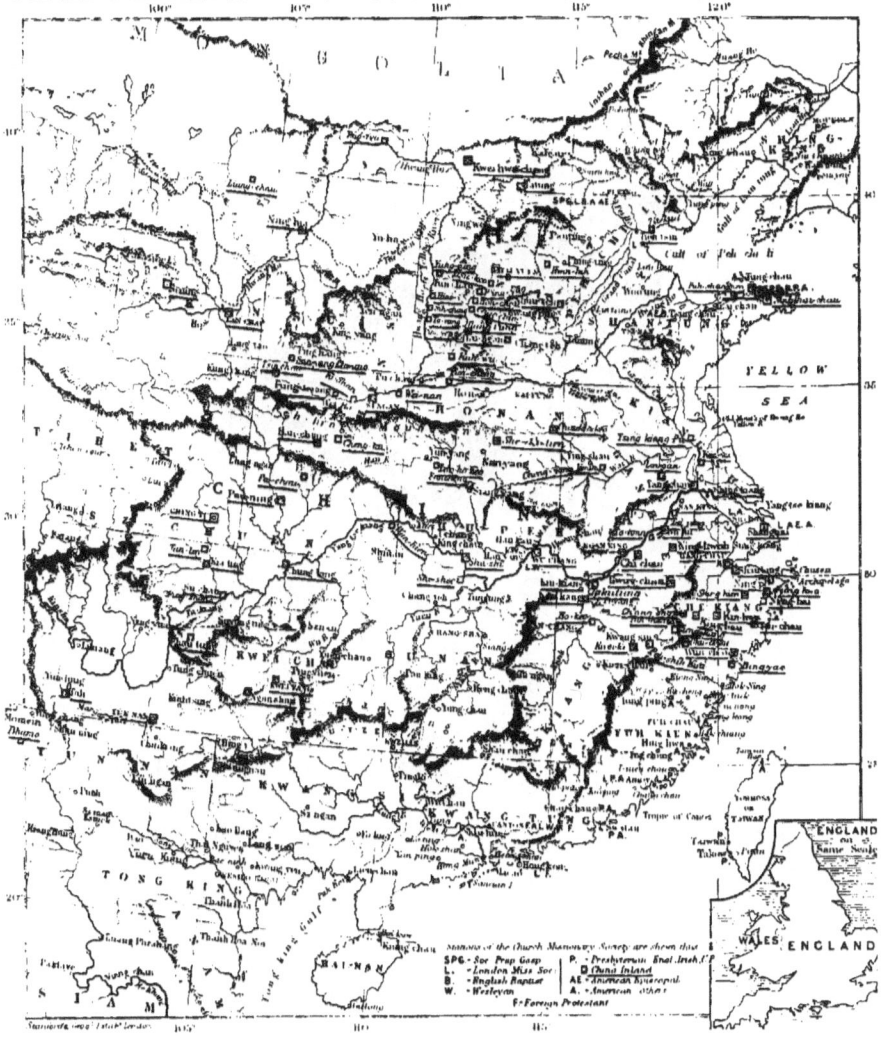

EDITED BY

J. HUDSON TAYLOR, M.R.C.S., F.R.G.S.

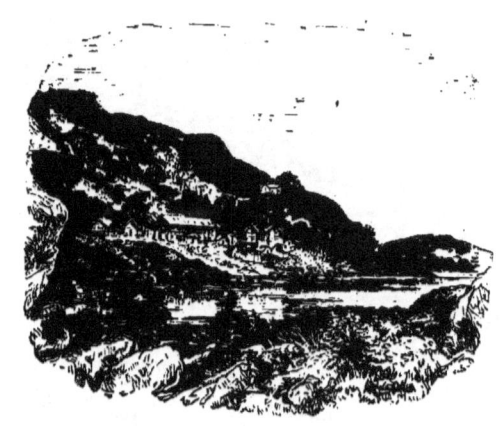

1890.

LONDON :

MORGAN AND SCOTT, 12, PATERNOSTER BUILDINGS, E.C.

CHINA INLAND MISSION, 4, PYRLAND ROAD, N.

HAZELL, WATSON, AND VINEY, LD.,
PRINTERS,
LONDON AND AYLESBURY.

Index.

A

	PAGE
"According to their Ability"	64
Accounts, Abstract of, for 1889	i-iv, 103
ANNIVERSARY MEETINGS, THE	83-99

AFTERNOON MEETING—

Address by Geo. Williams, Esq. (Chairman)	83
Letter from Mr. Hudson Taylor, read by T. Howard, Esq.	83
Address by B. Broomhall (Secretary)	85
,, Mrs. Hudson Taylor	85
,, Mr. Geo. Andrew	86
,, Mrs. Parker	88
,, Rev. A. T. Pierson, D.D.	88

EVENING MEETING—

Address by J. E. Mathieson, Esq. (Chairman)	90
,, Theodore Howard, Esq (Home Director)	91
,, Colonel J. F. Morton	91
,, Rev. E. Pearse	92
,, Rev. A. T. Pierson, D.D.	93
,, Rev. J. H. Horsburgh	95
,, Miss F. Campbell	98
,, Mr. Geo. Parker	99
,, Mrs. Geo. Parker	99
Annual Meetings, Announcement of	68

APPEALS FROM THE SHANGHAI GENERAL CONFERENCE—

For Ordained Missionaries for China	129
,, Lay Missionaries	110
,, One Thousand Men	111
To the Christian Women of Protestant Countries	121

ARRIVALS FROM CHINA—

Pearse, Mr. and Mrs. and two children	54
Parker, Mr and Mrs. and children	54
Crewdson, Miss R.	54
Wood, Mr. and Mrs.	114
Broomhall, Miss...	114
Seed, Miss	114
Ewing, Mr. and Mrs. A. Orr	168
Burnett, Mr. and Mrs.	168
Cheney, Mrs.	168
Judd, Miss H.	168
Arrival in China, Rev. C. Parsons	103
At the Front—Where are the Helpers?	150
Australasia, Mr. Hudson Taylor's visit to	158

B

Baptisms, etc. (see Stations, News from the)	
Blessed Prosperity, Meditations on Psalm I.	41, 55, 69
Boyd, Extracts from Last Letters of Miss Fanny	148
Breaking New Ground (S. KIANG-SI)	165
Bright Side and the Dark, The	136
British Mercantile Communities, The	163

C

	PAGE
Chefoo, Native Schools in	77
Cheng-ku, Baptisms at	29, 134
Cheng-yang-kwan, More about the First Convert in	8
Chen-tu, Progress at	43
China and the Language of China	162
China, Experiences of Life in	30
China, Fertility and Prosperity of	163
"China's Sorrow"	162
Chinese, The Attitude of towards Innovations	163
C.I.M. List of Missionaries	169
,, Stations and Missionaries of the	45
,, Statistics, January, 1890	101
Christians in Prison at Chu-ki	100, 112

D

DEPARTURES FOR CHINA OF MISSIONARIES AND PROBATIONERS—

Hunter, Rev. Geo., M.A., and Mrs.	14	Lowenadler, Miss	142
Evans, A. F.	14	Hol, Miss	142
Sharp, F.	14	Nicss, Miss	142
Willett, T.G.	14	Reid, Miss F. M.	156
Britton, Miss (returning)	26	Cundall, Miss	155
Forster, Miss	26	Broomhall, Marshall, B.A.	156
Legerton, Miss	26	Cormack, J. G.	156
Leggat, Miss	26	Goodall, T.	156
Burt, Miss	26	Ridley, H. F.	156
Baller, Mr. and Mrs. (returning)	26	Talbot, Jno.	156
Todd, Miss	26	Williams, J.E., M.R.C.S.	156
Taylor, F. Howard, M.D., F.R.C.S. E.	26	Berg, A.	156
		Hahne, A.	156
		Gjerde, S.	156
Graham, Jno.	26	Taylor, Mrs. Hudson (returning)	168
McConnell, Geo.	26	Marler, Miss	168
Carter, Jno.	26	Tanner, Miss	168
Tremberth, Wm.	26	Fowle, Miss	168
Hattrem, Miss	26	Ohlson, Em.	168
Fairbank, Miss	39	Carlson, N.	168
Miller, Miss	39	Bender, Jos.	168
Ross, Miss	39	Baumer, Miss	168
Power, Miss	39	Schmitgen, Miss	168
Scott, Misses (2)	39	Thor, A. F.	168
Kay, Miss	39	Duff, J. E.	168
McBrier, E. M.	39	Logerquist, A. W.	168
Stevens, C J.	39	Marshall, G.	168
Randall, R.	39	Taylor, W.	168
Pruen, Mrs.	142	Turner, Miss E. (returning)	168
Groves, Miss C. (returning)	142	Pook, Miss	168
Lang, Miss A. M.	142	Porter, Miss	168
Querry, Miss	142	May, Miss	168
Basnett, Miss	142	Rayer, Miss	168
Roberts, Miss	142	Sauzé, Miss	168
Stedman, Miss	142	Foucar, H. E.	168
Prytz, Miss	142	Gilmer, W. T.	168
Janzon, Miss	142	Prentice, Geo.	168
Dunn, The Last Days of Miss Annie			115

INDEX.

E
	PAGE
Eclipse, An	164

F
	PAGE
Feast of Lanterns, The	71
Floods in China, The	159
Foreign Communities in China, The	164

G
	PAGE
GAN-HWUY, A visit to scattered converts in	57
" Blessing in North	8
" Ploughing and Seed-sowing in	154
Gan-ren, The little flock at	62
Gan-shun, Baptisms at	155
Good and Faithful Servant, A (Miss F. Boyd)	148

H
	PAGE
Han-ch'ung, Converts examined at	4
" Good Tidings from	133
Happy Service	31, 59
"Here am I, send me" (Poetry)	76
Ho-k'eo, Baptisms at	136
HO-NAN, Itinerant work in	154
" Prepared Hearts in	51
HU-NAN, An Evangelistic Journey in	49
" On the Borders of	79

I
	PAGE
Idolatry	74
"I never heard before" (Lines for the Young)	153
IN MEMORIAM—	
Boyd, Miss Fanny	132
Carter, Jno.	147
Dunn, Miss	111
Racey, J. H.	78
Randall, R.	146
Sharp, F.	132, 146
Souter, Wm.	111
Instant in Season—Work in S. SHAN-SI	152
Items of Interest (J. W. Stevenson)	3, 17, 28, 43, 56, 99, 111, 119, 132, 145, 159
" " (J. H. Taylor)	100
I-yang, How the City was opened to the Gospel	136

J
	PAGE
Joy of being on China's soil, The	137

K
	PAGE
Kao yiu, Tidings from	49
KIANG-SI for CHRIST	9
Kwei-k'i Converts, The	60

L
	PAGE
Language of China, The	164
Lao-ho-k'eo, Experiences at	72
Life in China, Experiences of	30

M
	PAGE
Making Friends	138
Missionaries of C. I. M., List of	169
MISSIONARIES, CORRESPONDENCE OF, ETC.	
Adam, Jas.	128, 155
Bardsley, Miss	128
Beauchamp, M.	13, 100
Begg, T. D.	81
Belcher, W. T.	36
Beynon, W. T.	37
Black, Miss M.	12, 81, 114
Bland, A.	73, 113, 127, 150, 160
Botham, T. E. S.	24, 79, 150
Botham, Mrs.	65
Boyd, Miss	82, 148, 149
Bridge, A. H.	20, 37, 113
Brock, John	8
Brown, G. G.	61
Brown, Miss M. G.	12, 36, 113
Buchan, Miss	81
Burnett, W. E.	37, 65, 152
Carpenter, Miss S.	148
Cassels, W. W.	12, 127
Chilton, Miss	51
Clark, Miss C. P.	59
Clarke, S. R.	81, 156
Clarke, Mrs. S. R.	13
Cooper, W.	67
Cooper, Mrs. W.	54
Coulthard, J. J.	3, 38, 66
Coulthard, Mrs.	38
Culverwell, Miss E.	127, 168
Culverwell, Miss F. H.	54, 168
Curnow, J. O.	67
Darroch, John	81
Doggett, Miss	81
Donald, J. S.	122
Douthwaite, Dr.	53, 80
Drysdale, I. F.	8, 168
Easton, G. F.	79
Edwards, Dr.	24, 139
Elliston, Mrs.	65, 141
Ellis, Miss C.	25
Ellis, Miss F.	82
Ewing, A.	71
Eyres, Thos.	39
Faers, A. H.	12, 54
Fitzsimons, Miss C.	9, 138
Forth, Miss	25
Gardiner, Miss J.	136, 156
Gates, Miss C.	13
Gibson, Miss A.	26, 68, 136
Gillham, Miss A.	124
Grabham, Miss	136
Grierson, R.	14, 63
Griffith, M. L.	156
Guex, Miss	82, 137
Guinness, Miss	38
Hainge, Miss	67
Harding, Miss	34
Heal, J. A.	82
Hibberd, Miss	114
Hogg, Chas. F.	100
Horne, W. S.	165
Horobin, C.	24, 36, 53
Horsburgh, Miss	13
Hoste, D. E.	25, 37, 65
Hunt, H. W.	3, 100, 126, 165
Hunt, Mrs. H. W.	65
Huntley, A. H.	29, 79, 134
I'Anson, C. S.	25
Jakobsen, Miss	80, 141
Johnson, Miss	4, 133, 164, 166
Judd, C. H.	25, 38
Kay, Duncan	135
Kentfield, Miss	49
Kinahan, Miss	140
King, George	66, 74
King, Mrs. G.	72
Kolkenbeck, Miss	161
Lachlan, H. N.	13, 154
Laughton, Wm.	12, 113, 150
Laughton, Mrs.	12
Lawson, Mrs.	79
Littler, Miss C.	14
Lutley, A.	25, 141
MacGregor, H. N.	67
Mackintosh, Miss	14, 142
Marchbank, Miss	128
McFarlane, Miss	18
McKee, Stewart	37
McKenzie, Miss H.	62
McNair, M.	49
Meadows, Jas.	19, 118
Meikle, J.	26
Miles, Miss	31
Mills, D. J.	54, 154, 168
Muir, Miss G.	12, 100, 140
Munro, Miss	59, 114, 125
Ord, Miss	18, 26, 169
Owen, R. Gray	12, 34, 43, 114, 120, 153
Parry, Dr.	6, 168
Peat, W. G.	152
Polhill-Turner, A. T.	18, 81
Polhill-Turner, C. H.	24, 140
Pruen, Dr. W.	54, 114
Pruen, Mrs.	54
Ramsay, Miss I. W.	114
Randle, Dr.	156
Redfern, F. A.	113
Ririe, B.	12
Rudland, W. D.	33, 119
Sanderson, Miss	12
Saunders, A. R.	23, 25, 36, 126
Say, Miss	26, 60, 156
Scott, Miss M. E.	32
Simpson, Jas.	66, 122, 141
Simpson, Mrs.	38, 52, 80
Smalley, Miss R. L.	140
Smith, Stanley P.	37, 141
Steven, F.	67
Stevenson, O.	142
Stewart, D.	53
Stooke, J. A.	38, 76
Taylor, Dr. Howard	114, 142
Taylor, H. Hudson	141
Taylor, Mrs. H. H.	12, 80
Thirgood, Miss	156
Thompson, Mrs. D.	14, 39
Thorne, S. T.	67
Tomalin, E.	66
Tomkinson, E.	142
Turner, Miss H.	14, 68
Vanstone, T. G.	126
Webb, Miss E.	5
Webb, Miss J.	26
Wellwood, R.	25, 44, 127
Whitchurch, Miss	65
Williams, E. O.	30, 66, 141
Williams, Miss F. M.	65
Williamson, J.	68
Windsor, T.	13, 81, 127
Wood, F. M.	57
Wright, A.	82, 119
Missionary Methods	36

N
	PAGE
Nan-k'ang Fu, Riot in	18
" Back at	34
New Year, The	1
Niog-kwoh Fu, Conference at	7

O
	PAGE
"O-mi-t'o Fuh" (Lines for the Young)	34
Opium Patients, Visiting old	77
"Other Sheep I have" (Poetry)	168

P
	PAGE
Persecutor Saved and Taken Home, A	118
Poetry—	
"Here am I, send me"	76
"I never heard before"	153

INDEX.

	PAGE
"JEHOVAH SHAMMAH"—Lines written in New Mission House	112
"Other Sheep I have"	168
"Whatsoever"	145
Power over all the Power of the Enemy	30
Po-yang Lake, Visiting round the	124
Prayer, A Heathen's Testimony to the Power of	122
"Praise Him all the Time"	125
Preparation for Work	20
Private Letter, Extract from	128
Progress	27

PROVINCES, THE WORK IN THE—
- Cheh-kiang   3, 14, 18, 19, 33, 39, 82, 100, 108, 116, 119, 128, 159
- Chih-li   37, 52, 80, 104, 113, 141, 156
- Gan-hwuy   7, 8, 13, 26, 28, 39, 54, 81, 106, 114, 142, 154, 159, 168
- Ho-nan   12, 17, 28, 30, 38, 51, 53, 80, 100, 105, 141, 154, 167
- Hu-nan   49, 79, 107
- Hu-peh   13, 72, 81, 106, 114
- Kan-suh   3, 12, 24, 36, 53, 82, 100, 103, 113, 126, 140, 150, 165
- Kiang-si   9, 14, 17, 18, 26, 28, 34, 43, 81, 107, 114, 124, 125, 128, 136, 137, 138, 142, 156, 159, 165, 169
- Kiang-su   13, 26, 39, 49, 81, 107, 156, 161
- Kwei-chau   13, 81, 86, 107, 114, 127, 155, 156
- Shan-si   3, 23, 25, 31, 37, 43, 53, 71, 77, 80, 103, 113, 126, 135, 141, 152
- Shan-tung   3, 12, 25, 38, 53, 76, 77, 80, 104, 114, 156
- Shen-si   3, 4, 29, 73, 79, 103, 113, 127, 133, 134, 150, 164, 166
- Sï-ch'uen   5, 12, 17, 25, 30, 39, 43, 44, 54, 81, 100, 105, 113, 114, 120, 127, 141, 153, 162, 167
- Yun-nan   107, 112, 126, 142, 162

R

Report for the Year 1889	101
" of the Six Northern Provinces	103
" " Four Central Provinces	105
" " Five more Southerly Provinces	107
Roman Catholic Missions in China, Table of	40

S

Schofield Memorial Hospital Chapel, T'ai-yuen	51
Shanghai General Conference, The	10
" " Appeals (see under Appeals)	
" " Opening Sermon	129, 143
" " What shall be the Result of	59
Shanghai Prayer Meeting, Testimonies at the	112
SHAN-SI, Village Work in North	152
" Work in South	152
Shantung Promontory, A Visit to the	76
Shao-hing and its Outstations	19
SHEN-SI, Evangelistic Journey in	73
" Evangelising in the Si-gan Plain	150, 160
(For Sketch Map to trace these two journeys see p. 151.)	
SI-CH'UEN, A Family Itineration in	120
" Visiting Villages in	44
" and YUN-NAN	163
Stations and Missionaries of the China Inland Mission	45

STATIONS, NEWS FROM THE—

Bhamo	3, 28, 43, 107
Bing-yae	132
Chau-kia-k'eo	38, 43, 51, 100, 105, 145, 154, 167
Chau-tung Fu	107, 112
Chefoo	12, 38, 53, 77, 80, 104, 114, 156
Cheng-ku	18, 29, 103, 132, 134
Cheng-yang-kwan	3, 8, 28
Chen-tu	3, 12, 28, 43, 54, 105, 114, 120, 153, 159, 167
Ch'i-chau	106
Chinkiang	107, 116
Chu-chau	82, 120, 132
Chung-k'ing	12, 17, 26, 43, 54, 106, 114, 119, 132

Chu-sien-chen	53
Fan-ch'eng	13, 43, 81, 106, 114
Feng-tsiang Fu	3, 79, 103, 113, 127, 150
Fuh-shan	13
Fung-hwa	3, 18, 29, 119
Gan-k'ing	13, 17, 26, 43, 54, 106, 112, 114, 142, 159
Gan-ren	107, 119
Gan-shun Fu	28, 107, 128, 145, 155
Han-chung	3, 4, 79, 103, 132, 133, 164, 166
Hankow	106
Hiao-i	104, 141, 145
Hoh-chau	3, 25, 80, 104, 141
Ho-k'eo	119, 136
Hung-t'ueg	3, 25, 37, 104, 126
Hwuy-chau	18, 28, 43, 81
Hwuy-k'ing	53
Hwuy-luh	43, 80, 104, 141
I-ch'ang	3, 106
I-yang	26, 136, 156
Kao-yiu	17, 49, 107
Kia-ting	12, 106
Kin-hwa	120
Kiu-chau	14, 39, 82
Kiukiang	107
Ku-chen	81, 99
K'ih-tsing Fu	107, 119, 142
K'uh-wu	104, 132, 135
Kwang-feng	13, 107, 138
Kwang-yuen	17, 105, 127, 167
Kwan-hien	17, 105
Kwei-hwa-ch'eng	17, 37, 53, 71, 104
Kwei-k'i	26, 43, 107, 114, 119, 125, 156
Kwei-yang	3, 13, 35, 43, 81, 86, 107, 114, 119, 127, 156
Lan-chau	12, 36, 100, 103, 113, 140
Lao-ho-k'eo	72, 99, 106
Liang-chau	12, 103, 113, 150
Lu-ch'eng	37, 104, 141
Lu-chen Fu	106
Luh-gan	168
Nan-k'ang	17, 18, 25, 28, 34, 107, 167
Ning-hai (SHAN-TUNG)	3, 25, 28, 38, 105
Ning-hsia	3, 18, 24, 36, 53, 103, 111
Ning-kwoh	3, 6, 28, 39
Pa-chau	13, 81, 106
Pao-ning	12, 30, 39, 100, 106, 113, 127, 141
Pao-t'eo	37, 104, 152
Pch-shih-kiai	14
P'ing-yang	104, 127, 132
P'ing-yao	77, 104, 113, 119, 152
Shanghai	39, 100, 107, 111
Shao-hing	17, 18, 19, 118
Sha-shï	106
She-k'i-tien	12, 18, 38, 80, 105, 141
Shih-sheo	79, 106
Shun-teh Fu	104, 113, 156
Si-gan Plain	29, 73, 150, 160
Sih-chau	3, 25, 104
Sin-ch'ang	82, 119
Si-ning	24, 103, 140
Sui-fu (Su-chau)	25, 44, 106, 127
T'ai-chau	33, 111, 112, 119, 128, 132
T'ai-yuen	23, 25, 51, 104, 139, 141
Ta-li Fu	107
Ta-ning	28, 31, 104, 113
Tan-lin	3, 5, 6, 105, 106
Ta-t'ung	3, 25, 37, 104
Tientsin	3, 104
Ts'in-chau	3, 24, 82, 99, 100, 103, 126, 140, 145, 159, 165
Ts'ing-kiang-p'u	132
T'ung-shin	104
Wan-hien	104
Wu-ch'ang	106
Wu-hu	29
Wun-chau	3, 14, 28, 119, 128, 132
Yang-chau	13, 26, 81, 107, 156, 161
Yang-k'eo	128

	PAGE
Yuen-ch'eng	104
Yuh-shan... ... ... 9, 14, 81, 119, 132, 137,	142
Yun-nan Fu 107, 132,	142
Statistics of the China Inland Mission	101
Sweden, A Visit to (J. H. Taylor)	2

T

T'ai-chau, Baptisms at	119
,, Tidings from	33
T'ai-yuen, The Men's Bible-class in	23
,, Converts	139
Tan-lin Hien, Visit to	5
,, Progress in	6
Taylor, J. Hudson, Articles, etc. by—	
Blessed Prosperity 41, 55,	69
Opening Sermon, Shanghai Conference ... 129,	143
Progress	27
"To Every Creature" 15,	43
Visit to Australasia (Extracts from Letters) ...	158
Testimony, A Frequent	79
Tidings from Scattered Workers, 12, 24, 36, 53, 64, 79, 100,	
113, 126, 140, 156,	166

	PAGE
"To Every Creature"	15, 43
Ts'en, Letter from the Evangelist (K'vei-yang Fu) ...	35
Ts'in-chau, Native Jewels in...	7
,, Six Months' Work at	165
Ts'u, The Story of Mr.	122
Two Terribly Sad Cases	161

V

Villagers of North China	24
Visit, An Interesting (CHIH-LI)	52
Visiting a Fresh Village	135

W

"Whatsoever" (Poetry)	145
"What wilt Thou?"	157
Wun-chau, God's Work at	63

Y

Yung-k'ang District, The Work of God in ...	110
YUN-NAN, A Year's Work in	126
Young, Pieces for the	34, 153

List of Illustrations.

	PAGE
The Old French Consulate on the Tientsin River	7
Entrance to a Gentleman's House in Lan-chau	11
Eastern Building of the French Legation at Peking	21
Villagers of North China (from Photograph)	24
Pavilion for Picnics at Wan-show Shan, Peking	33
Shaven Monk, and Si-ch'uen Coolies carrying Tea (Sketches)	34, 35
Schofield Memorial Chapel at T'ai-yuen Fu (from Photograph)	50
Passenger Boat and Gunboat, Kiang-su	52
Entrance to the I-chang Gorge of the Yang-tse River	57
Group of Kwei-k'i Christians, Kiang-si (from Photograph)	61
Lantern Procession	71
Itinerant Needlewomen	75
A Sampan	108
Part of New C.I.M. Premises at Shanghai: A Social Reunion of the General Conference (from a Photograph)	121
The Collapsed Staging, Missionary Conference, Shanghai (from a Photograph)	124
Tung-ling Rapid on the Yang-tse River	135
T'ai-yuen Converts (from a Photograph)	139
Memorial Portal	147
River Boats	149
Sketch Map, Western Half of the Si-gan Plain, Shen-si	151
Si-ch'uen Grandmother and Grandson (Sketch)	153
The Niu-kan Gorge, Yang-tse-kiang	163
On the Street	167

Frontispiece.

Map of China, showing the Stations of the C. I. M.

CHINA'S MILLIONS.

The New Year.

"I will go in the strength of the Lord God"—Ps. lxxi. 16.

ONE thousand eight hundred and ninety! Thoughtless indeed should we be if we could enter upon the last ten years of this century without a solemn feeling of awe. It has been a wonderful century, the most wonderful on record. Progress in many ways has been very rapid, and the world seems going on at an almost maddening rate. Steam has superseded the slow and cumbrous posting system; but even steam is not quick enough for our correspondence, for which the telegraph and the telephone are increasingly in request. Parts of the world that were unknown at the beginning of the century are now linked to us by the electric cable. Roman Catholic countries of Europe and long closed heathen empires, like India and China, have been marvellously opened to the missionary. But Satan still reigns; the god of this world is not dethroned. Increasing knowledge of science has increased the fearful power of our weapons of destruction, and the armed millions of Continental Europe indicate but too plainly that man fears man no less, and loves man no more, than when the century commenced.

Who can foresee the events and the changes which a few years may now bring should our LORD delay His coming? We truly live in perilous times, whether we look at things political or things religious. Never was there a time in which it was more important to walk with GOD and to abide in the secret place of the MOST HIGH, nor in which it was so urgent to be up and doing; for our MASTER is at the door, while the Church is only now beginning to wake up to the realisation that the work of evangelisation for which she was left in the world is yet but barely commenced.

Let us enter the New Year in the spirit of him who in time of great difficulty and danger begins the 71st Psalm with "In Thee, O Lord, do I put my trust; let me never be put to confusion," and determined (in v. 16), "I will go in the strength of the LORD GOD: I will make mention of Thy righteousness, even of Thine only."

While in the great day of atonement the Israel of GOD recognised their own sin put away and forgiven through the acceptance of the sin-offering, their perfect acceptance in virtue of the burnt-offering, and their fellowship with GOD in the peace-offering, yet it was pleasing to Him that morning by morning and evening by evening a lamb for a burnt-offering should be a constant reminder of the sacrifices of that great day, and that offerings more numerous and full should be presented at the beginning of each month, and at the special feasts of the year. In like manner shall not we, who are already CHRIST'S, at this important epoch remind ourselves afresh of our acceptance in and through Him, and of our privilege to present ourselves as living sacrifices to Him, whose we are, and whom alone we can rightly serve? In the measure in which we truly recognise Him as our LORD and ourselves as His possession will it be easy to "put our trust" in Him. Do not we all take the charge of those things that we purchase? If the shepherd purchase a flock of sheep, does he not intend to provide for and take care of them? And the more they cost the more carefully will he tend them. Our good SHEPHERD has paid for us an infinite price, and we are not merely the sheep of His pasture and the subjects of His Kingdom, but are members of that Church which is the bride whom he loves. Well may we "put our trust" in Him who loves us with love so unique and unparalleled!

JANUARY, 1890.

Then having afresh " put our trust " in Him, let us further " go in the strength of the LORD GOD," thankful for all our weakness and insufficiency that His strength and sufficiency may have the fuller scope. We need never be afraid to recognise our own incompetence, and we have no need to minimise or hide from ourselves the magnitude of the difficulties that beset our path ; exulting faith will go in the strength of the LORD, singing : "If GOD be for us, who can be against us ?" As Abraham deliberately considered (revised version, Rom. iv.) the natural impossibilities of his having the promised seed, and in face of these difficulties waxed strong in faith, giving glory to GOD, so may we in the strength of the LORD meet each circumstance as it arises, expecting to find GOD glorified and His will accomplished.

The rest of faith, however, is not the rest of apathy or inaction ; for missions in general, and for the China Inland Mission in particular, we would earnestly crave the prayers of our readers. The more GOD enlarges the work, the more earnestly and constantly will the enemy attempt to hinder and mar. Pray, beloved friends, that the wisdom that is profitable to direct and all needed grace may be given to those who have the guidance of the Mission at home and abroad ; that GOD will preserve the dear missionaries in health of body and in full spiritual vigour; that He will bless all the native converts with increasing light and spirituality, delivering them from the snare of the fowler, and strengthening the persecuted and tried. Pray that He will speedily open the as yet unopened parts of the empire to resident missionary work, and that He will speedily thrust forth large bands of missionary evangelists *determined* to reach every family in the empire—a subject on which we hope to say more in our next. Ask that, as in previous years, the LORD will supply the ever-increasing pecuniary needs of the work, and will add to our numbers every willing skilful worker for every department of service. May He thus glorify His own great Name and encourage the faith of His people, proving again how wise and how safe it is to " put our trust in the LORD GOD and to go in His strength."

A Visit to Sweden.

IN response to a long-standing invitation, the Editor and his son, Dr. Howard Taylor, paid a visit to Sweden in November. The steamer arrived at Gothenburg on the morning of Sunday, November 3rd, and a large congregation was addressed the same evening through the interpretation of Pastor Holmgren, the Secretary of the Swedish China Mission. He had kindly come from Stockholm to meet and interpret for Mr. Taylor, and had not only arranged the whole tour, but went with the travellers, assisting in numberless ways, as well as interpreting the addresses. His soul is full of missionary fire, and his own earnest words added much to the value of the meetings.

The Monday and Tuesday were profitably spent in the same town, after which Helsingborg, Copenhagen, and Malmö were visited in turn. At Malmö the travellers divided, Dr. Howard Taylor going to the university town of Lund to address the students, and proceeding thence to Linköping, where he spoke five times on the Sunday. Mr. Hudson Taylor first had a crowded meeting at Tranas, and then proceeded to Norrköping. On Monday morning, joining his son at Linköping, he also had a meeting there, after which the following towns were visited on the way to Stockholm : Nässjö, Jönköping, Skara, Lidköping, Mariestad, Christinehamn, Carlstad, Kumla, Orebro, and Linde.

In Stockholm, which was reached on the 20th, the party were kindly met and entertained by the committee of the Swedish China Mission, and the first meeting was held that night in the large church of the court chaplain, Pastor Beskow. This church was built after the pattern of Mr. Spurgeon's Tabernacle, and it was pleasing on a week evening to address a gathering of more than 3,500 persons on the missionary question. Full, busy days were those of the stay in Stockholm, drawing-room meetings during the day being followed by meetings in churches at night. Sunday, the 24th, was spent at Upsala, and on Monday morning a drawing-room meeting was held in English before proceeding to Gefle, Hedemora, and Christiania. In the latter city the party were met and entertained by the committee of the Norwegian China Mission, and at the meeting on Thursday night they had the pleasure of seeing two missionary sisters who were embarking immediately for England *en route* for China. Next day, beside a general meeting in the Bethlehem chapel, the theological students were addressed. Then proceeding to Christianssand, where Saturday and Sunday were spent, at an early hour on Monday morning, Dec. 2nd, the return journey was commenced.

The weather was mild and favourable ; the country beautiful even in winter ; but the kindness and Christian love shown to the visitors, and the warm interest evidently taken in missions, were both surprising and delightful. The churches and chapels are very large, and the meetings were usually crowded, hundreds patiently standing for two or three hours, though the kindness of those who were seated in exchanging places was very noticeable. Collections were generally taken for the Swedish China Mission, and the making of these collections was no easy task, but the eagerness with which many of the poor called out or pressed forward to make their little gifts was very amusing and pleasing. One dear old sailor, who did not look as though he had much to give, put in the collecting box his snuff box, snuff and all. We were told it had probably been his constant companion for the last forty years. It was made of a shell, and had a heavy silver top and lid, and sold that night for twenty crowns. At another town, a lady who had been much moved in the meeting, came to Mr. Taylor, and putting a beautiful watch into his hand, began to speak in English, but her emotion prevented her completing the sentence in that language, "It—is—for—Herren JESUS" (the LORD JESUS), and several times she repeated, " The LORD JESUS, the LORD JESUS, the dear LORD JESUS." At another place a watch was given to Mr. Holmgren. The LORD bless the loving donors; how His heart must have been gladdened!

Reviewing the month thus spent, it is impossible to be too grateful for journeying mercies. For suitable weather, for unbounded kindness, for large attendances (at least 50,000 or 60,000 must have been present at the various meetings), and for unmistakable evidence of spiritual blessing, thanks and praise are due to GOD. In Scandinavia there are surely 100 of the 1,000 additional missionary evangelists needed to carry the Gospel to every family in China.

Items of Interest.

FROM REV. J. W. STEVENSON.

SEPT. 13th.—The following 27 baptisms are reported: at Han-chung, SHEN-SI, on July 30th, 9; at Wun-chau, CHEH-KIANG, on Sept. 1, 7; and at Tan-lin, SI-CH'UEN, 11.

Oct. 4th.—Since my last I have heard of the following 23 baptisms: at Hung-t'ung, SHAN-SI, on Aug. 18th, 4; and at Sih-chau on Aug. 28th, 5; at I-chang, HU-PEH, on Sept. 14th, 1; and in CHEH-KIANG, at Yung-k'ang, on Sept. 1, 8; also at Fung-hwa on Sept. 15th, 3.

Brothers Bland and Redfern are still living in Fung-tsiang Fu, in an inn, where they are allowed to reside quietly, though they are meeting with great opposition from the officials. They have plenty of opportunities of serving the LORD in itinerating, and it is a joy to find them full of hope, notwithstanding all the difficulties of their service.

Mr. and Mrs. G. W. Clarke and Miss Dunn arrived safely on Sept. 21st, and the former left for Tien-tsin on the 26th. By to-day's mail Messrs. Selkirk and Lambert leave to take up the work in Bhamo.

Oct. 16th.—Since writing last on the 4th inst., I have heard of the following 98 baptisms:

On July 27th at Ning-hsia, KAN-SUH ... 4
,, Aug 13th ,, Ta-t'ung, SHAN-SI ... 1
,, ,, 17th ,, Chen-tu, SI-CH'UEN ... 2
,, Sept. 3rd ,, Kwei-yang, KWEI-CHAU ... 3
,, ,, 14th ,, Hung-t'ung, SHAN-SI ... 47
,, ,, 15th ,, Cheng-yang-kwan, GAN-HWUY 2
On Sept.21st ,, Hoh-chau, SHAN-SI ... 10
,, ,, 22nd ,, Ning-kwoh, GAN-HWUY ... 9
,, ,, 29th ,, Yung-k'ang, CHEH-KIANG ... 3
,, ,, 29th ,, Wun-chau CHEH-KIANG ... 11
,, Oct. 6th ,, Wun-chau outstation ... 2
Ning-hai-chau, SHAN-TUNG ... 4

Total 98

In the two first, Ning-hsia and Ta-t'ung, these are the first baptisms at the stations.

We have had heavy rains here for three weeks, the Yang-tse valley is flooded, and I fear that there will be a great deal of sickness and distress this autumn and winter. In Han-kow there are several feet of water on the streets and bund. This will delay parties going west for a time. Dr. Pruen has asked to be transferred to Kwei-yang, Mr. S. R. Clarke greatly desiring it. Mr. James has also asked to be transferred to SI-CH'UEN. Both these requests have been acceded to. Mr. James will probably open Lu-chau Fu, an important city between Chung-k'ing and Sui-fu. I am sorry to hear from Hwuy-luh that the house had to be given up. Mr. Hoddle is now living in an inn, and Mr. and Mrs. Simpson have gone to the country station. It is cheering, however, to hear of the friendliness of the people there. Our Brother Cardwell has been ill, but I am thankful to say is now recovering, though weak.

A Few Native Jewels in Ts'in-chau, Kan-suh.

FROM REV. H. W. HUNT.

"*For behold your calling, brethren, how that not many wise after the flesh, not many mighty, not many noble, are called: but God chose the foolish things of the world, that He might put to shame them that are wise; and God chose the weak things of the world, that He might put to shame the things that are strong; and the base things of the world, and the things that are despised, did God choose, yea, and the things that are not, that He might bring to nought the things that are: that no flesh should glory before God.*"—1 Cor. i. 26-29 (R. V.).

1. Mrs. Chao (No. 1).—Before conversion a timid woman, almost afraid to come to the services, and more afraid to say anything. Born again in 1886, filled with the SPIRIT in 1887. A voluntary and bold worker ever since, not only the means of bringing many women to hear the Word, but persuades some men to come also. Literally *shines* for JESUS, and gives Him her little all gladly.

2. Mrs. Chao (No. 2).—Natives are generally supposed to go mad at conversion; this woman is an exception to the rule. Most strange in her mind before she believed, and often appearing really mad during violent outbursts of temper, she completely changed when the HOLY SPIRIT enlightened her. A mind that once could not comprehend a simple idea, grasped in a wonderful manner the plan of salvation, and is now comparatively clear. This woman's prayers, though somewhat original, and her consistent life, prove the miracle that has been wrought in both soul and body. Baptised in 1888.

3. Mr. Suen.—An old blind man. Came to the services for many years. Saw himself a poor sinner and nothing at all, and JESUS CHRIST as his all in all. Bed-ridden last year; when visited declared his soul was in perfect peace. Fell asleep in JESUS in the autumn, two years after he entered the Church.

4. Mr. Chang.—Another old blind man, and a beggar withal. Having nothing, he possesses all things, and drinks in the treasures of wisdom and knowledge as much as he is able every Sabbath Day. He says he sees JESUS now, and is looking forward to the time when

blindness and poverty will be included amongst the "old things that are passed away." Baptised last year.

5. Mrs. Chang.—One of the poorest but brightest of the female converts, called to much suffering from the early months of last summer, and now has entered into rest. In the greatest pain she testified of her peace in JESUS, and during her last hours exhorted her unbelieving relatives (1) To repent, and follow the same road as she had walked ; (2) To allow her to be buried after the manner of Christians ; and (3) To have nothing to do with idolatry after her decease. We regret to say that her dying wishes were disregarded, but rejoice that idolatry and devilry can do her no harm. She is now realising the sweets of the eternity where pain and poverty are never known.

6. Mrs. Huang.—A rough diamond. Converted through meeting Mrs. Hunt during one of our journeys. Early in her Christian career in 1886 brought many women in to hear the Gospel, the first-named Mrs. Chao among the rest. Still persuades people to come on Sundays. Always answers questions at the services quickly and correctly. Her mother and two children believed soon after herself, and she is longing for her husband to be brought in. Most opposed at one time, he has now asked for baptism. Mrs. Huang's only son was called away last year, and neighbours said it was because she had followed the foreigners. But she remained steadfast, though sorely tried. She is a big-footed woman, whose home is in SI-CH'UAN, but has lived many years in KAN-SUH. Very blunt in manner, but with decision of character, and true as steel.

7. Master Huang.—Son of the last-named. A bright Christian boy, who fell sick and died early last year. He declared his belief that he was bound for glory, and his end was peace, which peace was after his death strikingly depicted on his countenance.

8. Mr. Chao.—Husband of the first in this list. One of the few Chinamen who think a great deal of their wives. Naturally dense, the SPIRIT of GOD has opened his heart and mind, and he rejoices in the wisdom obtained by the glorious Gospel. Does his best to influence other men, and maintains a consistent walk day by day.

Converts Examined at Han-ch'ung.

FROM MISS JOHNSON.

JUNE 24th.—Yesterday I attended the church meeting after the service, and had the pleasure of seeing one of the women of my class and one of my elder girls accepted for baptism. Another of my women came before the church, but her baptism is to be delayed as she needs more teaching ; one man was also accepted. Praise GOD ! To-day a third woman from my class came to me and asked if she might make application to Mr. Easton for baptism ; she had been an inquirer for two years. I spent a long while catechising her in the afternoon, and found her satisfactory ; she will perhaps come before the church next week.

June 25th.—To-day two more women from my class and the two elder girls who have not yet come before the church, came to spend the day with me. We formed a little class in the afternoon, while I carefully examined them on all the vital points, and found them all thoroughly satisfactory except *one*, the elder woman, Mrs. Lo. Although she answers well and understands, yet she is too glib of tongue, too sure of herself ; the heavenly road is so easily trod and salvation so easily obtained, that I am a little afraid. Of the other three I can truly say I have seen for many, many months evidences of a real, true change of heart. To GOD be all the glory !

July 1st.—Yesterday had a very large Sunday-school class. Such a number of fresh women and men, who are really interested. In the afternoon there was a church-meeting, when three more men, a dear boy of fourteen, a woman from my class, and the other two of my children, were received. It would have done your heart good to have heard those children answer when catechised ; it was almost too much for me. Little Chü-hsiang was asked the nature of sin, original and personal, and the question was put, "And have you sin?" Looking up with a smile, she answered, after a pause, "They are all forgiven!" Dear child ! what a change has taken place during these eighteen months ! The GOOD SHEPHERD has sought this little lamb *till He found her.*

Fung-ing answered so clearly and bravely that there was no mistaking her testimony, nervous as I could see she was. Poor children ! it was an ordeal that needed much grace to sit before a long double row of elders and deacons, besides native Christian women and some foreigners. Fung-ing said afterwards that, while waiting her turn to come, she got more and more nervous, and her heart beat so much when her name was called that she hardly knew how she would get on, but she kept praying for strength, and when she entered the door and took her seat she was quite surprised to find how the nervous beating of her heart was all gone, and she felt quite calm and reassured. When Kin-hsiang was being examined last week her voice got lower and lower, and her eyes filled with tears, till Mr. Easton could see it was getting too much for her and let her go. It is far harder for these Chinese girls than it would be for English ones, and is a very real test of their faith and love. Mr. Easton was so kind and gentle and loving as he catechised them, which he did most *thoroughly*. It was nice to hear the questions put here and there by church-members ; they were very much to the point. The three men received were splendid in their answers. It does one's heart good to see and hear this sort of thing. But this is only the beginning of wonderful things which the LORD is going to do. Let us "*watch* and *pray*."

AN EMBROIDERED HANDKERCHIEF.

Tuesday, 9th.—Three new children have come to school to-day. It was so good of the LORD to send them !

Wednesday, 10th.—To-day an old girl has come who left school because her mother said she was too old (eleven !). I was so glad she stayed to the afternoon class, and I had another opportunity of preaching the Gospel. After class, seeing all the girls at needlework, she asked if she might do some. So I got a square of English calico, and drew an elaborate pattern in the centre for her to work over with dark blue cotton like a Chinese handkerchief. She was *delighted*, and asked if she might take it home to finish. I said no, she might not. Then she said, "Cheo Ku-niang, do give me a square of English calico like this and flower it for me." Then I was suddenly struck with a new idea, I am sure it was of the LORD, and I said, "Perfect perfume, if you come every day and read, and then work this handkerchief in the afternoons, you shall have it when it is finished." Her eyes glistened, and she said, "I'll ask mother." I feel sure she will come ; and won't I make that pattern elaborate so as to take a long while! I often wondered how I could use my talent (a very small one!) for drawing out in China.

Monday, July 15th.—"Perfect Perfume" has come regularly every day since, and I have added to the pattern every day; that handkerchief will be unique when finished! Praise GOD it is only half done as yet!

MORE SCHOLARS.

Last Friday I had a very pressing invitation to go and see one of the mothers of two girls who have left off coming to school. It was not very convenient, as school was not dismissed, and I was very busy; however, I thought perhaps it was the LORD'S will that might result in one or both returning to school. So I took my woman, and off I went, and had a very happy time; and it *did* result in the youngest coming to school the very next day, praise GOD! On Sunday (yesterday) I had (in spite of rain) such a good class of women, and I never felt more power in the language; the lesson was Jethro's visit to Moses in the wilderness, and the lessons drawn were *grand!* I had no idea it was such a full subject.

ANOTHER GIRL CONFESSING CHRIST.

After school another of my elder girls, "Rare Perfume," who has been obliged to leave to nurse her mother (who, to all appearance, is in the last stage of consumption), came up to me and said, "Cheo Ku-niang, I *do* want to be baptised." I was so surprised, for *this* girl had always been so very troublesome, and though I have besought her and prayed for her, yet I felt often, "I wonder *when* she will give her heart to JESUS?" So now I sat down by her and had a long talk. She told me she obtained salvation last year, and has long been wanting to be baptised, but did not like to ask. I asked if she knew what baptism meant? She replied, "It is a confession before all men that I am JESUS' disciple." I said, "You say you are saved: do you know that those who have obtained eternal life are very, very different to those who have not? Their words, their thoughts, their actions are utterly unlike. What outward, every-day sign is there that you have passed from death unto life?" She looked up after a short silence and said, softly, "The old sinful ways and habits are broken off." I said, "What advantage will you gain by becoming a member of CHRIST'S church?" "A heavenly advantage," she answered. I put a great many more questions, and then she was called away to attend to her sick mother. I did shout for joy in my heart! I had noticed for some time back this girl very quiet, gentle, and subdued, and most thoughtful in her attentions to her mother, but I am naturally of a very doubting disposition, and there must be very palpable proofs before I will believe in a person's conversion. This girl's parents are both Christians of some years' standing and members of the Church; she is not yet engaged. I can only exclaim, "What hath GOD wrought!"

A NATIVE EXPOUNDING SCRIPTURE.

I was very much struck with the explanation given by one of the native Christians yesterday; when preaching about the demoniac in Mark v., he said, "The devil, you know, *must* hurt something—that is his one aim and object, to hurt and destroy; he did his *best* to hurt that man, but he *could not* when JESUS was there. When JESUS came, as he could not destroy the man, he went and destroyed the pigs! This is splendid teaching for us, and lays bare the very nature of the devil—a destroyer: that is what he wants to do with all of us; but he cannot if *Jesus is there!* JESUS gave an optical illustration of the *design, purpose,* and *power* of the devil in permitting him to enter the swine!" This was quite a new light to me. I had never heard *that* explanation before! He threw a new light too upon the fact of the man wanting to follow JESUS. I always thought he wanted to follow Him, because He was so full of grateful love; but Mr. Liu said, "He wanted to follow JESUS because he was afraid to be alone in the city; he was sure to be persecuted because of the pigs, and he thought if JESUS would take him with Him, he would escape it; and JESUS, seeing that *that* was his motive, would not permit him to go with Him, but sent him back to witness in his own family." This, of course, may or may not be the right interpretation, but it showed that the subject had been well thought out.

Visit to Tan-lin Hien, Si-ch'uen Province.

FROM MISS LILY WEBB.

APRIL 28th.—I arrived at Tan-lin to-day, and I received such a hearty welcome from all the Christians and inquirers here, and as I see them and think of them, I can only say, "What hath GOD wrought!" When I was staying here in an inn, six months ago, there were in all three baptised Christians; now there is a house in the city, and a happy little church of sixteen Christians and twenty-two inquirers. They have had to bear a good deal of persecution for the truth's sake, and so far have shone brightly and bravely. Now the persecution seems to have ceased to a certain extent, and we need to pray very earnestly that the GREAT SHEPHERD will keep His little flock here pure and true to Himself. It is so refreshing to be at morning and evening prayers when a good number come. The singing would certainly shock ears unaccustomed to Chinese attempts, but it is evident the praise comes from the heart.

April 30th.—My heart is filled with joy and thanksgiving for to-day's experience. I have been spending the day at the inn where I lodged while staying here six months ago, and I feel I must write down a sketch of the

"BEFORE" AND "AFTER"

of that house. The household consists of the landlord, his mother, his wife and children, besides several servants. Before, when you entered, straight in front of you was a rather elaborate arrangement for idolatry, consisting of several idols, and all the usual idolatrous scrolls and tablets; and although on the part of the landlord and his wife there was then an evident interest in the Gospel, and especially was the mother interested, yet every evening regularly I was saddened and sometimes discouraged by the practices of idolatry diligently persevered in.

Then, when about to partake of a meal, there was no recognition made of the Giver of all good gifts, and at that time the landlady was observing the usual nine days' fast very strictly.

Now all is changed. On entering, a blank wall meets the eye, relieved only by a red scroll, explaining away the usual tablet, and pointing the reader to the one true GOD, while on the side wall hang several scrolls, with the commandments, etc. This is all in the public tea-shop of the inn. The idols, etc., were all made into a bonfire some time ago. Meal-time comes, and around the table in this public shop, open to the street, we all stand and sing our thanksgiving to GOD. At dusk all gather round a table just by the place where the regular idolatry was practised, and the landlord leading, we have a quiet family worship of singing, reading the Word with exposition and prayer, followed by the Doxology. I did not know how to thank GOD enough as I joined with them, and some of the other Christians who came in, but felt "This is the LORD'S doing, and it is marvellous in our eyes." Passers-by stood and wondered, and well they might, knowing what it had been only such a short time before.

The landlord is not yet baptised, but is going to be shortly; his wife and mother have both been baptised, also one of the servants. A bolder witness for CHRIST than the landlady I have never seen. When I was speaking to the guests during the day, she invariably gave her testimony brightly and clearly, and not only so, but she *never fails* to speak of JESUS to any one she meets. In the afternoon several of the Christians (the landlady included) and I went for a walk, and on the hillside we sang several hymns, at their own suggestion, and then we sat down, and I taught them the words of a new one. I feel so much that they need our earnest prayers that they may be kept, for the great enemy will be very busy to cause them to stumble.

May 2nd. This afternoon some of the Christians and inquirers came and I had a long class with them. They never seem to get weary of learning, difficult as it is to them, but persevere and are so pleased when they have conquered.

May 3rd.—I joined the Christians at the inn at family prayer this evening, and we had a good time. Between thirty and forty people were there altogether, and there was real attention. The Gospel was very clearly preached by the landlord.

May 4th.—I spent most of the day at the inn. Outside women came, who heard the Gospel, and I had other opportunities of teaching the Christians. We returned to the "Gospel Hall" to prayers. After we had finished, our hearts were gladdened by a man who is much respected in this city for his learning, putting down his name as a candidate; he has read the Scriptures and knows them well, and I think he will in time be a useful and bold servant of the LORD. It is no wonder that souls are added to the Church here, for the Christians are in real earnest about the salvation of others.

May 6th.—To-day I went with some of the Christians to a village about eighteen *li* from this, the home of one of the inquirers. A good many women came to see the foreigner, but unhappily some of them having heard the bad reports which some of the "baser sort" had circulated about us, were afraid to come into the room where I was, fearing I should bewitch them in some terrible way. However, they heard the Gospel. One dear old woman seemed much impressed, and assured us she believed the Gospel, and when we were kneeling down to pray she knelt also, saying to an old woman near her, "Let us all worship too."

On my return I went to the inn again, and met a woman in whom I had been very much interested on my last visit here. She is a relative of the landlord of the inn, a devout worshipper of Buddha, a vegetarian, and moreover, an opium smoker. It is not too much to say that for two hours the landlord and his wife just worked for that woman's soul as they preached to her with all their hearts, not only as a mere theory, but as a living experience.

May 10th.—Some of the women came to-day to say good-bye, as I return to the capital to-morrow. I go with a heart full of thanksgiving and praise to my Heavenly FATHER for allowing me to see His work in this place. Please pray much for Tan-lin Hien. Praise the LORD!

Progress in Tan-lin Hien.

FROM DR. PARRY.

MONDAY, *August 5th*, 1889.—By GOD's goodness I reached Tan-lin on Wednesday last, on another short visit, and I can best set forth the progress that I find by giving at once a little account of eleven persons who have this morning confessed their faith by baptism.

(1) Chang Ting-wan, sixty years of age, (2) his wife, (3) their son. These are three of a family of farmers about twenty-five *li* off, of whom four generations, including a little girl, are all of one mind to turn from idols and serve the true GOD. The son was the first to come—a fine, strong, open-faced man, who came to give up his opium, and in doing so, according to the custom which the evangelist has made here, first attended for several Sundays, and then came along with a whole basketful of idols, the clearance of their home; the idols, except two, were used to cook rice, and he came in and gave up his opium, and showed an evidently sincere interest in the Gospel. He cannot read, but there seems no doubt as to the sincerity of his simple faith in JESUS as SAVIOUR. When he went home to take way the idols, the whole family were of one mind; six persons all came together to give in their names as inquirers. I paid this family a visit last Friday in the substantial farm home, and saw for myself the evidences of the defeat which idol-worship has met there; thank GOD, the sight is getting less and less rare, of family halls, where idols have reigned for generations, now cleared out. In this case the motto put up was, "As for me and my house, we will serve the LORD." We had public preaching in their house, and it was most evident that, very simple as the knowledge which they have is, their testimony for God is open to all.

How we should and do praise GOD for this first instance of a whole family coming out at once!

(4) Kweh Chen-mei, about sixty, a farmer and oil-seller, who lives not far from the above family. He also is a token of GOD's marble blessing given to the thoroughly evangelistic opium-curing that has been going on under the care of the evangelist. Though so old, GOD helped him through the fight, and he with others is rejoicing in fetters loosed by the grace of GOD. This man, too, is a notable character, for he has been for nine years in earnest pursuit of a way of truth as a Buddhist, and is, or has been till lately, a sort of precentor in the temple on days when the idols are publicly worshipped. Now we trust he will lead many in the way of life. I visited his home on Thursday last, and saw there too a home emptied of its idols and incense altar, and the Bible on the table ready for use. He told me how he wished he had been earlier in finding this True Way, for he had tried four other ways, but had one day given them up as false.

There are two inquirers whose homes are near his, and I hope he will, as the most intelligent of them, be a help in leading them on. These other two are also cured opium-smokers, who have renounced idols and desire to be disciples of CHRIST.

(5) Kweh Ta-yie, the father of a young man baptised on my last visit, and another of the cured opium-smokers. He is a quiet, unassuming man, no scholar, but, I trust, will prove a steady Christian.

(6) and (7) Shiao Ta-yie and his wife, a couple who live a little way outside the city. Before-time they so disagreed that they used separate pans to cook their rice. Now they are fellow-heirs of the grace of life, and the husband is going to teach the wife some characters. They are very poor, but independent, and, like the rest here, are very outspoken in confessing the LORD.

(8) Ch'ing Feng-chiu a carpenter, who has been an inquirer for several months. He, too, is an unusual man—in manner most unpretending and few in his words, yet evidently a man in earnest, for he is one of those who have for years together given up the natural position of rest in sleep, and used the Buddhist posture of meditation, squatting with legs folded over one another and hands clasped.

(9) Kweh Ching-shih, the wife of the young man whose father is mentioned above (No. 5).

(10) Ch'en Tsuen-shih, a young woman who is sadly afflicted with lupus of the face, which medicine can barely keep in check. She has heard and believed for a good while now.

(11) Wong Ting-sung, the only remaining son of our evangelist here—a boy of twelve, bright and intelligent, and who has for some time expressed his desire to be received and to grow up a good servant of GOD.

We are sure prayer will go up to GOD for these eleven persons that not one may fall back, but all be found in the day of JESUS CHRIST, to His praise and glory.

At the time of my former visit, when seven persons were baptised, you will remember that it was in the face of much of Satan's roaring and opposition from without, that this grace of

God appeared ; this time I have to tell, with a mingled feeling of

SORROW AND THANKFULNESS,

that the baptism and adding to the Church of these eleven persons is in despite of a far more successful and subtle assault of the enemy from within our little citadel ; truly we recognise the same great ceaseless foe in either case, and our trust is that the same STRONGER than he will gain in this case as in the first defeat of him.

I must explain a little. The fierce storm of heathen opposition has passed over since the official proclamations were issued ; the feeling with which the Gospel Hall is regarded by the people generally is much changed. Now they are speaking well of us as people of good works, who are not harming but seeking to save the people.

Along with this change without, a different change has been working from within, and a dark cloud has risen between the evangelist and the most prominent family of members and inquirers. Satan has made good use of his opportunity, and the little church has been in more serious peril than ever it could be from outward trials.

The story in detail I cannot go into, but having heard both sides, I feel that in spite of faults our evangelist has been in the right, and has not departed from the desire to serve GOD and man truly. I have also seen clearly that the chief cause of the trouble has risen from the headstrong self-confidence and perhaps pride and ill-speaking of one woman—[the landlady]. I will only say that I felt no other course could be right than to suspend her for a time, in the fervent hope and prayer that she may yet be a restored and humbled, as well as zealous member.

You may be sure that these events have been a blow to us all, but we sorrow in humble confidence that all these things will yet work out the true and lasting good of the church there. Is it not a token for good that at such a time there should be these souls all desirous of confessing their faith ?

You will see by my notes that the opium-curing is thoroughly evangelistic ; the evangelist does not receive payment, but each one who comes finds his own rice, and, moreover, is first expected to show his interest by attending for several Sundays, and then, when possible, to declare himself as truly anxious to worship GOD by the open removal of his idolatrous objects.

While with them last week, three grateful patients presented Mr. Wong with a sign-board and two banners, on each of which are words of Truth for all who see them.

THE OLD FRENCH CONSULATE ON THE TIEN-TSIN RIVER.

A Conference at Ning-kwoh, Gan-hwuy.

FROM MR. MACGREGOR.

SEP. 18*th*.—In two days' time we are (D.V.) to open our conference. We are all praying much for marked blessing, and GOD is preparing our hearts. We expect a party of some half dozen from Wu-hu. We trust such an impetus shall be given to the Christians as shall send them through the winter earnestly seeking and finding more of the love and will of JESUS. The last three weeks have been the best in my life of communion with the LORD JESUS and delight in GOD. The LORD has given me such absolute rest concerning my work, and has been answering prayer for certain things I lacked, so that I seem as though on a new way.

Sep. 21st.—Let me tell you of the Convention ; I am writing at the close of its second day. In spite of continuous rain for four days, which has prevented some from coming whom we expected, we have mustered about sixty-six, all children of GOD, and the happiness that prevails is just what one meets with in a convention at home. Praise His Name ! He leadeth and feedeth and uniteth His own sheep. On Thursday some friends came, and we had a prayer-meeting at seven. I was called away to an opium case, and, alas, had much cause to rebuke myself for not at the moment accepting it as GOD's will, for I wanted to go to the meeting. I felt the effect of that momentary unwillingness for hours. Oh, how careful we should be in our wills, in our ways, in the slightest things, lest offending we lose the sweetness of our fellowship and communion with the blessed Saviour.

One of the Wu-hu friends prayed very nicely; he is grandson to the good old Elder who died a year ago, a very nice, discreet young lad, I believe he will be a pillar to the church there. With him was a countryman whose parents are still unsaved, but who, with his wife, glorifies GOD and suffers persecution. When I spoke to him he answered very cheerfully; he looks a simple, bright fellow, such as can bear good testimony for GOD. Last night I gave an address, and Mr. Miller followed me. The LORD very much helped me; I had made the matter one of much prayer. After retiring for the night, we could hear the voices of Chinese saints prolonging worship by singing and praying in company in their sleeping apartment. Praise GOD for His goodness. Cannot we reckon on Him to bless the Chinaman as much as the Briton?

This evening Wang came back from his home with his old father of seventy, who is a thoroughly converted man. He walked twenty miles to-day in the wet, and so fast that his serving man could scarcely keep up with him. Wang said, "If it were not for GOD's help my father could not walk like that." He says his father is much given to prayer at his home. Wang is himself growing in grace, ripening and steadying down. He told Mr. Miller he felt the importance of living a holy life, so that none could point to him and spoil his testimony.

Sep. 25th.—On Saturday night Mr. Miller gave a missionary address, the meeting lasting two hours. He had a map of the world and one of China, and there seemed real interest. I wished he had continued.

On Sunday, prayer-meeting at eight, service at eleven, and the baptism of nine candidates, six men and three women. On Monday morning, a prayer-meeting at eight, and in the evening a magic-lantern on Elijah. The old man Li was projected staff, teapot, and all on to the sheet. Of course there was some merriment. He is eighty-six, and was once one of the richest men in Wu-hu, but lost his money in lawsuits. He is well known there. It made us thankful to GOD to see the happiness of everyone.

More about the First Convert in Cheng-yang-kwan.

FROM MR. DRYSDALE.

JUNE 14th.—In the evening we had the pleasure of speaking with Wang. The peace he is enjoying is really a marvellous proof of what the Gospel can do for any one. He is realising the truth of Heb. xiii. 5: "I will never leave thee nor forsake thee;" and of the SAVIOUR'S promise: "Lo, I am with you alway," etc.

He had suffered much since the Sabbath. He was taken before the Mohammedan priest, and questioned as to his doings, when he boldly witnessed a good confession in their presence, and fearlessly reminded them of the sins they indulged in, such as opium-smoking, gambling, drinking, etc. They expelled him by saying that when his old father died he was not to look to them to give him burial, or to ask them to kill his fowls. This, to our mind, is perhaps a trifle, but in the minds of this people a most serious thing, and the greatest test to a Mohammedan. The old father was next called, and accused of not instructing his son properly. He was told that he was now separated from the true faith, and that they would do nothing for him after death. This meant no reading of the Koran, no special box for carrying the body to the grave, and no bringing down of blessing upon it, etc. The old father replied, "We will follow the doctrine of JESUS."

The message which came to us on the Monday that some were waiting to take the life of dear Wang was quite true. Between one and two hundred of the baser sort of fellows assembled near his home. Some wanted to drown him in the river, others wanted to beat him to death, but were hindered by his old mother, who took her place at the door, and threatened to take her own life in order to repay those who should lay hands on her son. The haunting by the spirits of the dead in such cases occupies a very prominent place in the minds of, and is a terror to, the Chinese.

In the midst of all this our brother was kept in perfect peace, without fear, rejoicing in the LORD JESUS. It is true he has lost nearly all worldly friends, and made many enemies, but it is equally true that he has gained the favour of the FRIEND that sticketh closer than a brother.

We are assured that this bold testimony will not be without blessing to others. "May the LORD grant it for His Name's sake." Please remember this our first convert in North GAN-HWUY specially in your prayers, and not him only, but also the Mohammedans, Buddhists, Taoists, and the many admirers of Confucius that we are living amongst here.

We have others who desire baptism.

"There shall be showers of blessing:
This is the promise of GOD."

Blessing in North Gan-hwuy.

FROM MR. JOHN BROCK.

CHENG-YANG-KWAN, *September 18th.* You will be glad to know that two men have publicly confessed their faith in CHRIST. They were baptised on Sabbath last. I do praise and magnify the LORD for allowing me to receive these dear brethren into the Church.

One of the two is a teacher, seventy-one years of age, and comes from a village 117 miles from here. Over ten years ago he saw one of our books, which a friend of his had bought from a colporteur, and he had often thought of going to Gan-k'ing to learn more of the doctrine, but the distance being so great he had never managed it. Time passed on, and the Romanists opened an outstation in his village, the result being that he was led to disregard idols and to adopt their worship. Still he was not satisfied; he could not believe that the French Holy Fathers had all the power that they professed to have, and prostrating himself before them was specially objectionable.

A short time ago "The Gate of Virtue and Wisdom,"

a book by the Rev. Griffith John, was given him by a friend, and he was told that at Cheng-yang-kwan there was a gospel hall; so he came to us two months ago and gave himself to the study of our books. The amount of reading he did was remarkable; it included the Old and New Testaments, two volumes of Church History, "Pilgrim's Progress," "The Holy War," "Martin's Evidences," etc., besides the smaller books and catechisms suitable for inquirers.

He soon learned to pray, and daily he might have been seen in his little room kneeling in silent prayer. He won the respect of all, and used every opportunity to speak to visitors about the Gospel. He had come for a month, and at the end of that time he sought for baptism, but as Mr. Reid was absent I got him to stay on. As Mr. Cooper could not come up, I baptised him last Sabbath, and he left for home the following morning in company with his son, who is a hopeful case, but needs teaching. They have taken Scriptures with them, and hope to lead some of their friends to JESUS. They greatly desire to see Poh-chau opened, which is but 70 *li* from their home.

The other convert is a young HU-PEH man, aged thirty-one, who was first led to think of the true GOD through hearing another man say that the foreigners in Cheng-yang-kwan taught a good doctrine, and told of the true Creator. He came to hear for himself, and having a fair education, the more he read, as well as heard, the more interested he became. About four months ago he began attending Brother Reid's inquirers' class, and about three months ago, when the greater part of the city was flooded, he came to our premises and stayed with Mr. Yang, going daily to earn his living and attending worship in the evening.

On Monday last he went to Sheo-chau, and tried to find the man who recommended the Gospel to him, but did not succeed. I hope to seek him out soon; he was here but once; I believe he is one of the LORD'S elect. On the way to Sheo-chau our young convert spent a night in the home of one of our inquirers, a doctor, and also a HU-PEH man; they had a season of prayer together. Wen starts for his home in a day or two; he means to win souls. I am glad to learn that the London Mission have a station in Hiao-kan Hien, which is not far from his home.

The prospects of a good work here are very bright at present. We have an out and out HO-NAN man witnessing boldly for CHRIST. A month ago cholera was raging in our midst, and this dear fellow, who had cheered us much by the way in which he received our message, was attacked, and had we not taken him in would probably have been cut off. Our landlords were very much opposed to his being on our premises, lest he should die, but we determined that whether he lived or died we would do our part. The outsiders said we wanted his eyes and heart for medicine, so we called upon GOD, and our Evangelist felt sure he would not die, although all the medicine which he attempted to take was rejected. Praise the LORD, he did get better, and now he delights to tell that he was raised up in answer to prayer, and that he feels he must witness for JESUS. He gets called foreign devil, etc., but none of these things move him. Though not a reader, he is quite an able speaker.

Praise the LORD for a recent persecutor joining the ranks of the persecuted. Until last week a man named Huang ridiculed the one mentioned above, but now he comes regularly to evening worship, and has to defend himself from the taunts of others. Persecution is indispensable, as it makes the real inquirer speak out for the Gospel sooner than smooth sailing would.

The young Mohammedan whom Mr. Reid baptised three months ago is very much tried, but he says he will never give up JESUS. Praise GOD, there is no fear that JESUS will give him up.

Last Sabbath evening we turned the service into a testimony meeting. We had a word from the two colporteurs who were to leave on the Monday; then the late vegetarian gave GOD glory for raising him up from the gates of death, and Wen, the melon-seed vendor, spoke very nicely for a short time. I believe all present enjoyed the service. I brought the meeting to a close by urging the unsaved to accept this fourfold witness to the reality of the Gospel.

Kiang-si for Christ.

THE following letter, to her friends in Canada, from Miss Fitzsimons, who went to China in our first American party, will, we feel sure, interest English friends also. We extract it from *The Faithful Witness*.

YUH-SHAN is a large city in the north-east of the KIANG-SI Province, beautifully situated at the foot of a mountain, and on the Kwang-sin river.

I cannot realise that two months have gone since I sailed up this river to my first inland home, where the strange sights and sounds have so taken up my attention that time has gone almost unconsciously. Although time has gone so speedily, it has not gone vainly, for GOD has taught me many precious lessons. I have learned to "look up," to trust as never before. I know the dear natives better, and the more I know about them, the more I love them, and determine to spend and be spent for them.

Here in Yuh-shan, with Miss Mackintosh, we are *one* with the people. For this I thank and praise GOD, as I believe it is the secret of winning many precious souls.

When we were in Yang-chau, we met daily at noon to pray for the different provinces and their cities. Thursday was the day we prayed for KIANG-SI, and my heart went out especially for Yuh-shan. I do not quite know why, unless it was hearing so much about the work, and how Miss Mackintosh lived amongst the natives. I prayed very much about it, asking GOD to send Miss Turner and myself there, if it would be for His honour and glory. I waited patiently on Him to give me the desire of my heart, quite willing to go wherever He should send me, knowing *He* would go before me, yet hoping it would be His will to send us to Yuh-shan, and it was. Praise Him!

Now that I am acquainted with the dear Christians here, I feel led to write a little about them, so that those in the quiet home land who pray for us and the natives, may know just what sort of people they remember before the throne of grace.

I shall never forget my first Sunday in Yuh-shan, as from early morning until evening I mingled with redeemed souls, who once bowed down to idols, and knew nothing whatever about the LORD'S day of rest.

When we came down stairs to breakfast, there was four or five dear women sitting in the Worship Hall, who had walked from ten to fifteen *li* to the morning prayer-meeting. After breakfast we had the joy of meeting an old woman of sixty-eight years, who had walked thirty *li* (ten miles) with her tiny feet, accompanied by her husband of sixty-five; he had prayed for twelve years that she might believe in the LORD JESUS, observe the Sabbath, and worship the true GOD. GOD honoured his simple faith, and now he is reaping the benefit of persevering in prayer. I never knew I was so faithless and unbelieving until I met with Chinese Christians.

As the day passed I saw many strange and happy sights, which I have not time to mention. But I must tell about the little boy who was sitting in a quiet corner of the "Worship Hall," looking so pale and ill with dropsy. He was about sixteen years old and had only heard the Gospel for the first time the week before, but he had learned to trust the loving SAVIOUR who "had gone to prepare a place for him." He was so happy, and forgot all about his pains and aches when talking about heaven and JESUS. He came every day for another week, and then went home to be for ever with the LORD.

There are many cases similar to this one, of persons being saved and never reckoned church members. Miss Mackintosh says she is quite sure that there will be many children, blind men, and beggars around the throne of GOD, whose names were never on a Church-book.

This reminds me of our old blind man who has been to church, and to the Wednesday afternoon class regularly since we have been here. I love to look into his old wrinkled face, there is such a look of trust and peace upon it, and when he gets even a cold cup of tea, he kneels down, and thanks GOD for it.

A LOVING COUPLE.

Outside the city wall, in a little hut by the "great west gate," live a poor old couple whose history would be most interesting if one had time to relate it minutely.

The woman's first husband was a man of position and wealth. When he died she married one of the workmen in his place of business. Her husband's friends were so much disappointed, they turned her out into the world with him. So they came to Yuh-sban to live, and although very poor, they have been very happy. Last year the little woman came to the hall, and became deeply interested; came regularly to hear more, and the Gospel at once made a change in her, she looked cleaner, brighter, and did not beg anything. She is a member now, and comes to all the services. Miss Macintosh, when out visiting one afternoon, chancing to call at her home, found her out, but her husband at home. When she asked him if he knew about the true GOD, he said his wife talked about one, but *he* did not understand. He said his wife prepared the rice, and then went outside the door, knelt down and thanked GOD for it, thinking GOD could see her better outside. "I do not understand this," he said, "but I let her do it, and I just nod my head. She has always been so good, I let her do what she likes." He sings her praises, and she tells how good he is. They are so simple and loving. This is a case of real love even in China. Her friends in Ho-k'eo want her to give this man up and go back home, but she will not, and so lives on in poverty with him. The husband comes to prayers every night now; he is not yet baptised, but very bright. Although these old creatures do not know sometimes where their next meal will come from, they never ask from us.

Dear home friends, the hearts of the Chinese are very similar to our own after all. We are so apt to think that because they are heathen, they are heartless, but such is not the case. The love the dear Christians lavish upon us is so sweet. They pray continually for us and for those at home who are sending the Bible to them.

RICH BLESSING.

GOD has blessed this work so richly. There have been ninety-five persons baptised. At present there is a Church-membership of eighty-eight. Some have gone home to heaven, and others have gone to different cities. There is a good earnest pastor here, Mr. Chang, and two itinerating evangelists. The Lord has blessed the work of our dear sister Miss Mackintosh abundantly. Since He called her here about three years ago, at each baptismal service the number to be baptised increases. The last time there were twenty-four; we are looking for thirty next time, "according to *our* faith." One of the last number was Miss Mackintosh's teacher, Mr. Li, and a real trophy to lay at the feet of JESUS. He was a doctor, and worshipped a small black god of medicine. His father and grandfather had worshipped it, and it was thought to have cured many, many diseases. He gave it to Miss Mackintosh, and it is now on its way to her friends in Scotland.

This is how the devil's strongholds are coming down, as one after the other turn to the true GOD, and give up or burn the idols their forefathers worshipped. Oh, the joy of taking part in such a work as this! By-and-by *we*, too, shall be helping to burn idols and ancestral tablets. "For this purpose the SON of GOD was manifested that *He* might destroy the works of the devil."

CHANGED HEARTS AND HOMES.

When our superintendent, Mr. McCarthy, was visiting us, we spent a day in the country visiting the homes of a few Christians. It was a truly happy and blessed day. We dined in a home where every member of the family were followers of the LORD JESUS. As we went from house to house, seeing the ten commandments hanging up where the ancestral tablets used to hang, and scrolls on the walls with texts telling of GOD's love for sinners, and how willing and able *He* is to save, our hearts were so full.

What a change the love of CHRIST makes in these homes and in these poor hearts. Hallelujah! what a SAVIOUR! Who would not carry the story of *His* life, death and resurrection to those who have never heard? Praise His glorious Name for the privilege of doing so, and this is *mine*.

Dear friends, GOD has heard and answered your prayers for us as a party, and for each one individually. *I* cannot begin to tell what He has done for my soul, or how He has helped me with the language. Each day I have been conscious of His presence and help, and now I ask for your prayers, that I may only use the words GOD has given me for His glory, and be continually filled with His HOLY SPIRIT, without which all my words would be in vain.

KUANG-FENG.

I also ask your prayers for Miss Turner's and my city, "Kuang-feng," where we expect to go (D.V.) in a couple of months. At present the house is being prepared for us.

This, too, is in answer to the prayers of our home friends. Is it not good of the LORD to send us forward so soon? "We will go in the strength of the LORD GOD, and we will make mention *only* of *His* righteousness."

There is a young evangelist, his wife, and a Bible-woman there now, and many interested in the Gospel. We are believing "for great things" in that city.

Dear friends, there are still many great cities in KIANG-SI without one gleam of Gospel light, and doors are standing open on all sides.

Do you realise *your* individual responsibility? Are you seeking a knowledge of GOD's will concerning *you*? Do you not feel burdened when you think of the fifteen millions in KIANG-SI, without even referring to the other great provinces?

The LORD is truly blessing KIANG-SI, sixty-six of His precious souls were baptised on confession of their faith in CHRIST last month. The time is short; CHRIST is coming! "Let us, *then*, lay aside every weight, *and the sin* which doth so easily beset us." "Let us awake to righteousness, *and sin not*." Why? Because "some have not the knowledge of God." (1 Cor. xv. 34).

THE ENTRANCE-COURT TO A GENTLEMAN'S HOUSE IN LAN-CHŬ, THE CAPITAL OF KAN-SUH.—ARRIVAL OF THE FOREIGN VISITORS.

Tidings from Scattered Workers.

Kan-suh Province.

FROM MISS MAY GRAHAM BROWN.

Lan-chau, July 6th.—Round this place most of the ground is at present occupied in growing opium; people remember when there was no such thing in the province, and now there is a town not far off where we hear that every man, woman, and child of any age take it in some form. Only GOD can help.

Both men and women are coming in larger numbers to service on Sundays, and the interest in the open-air preaching in our yard continues. Many seem to come near and then draw back from decision for GOD; but the work is His.

FROM MISS G. M. MUIR.

Lan-chau, August 16th.—Of course, you have heard of our removal to a very suitable house inside the city. I never saw anything more strikingly of GOD from beginning to end; the house is truly His gift, and we take it as an earnest of blessing in Lan-chau. May we see very many souls brought to GOD here. Pray for power from on high to rest continually on us. The sound of reinforcements for Kan-suh is a very refreshing one. May they bring mighty blessing with them.

FROM MR. LAUGHTON.

Liang-chau, June 7th.—What a city with opium and opium-smokers this is! Quite a hell upon earth! If our opium traders and all who have anything to do with the trade or who derive any benefit from it could just see these poor people, then, if they have a conscience at all, they must give up this awful trade.

FROM MRS. LAUGHTON.

June 9th.—We have been at two opium-poisoning cases lately; one a little girl of only thirteen; we were called to her too late, she died in a short time. The other seemed a nice quiet woman in a family I had visited; she was beaten by her husband when under the influence of drink, and, as is usual in such cases, took opium; I am thankful to say we were able to save her. I have been without a woman since coming to Liang-chau. I feel it a great difficulty, but we believe that this need will be met at the right time.

Shan-tung Province.

FROM MISS SPARK.

Che-foo, Aug. 14th.—Let me say a word regarding my opinion of the influence and working of this school (English Girls' School). I cannot speak too highly of the standard of education; it is well equal and in many ways supersedes a first-class English school with masters. Girls are not crammed, but are taught to think, and so to a large extent to learn independence and self-help. As regards the spiritual tone, for more consistent lives in young Christians, you might look through fifty or a hundred English schools, and not find more conscientious girls, as a whole. The teaching brought to bear on them is the practical, daily-life side of Christianity, and not the more frequent sentimental side.

FROM MISS SANDERSON.

Che-foo, Aug. 17th. The results of school work, as far as the credit of the girls was concerned, were very pleasantly rewarded on prize-giving day. The music and singing, which was the first part of the performance, seemed to be thoroughly enjoyed by a goodly company of people. The girls did their part in a way to make *us* feel quite delighted with them, especially knowing as we did that in their hearts as well as by lip the glory was given to GOD. At their prayer-meeting the previous evening earnest prayers ascended that they might be very humble, and do everything for GOD's glory only. This is the secret of the marked success that attends the studies of so many of them.

Ho-nan Province.

FROM MRS. HERBERT TAYLOR.

She-ki-tien, Sept. 24th. We have real encouragement in the work; the men are studying their Bibles more; some of them come and help in speaking to the unsaved in the chapel. How different it is now from what it was when we first came; we can go where we like now and no one follows us; at first what crowds! The five women who were accepted for baptism are growing brighter, and there are others, who, we believe, really love JESUS, and are trusting Him for salvation. Last Sunday morning I had such an attentive class of women, and the LORD was manifestly with us. If you had only seen these dear women's happy faces, as they forgot f r the time all their home troubles, and were occupied with GOD the FATHER's love, My heart was filled with joy. Two new women have come these last two Sundays; they are vegetarians, but now most interested and eager to hear about the SAVIOUR.

Si-ch'uen Province.

FROM MR. GRAY OWEN.

Chen tu, Aug. 10th.—I have great hopes of seeing the first little out-station opened on the Chen-tu plain ere long, the preaching and expenses mostly devolving on the church here. I do long to see the great plain dotted with red dots, denoting the presence of a few saved ones under each mark.

FROM MR. RILEY.

Kia-ting, July 20th.—Our work is discouraging to sight just now, but we must not doubt GOD's promise and power. Some who have attended are convinced of the truth, but lack courage and need our prayers; some who have plenty of courage lack reality. Oh, how we need the power of the Holy Ghost! We are thinking of working the Hien cities regularly, D.V., during the coming autumn and winter, taking a city at a time and visiting all the markets in connection with it, spending say ten days at each, and taking it in turns. If the native helper is still with us we could do this and keep at work in this city, too, preaching outdoors and visiting.

FROM MR. FAERS.

Chung-King, Aug. 15th.—Our work here is hampered for want of more men; when will they come? when will they come? We are hoping soon to enlarge the present chapel by throwing two more rooms into it, which will make it capable of seating over 400 people; at present it seats about 280, but we generally have over 300 to the services, and these remain the whole time. During the week we have two large evening services, at which we get one half side of the chapel well filled. One of these meetings is for prayer especially, and the other for expounding the Word to the Christians and enquirers; very few outsiders attend these meetings. One other evening is set apart for instruction in fundamental truths, and on the other evenings we have gospel meetings.

FROM REV. W. W. CASSELS.

Pao-ning, September 12th. The autumn is now upon us, and we are looking forward to some hard work. Already we have encouragement in one or two directions. Feeling there were special needs, on Wednesday 4th we had a meeting for prayer and fasting. We specially sought from the LORD that the excessive rain might cease; that dear Mrs. Williams might be restored to health; and that the LORD would revive His work in our midst. Before we separated, Mrs. Williams was reported to be better, and steady improvement has continued. That evening the rain ceased, and we have had beautiful weather since. The next day one backslider returned, and another returned on Sunday, on which day the LORD gave us manifest blessing. At our half-monthly early morning prayer meeting we had an unusually large attendance. The Lord be praised for the past and give us greater things for the future. The news from our sisters at Kwang-yuen is encouraging. They are hard at work—go out visiting daily and find open doors.

FROM MR. BEAUCHAMP.

Pa-chau, Sept. 7th.—I have enjoyed my preaching here at the ya-men gates so much ; it reminds me of the spell at Wan-hien this time last year. I have been almost daily there, the rain being the only thing that has stopped me. The people are so nice. I do earnestly pray that GOD will bless the Word there ; several faces are getting familiar, yet I do not see them come to the Gospel Hall.

FROM MR. A. P. TURNER.

Sept. 7th.—I feel that we must do things on a different scale if China is to be evangelised ; though we rejoice in a band of thirty-three workers in SI-CH'UEN, what is that among the millions of souls? Still we must use the means GOD has given to feed the multitude, and He will surely give the blessing and increase. Pray that we may have that patient continuance in well-doing, expectant for the future, but living and working in the present.

The LORD's work at Pa-chau is going ahead in the way of seed-sowing and willingness to hear the Gospel, and the Boys' School is flourishing. We have taken down the names of three women who are candidates for baptism. We have been disappointed in the old women of last year ; only one of them now comes, the one baptised, and she is cold, I fear. We are anxiously awaiting reinforcements.

Hu-peh Province.

FROM MISS GATES.

Fan-ch'eng, June 25th.—I was talking to our woman on Sunday afternoon ; she understands the plan of salvation, but whether she is trusting wholly in JESUS for salvation I cannot yet say. I am sure she is not far from the Kingdom. I believe she often speaks of the one true GOD in her own home. She says they will not listen to her, but tell her " she is with the foreigners, and she may eat the foreign doctrine, but they won't ; that if half the people in Fan-ch'eng believed, then they would." I am glad to say the school children come regularly, and to-day I have had another new one brought. Pray for me, and for the little ones also, that some of them may very soon know JESUS as their SAVIOUR.

July 15th.—I am thankful to tell you that my school is gradually increasing. I now have nine children, and the promise of another. We have been asking that they may tell out in their own homes all they learn here, and last week in visiting one of the homes of the children, I was much encouraged on hearing the mother and a girl of nineteen repeat what the little one of six had learned ; the mother also told me that she had taught her baby brother to repeat "JESUS loves me." I do praise GOD so much for this little encouragement, especially in that home, as they are Mohammedans. Do pray much for me. I want life more abundantly, to be filled with His fulness.

FROM MISS MARY BLACK.

Fan-ch'eng, Sept. 2nd.—I have been able to keep up my outdoor work all through the heat, and have not been without encouragement. There is a stirring among the people ; only this morning an old woman invited me into her house, and there and then professed to believe the Gospel, promising not to worship idols any more. Yesterday, in consequence of the floods, few people were able to come to the chapel, but on the three previous Sundays the average attendance of men at my class was nineteen.

I am very thankful I was led to open the front chapel. Scarcely a day passes without our dear old blind friend having several opportunities of telling the old, old story, which he loves to tell to eager listeners in that chapel. The good man's loving, gentle words and ways make me think of the Apostle John ; he certainly is a treasure. The women, too, are gathering round me, and I trust we shall ere long see showers of blessing.

Sept. 21st.—The possibilities of usefulness here are unlimited, and it is a great joy to have one's entire time free for the LORD's work. My day generally begins about 4.30, and I am occupied almost all day long visiting, receiving visitors, teaching classes, etc.

Gan-hwuy Province.

FROM MR. LACHLAN.

Gan-k'ing, September 2nd.—A man named Li, who was baptized here last autumn, and who lives about 170 *li* from here, gave a very bright testimony in the chapel yesterday afternoon, and again to-day. His happy face spoke volumes. He is, amongst other things, a herbalist, and makes occasional visits to Gan-k'ing to dispose of rare herbs.

Sunday, September 8th.—Yesterday Wang the mandarin's son came in, and from some questions he put, seemed to have been reading the Gospel of John, and to be puzzled as to who CHRIST was. Li told him always to ask for the HOLY SPIRIT's guidance before reading, and then spoke with great power on our LORD's sufferings, death, and resurrection, and the sending of the HOLY SPIRIT as proving our LORD's divinity. At the prayer meeting in Gan-k'ing we had prayed for this Wang and some others. To-day, Sunday, Mr. Wood's little boy being unwell, I took the morning service to relieve him. The LORD helped me very much. [Mr. Lachlan only reached China on January 13th.] Two more of those we prayed for on Saturday came in, and some others whose faces are familiar to me. May we wait only upon GOD.

Kiang-su Province.

FROM MISS HORSBURG.

Yang-chau, Aug. 21st.—I feel every day how good our FATHER is to have brought me to China. I think it is impossible to realise one's utter dependence on GOD at home, where we have so many loved ones, and so much of earth's comfort, in the same way that we do here. It is so sweet. Very often I have thought, "If I could only fly home and gather all my loved ones and fly back with them so that they too could share all these blessings !" I hope just as many as are required the LORD will make willing to come, but only those whom He calls, those not only willing to come to China, but willing to live for Him here and just to trust and obey.

The new addition is making progress. My window looks north, so I get the benefit of the sight and sounds too. It is most interesting to watch how they build ; it is all so different to our ways. All the men, forty in number, come to prayers every morning. I do pray that many may be brought to JESUS before its completion.

Kwei-chau Province.

FROM MR. WINDSOR.

Kwei-yang Fu, Aug. 22nd.—Bro. Adam and I left the capital together on July 29th, travelling together as far as Tsa-fao, where I stayed two or three days, having encouraging times in the city and at two markets. The people in the city listened attentively, and readily bought books.

I spent three happy days at T'ung-chau, and was exceedingly pleased and encouraged with my visit. To my great joy and surprise I found an apparently true disciple of CHRIST living here. He is a relative of the evangelist at Gan-shun, and named Mao. Mr. Andrew had stayed at his house on former visits, and about two years ago he came to the capital to hear and learn more of the Doctrine. Upon his return home he cleared his house of all idolatry, but some months afterwards we heard that he had again put up his idols because a relative had beaten him for removing them. It turns out, however, that these rumours are unfounded, and appear to have been circulated about the time the boys' school teacher was desiring baptism, with the intention to frighten the teacher from joining us.

FROM MRS. S. R. CLARKE.

Kwei-yang, July 8th.—We have eleven baptised women here, and three enquirers. I like the school work and the girls. The teacher is the first Chinaman who has fed my soul by his discourse. He has opposition in his family, which, no doubt, helps to keep him bright. Pray for us in Kwei-yang.

Kiang-si Province.

FROM MISS HATTIE TURNER.

Yuh-shan, Aug. 13th.—We do rejoice that such rich blessing is being given to the work in KIANG-SI. May each convert be kept very near the SAVIOUR. It is grand to know that He is KING, is it not? Who would not leave loved ones and home lands to carry the message and bring joy, everlasting joy, to these dear women? We are repaid *often* when we see how happy these people are now they love JESUS; their whole life is changed. The more we live among them and the more we see and know them, the more we love them with our whole heart. Truly the LORD was good to allow us to come here; we praise Him daily. Miss Fitzsimons and I had been praying that we might live right in among the natives. Sunday after Sunday such a goodly number meet, and when we saw an old woman of sixty-eight years arrive, after walking on her small feet thirty *li* (ten miles) to hear more about JESUS, how our hearts went out in praise!

You will have heard of the house being rented at Kwang-feng for ten years. Miss Fitzsimons and I expect to go there to work before long. The city is so thickly populated. It is one of those the rebels did not enter. At daybreak on Monday, July 22nd, Miss Mackintosh, the Pastor Chang, and I took chairs, arriving at Kwang-feng at about five in the afternoon. The Evangelist Hu, wife, and Biblewoman were very pleased to see us. We sent our cards and passports to the mandarin on our arrival, by the pastor, who was kindly received, and asked how long we were going to stay. The pastor told him only a few days now, but that later on we were coming to be guests in his city. He said that he was glad to hear it, and would always protect us. He sent two of his soldiers to see that the people did not crowd too much or disturb our peace. Though it rained from the time we arrived till the time we left on Thursday morning, people did not cease to come from early morn till dark each day. We were very well received, and already the women's work has begun. The old Biblewoman is faithful in teaching hymns to some women who come regularly, also some portions of the Word and prayer. How good it was to hear them say that they prayed morning and evening and whenever they ate their rice. The house there is now being fitted up, and when finished will be very comfortable for two sisters. God supplies all our need.

FROM MISS MACKINTOSH.

Last week Miss Turner and I visited Kwang-feng. It was so nice to hear several dear women say that they prayed every day, and were teaching their children to pray to JESUS too. One has a little boy of six or seven, and she said, "He knows about JESUS, and always kneels down beside me." I am sure the LORD has many precious gems in Kwang-feng, and our dear sisters are looking forward with joy to gathering them in. What a glorious privilege is ours!

Cheh-kiang Province.

FROM MR. GRIERSON.

Wun-chau, Aug. 26th.—At our last monthly church-meeting here I had the joy of examining ten candidates for church-membership, and on LORD'S Day, July 28th, baptized four of the ten, three men and a woman, who have all given good evidence of being born again. The other six are good cases, I believe, but want some further testing. I look forward to having a royal time at our next church-meeting on Saturday, and expect a number more baptisms on LORD'S Day.

On Wednesday I leave Wun-chau for a thorough visiting of our Dong-ling members, whence I go to Bing-yiu. The only Hien city in this prefecture which has not yet received the Gospel is now being laid siege to. I hope to spend some considerable time at Bing-yiu, and to make extensive journeys over the several plains near and around the city.

FROM MISS LITTLER.

Peh-shih-kiai, Sat., July 30th.—Mr. Thompson baptized our six candidates this morning, with two Chang-shan candidates. We had a very nice service, with the communion at the close.

Request for Prayer for Kiu-chau.

FROM MRS. THOMPSON.

KIU-CHAU, *July 15th.*—You will be glad to hear of four being baptized here yesterday. The first was the old blind woman who lives fifteen *li* away, and first heard the Gospel from dear old Chuh-ma over two years and a half ago. Before Chuh-ma was baptised she took the Gospel to her village, and the old blind woman seemed to believe from the first. From time to time we have been to see her. We thought it would be well for her to come here and learn a little more, so I have been spending a little time each morning in teaching her and others, and it is encouraging how much she has learned. She is very poor, but very bright.

Number two was a woman who has been living here for some time, and at first was very opposed to the Gospel. At our little convention this time last year this woman was especially prayed for, and dear Miss Boyd asked if Mr. Thompson and I would join in praying for her every day. Soon after, without anyone speaking to her, she told one of the Christians that she had wakened in the night and had felt obliged to pray to GOD to forgive her sins. May the LORD keep her and bring her out still more brightly is now our prayer.

Number three was one of the schoolgirls married a few months since; she, of course, has been prayed for for years. She is a very promising girl. Her husband and another Christian brother are farmers, and live seven *li* outside the city. Praise the LORD, they are quite a bright light in that little place. They come every LORD'S day for the day, and a man they employed this year was received yesterday as a candidate. He had never heard the Gospel till he went to live with them, but he answered so brightly and understands a great deal.

Number four was an old man of this city, who, after our Convention last year, asked to be received, and has a clear knowledge of the Gospel. It was a very happy time. We have another woman a candidate and others coming regularly, for whom we are praying.

Sept. 17th.—We are looking to the LORD about new work for this autumn. We had a meeting with the Christians to talk over what they thought we could do more for the extension of the Gospel. GOD'S Word was read, showing that without the HOLY GHOST we could do nothing, and we had quite a holiness meeting. May our GOD help us to be entirely given up for Him to work in us. Will you remember us in prayer? We are only two here, but we desire to do all we can in the strength of the LORD.

You will rejoice to hear that Kiang-san, another Hien city, has the Gospel of GOD'S love. A young man who had lived with us since we came here, and has been a Christian ten years, was commended to the LORD for that city, and has been there about two months.

Departures for China.

On Dec. 12th, per P. and O. s.s. *Khedive*, Rev. GEO. and MRS. HUNTER, and child, also Messrs. A. E. EVANS, F. SHARP, and T. G. WILLETT.

On Jan. 9th, per P. and O. s.s. *Peshawur*, Miss F. M. BRITTON returning, also Misses H. POLHILL-TURNER, A. J. FORSTER, E. G. LEGERTON, and BESSIE LEGGAT.

CHINA'S MILLIONS.

"To Every Creature."

SHALL CHINA HAVE A THOUSAND EVANGELISTS WITHOUT DELAY?

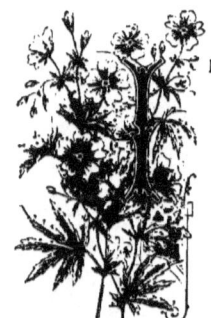

IN our December number we pointed out that a thousand evangelists, each presenting the Gospel to fifty families a day, might, within three years of such work (a thousand days), reach every family in China. We also pointed out that if Europe supplied 500 of these evangelists, the U.S.A. and Canada might well supply a similar contingent; and that the workers should be looked for from no one branch of the Christian Church, but should be the outcome of the harmonious and united co-operation of the whole body of CHRIST, for the perfect work of the body can be effected by no single member. We did not, therefore, ask for a thousand evangelists for the CHINA INLAND MISSION, but for prayer that the LORD would thrust forth that number of workers in such ways as He should see best. We deferred to a future number the consideration of the real value of such a proclamation as we proposed. To careful readers of CHINA'S MILLIONS this question scarcely needs dwelling upon, so many instances having been given from time to time of lasting good resulting from the first hearing of the Gospel. Still, as the question will arise in many minds, we will devote a little space to its consideration.

What, then, may be the real value of a single proclamation of the Gospel to the millions of China?

I. The command of the LORD JESUS will have been obeyed; in the keeping of His Commandment there is great reward. It is not for soldiers to question the expediency of a general's commands, but to obey. Unbelief might well have asked, What is the good of marching round the city of Jericho—are we not simply making ourselves appear ridiculous? The issue proved that the obedience of faith was the wise and right course. Or, to take another illustration, when JESUS said of the hungry multitudes in the desert, "Make the men sit down"; how they were to be benefited was still a mystery, yet the wisdom of obedience was soon proved. If, therefore, we could not *see* the benefit to be derived, our duty to every creature would still be plain, and if there were no other result, the reward of obedience would be ours.

II. Thoughtful readers of the Acts of the Apostles will have noticed that the triumphs of the Gospel through the preaching of the Apostle Paul, were in many instances very rapidly accomplished, as he passed from place to place. If, to the conversion of Lydia, it be objected that she was probably a Jewess, and certainly a worshipper of GOD, that can scarcely be predicated of the Philippian jailer and his family, or of the worshippers of the unknown god in Athens, among whom was Dionysius, the Areopagite.

III. To turn to China itself, multitudes of examples of GOD's blessing on the first preaching of the Gospel are to be found in the history of its missions. In some cases the results have been immediate, in others they have not appeared till after many days. The thousand evangelists would, of course, avail themselves of their daily opportunities of circulating everywhere Scriptures and Christian tracts, and of posting sheet-tracts on walls in suitable positions, from which kind of work alone great blessing has already resulted. It was stated at the Shanghai Conference of 1877, that the Presbyterian church at Chi-mi, in SHAN-TUNG, owed its origin, under GOD, to books or tidings taken from a street chapel elsewhere.

FEBRUARY, 1890.

"Dr. Medhurst, in 1835, landed on the island of Lam-yit, and left books; in 1868 a native preacher visited that island, and was preaching on the sea-shore, when two men said, 'Come up to the village, we have books that contain the same doctrine; our father charged us before his death to take good care of these books, for by-and-by, some one would come to explain them.' In six months more than sixty persons were baptised on that island."

The first convert in the Presbyterian church at Yü-yao read a sheet tract posted on the city wall, and not liking the position assigned to Confucius, as compared with the LORD JESUS, took the first opportunity of going to discuss the matter with a native preacher, which issued in his conversion.

The first convert the LORD gave us in Ningpo rose up and testified to his acceptance of the Gospel the first time he heard it. He subsequently became a native preacher, and died, I believe, in the service of the United Methodist Free Church.

The oldest native helper in connection with the C.I.M. is Mr. Wong, of Ho-zï. A native Christian, thrown out of employment for refusing to work on the LORD's day, went on the Monday afternoon to a tea shop to preach the Gospel. Mr. Wong there and then accepted it, and after some time returned to his native district to seek the conversion of his family and neighbours, while working on his own farm. After several years of such work, a lady in England, recently deceased, sent him a small sum of money, to enable him to hire partial help on his farm, that he might be more free for evangelisation. The old man has been preaching the Gospel there for twenty-nine years, and for over twenty years has shepherded a little church in his house of twenty or thirty native Christians, the fruit of his labours.

A missionary, not connected with the C.I.M., passing through a city in the north of KIANG-SU, preached the Gospel there. One of his hearers was much impressed, and obtained a couple of tracts from a native helper. After studying them carefully, he went to the inn where the missionary had stayed, to seek further instruction, but found that he had gone. In deep hunger and thirst of soul, after weeks of vain enquiry, he learnt that we had an out-station, four days' journey to the south. Thither he repaired, and received much instruction, but failed to find rest to his soul. Journeying four days further to the south in search of help, Mr. Tomalin, of the C.I.M., had the joy of being instrumental in his conversion, and he returned to his duties with Christian tracts and books, a rejoicing believer. Before he left that neighbourhood, he was the means of interesting about a dozen people in the Gospel, who subsequently became the members of a native church when one was formed there. Leaving the city, he went to his own native district, where he was greatly used of GOD, and three or four village churches exist to-day, the outcome of his work in the Lai-gan district of the GAN-HWUY province.

One of the most remarkable helpers we have ever had in CHEH-KIANG, was a literary man, Mr. Nying, whose conversion was the fruit of a single conversation with Mr. Stevenson. Eternity only will show all the fruit of that man's conversion.

One of the most devoted native pastors we have in SHAN-SI received his first leading to the truth through a Gospel given him by a man who procured it from one of our missionaries on the occasion of a solitary visit to the neighbourhood.

Time would fail to tell of scores of similar cases, which might easily be collected, showing the blessing received through once hearing or through receiving a book.

IV. Apart, altogether, from cases of distinct conversion by visits of the kind proposed, the whole Chinese mind is being enlightened, and subjects for thought are suggested that cannot be forgotten, and will surely bear fruit in days to come. The Chinese nation had lost the knowledge of one living personal GOD. Without GOD there can be no true idea of sin, and there is no place for forgiveness or atonement. A single visit may set hundreds of people thinking, and talking, and prepare the way for a great work later on, even where no immediate good is apparent.

But though, as we have shown, so much may be effected by once hearing, the proposed work would give the opportunity, as a rule, for much more than a single hearing of the Gospel.

Those who are accustomed to preaching the Gospel in the streets know how, frequently, interested hearers follow them from place to place, visit them in their inns or boats for further enquiry, and often, in the course of a few days, obtain a considerable amount of Scriptural knowledge. Our sisters, too, preaching the Gospel to the women, in their homes or in the courts, around which the houses are built, remark how some of their hearers follow them from court to court, and often carry on their enquiries and conversation till quite late at night. An evangelist would need to spend, at the rate proposed, four days in a village of 1,000 inhabitants, or two such workers would need to spend ten days in a market-town of 5,000 people. In most parts of China the people are collected in towns and villages, clustered round some large mart or city, of, perhaps, 20,000 to 50,000 inhabitants. Now, as an evangelist deputed to reach all the families of such city or mart would take four days to reach 1,000 people, it would take one worker from three to six months to reach the people of such a city. During all this time, the evangelists working in the villages around the city, when they left, could direct enquirers to the city in which one of their number would be found for weeks or months to come. The books and tracts sold, too, would contain the address of the nearest permanent mission-station, where enquirers might obtain help all the year round.

In conclusion, it may be well to mention that such work as is here proposed is not only possible, but has been proved to be practicable in different provinces. So long ago as the years 1855 and 1856 the editor spent many months in work of this kind, in company with the late Rev. W. C. Burns. When visiting a village, town, or city, the Gospel was systematically preached in all the principal streets, first of the suburbs and then of the city itself. Every shop was visited with tracts and books; six to eight hours were spent daily in speaking, alternately, in the open air; and not less than 500 to 1,000, as a rule, had the offer of the Gospel each day. When night came on, at a previously announced tea-house, enquirers and those interested were met for conversation; while a few were received into our boats for prayer and still more personal dealing. Similar work has, no doubt, been frequently done by other evangelists; our missionary sisters located in some of our inland stations pay itinerant visits to villages around, and do precisely this kind of work; but, of course, not in the thorough and systematic way we here propose, because their district is too large, and the duties of their station limit the time they can give. For the work now proposed, workers must be entirely free, and their districts clearly defined.

It seems to us that the present is a peculiarly appropriate time to raise this question; in May next delegates and representatives of all the Evangelical Protestant Missionary Societies will meet together in Shanghai, and one of the subjects to be discussed is the division of the field. We would ask for much prayer that this Conference may be made a time of great blessing, and that such steps may be taken as shall hasten the day when the Gospel shall have been brought within the reach of every creature in China. We have already entered on the last ten years of this century; surely, ere its close, we shall see this accomplished. We are thankful to find that the hearts of many of our correspondents have been stirred to prayer and effort; let us all persevere; a book of remembrance is kept, and our LORD has said, "Whatsoever ye shall ask in My Name, that will I do, that the FATHER may be glorified in the SON."

Items of Interest.

FROM REV. J. W. STEVENSON.

SHANGHAI, *Nov. 1st.*—Since last writing I have heard of 4 baptisms at Chung-k'ing on Sept. 30th. Messrs. Johnston and Mills, itinerating in the north of HO-NAN, are having a good deal of encouragement. They went into the capital, Kai-fung Fu, and freely walked about the streets, preached, and sold books, and stayed one night inside the walls.

From SI-CH'UEN I hear that Miss Foshery is living in Kwan-hien, a city four or five days north of Chen-tu. She has secured a house, and is quietly settled there, and writes very hopefully. Mr. Cassels, however, writes of his failure in opening I-lung Hien, a city near P'ao-ning. The people were so unruly that it was thought wise to give up the house and retire. Although this door is closed, there are many open doors in the neighbourhood which he and his fellow-workers hope to enter.

On Oct. 15th I left Shanghai with Mr. and Mrs. Steven and Mr. Tjäder, and we reached Gan-k'ing on the 20th, where I was greatly encouraged with the progress of the brethren, and with the spiritual tone prevailing. Mr. and Mrs. Steven, and Messrs. Meikle, Duff, Horne, J. Lawson, Souter, and Rough left there on the 29th by native boat for Ta-ku-t'ang. Mr. Steven will take the superintendence of these American brethren in the south of KIANG-SI. They have gone with many prayers and much hope. We shall be thankful for special prayer on behalf of this forward movement.

Nov. 13th.—I am sorry to report a serious riot at Nan-k'ang. It appears that the students who have been up for examination have been very rowdy for some time. On Nov. 6th they came to the house where Misses McFarlane and Harding were living, and wrecked it. Our sisters got safely into the Ya-men, but lost everything except what they had on. Then the rioters went over to the Opium Refuge, where Misses Ord and Bradfield were, and soon wrecked that place too. Misses Ord and Bradfield went into a neighbouring house before the work of destruction began, and about an hour afterwards the magistrate came to take them to the Ya-men. They were escorted by soldiers to Ta-ku-t'ang, and arrived safely.

I have to report the following 11 baptisms: Oct. 27th, Wun-chau, 8; Nov. 3rd, Shao-hing, 3. Looking at the work all round, we have much cause for thankfulness.

Nov. 29th.—We have, after a good deal of difficulty, secured a house at Kao-yiu, on the Grand Canal, and Misses Kentfield and Oakeshott are quietly settling in there. I receive most encouraging tidings from the Kwang-sin River, KIANG-SI, from both Misses Gibson and Mackintosh; the work is extending rapidly. The younger sisters who have gone there lately are getting on very well. Mr. Cassels is meeting with difficulties in his pioneering work. Misses Culverwell and Bastone, who are living at Kwan-yuen, meet with the greatest friendliness from the people, and yet there is some opposition. At Chao-hwa also, a station south of Kwan-yuen, there are serious difficulties, though the people there, too, are very friendly. Mr. Beauchamp has gone to Chao-hwa to assist Mr. Cassels.

I hear from Kwei-hwa-ch'eng, SHAN-SI, that they were having nightly meetings, and very attentive audiences.

Mr. Horobin, in Ning-hsia, KAN-SUH, writes urging for reinforcements. The work in the city and district is very promising, and I am sure there is ample room for a dozen missionaries in that large and important district, but with our small numbers it is impossible to do anything at present. I have the pleasure to report the following baptisms:—

Oct. 22 — Cheng-ku, SHEN-SI	...	...	...	16
,, 29. — She-k'i-tien, HO-NAN				8
Nov. 10. — Fung-hwa, outstations, CHEH-KIANG	...			2
,, 18. — Shao-h'ng	,,	,,	...	10
				—
				36

Messrs. Begg and Ewbank are encouraged at Hwuy-chau Fu, GAN-HWUY. From Mr. Huntley I gather that the work at Cheng-ku, GAN-HWUY, is very promising. GOD has greatly blessed Mr. and Mrs. Pearse during their residence in that city. Misses Ord and McFarlane were called upon by the British Consul at Kiu-kiang to give depositions with regard to the riot at Nan-k'ang. He intends to ask the Tao-t'ai that the officials shall invite our sisters back to the city. I hope that they may soon be able to return. It is very cheering to hear how the Christians have acted.

Misses Priscilla and Florence Barclay, F. H. Culverwell, Martin, and Bangert, with Mr. Hayward, left Hankow on the 21st inst. by steamer for I-chang. They would be joined there by Mr. and Mrs. James, and go on to SI-CH'UEN with them. Mr. Meadows has just returned from a most interesting tour of his outstations, CHEH-KIANG. In one, Yih-kō-chün, 103 sat down to the LORD's table.

Riot in Nan-k'ang Fu, Kiang-si.

FROM MISS C. McFARLANE.

KIU-KIANG, *Nov. 26th.*—For the last two months at Nan-k'ang, we have had a considerable amount of trouble with some students who were in the city for examinations. Several times during September we seemed on the point of having a riot. The officials did all they could to prevent anything of the kind by issuing proclamations, and several times sent men to guard our houses. On Wednesday, the 6th Nov., just as Miss Harding and I had finished our evening meal, stones were thrown at our windows. We did not think much of this as it had happened so often before. We closed the shutters and went on with our work, and for a time the stone-throwing ceased.

About half an hour afterwards Hu Sien-seng, the evangelist, came and told us the people were gathering in crowds in the street at the front of the house, and that he had sent to the ya-men. We heard almost immediately afterwards that the "hien" mandarin* had arrived. We then had some prayer together, and commended ourselves and the others to the care of our GOD. He *did* keep us *resting* in *Himself*. The stone-throwing began more vigorous than ever, and soon the stones came flying in from all corners, making it unsafe for us to stay upstairs. We then went downstairs into a room behind the chapel and were there for some time. Meanwhile the "hien" mandarin had arrived, and also a military mandarin; they kept at the front of the house, just at the door of the chapel, to prevent the people coming in, and they had soldiers going about with lighted torches trying to disperse the crowd.

Very soon part of the wall at the back of the house gave way, and the rioters got in and began smashing up everything they could lay hands on. The officials then gave the word for Miss Harding and I to leave the house and go to the ya-men. The "hien" led the way through the crowd, we following, surrounded by some soldiers and a few of the native Christians. How we got through that mob I cannot tell you, but we *did* without being hurt in the least, although stones were flying all around. Praise the LORD. We reached the ya-men safely, and spent a long, anxious two hours waiting for our two dear sisters from the other house. When we saw things were so serious at our house, we sent word to them and they took refuge in their landlord's house next door.

As soon as the rioters had destroyed the Ye-su-tang, they made for Miss Ord's house. Miss Bradfield had been in bed for two days poorly, and fortunately was up and out of the house before the great mass of the rioters got there. They had a very trying time on the way to the ya-men; they had a long walk, and the mob tried to get them away from the soldiers who were guarding them, but the LORD kept them wonderfully.

You can imagine better than I can tell you what joy it was to meet all safe in that ya-men; we did praise GOD with *very* full hearts. The native Christians, too, were *so* kind, I shall *never* forget their love and care over us. The LORD will reward and bless them for it.

We had a room given us, and went to rest some time in the early morning. We were in the ya-men all the next day until eleven o'clock at night. It seemed a long day, but we could not leave earlier; the weather was too stormy to cross the lake. The officials escorted us to the boat, which belonged to the Fu,† and several soldiers were sent with us to Ta-ku-tang, when we were received by the friends there who have been *so* kind to us. May GOD be glorified through it all. It is very blessed to KNOW "*He rules" over all*, and will cause this to be the means of extending, instead of hindering, His Kingdom.

EXTRACTS FROM A LETTER FROM MISS ORD.

TA-KU-TANG, *Nov. 8th.*—On Wednesday, Nov. 6th, we had a serious riot at Nan-k'ang Fu. I wrote you that morning telling you of a disturbance at the Opium Refuge on Sunday morning, but that letter with others was lost in the riot. The riot began at the chapel about six o'clock in the evening, and after the rioters had destroyed the house and everything in it, they then came on to my house (Opium Refuge about eight o'clock. The first intimation we had was a note from Miss McFarlane, begging us to get a boat and start for Ta-ku-t'ang, they being in the ya-men. This was out of the question as the mob was fast coming, so we went into the landlord's house adjoining ours. Our servants brought our coverlets and a few things that were at hand. The landlord took us into his back room, and all were so kind. In about ten minutes the students (estimated at about 7,000) came along literally yelling like wild beasts. They soon broke in, smashing and carrying off everything, except the few things in the landlord's house. The dear sisters at the other house — Misses McFarlane and Harding have

* The District Magistrate or Mayor. † The Prefect.

saved nothing but what they were wearing. In about an hour's time, nine o'clock, the mandarins, the Prefect, the district magistrate, two others, and one military mandarin came with the soldiers to take us to the Prefect's ya-men nearest to our house. We walked, guarded by soldiers on each side, but the students would not let us get in there, and broke the Prefect's chair in pieces; so we were taken through the streets to the district magistrate's ya-men, where we stayed until last night (7th), whence they escorted us to the mandarin's boat and sent us here under escort. We cannot speak too highly of their kindness; they did everything they could think of for our comfort. Indeed, we received kindness from so many, and the native Christians were just splendid; so bright, kind, and affectionate, and not ashamed to confess the LORD.

For myself, I can say I would not have missed this riot on any account. I never in my life had such joy in the LORD, or such a sense of His presence. I seemed all the time to be just seeing His face shining upon me. We all feel it an honour to have been privileged to suffer for His dear sake. May this experience draw us nearer to Him and make us more in earnest for souls. I do feel leaving Nan-k'ang Fu so much and the dear ones there; I have got so attached to them and the place. The kindness of everyone here is so touching, and the Canadian brethren have subscribed and given us a handsome sum in money, besides blankets, pillows, etc. The LORD will reward them a hundredfold.

I am sure we have the sympathy of many at Nan-k'ang Fu. I trust the LORD will soon let us return there, and that he will yet get great glory to Himself in this matter.

AFTER THE RIOT.

Mr. F. A. Steven, who visited Nan-k'ang Fu on Friday morning (8th) to render assistance, found on arrival that the sisters had already left for Ta-ku-t'ang. He had prayer with the native Christians, and was gratified to find them bright and hopeful, notwithstanding what had happened. He visited the scenes of the riot, and found both houses in ruins, and that everything had been carried off. Loot was evidently one—if not the main—object of the rioters.

Shao-hing and its Out-stations.

ON November 3rd, three persons were baptised in Shao-hing. Three days later Mr. Meadows started with the native pastor on a visit to the out-stations, where ten persons were baptised. The following extracts will be read with interest:—

FROM REV. JAS. MEADOWS.

BEFORE we started for Shing-hien we prayed for fair wind, for an uncrowded passenger boat, and for a comfortable seat for the *ten* hours in the usually slow boat up the mountain stream. GOD gave us all three, and we were thankful: so would most people be if they knew what it is to sit upright among a crowd of Chinese for ten hours! We preached salvation by CHRIST to our fellow-passengers, and trust many of their silly prejudices were removed, for our pastor knows how to answer the gainsayers well.

I took three services on LORD's day, November 10th. We had a prayer-meeting at night. There were six inquirers here. The pastor went to Mô-kô and held two services.

Saturday, 16th, we had to prepare for our great gatherings at *Yih-kô-chün* on Sunday and Monday, 17th and 18th. There are no shops at Yih-kô-chün, so everything had to be hired or bought, and brought from a city twenty-five *li* off, or from a large town ten *li* off. We had to provide rice for 150 persons for two days; this was paid for by the natives, or most of it. We had to hire bed-quilts, mats, basins, cups, and dishes, all brought on men's shoulders from the city, and the vegetables, meat, and bean curd had to be fetched from the market town 10 *li* off. We had not sufficient accommodation to lodge so many people in the city, so were obliged to hold our gatherings here in the country. The heads of the clan lent us their large ancestral hall in which to lodge our male friends, to cook their food, and to hold services for all. There must have been nearly 300 people present the first day.

On Sunday morning, directly after an early breakfast, we had a prayer-meeting, conducted by the pastor. After this fourteen candidates were examined; out of that number ten were accepted for baptism, six women and four men. Two brethren preached; the first subject, "How to Promote the Spread of the Gospel through our Church Members;" and the second subject, "How to Help one another to Seek *first* the Kingdom of GOD and His Righteousness;" both discourses very good. After this service came the baptisms.

The attitude of the clan and villagers is quite different from what it was a few years ago. Just fancy the boldness of our preacher to ask these heathen folks for the loan of their historical ancestral hall. Blessed, ever blessed be our GOD and FATHER, who hath made even our enemies to be at peace with us.

In the afternoon we had another service; two brethren preached. The first subject was, "The Importance of a Prayerful Study of the Scriptures." The speaker drew a very good picture of the benefit and blessing of searching the Scriptures, and thus tried to induce the hearers to fall in love with them. The second subject, "The Duty and Privilege of Keeping the LORD's Day." Our farmers, field labourers, and artisans are very much exposed to temptation in this matter, and the address was very seasonable. At night 103 sat down to the LORD's Supper. Many of our members could not attend, on account of distance and domestic duties.

It is easy to lodge 150 Chinese, for they are the most matter-of-fact sort of people in the world in this matter. Our female members and friends had the room over the little chapel; not a single article of furniture in it, not even a stool. On the old partly rotten floor was strewn some paddy straw; over this was spread some matting, and on the matting the cold-looking cotton quilts. The room was open on the south side; there was no door to keep them snug and private for the night, and the nights were very cold. The men spread straw on the bare ground in the ancestral hall, much of the place open to the sky, and with their bed quilts slept soundly half the night, for the first half was spent in discussing what they had heard during the day.

The next day, Monday, the 18th, we met again, and had prayer, singing, and four addresses. One address was on "How to Maintain and Foster Love and Harmony amongst the Brethren;" another, "How to Cultivate a Love for prayer;" a third was on "How to Induce the Churches in general to Give more Liberally to the Cause of GOD;" and the fourth was on "The Duty of the Members to *Aim at* the Support of their Particular Preachers." The speaker proposed *four* ways by which to raise the salaries of the preachers, namely, (1) reduce the quantity of tobacco, (2) the quantity of wine ; (3) young women to give up a certain kind of hair-oil ; (4) that each church should form a sort of shaving-club, and instead of going to the ordinary barber and paying twenty-four cash (one penny), that they should shave each other, and put two-thirds of this sum into a common box for the cause, thus saving one-third of the price and helping the LORD'S work at the same time.

Pray for *Shao-hing* city, that GOD may show to the churches here that He is stronger than Satan and superior to all hindrances and hard-heartedness on the part of the heathen, that the name of the LORD JESUS may be magnified and our FATHER'S name hallowed and glorified by many in this place.

Preparation for Work.

WE trust that many hearts are being stirred up to feel China's need of the Gospel, which has *never reached* a large part of the people. Some may long to go, and not see their way to the needful training. To such the narrative of how our brother Bridge was led may be helpful. He argued, If I am to trust GOD for support in China, may I not trust Him for help here, while preparing myself for the field? He first by prayer made sure he was following GOD'S will in leaving his work to prepare, and then went forward in faith ; and the GOD he had trusted and was serving did not fail him. When did He fail any who, sincerely desiring to serve Him, trust Him fully?

LETTER FROM MR. A. H. BRIDGE TO MR. THEODORE HOWARD.

ACCORDING to promise I write you an account of GOD'S dealings with me. I received an early training in the truths of the Gospel. My father died just before my fourth birthday, so that I am chiefly indebted to my mother for the said training. Still, I owe much to the prayers of my dear father ; for, since my conversion, my mother has often told me that he ceased not to pray for me, from my birth until his death, that I might be brought, while young, to a saving knowledge of the truth as it is in JESUS, and be made an instrument in His hands for good to the world.

Notwithstanding all this, I early wandered far away into sin. A consciousness of wrong would sometimes fill me, but I stifled it.

When between fourteen and fifteen, I chanced to form the acquaintance of a person a little older than myself, whose aspirations and tendencies were loftier and purer than mine, though he was not a Christian. Association with him affected me considerably, and revived oft-stifled desires to become a Christian ; but I did not see myself as a sinner, lost and ruined.

A few months afterwards GOD blessed the church which I attended with "showers of blessing." Numbers were converted and added to the church every month. I have since been informed that our beloved pastor wrestled much with GOD for my companion and myself. GOD answered those prayers, and brought both of us to Himself. My friend decided for CHRIST about a month before I did. The Sunday night that he did so, the minister had a little conversation with me, which set me thinking more than ever ; but the devil stepped in, and filled me with the thought that to join the church, read the Bible, and say prayers regularly was all that was wanted. It was not long ere I made up my mind to do this, and, as I thought, to be a Christian with my companion. GOD, however, interposed the same week that I thought of seeking admission into the church, and brought about a conversation in my presence between two men who knew nothing of my state of mind which completely overthrew my ideal of a Christian. Thus GOD saved me from becoming an unsaved member of a Christian Church. I then tried to banish all thoughts of religion from my mind, and endeavoured to quench the pleadings of the HOLY SPIRIT.

My work in the coal-mines in which I had laboured since I was twelve—was usually very hard and tiring, but about this time it was unusually so. A night's rest not being sufficient under the circumstances, it was with difficulty that I walked or moved in the morning until I had perspired freely. This led me to think of life : Why have I been brought into existence? etc. I concluded that man was created for a higher purpose than to work, eat, drink, and sleep. This revived old ideas of a life beyond, for which this one is a preparation. A line of poetry, from a piece entitled "Little Bessie Vane," which I had recited in the quarterly meeting of the Sabbath-school a few weeks previously, now came to my mind. The line ran thus :—

"For in that land the weary are at rest."

At first it gave me consolation and hope ; but when I mused on it, the thought came home to me that the "Land of Rest" was not for me it was a prepared place for a prepared people. I then realised, as never before, that I was lost. All my past came up before me : I had rebelled against GOD who wanted to do me good. This thought filled me with agony of soul. Strange to say, I scarcely thought of hell and its terrors : all my thoughts were of the wrong I had done towards GOD. The SPIRIT of GOD led me to contemplate CHRIST JESUS, and Him crucified—crucified for me! I was then at a loss to know how to appropriate this to myself, until, as the flash of a meteor, came the words to my mind, "Believe on the LORD JESUS CHRIST, and thou shalt be saved." The HOLY SPIRIT made it plain to me, and I then and there rejoiced in a present salvation.

Not half-an-hour afterwards, that old serpent the devil appeared on the scene, and tried to upset me. He intimated that there was no change in my person. I had experienced no extraordinary feelings of transformation, etc. But I was now one of CHRIST'S own, in possession of eternal life, and therefore should never perish. The HOLY SPIRIT gave me to realise that my assurance of salvation was in His Word, and not in any personal feeling. I answered Satan accordingly, and he never troubled me again on that score. I now "joined the church"—a saved soul.

All my heart's desires went out to GOD—I longed to please Him. I laid myself at His feet, and asked Him to use me as He thought fit. He laid it on my heart to tell others the glad tidings and to distribute tracts. It was a great delight and blessing to me to walk among the crowds who frequented the public-houses on Saturday evenings, and give them tracts and a few personal words. I cannot point to any conversion resulting from this work, but I have no doubt that the GOD who has said His Word "shall not return unto Him void" has caused it to accomplish that whereto He sent it. After a while GOD led me to speak for Him in public. Step by step He drew me on, until my eyes rested on the pulpit. I saw my fellow-men lying in darkness, strangers to GOD and His saving grace, and I longed to devote my life to preaching the Gospel to them. I prayed about it, and became convinced that

and expressed to Him my willingness to let His will be mine. I did not let my friends know anything about it for five or six months; I wanted to be sure that GOD was leading me to China; that He was leading me somewhere, I felt certain. The following verse of a beautiful little hymn called "GOD leads me," often came to my mind in those days—

GOD leads me; where I cannot tell;
But this I know,
If I within His path do go,
All will be well."

I prayed daily about it; it was the one thought of my life. GOD gave me a longing to take the Gospel to the heathen. The desire grew upon me; it burned, until I

THE EASTERN BUILDING OF THE FRENCH LEGATION AT PEKIN.

GOD wanted me to become a minister of the Gospel. My friends were delighted; it was just what they had hoped and expected. They gave me every encouragement. According to the usual custom, I preached twice before the church and pastor, and was set apart as a local preacher. As I had opportunity, I preached in the churches of our denomination in surrounding districts. In addition to this, it was a great delight to help others in cottage, prayer, and open-air meetings. GOD was with me, and gave me much acceptance and blessing. At the same time I sought to improve my education, my pastor helping me, so as to prepare for college. My mother, church, and personal friends intended to defray my college expenses.

About this time the Cambridge party went to China. I read in the Christian papers a little about them, and of the millions in "the regions beyond" who pass into eternity without hearing a word of salvation being brought nigh by CHRIST. This so weighed on my mind that I thought it my duty to go to the heathen. At first I did not like the idea. I had a bright prospect before me, which I did not want to give up; and besides, there were hardships, privations, and difficulties not a few for a missionary's lot. However, I prayed about it, and the more I did so the more plain did it seem to me that GOD wanted me for the heathen. I laid myself at His feet,

could not contain myself any longer, and so told my friends. My mother at first objected, but soon came round favourably. My step-father thought it a passing fancy of mine. My friends said nothing, thinking it best to leave me to the leadings of the HOLY SPIRIT. I continued to wait upon GOD for guidance; but, realising that all prayer must have a corresponding action, I pushed forward more than ever with my studies, and sought in every way possible to improve myself physically. In February of the following year (1886), after much waiting upon GOD about it, I made an application to the C.I.M. Our correspondence gave me considerable help.

Now came the time of real trial. Difficulties arose, circumstances changed, I had to leave home and support myself. But feeling assured more than ever that GOD wanted me in China, I resolutely set my face thither, and determined at all costs to go. I left home on October 19th, 1886, and obtained employment in the coal-mine of a village called Watt's Town, three miles lower down the valley, where I settled for the time being. I asked GOD to show me how best to prepare myself for China. Two things were brought before me. First, an opening for colportage work presented itself, which would give practical training, more time for study, and financial help. Then, second, I thought it best to give up my employment and devote my whole time to study. This would mean my leaving my every means of support, besides bringing upon me additional expense; but I thought that He who feeds and clothes the birds so well would look after me too. I had no one else to look to, so that I was cast absolutely upon Him. I prayed much about it, and became convinced that the latter was what GOD wanted me to do.

I immediately gave up my employment, and on November 15th, 1886, went to Pontypridd Academy, and commenced a course of study. The principal gave special advantages to ministerial students, so that, instead of having to pay two guineas per quarter, I only had to pay one. My lodging amounted to 10s. per month. I boarded myself, thinking to get on better. From a little book in which I sometimes entered special events (I am sorry I did not keep a diary) I extract the following:—

"*November 29th.*—I have been led to give my case into the LORD'S hands, with regard to an education to fit me for the mission field in China. Consequently I have been led to go to school. I gave up my employment a fortnight ago, and went to Edward's Academy, Pontypridd, and had myself enrolled as a day scholar. For my sustenance I look to Him who feeds the birds of the air and clothes the lilies of the field. So far I have lacked nothing; the LORD has met my every need. I am now to have lodging for nothing as soon as Bro. —— can get a house. So upon past 'Ebenezers' I build *my* 'Jehovah-Jireh' for the future."

I had intended to remove to Pontypridd, but my friend, who then lived in apartments, desiring to help me, came to see me the same week that I went to the academy, and promised me lodging free as soon as he could get a house. This he did in about a fortnight after the entry of the above, and I went to live with him. I walked to Pontypridd and back—a distance of six miles —five days a week, through the frost and snow of the winter; but when it rained I rode. This exercise did me much physical good. I remained with my friend, lodging without expense, till the following January, when I removed two miles nearer the academy, and remained there until May. Then, my health failing me, some friends advised me to go to Wiltshire, offering to pay my expenses. Having spread the matter before the LORD, I became convinced that it was His will that I should go. Then they gave me my travelling expenses, and I went to Wilts on May 3rd.

I have been repeatedly asked,

"HOW WAS YOUR NEED SUPPLIED?"

Well, when I was in need I made it known to the LORD, and He cared for me. For instance, when I was obliged to pay for my lodgings again, my supplies were nearly run out. I had sufficient food for the week, and 5s. or 6s. in my pocket. I intended removing on the Saturday, but had no human guarantee that my lodging money would come in. However, I doubted not, for I had learnt from experience by this time that "He *is* faithful." On the Thursday I had an invitation to preach the following Sunday in Monmouthshire. I removed to Cymmer on Saturday morning, and went to Monmouthshire in the evening, expecting GOD would there supply my need; but He did not, and I came back to find that 3s. had gone for travelling expenses. Having occasion to go to Ferndale, my old home, the same evening that I came back, a few friends who knew nothing of my need gave me sufficient to buy provisions for the week. Before the week was out I received an invitation to preach on the following Sunday at Llwynpia. I went, and the friends gave me 10s. On the Friday of the same week the pastor of Porth Church asked me to take his place on the Sunday, as he was called away. I did so, and he did likewise. This, with small sums given me by friends who had endeavoured to help me from the beginning, supplied my need.

The said friends were not in a position to render me much help being only poor miners—but from the time I went to the academy, they often sacrificed personal comforts that they might have wherewith to help me. Some of them asked me in the beginning to let them know when I was in need, and I should share whatever they had; but this, I told them, I would never do: GOD was the Supplier of my need, and I would "make my requests known to Him." However, they always endeavoured to help me, and it happened that when they did so it was just when I was in need. I owe these friends a debt which GOD alone can repay.

My destination in Wilts was the house of my beloved pastor, who had removed to Malmsbury a few weeks before I left home. A few days after my arrival there, I found myself with only a few pence, and sadly in need of a certain garment. My only expenses now were clothing, so I asked GOD to send me sufficient for the occasion. The following Sunday evening I was privileged to address the Y.M.C.A. public meeting on "The Need of the Foreign Mission Field." Just a little of how the LORD led *me* and opened up the way came out in the address. I know not whether my pastor told them of how I had lived for the past few months or not, but I was quite surprised to receive from him, the following Tuesday evening, on his return from the committee meeting, between sixteen and seventeen shillings, subscribed for me by the members that same evening. This supplied the said need and a few other necessaries.

My programme for the future was a few weeks' rest with Mr. Jones and my relatives—who lived a few miles away—to recruit my health, and then settle down somewhere to study again; but somehow there came an inclination to go to London.

THE ANNUAL MEETINGS OF THE C.I.M.

were drawing near, and I seemed to hear a voice saying, "Go up to London for these meetings." I became filled with a strange desire to go up, but couldn't see that it would do me any good, unless, maybe, the C.I.M. would see fit to do something further with my case.

I prayed much about it, and the voice seemed to be more distinct calling upon me to go up. I concluded GOD wanted me, so I wrote home telling my mother and friends that I should be in London the following week. I was now all expectation for the means wherewith to go. Friday came and passed away, and no money came. I reminded GOD of my need, and expected it by the next morning's post. Saturday's post came, but I received nothing. I began to feel queer, and to ask myself, What shall I do? Louder seemed the voice, 'Go to London for the meetings next week." After a little time of prayer, the thought struck me that GOD wanted to test my determination to work for Him. I immediately cleaned my old working boots (which I happened to have by me), and selected a few things for a walk to London, to commence at daybreak on Monday, expecting to reach Pyrland Road on Wednesday evening. I was not without money for the end of my journey, but I had not any to spend by the way; I felt sure GOD meant me to go, and that He would minister to my need. I finished my arrangements by dinner-time, and told my uncle and aunt, whom I was visiting for a few days, that I was going. They knew nothing of my need. Late in the afternoon I went to see a friend, when two sovereigns were dropped into my hand. So I discarded my working boots, and rode to London on the Tuesday. I repaired to Pyrland Road, and Mr. Broomhall kindly made arrangements for my stay with him. After the meetings, which were a great blessing to me, I spoke to Mr. Broomhall about leaving, but he asked me to stay a little longer. I proposed leaving two or three times after that, but he answered, "Are you tired of us?" GOD had lessons many and deep for me to learn in London. I trust they will be retained.

In a few months the remaining difficulties disappeared, and I found myself at the door, as it were, of China. I asked GOD daily to open the door, but He did not. Becoming engaged with lodging-house work in the East End and studies with Mr. Barfield in Inglesby House, and the door not opening, led me to think that GOD meant me to stay in England longer than I expected. So upon a certain Monday evening in November last I had a little prayer about it. I told the LORD I expected to stay till the spring at least, and asked Him to help me in the things referred to. The very next morning before breakfast I was asked if I was prepared to go to China. I scarcely ate my breakfast after that, so great were the surprise and the joy. In a week's time it was decided that I should be one of "the hundred." So on December 1st, I started in the S.S. *Brindisi*; and after six week's sailing and a very prosperous, enjoyable, and profitable voyage we reached China.

The Men's Bible-class in T'ai-yuen.

FROM MR. SAUNDERS.

T'AI-YUEN-FU, *Aug. 6th.*—Knowing the interest you take in Bible-classes, I thought a little about my Bible-class here would be of interest. We hold it on Monday evenings, meeting in a room which we use as parlour, dining-room, and for almost every other purpose except sleeping. Five natives attend, who form the male portion of our church membership at present.

No. 1 is an old man, converted from Buddhism several years ago. For some time he was employed as an evangelist, but when the mission decided to employ very few natives, he was given a pension as he was not able to do much. He has some very peculiar notions as to how work should be carried on, and, converted as he was an old man, he clings tenaciously to them, making it at times a little difficult to deal with him; yet the old man has new life burning within him, and we trust that many will be led to our LORD JESUS through him. I would ask your prayers on his behalf; his name is Tong.

No. 2 is a young man who during the famine in SHAN-SI in 1877 was taken into the boys' school then opened. He has been living with the missionaries ever since. For a few years he had acted as Dr. Edward's assistant in the dispensary; he has been a Christian several years. We call him Heh-nin.

No. 3 is an old man named Wang, who came from Wu-t'ai, a district over 100 miles north of this, to see the doctor about his eyes, he being almost blind. Nothing could be done for him, but Dr. E. kept him on giving him odd jobs to do, such as carrying water, etc. He accepted Christ, and was baptised about two years ago.

No. 4 is a boy, also blind, who came from a village about fifty miles north of this, to see the doctor about his eyes. Nothing could be done for him; but while here he believed in JESUS, and was baptised. Being an intelligent lad, Dr. Edwards took a deep interest in him, and after getting the consent of his old mother, sent him to Peking to learn Mr. Murray's blind reader's system. He spent nine months there, and has recently returned. Nothing has been decided as to what he will do in the future, but it is proposed that a work for the blind should be started. Will you join us in prayer about this?

No. 5 is the only church member (male) that we have who is not employed by us; there are several others, but they are not in good standing, so cannot be counted. He is a bricklayer and stonemason by trade, but was formerly a soldier. He was brought to the Lord through the instrumentality of the late of Mr. Sturman, and is one of the brightest Christians we have. He comes to the services on Sundays with an entire change of clothing, etc., which, to my Scotch idea, is what ought to be. His name is Iloh. So now you have a brief account of each member of my Bible-class; now a little about the class itself. We have an opening hymn—the one last night was, "I once loved the pleasures which earth has to give"—then one of the native brethren engaged in prayer, remembering specially the thousands and millions of China who know nothing about our SAVIOUR; then comes the lesson, which last night was Lot's separation from Abraham. Our system of teaching is usually by questioning and expounding; after the lesson comes another prayer by one of the native brethren, and we are done, having been together for nearly an hour and a half. Will you pray for this class that it may be the means of great blessing and strengthening to the few Christians?

I send you enclosed with this

FOUR PAPER GODS,

all of them commonly worshipped in China.

No. 1, called T'ien-ti, or Heaven and Earth, almost universally worshipped in China; in fact, in houses where there are fewest idols you will always find Heaven and Earth. Heaven is the great father, and Earth is the great mother.

No. 2 is Tsao-uan-ie, a household god, almost every family having an altar on the stove dedicated to him. He cares for all the members of the family, and will report what they have done to the Great Emperor (the highest god). He is supposed annually to ascend to heaven on the 24th day of the 12th Chinese month. Offerings are made on that day of rice, flour, fruits, and sugar; for "sugar will cause his mouth to stick, so that he will not be able to report any bad actions of the family to the Great Emperor." Paper chairs are sold in quantities at this time "to assist him in ascending to heaven." He returns to his duty on the 15th of the 1st month.

No. 3, "the God of Riches." This god is greatly venerated in China—more so even than the great philosopher Confucius, "because he possesses the power of enriching those whom he likes." He loves playthings. On the 5th day of the new year, before the recommencement of business, he is sacrificed to; this is called "welcoming the wealth god." Other gods are sacrificed too with male fowls, but this one with hens, eggs, game, fireworks, etc. The fish offered are a pair of carps, but the name on this occasion is changed to "silver ingot fish." After sacrifice, some of these fish are released and put into a pond or river, that the business may be as profitable as the spawn of the carp is plentiful. In a merchant's house, if persons employed by him are invited to the sacrificial ceremony, they will still be employed for the ensuing year; if not invited, they will be dismissed. Scarcely a shop has not a small altar to this god.

No. 4. This is a god also controlling man's fortune, but differing from the wealth god in being only temporary, and not being put up in shops, but generally by the side of doors of private houses. It is called the "Earth God," and is connected chiefly with the farming classes.

Villagers of North China.
FROM DR. EDWARDS.

THE two men on the right are brothers, and hold in their hand Christian tracts which have been given them. These two men migrated from their home in Chu-lu to a village in north Shansi, where Mr. and Mrs. Pigott made their acquaintance. Subsequently Mr. and Mrs. Pigott removed to Chu-lu and opened a station at Shun-teh Fu, ten miles from the home of these men. Last (Chinese) New Year, the men went home for a holiday, and took a number of their relatives to see Mr. and Mrs. Pigott; and through this introduction there is a very friendly feeling on the part of the people of that village towards the missionaries.

The third man holds in one hand a packet of medicine just given him by the missionary, and in the other his pipe. Over his shoulder is his cash-bag or purse, on which is written the name of his village and place of business.

Tidings from Scattered Workers.

Kan-suh Province.
FROM MR. C. POLHILL TURNER.

Si-ning, Sept. 24th.—We have only just returned from Maying-tsi, a little place, three days' journey from here. We met the principal of the monastery at Ta-si last year; he then invited us to pay him a visit and spend as long as we liked with him, when he would help us with the Tibetan language. He is an old gentleman of seventy, and has a degree equal to the highest literary degree of the Chinese; his reputation as a sage is great among the Tibetans. Tha monastery is small, having about forty lamas; the buildings consist of one large hall, surrounded by smaller rooms in which the lamas live. The large hall contains idols and several rows of pillars, and at the base of each row slightly raised platforms, on which the lamas sit as they recite their prayers. The whole building is elaborately painted and gilded and lies in the midst of a mountainous district. The lama gave us useful lessons in Tibetan, writing sentences and explaining them, while we endeavoured to help him with English; he took much interest in foreign customs, sciences, etc. We hope to visit him again soon. The first three weeks we lived in a black tent which the lamas erected for us, as they were then engaged in prayers, and no woman might enter the precincts of the monastery until their conclusion. I had my meals daily with the lama, and then carried my wife's to her. The latter part of the time we lived in a nice room next door to the old gentleman's little house. My wife is ever so much better for the change and fresh mountain air. Please pray for the lama; he was so kind to us, and would take no remuneration for the six weeks we spent with him, giving us a present in addition.

FROM MR. HORObIN.
Ning-hsia, July 6th.—On June 24th I left for the Ling-chau district. On arriving at Yeh-shen-p'u I went on the street preaching, and the following day being market day, I spent a good time in preaching and selling books. But of all seasons of the year this seems the busiest, as the opium is being gathered. The people rush to market and rush back again. I was on the street soon after five, and at that time it seemed like noon. I was surprised to find Chin-chi-p'u such a large walled city with shops as large or larger than we have in Ning-hsia. My man had been there only a few days before and sold 150 books, and I sold a similar number, chiefly in the shops, most of which I visited. This would be a fine place for a missionary, nine markets being held during the month; the Yellow River lying between, it would be difficult to work from our side of the river. At Wu-tsung-p'u, too, there are also nine markets a month, and on the streets I should think there were several thousand people. In that district, at least, nine-tenths of the ground is burdened with opium.

Aug. 11th.—You will be glad to hear that we have had a few baptisms at Ning-hsia, though not so many as I anticipated; we are praying that the halting ones may yet come out fully on the Lord's side. Our life truly is a life of faith, which seems often to be tried as by fire. Of the four baptised, three had passed through the refuge, and one assists in it; one is a tailor and was the first to enter the refuge; another was a carpenter, to whom the Sunday question has been no small test, seeing he has two young fellows in his employ. It is the Sunday question that has kept several of the others back. Our greatest disappointment is in a young man who has been in our employ for several years; he wept on the evening previous to the baptisms as I dealt personally with him. He being the eldest son in the family, his father, a well-read man, was very much opposed, and asked him if that was filial piety to listen to an outsider rather than to his father. Please pray for him.

FROM MR. BOTHAM.
Tien-chan, July 26th.—We find going to villages together succeeds splendidly; the women soon gather round my wife, and take her to a house where she can speak to them, while I get

the men on the street or in the tea-shops. We wish to get more at the poorer classes of people, so we are arranging to travel in the simplest way, and intend to stay at all the villages to thoroughly preach CHRIST, letting them see that we have a Doctrine for every one of them.

FROM MISS CLARA ELLIS.

T'sin-chau, August 25th.—I have felt much better since coming here, praise the Lord. The climate seems more genial than that of Si-ning. My sister and I are living with Miss Sutherland at the ladies' house; we are looking forward to being really settled down here; may our work be in the power of the SPIRIT. There is much here to encourage, but there are many discouragements too. Were we not sure that the Almighty One works with us we should be inclined to cry out, Who is sufficient for these things! Mrs. Chao, the Bible-woman, is a power for good, and even in persecution is not ashamed of the testimony of JESUS. To speak to her helps one; JESUS *only* seems to be the centre and object of her life. We long to see other of the native Christians more earnest, and sitting more loosely to the things of time. Our life really needs to be one of unceasing intercession for these people.

Shan-si Province.

FROM MR. I'ANSON.

Ta-t'ung, August 9th.—We have had a rainy season which has done damage to several places around here. To the west a village was submerged and swept away. To the S.E., the west suburb of Ilwen yuen-chau, 120 *li* from here, has also been swept away by the floods. On Monday I started off for Chu-loh, and found the roads in places cut into gullies of two feet deep. Chu-loh is sixty *li* N.W. from Ta-t'ung, and is a small walled town of 300 families. I reached there early in the evening, went on the streets with some books, and had a very good time. The people were so eager to buy gospels; I do trust the Lord will bless His own Word to these people. Next day at the place where I stopped at noon I had such a grand opportunity of scattering the good seed that I did not go further, as I had intended. Here, in contrast to Chu-loh, I could hardly sell one gospel—the people chose all the other books. Some time ago I spoke of a man named Li; praise GOD, he is coming out very brightly, but he has a tremendous trouble in his wife, who does all she can to withstand him. We found that he was going to *sell* her to another man! but after reading the Word together, and prayer, he said he would not do so.

FROM MR. SAUNDERS.

T'ai-yuen, August 15th.—The Lord has been leading me through many experiences since coming to China. Whilst studying, I have had opportunity of watching the work in its various aspects, and oh, how saddening to see how depraved the human heart is, and how men will seek after earthly gain rather than eternal hope. How sad to see men professing Christianity in the hope of gaining some earthly advantage! It shows how we must lean on the power of the HOLY SPIRIT to convince men of sin and to convert them. Well, praise the LORD, He reigns, and the chosen ones will be gathered out; though there may be tares, the wheat will also be there. It has been blessed to read the life of Paul by the HOLY SPIRIT; it encourages one to know that he met with difficulties, and many a time I daresay he wept over erring believers—and so must we.

One thought has been impressed upon me very much, and that is that we must get nearer the people; we must come down to them, as the Lord did to all mankind. I am sure that we in T'ai-yuen, at any rate, are living too much above the ordinary people.

FROM MR. LUTLEY.

Sih-chau, Sept. 17th.—You will be glad to hear of five more baptisms at Keh-ch'eng, three women, one man, and a son of one of the Christians, a bright Christian lad about sixteen years old. Mr. Key is hoping to baptise several others at Ta-ning in a few weeks. While Miss Scott and Miss Miles were away for a little change I spent about six weeks there, and had a very happy time, although as I had to get some repairs done to the house, etc., I was not able to spend so much time in the villages as I could have wished. It is a real joy to get about among the Christians in the villages, they are so simple, warm-hearted and kind; there is a spirit of enquiry abroad too in some of the villages, and some of the people come together splendidly to the meetings. I returned here about a week since. While there is much cause for praise, there is also much cause for sorrow; several of the Christians I found were not keeping the Sabbath; and one or two had gone back to their opium, the temptation having proved too strong for them in time of sickness.

FROM MISS FORTH.

Hoh-chau, Aug. 7th.—Miss Jakobsen and I have been here now for more than six months; we are very happy together. Many families have taken down their idols, principally in the villages, and one or two we hope have received the SPIRIT, and been born again. Experience however teaches us to rejoice with trembling; we have had some most bitter sorrow in seeing those whom we had hoped would be His "in that day when He shall come to make up His jewels" going backwards and not forwards.

FROM MR. HOSTE.

Hung-t'un , July 10th.— I and my boy started early and travelled leisurely to Yo-yang Hien, seventy *li* distant. We had lunch, such as it was, at the remains of an inn at a place called Kao-p'en, forty *li* from Hung-t'ung. The people and houses in the place were alike miserable; the ravages of opium in these wretched hamlets among the hills are horrible.

Yo-yang, July 14th.—Had a long visit from a young man of the reading-class, who seems most interested in the way of salvation from his opium and other sins. Mr. Li knows him and has often spoken to him on the subject. Mr. Li's influence in this neighbourhood is very widespread. GOD uses him remarkably in healing the sick in answer to prayer. I had much conversation with him which was very helpful to me.

July 15th.—To-day it rained unceasingly; as a consequence I had quite a number of visitors, agricultural people who were kept from their work by the rain. It was very nice to hear dear Li explaining to them the things of GOD, and in some cases there was close and patient attention given.

Shan-tung Province.

FROM MR. JUDD.

Ning-hai Chau, Sept. 26th. We are thankful to see a few more souls in this place wishing to follow the SAVIOUR. Ten women and one man asked for baptism last Sunday; we have good reason to believe that about half of them are true believers in the LORD JESUS; of the others we need further evidence of their conversion. Some of them, we think, have been converted for a year or so, but we, as a rule, do not propose baptism until they ask for it. Last Sunday week I was urging two women to cry to GOD for their husbands' conversion; they were opium-smokers. One said she feared it was hopeless, as her husband seldom came home, and then he often beat her. Another Christian woman on hearing this, said, "You should see the difference in *my* husband since he believed; he used to fight with me and throw the stool about, but now he never does, and we are happy." The same woman got up last LORD's day with two or three others, and testified to the change in their homes and to their happiness since they knew the LORD JESUS. The women here seem to get a-head of the men. Two of the men have fallen out about their business; I trust it will be put right quickly. Another man who came to us from Fuh-shan has turned out a desperate rogue. We are not without our trials. I am more and more impressed with the deep importance of love as the chief factor in winning souls. Oh, how possible it is to preach with wonderful eloquence, earnest zeal, and convincing logic, and yet every soul be untouched, because love was lacking.

Si-ch'uen Province.

FROM MR. WELLWOOD.

Sui-fu, Aug. 10th.—The work here is progressing; leavening is going on, and the good seed of the Kingdom, which is sure to bear fruit, is being sown every day. It needs grace to keep one patient, waiting in hope. Just now we have gone over the city thoroughly with tract distributing; there is scarcely an alley or house in Sui-fu where the news has not entered.

From Miss I. W. Ramsay.

Chung-k'ing, Aug. 15*th.*—To-day we have had a good many women in. All the neighbours when they have visitors bring them to see us.

Aug. 18*th.*—As Dr. Cameron is away, Mr. Chu, our native evangelist, takes the services. He preaches spiritually and simply; the people could not fail to understand. He seems to be growing in grace.

We have been much in prayer about the wife of Miss Hook's teacher, who was our first opium patient. She is a Christian, but very timid; on asking her if she would be willing to go out visiting with us, to our surprise and joy she readily assented.

Gan-hwuy Province.

From Mr. Meikle.

Gan King, September 23*rd.*—I had the pleasure of visiting Ning-kwoh with Mr. Souter this summer. We stayed three weeks, and I gained much valuable experience. I visited several of the villages where there were native Christians. One day the evangelist and I went to Lang-ting, 15 *li* from the city. A number of Christians gathered together for worship in the house of one of them, a farmer, whose wife and mother are also Christians. We had a very blessed time in that home. I felt the presence of the MASTER very near. There are twenty converts in this place.

Another day I went with Mr. Miller to Seng-kia-p'u, thirty *li* from the city. We had a very blessed time there. There are no Christians there except the evangelist and his wife; but, praise GOD, there are six enquirers. We stayed the night and had a good gospel meeting, the little hall was filled.

Mr. Eyres and I went out a great deal in the streets, and while he preached I sold gospels and tracts, and got on very well.

Kiang-su Province.

From Miss J. Webb.

Yang-chau, Oct. 12*th.*—On Wednesday last Miss Kentfield and Miss Oakeshott started for Kao-yiu; they have gone to take possession for a time of the new house there. I have just had a letter from Miss Oakeshott, in which she says "Ling Nai-nai and a girl have been talking about Miss MacKee, how they asked her when she was going to leave them, and she said, 'I am not going back; when I die, I die here,' and telling me that many people in Kao-yiu knew her, and all who did loved her and grieved when she died. Her little while here I am sure must have been a blessing."

Tsang-tsi, who has been very ill, is now nearly well; he has had a trying time; his parents have been troublesome, but he is praying all the more earnestly for their conversion.

This morning we had a special time of prayer together for the LORD's help and blessing upon all the work in China and at home; we felt it good to wait upon GOD, and to remind ourselves of the many promises of blessing in GOD's Word. We were dwelling upon the blessings Abraham had because of his obedience. How often our MASTER calls for our obedience, and when we see Him how easy to obey, is it not?

Miss F. H. Culverwell has been to the old city this afternoon with Kao Lao-t'ai, and they had a real good time, all listened so well. Every afternoon one of us goes to the house in the old city; at first we could only talk to those who came in, and they would suddenly go and others come, now they sit and listen while we have prayer, sing a hymn or two, and read the Word of GOD.

Kiang-si Province.

From Miss Gibson.

I-yang Hien, Sept. 5*th.*—Nothing remarkable has taken place in our station this month. The Christians seem to be steadily growing in grace, and there are a few women inquirers, who say they truly trust in JESUS. One of them is from a village about ten *li* (three miles) from here, brought by a Christian woman who has been coming herself for some months, but is not yet baptised. Another woman from the same village, an opium-smoker, seems interested.

Three of our Christian women accompanied Miss Rogers to a village about 40 *li* from Ho-k'eo, where they were very kindly entertained by a woman who professed faith in JESUS when visiting Ho-k'eo. It gave us great joy to see these dear women of their own accord going to the villages to tell the Gospel. They returned so full of joy. GOD grant that a great many women may have the needs of their heathen sisters laid more heavily on their hearts.

Miss Gardiner and I spent a few days in a village about thirty-five *li* away. We stayed with a woman who *firmly* believes in JESUS; the HOLY GHOST has opened her heart, like Lydia's of old. Prayer is very real to her; her faith quite overstepped mine, which sometimes seems very small. She is very earnest about the souls of the people. We also visited another woman, Mrs. Ting; quite a number of women listened very attentively, and we trust some will gather every Sunday in that village.

Miss Rogers and I visited a village twenty *li* away, with Mrs. Cheng, a Christian, who went to visit her mother. It rejoiced our hearts to see how earnestly Mrs. Cheng testified for the MASTER.

Miss Gardiner and I left Ho-k'eo for I-yang Hien on Monday, so have been here four days; we are just returning, and intend coming again within a fortnight, as at present it does not seem advisable for any of us to stay here. One of the Ho-k'eo Christians, a very faithful follower of the LORD JESUS, is living in the house which has been rented for fifteen dollars a year. A good many seem very favourable to the Gospel, and we are looking to the LORD to save many souls here. We have visited the next city, Yen-san Hien twice, staying in an inn and receiving great kindness from the people; we are looking to the LORD to give us an opening in it; will you remember this city in prayer.

One wants to rest on the LORD as the work widens. We have been thinking a great deal about the sitting time when the LORD will burn up the wood, hay, and stubble. May all that we do be in the power of the HOLY GHOST.

From Miss Ord.

Nan-k'ang, Aug. 26*th.*—The Christians were never more warm than they are now. This morning I was so touched by one of them coming to say that he had heard that money that I was expecting from England had not come, and that I could not buy any more things until it did. He had six dollars; would I please accept it?

From Miss Say.

Kwei-K'i, Sept. 15*th.*—The work here is going on, souls are being saved, but only one here and there. I long to see tens and twenties coming out; perhaps the LORD cannot trust me with success. Please pray that all that would hinder may be fully cleansed. We had two more idols burnt a week or two ago, and their owner seems in real earnest about her soul. One of the women baptized when Mr. McCarthy was here promises to make a very good Bible-woman. I want two or three, if the LORD will give them to me, to help in the villages.

Departures for China.

On Jan. 9th, per P. and O. s.s. *Peshawur*, Miss F. M. BRITTON returning, also Misses A. J. FORSTER, E. G. LEGERTON, BESSIE LEGGATT, and M. J. BURT. (Miss H. POLHILL-TURNER was unable to go from illness.)

On Jan. 23rd, per P. and O. s.s. *Chusan*, Mr. and Mrs. BALLER and two children, and Miss TODD returning, also Dr. HOWARD TAYLOR, JOHN GRAHAM, and GEO. MCCONNELL; of the Bible Christian Mission, *John Carter* and *Wm. Tremberth*; and of the Norwegian China Mission, *Miss Hattrem* and her mother.

CHINA'S MILLIONS.

Progress.

SHALL China have a thousand Evangelists without delay? we have asked; and the question will naturally arise, How far can the friends of the China Inland Mission help in this movement? We are glad to find that some of them are already beginning in the right way—by prayer and by interesting as many of their friends as they can. We should like to suggest several definite topics for prayer.

I. That GOD will lay the need and the possibility of this work on the hearts of influential Christian leaders in different sections of the Church.

II. That in the approaching general Conference of Missionaries to be held in Shanghai in May, the subject of the division of the field may be so practically dealt with as to facilitate the carrying out of the evangelisation of the whole empire.

III. That, as to the China Inland Mission, GOD may give us suitable helpers to strengthen both our home and foreign work. When we first commenced the Mission we were encouraged by the promises given to Solomon for the building of the Temple in 1 Chron. xxviii. 20, 21. It was foreseen that as the work progressed, help of various kinds would become requisite; but as the work to be done was the work of CHRIST, our KING, the true Solomon, so the promises made to Him secured the raising up of every willing skilful man for any manner of service, and that, therefore, we might in faith apply to Him for whatever help might become needful. Hitherto our expectation has not been disappointed; signally suitable fellow-workers have been given to us. But our work at the present time cannot be largely increased without more help, both in the home and foreign departments. Our Council needs enlarging. One or two friends at home able to give their whole time to the work would be a boon; and several earnest, capable young men for business departments at home and abroad, and for shorthand and other clerkships, are desirable. We also need well-qualified male and female teachers for our English schools in Che-foo.

IV. While mentioning these needs we must not fail to give GOD thanks for the encouragement He has been giving us in recent developments, a few of which we may mention to help in thanksgiving. In our October number we spoke of the Council for North America and gave the address of the office, 14, Richmond Street W., Toronto, Ont. Since then a training home has been opened in that city at 30, Shuter Street, by the Secretary-Treasurer, Mr. H. W. Frost. One of the members of that Council, the Rev. R. Wallace, of Belleville, Ont., writing on November 12th, said:—

"I went up to Toronto last week to attend a meeting of the Council and spent the night with Mr. Frost in the new home. You will be glad to know that I was very much pleased with all I saw. I feel more and more that he is a prepared man for a prepared place. The house is most suitable, and Mrs. Frost is very capable. There are five young ladies with them at present, one of whom was accepted at our meeting. Two young men are at the Institute, and come in for meals, etc. So far as I saw, the home is a model, and is carried on in the most loving and wise way possible. The office arrangements are also well planned and systematised, and every detail is done in a most prayerful and devoted spirit."

From this home six sisters left for China on the 13th of January, and about the same number of brethren were expected to follow in February.

In the November number of CHINA'S MILLIONS we gave an account of the formation of an Auxiliary Council for Scotland, of which Mr. Wm. Oatts, of 70, Bothwell Street, Glasgow, is the Hon.

MARCH, 1890.

Secretary, to whom all applications of candidates from Scotland are now sent. We look for much help and blessing from this development.

A few months ago a Ladies' Auxiliary Council was formed in London, of which the members at present are Mrs. Theodore Howard, Mrs. William Sharp, Mrs. Broomhall, Mrs. Hudson Taylor, and Miss Soltau, the Honorary Secretary. We are now able to mention that the houses 41 and 41A, Pyrland Road, have been occupied as the office of this Council, and as a Ladies' Training Home, under the care of Miss Soltau. Those who know how largely Miss Soltau has been used of the LORD in Hastings, among young women and others, will rejoice with us in this accession to our strength.

In the report of our annual meetings for the year 1888, it was mentioned that a Home had been opened in Cambridge for those approved candidates who, having some means, wished to prepare for the Mission-field at that University; and that, as the sum charged for board and fees did not cover the expenses, the surplus had been provided by special gifts from Christian friends. For two years this Home has been carried on for the benefit of the Mission, but independently; its value having been proved, it has recently been thought desirable that it should be under the management of the Council of the Mission. Of the students at present studying there, four are preparing for medical missionary work. We shall be thankful for prayer for this Home, and that it should continue to be sustained by the special gifts of those who appreciate its value.

We have also to thank GOD for important enlargements in China, which will greatly facilitate the more rapid development of the work. As our readers know, we have long been needing more suitable accommodation in Shanghai. When we last left China, the far from satisfactory premises there were costing a monthly rental of over £30 (though nearly half this rental was paid for us by one of the members of the Mission). Now, through the munificence of a devoted servant of GOD, who has borne the whole expense of site and buildings, we have large and well-adapted premises of our own. We are also indebted to the same kind friend for the gift of mission premises in Tientsin.

In the training homes at Gan-k'ing and Yang-chau we were also needing additional premises for students. In each of these places new buildings have been erected during the past year, doubling the amount of our accommodation. The return of Mr. and Mrs. Baller after their furlough, will further facilitate the training of new missionaries as GOD gives them. In other ways which we cannot here particularize, there have been helpful developments; but the constant growth of the work brings additional pressure on already over-burdened workers, among whom Mr. Cardwell, our Secretary at Shanghai, and Mr. Broumton, the Treasurer and Accountant in China, are specially needing the help we have referred to. What definite part the China Inland Mission may be able to take in the work of the thousand Evangelists we do not yet see, and therefore while we shall be thankful for any suitable persons who may offer for this special service, we are not asking at present for any definite number for the Mission; but we cannot help feeling that GOD is leading us on to larger things than we have yet attempted.

V. In conclusion, we commend to the earnest prayers of our readers the members of the new Councils. For the Directors and officers of the Mission at home and in China, and for the C.I.M. Conference meeting in Shanghai, in April, special prayer is also desired, as many important and difficult matters are now under consideration. May GOD the HOLY GHOST guide to right conclusions, and answered prayers offered in the name of CHRIST bring glory to our Heavenly FATHER.—J. H. T.

Items of Interest.

FROM REV. J. W. STEVENSON.

SHANGHAI, *Dec.* 13*th.*— Since my last I have heard of the following baptisms :

Oct. 19th at Ta-ning, SHAN-SI	...	...	8
,, 26th ,, Gan-shun, KWEI-CHAU		...	1
Nov. 2nd ,, Chen-tu, SI-CH'UEN	...	...	2
,, 18th ,, Ning-hai-chau, SHAN-TUNG		...	2
,, 23rd ,, ,, ,,		...	1
,, 24th ,, ,, ,,		...	5
,, 24th ,, Wun-chau, CHEH-KIANG		...	4
			23

Mr. Bridge sends me an interesting report of a visit paid to North HO-NAN lately. Mr. Wood has gone into the country (GAN-HWUY Province) to help some Christians who were suffering persecution. I hear from Bhamo of the safe arrival of Messrs. Selkirk and Lambert. We have heard from Mr. Steven and his party in South KIANG-SI. Mr. James Lawson writes that he and Mr. Rough were settled in an inn, and hoped to work in that district, while Mr. Steven and his three companions have gone on further south.

Dec. 17*th.*—Mr. Cooper baptized two men at Cheng-yang-kwan lately; he has visited Ning-kwoh and has gone on to Hwuy-chau.

Dec. 27*th.*—We have had a hallowed season here and much to praise GOD for. Mr. and Mrs. Nicoll and the five sisters arrived safely to-day, all well. I hear that the four sisters have returned to Nan-k'ang. Mr. and Mrs

Botham have started on their wandering pilgrim life on the Si-gan plain. They expect to go from city to city to stay a week or a fortnight, as GOD may guide. I have heard of Mr. and Mrs. Pearse's departure from Cheng-ku, and also with sorrow of their wreck 175 *li* below at the Pu-tan rapid. I hear that they were camping on shore in huts made of rugs, and expected to be another week before they could start; their boat had been quite wrecked. I am sorry to hear from Mr. Meadows that seven men are in prison in the Chu-ki district, CHEH-KIANG, and being badly treated on a false charge—really a case of persecution for the Gospel's sake. Mr. Meadows is greatly distressed about it, and asks for special prayer for these men.

On the 14th inst. we had the pleasure of welcoming Messrs. Anderson, Stark, Alty, Allen, Dickie, Grainger and Hall; they left us after a very pleasant time here on the evening of the 18th inst., and I have since heard of their arrival at Gan-k'ing. We have heard of the following baptisms:—

Dec. 1st at Wu-hu, GAN-HWUY 2
 ,,   1st ,, Fung-hwa outstation, CHEH-KIANG 1
                                              —
                                              3

Baptisms at Cheng-ku, Shen-si.

FROM MR. A. H. HUNTLEY.

OCT. 20*th*, *Sunday*.—Very wet; but not sufficient to damp the zeal and love of those who are accustomed to meet on this day and worship the true GOD. Our little room was crowded out at the morning meeting, there being about forty present. In the afternoon we had another meeting, quite as well attended as that of the morning. It had been specially convened to examine candidates for baptism. This time, Mr. Pearse tried a new plan and examined them before the whole assembly, and not merely in the presence of the church. It seemed to answer capitally, for not only did the candidates by this means make a public profession of CHRIST JESUS as their only hope of salvation, but those present, I believe, were greatly benefited by the clear, unhesitating replies to the various questions.

GOSPEL TRIUMPHS.

It was grand to hear two carpenters, also the wife of one of them, tell how the power of GOD had enabled them to break off the habit of opium-smoking, which had held them in bondage for many years. Another, an *old* man, had been an enquirer seven months, and had succeeded in reducing his usual quantity of opium by more than one-half; in this way he was gradually giving it up. When he stood upon his feet and declared that he would yet have the full mastery over the enemy which now oppressed him, I thought younger ones present, who were addicted to the same habit, might well take courage. The old man will be retained as an enquirer, and will not be baptised until he is quite free.

The replies of those who came from a distance, and who, consequently, have but few opportunities of attending the means of grace, showed how truly they had been taught of GOD. One was a woman whose husband is not a Christian, and never comes near us. She walked ten *li* this morning, through mud and rain, such as many men would not care to venture through, in order to attend worship. After leaving her home and crossing several small rivers, she came to the large river, the Han, which, in consequence of the continual rains, was so swollen that no boats were crossing. Nothing daunted, she waited for several hours until a boat did cross, and then she came in time only for the afternoon meeting. Although she had received very limited teaching, she gave a reason for the hope within her, and showed every reason why she should be received amongst GOD's people.

A young man came from a place sixty or seventy *li* distant—the only witness in that place. He is to be received and sent forth again with the prayerful hope that he may "become a thousand." Already he has created interest in his native place, and his younger brother professes to believe. His answers showed that he had read much, and had acquired quite an intelligent grasp of the Gospel. With this he shows that change of life and heart which only can make him a living epistle. I might say very much more of individuals, but must forbear now.

About twenty were examined, of whom perhaps fourteen will be baptised on Tuesday and received into our little company of saints, beloved of GOD. Truly GOD is good to dear Mr. and Mrs. Pearse, and has greatly blessed and owned their labours. I trust as I take up this work I may be no hindrance, but an instrument "meet for the MASTER'S use."

October 22*nd*.—This has been a very happy day, inasmuch as we have seen with our eyes and have heard with our ears much that makes glad the hearts of those who truly desire that CHRIST'S kingdom may come. Sixteen precious souls have been added to our little church, and have publicly

CONFESSED CHRIST BY BAPTISM.

We commenced this morning with a service at which many attended, so filling our hall as to make us wonder where next we may move to, in order to accommodate worshippers and listeners. The sixteen candidates for baptism sat in front, and as we looked upon their bright and happy faces, how could we but praise GOD, and take courage in the grand hope that China may *yet* be "for CHRIST." At the top of the list was an old lady of seventy-nine years, whilst the youngest was a boy of only twelve, who gave unmistakable signs of true conversion, and is the third of a Christian family—his elder brother being baptised with him. Praise GOD, this grand old Gospel proves the salvation of the very aged and of those of tender years in this land. Both are drawn by cords of Love—*Love* so strong that the chains of darkness and sin have no power to withhold them.

Before the baptism, Mr. Pearse gave the candidates opportunity of openly confessing CHRIST as their SAVIOUR before all present. Various questions put brought forth beautiful testimony of the power of GOD to save and reclaim those who were apparently irreclaimable. Opium-smokers told how that by trusting only in GOD (and not taking any opium medicine) they had broken off the habit of years. A Vegetarian with joyful countenance—the index of the heart—made known to us, that now his trust was not in the merit of his several years of Vegetarianism but in the merit of the blood of JESUS his SAVIOUR. Others, in various ways, testified to saving grace, and then joined in a prayer, led by Mr. Pearse, in which they consecrated themselves to GOD.

Mr. Pearse gave a very practical address on assurance,

and then the baptism was proceeded with. During the ordinance, great reverence was manifested even by the spectators from without ; and, I trust, an impression was made for good upon those who have never yet thought of their soul's salvation. After baptizing four we sang a verse of "Oh, happy day that fixed my choice," and the same after each four candidates, finishing with the Doxology. All praise be to GOD, for He hath commenced doing great things : greater things are in store ; for these consecrated disciples will go forth, some to a distance, and, I believe, become fishers of men. Already the outlying districts within this hien are having the Gospel preached to their inhabitants by these converts. Shall not GOD multiply them a hundred-fold?

After the baptisms were over a man named Ho, from Yang-hien, who had been for some time treated by Dr. Wilson, in the Han-chung hospital, came in and said that he had burnt everything of an idolatrous character about his house, and that he and his wife had determined to serve the true GOD. Furthermore, a friend of his was also interested, but was too aged to come to Cheng-ku and himself hear of the doctrine, so he had deputed his son to accompany Mr. Ho, and after hearing the Gospel, to take back the message to his father. The son, however, did not arrive, having been taken ill upon the road, and hence obliged to return. Mr. Ho, after spending the night here, determined to return again to-morrow, and if the young man had recovered, to bring him to spend next Sunday. Mr. Ho has also agreed that worship shall henceforth be held in his house, and that two of our church-members shall go at intervals and hold Sunday Services. I hope sometimes to go myself, and then with GOD'S blessing upon our united work, soon to have a church in Yang-hien !

October 23rd.—I had a good time of preaching in the street chapel, and was much assisted by one of our earliest members coming in to help to tell the glad news. It is good to listen to this man—he so sincerely believes and is so earnest in his pleadings with his fellow-countrymen. This afternoon went out to dinner with Mr. and Mrs. Pearse—a farewell dinner given by one of the church-members. This evening a good prayer-meeting—four members from the Shih-pah-li-p'u Church to take farewell of Mr. and Mrs. Pearse, and also to send messages from that Church to the Churches at home.

Power over all the Power of the Enemy.

FROM REV. J. J. COULTHARD.

IN the March number of CHINA'S MILLIONS for 1888, an account was given of the formation, in November, 1887, of the first church founded in the HO-NAN Province, and mention was made of the distress of a bright convert that he could not be received until he had given up his business—that of making crackers for idolatrous purposes. Subsequently he threw up his business, was baptized, and returned to earn his living in his own village. It is delightful to hear the following account of him.

THE fire-work maker, who was baptized eighteen months ago, has just returned here, and is very bright. When he first went home he met with terrible opposition and persecution. At one time he was threatened with legal proceedings if he persisted in opposing the religion of his forefathers ; he went away to a solitary place a few *li* from home and prayed earnestly and wept. Almost immediately his prayer was answered, for his would-be accuser was in turn sued by another man for a sum of money.

A SORCERER POWERLESS.

At another time the whole village brought a sorcerer to bewitch him, or to drive out the devil which was supposed to possess him. He was singing at the time they arrived, and his Old and New Testaments and Commentary—his whole theological library—were spread out before him on the table. When they entered the room, Mr. Liu went to the sorcerer, and laying his hand upon his, said, "In the Name of JESUS of Nazareth I command you to leave !" Immediately the sorcerer was rendered speechless and powerless, the evil spirit within being quite subdued. The crowd urged on the sorcerer, beseeching him to exorcise Mr. Liu, who then said : "In the Name of the FATHER, SON, and HOLY GHOST I command you to leave," whereupon the man fled as if for life, shouting out, "he is too powerful for me, he is too great." The crowd wanted him to come back, but he said, "Do not take me to him, his SAVIOUR is too strong for me ; his prayer is too powerful and efficacious," so Mr. Liu got the reputation for being more powerful than the sorcerer, or the gods.

No less than three of his relations died in turn, after being faithfully warned by him ; but they were, alas, untouched by the SPIRIT'S power, and died as they had lived. Upon their death all opposition ceased. Now the *whole* of his family, including elder brothers, are converted. He did not like to leave them a year ago, as they were not strong enough in the faith, but now they are able to stand in CHRIST'S strength, he has left them.

Experiences of Life in China.

FROM REV. F. O. WILLIAMS.

PAO-NING, *Nov. 4th.*—Our Heavenly FATHER has been very gracious to us, and we have great cause to praise Him. We are all, through His goodness, now very well. I wish you could see how comfortable and happy we are here. I feel it to be a great privilege to be associated with Mr. Cassels ; and the other dear workers are so good and kind. Mr. Beauchamp has done so much for us ; the LORD reward him richly for all his kindness to us. It is very hard to believe one is really in the heart of this great Empire ; when I look at our surroundings, our comfortable home with so many presents from kind friends here, and so many things we used to have in our home in Leeds, our good food, our beautiful country, with splendid walks for the children, the happy intercourse with our fellow-workers, the mail coming and going about every week,—when we look at these and other things we wonder where the hardships are, in going through which our friends at home pity us so much. As things are at present, there are *no hardships* ; things are very different to what they were twenty years ago. And yet we may be called to pass through similar trials to those passed through by the early members of the Mission. If so, may the LORD keep us very close to Himself, trusting Him alone, and rejoicing to suffer for His sake.

Dear Miss S. E. Jones has been, and is still, an invaluable helper to us. I do not know what we should have done without her. She is so kind and willing to help in any way she can. She has got our new cook into firstrate shape, he cooks capitally, but the best news about him is that he is really interested in the truth. Miss Jones is teaching him to read, and believes he is truly converted. I do trust he will come right out and take a bold stand for the LORD. The work has been much hindered by some of those first baptised here having gone back ; one man especially has caused dear Mr. Cassels great grief. But I do believe the LORD is preparing the way for great blessing. Oh that He may work mightily in this city and district, and that we may not hinder Him by unbelief, or coldness of heart. Oh, how close we need to be kept to the MASTER for Him to be able to work through us.

Amongst others in whose hearts I believe GOD is working, is our landlady, a Mahommedan ; she has a proud spirit, and has not appeared interested in the truth until lately ; now she says she has no rest. Miss Jones goes into her house, which adjoins ours, and reads, and speaks, and prays with her and her relations and one or two friends each Sunday afternoon. Last Sunday she had mats all ready, and all of them knelt down for prayer.

Miss Jones has also been two or three times to another Mahommedan house near here ; when she was there the other day, one of the women asked her to come again and tell them more, because they could take in only a little at a time.

By Dr. Wilson's advice we brought out a magic lantern and a good number of Scripture slides, and we have used it several times. Last Tuesday I showed it at the ladies' house to a good number of women, and Miss Williams explained the pictures, and spoke so nicely and simply to the people.

Thank GOD for the ladies ; but oh ! we, or rather He, needs more men also. There is a grand field for work in E. SI-CH'UEN; a good climate, friendly people on the whole, and thousands and thousands who know nothing of the Gospel. Oh, if some of my brother clergy knew how blessed it is to be out here *for* and *with* the LORD, how quickly they would come ! Do tell any you meet how happy we are, and how happy the LORD can make them out here. Much as we love our dear ones at home, we have not a shadow of regret that we followed the LORD, nor do we expect ever to have. And do tell any that have little ones that they are *no hindrance*, but on the contrary a *great help* to getting near the people. Our dear little ones are such a comfort to us, and so well and happy; they have no roughing it, but are just as comfortable as at home.

Happy Service.

FROM MISS ALICE A. MILES.

TA-NING, SHANSI, *Sept.* 20*th*, 1889.—Here we are amongst our dear people again, and I need scarcely say how glad we are to return. We have had such a splendid change, and seen much in the work during our absence which we hope will prove useful to us in our winter's campaign here. In looking back one cannot but be thankful for wider experience gained during this summer, and one's heart's cry is for wisdom to win souls and to *lead* them. And the wisdom *is* coming ! We are asking for it, and expecting it. Will you, dear friends, ask that we may take GOD'S unerring guidance in every detail connected with the native Church ? for we are longing to see the LORD glorified in our midst. We had such a joyful welcome back again—nothing to sadden us, our SAVIOUR showing us that He is "mighty to save" and "able to keep." The night we arrived we found two presents of fruit and a pair of shoes each. The latter were most acceptable, as our "best" pair, to speak mildly, had lost *much* of their freshness on the journey. The next morning our dear women told us what she could of what had happened during our absence ; how she had dreamed of us ; how she had missed us ; and how she began to think we were never coming back again !

I think some of you may remember a young scholar named Uang, who was baptized here last spring. The head magistrate has several times tried to get him into trouble, and has at last succeeded. It appears that some of his relatives have not paid their taxes, and so the mandarin seized the opportunity and made poor young Uang responsible for them. He could not manage to pay more than his own taxes, and so he was beaten. The petty spite and deep hatred of this "great man" came out when Uang was being beaten, for he shouted, "Beat the foreigner I beat the foreigner !" [*i.e.*, the man who had joined the foreign religion.]

Elder Chang says there is nothing against this young man's character in the eyes of the people, except that he is a follower of JESUS. May the LORD make him strong in faith ! Blessed thought for the LORD'S children : "The LORD of hosts *is* with us ; the GOD of Jacob *is* our refuge."

When we came back we found that improvements had taken place in our cave-rooms, to prevent them from being so damp, so you see how lovingly our Heavenly FATHER has cared for us. It is a good thing to be a child of a KING !

We are trying to arrange some plan for more direct village work. In three or four villages the Christians are anxious to have a room set aside for worship, and have suggested that some one should go out to help the women and children and those who cannot get here for the services. The elder thinks that our man Yang, who has proved himself very faithful to us, would be the very one to undertake this work, but we have had no time yet to talk the matter properly over. He certainly has the confidence and affection of all who come here, and we feel the LORD must have raised him up from that serious illness last spring to do some special work for Him.

The old blind woman comes still ; she manages to get here at 7.30 in the morning for prayers. Mrs. Shan is as bright as ever, and looking forward to her baptism. We are thankful to report that those who broke off opium last spring have kept faithful, as far as we know, and one or two really seem changed in heart. A poor man, named P'ieh, who has broken off twice with us here, has, we think, gone back to his opium again. We have had many heartaches over this family, but the LORD has taught us many lessons in regard to them, and we can praise Him for *that.* You see, we are all led by "a way we know not," but it is TRUST !

Sept. 30th.—The last few days we have been experiencing what it is to rejoice, and joy in the LORD, in no small measure. Since our return we have had much to make our hearts glad in the work, and the many little practical proofs the dear members have given us of their pleasure at our return has *quite* overflowed our cup. Dates, grapes, and eggs from friends more than forty *li* away, and kind enquirers from still further, and now an old lady, from a place seventy *li* away, is staying with us and persists in using her spare moments in doing work for us. "My heart loves you, and I want to," she said, when I expostulated with her this morning, after our class, and so this afternoon she is sitting on the k'ang, making up some new bedding for us.

You will be glad to hear that Mrs. Ma (whom I mentioned some time ago, and who has suffered a good deal for the sake of JESUS) is still very bright. Praise GOD! He can keep these dear people happy, and make JESUS a "reality" to each one of us. She is very anxious to be baptized, but there are certain difficulties with her husband, which make us fear she may have to wait longer. But, as she said this morning, none of these things can prevent her believing in JESUS, and being happy, because her sins are all forgiven! Do remember this dear woman in prayer, for she has to face much trial and ridicule, and her faith is so young.

When I was visiting last Thursday, I met a poor woman whom I do not remember to have seen before. She gave me an account of her life, and it made me realize more than ever

HOW DREADFUL HEATHENISM IS,

and *how* much the glorious Gospel is needed in these ruined, black hearts. The woman's husband is an opium-smoker, and keeps a shop. When I asked what he sold, the answer was "Everything!" but if you knew what sort of place Ta-ning was, you would agree with me that the "everything" in question must be a decidedly limited everything. Anyhow, he sells cloth, and his wife slaves day after day to weave for him, and makes him socks and shoes and other garments for sale. She seldom does enough to please him, and often, very often is dreadfully beaten because she cannot get through more. While she was telling me this, and I was explaining to her a little about the LORD's love, she was mechanically stitching away at a sock; and when I asked her to put it down and repeat a prayer after me, such a very delighted look passed over her face, and she said, quite excitedly, "Do you think GOD will hear *me?*" Before I left the house I told her that I should go and see her in her own home, as her husband would not let her come to us, so on Saturday Miss Scott and I called upon her during our visiting. She was working, of course, but immensely glad to see us; and we were pleased to find that she had not forgotten what we had said about JESUS.

Oct. 5th.—The other day when I was writing I meant to tell you of Yang's visit to some villages. He spent a night at Ho-ti, where two Christians were baptised last spring, and since his return we have heard of a man destroying his idols. He came in on Sunday to the services, and appeared much in earnest. At a second village, called Ma-shu, dear Yang had much encouragement, and came home so bright and happy, with many tales of the LORD's love. You will be glad to hear that there are four women in this small village much interested in the Gospel, and one of them has made quite a stand for the LORD. having given up wine-drinking and tobacco-smoking. Four or five of the Christian women here have put away their pipes, and the fact of its having been done quietly, without our knowing it at the time, makes us all the more glad. The more these dear people see the love of GOD to them, the more earnest will be their desire to follow Him.

BAPTISMS.

Oct. 26th.—Last Saturday we had a large gathering here, and eight people were received into the Church. We had the pleasure of welcoming Mr. and Mrs. Key and their two children; and Mr. Orr Ewing also came down and took part in the services. We were rejoiced to see the happy spirit of unity and love which prevailed amongst the Church-members, all doing their best to make things pass off comfortably. Of the eight received into fellowship five were women, all of whom we have had the privilege of teaching, and there are still a few waiting over for further instruction. Friends who have seen former diaries will be interested to know that our old blind woman was one of those baptised. She was very bright and happy, and answered the questions put to her very satisfactorily. Mrs. Shan was also received, and we can thank GOD upon every remembrance of her intelligent faith. There were also two women, named Ho, wives of Church-members, and a dear woman named Yuen, whose husband was baptised at the same time. These two are, as far as we know, the first Christians in the Chi-chau district; their home is about 70 *li* from here, and we would ask prayer that the LORD will make them true witnesses for Himself. Of the other two men one was Mrs. Shan's husband, who broke off opium when with Mr. Cassels, and the other was a relative of Pastor Ch'u, who was here last spring, breaking off opium. On the LORD's Day we had a happy time, when these dear natives joined with us for the first time in remembering the death of JESUS. On Monday morning most of the friends returned to their homes, and we gradually subsided into our old quietness. Before closing we would like to ask special prayer for the fifteen who have entered the Church at Ta-ning this year, and that we may have a great blessing on the winter's work.

FROM MISS MARY E. SCOTT.

TA-NING, *Oct. 3rd.*—I see, on looking back, that my last regular diary was dated Hiao-i, June 25th, and now it is the beginning of October. Well, we had a truly happy and very helpful visit to the dear Sisters at Hiao-i, and then we went on to T'ai-yuen Fu, and spent a pleasant time with Mr. and Mrs. Bagnall. We also spent a few days on the East Hills with dear Gertrude Broomhall. We seem to have had a long holiday, but we are feeling the benefit of it in every way, and I think specially perhaps with regard to the language, for though we did not actually do very much study, yet it was a great help to us to hear so many other foreigners speak in Chinese. We have gained a great deal, too, from seeing the methods of workers so much more experienced than ourselves, and are seeking to do more to *teach* our dear people the Word of GOD. For one thing we are now, from dear Elder Chang downwards, daily committing a verse to memory, which is repeated in company with the former ones at morning worship, to which, I am sorry to say, hardly any outsiders are coming just now; but still this very fact is giving us the opportunity for taking up Genesis; then, to the great delight of the good old Elder, and some of the other members of the household, Miss Miles and I take the Bible-reading on alternate mornings, while the Elder always conducts evening worship.

Ever since our return (on Sept. 16th) we have had constant cause for praise and thanksgiving. To begin with, our welcome home was a truly warm one. Then, remembering that when we left Ta-ning, early in June, poor Yang was just struggling back to life again, after his serious illness, we can scarcely thank the LORD enough for his restored health; his bright face is a continual cheer. Last week he was out at two villages, trying to help some of the Christians, some of whom as yet know very little; and to-day he is at another village, looking up old friends. Last week, at one of the villages to which he went, an extremely interesting incident occurred.

I think you know already how very hospitable these dear village people are. Well, one very nice woman, who is interested in the Gospel, and a warm friend of ours, determined that Yang must have a meal at her house. Accordingly she was up betimes, and in the course of her preparations was badly stung on the finger by a scorpion. The poison must have circulated very quickly, for soon, not only was she in pain all over, but seemed to lose consciousness. In alarm, Yang was called for, who laid hands on her and prayed, and she *very** soon recovered. There was still some pain, however, in the arm and hand. So he prayed again; and when he left, soon afterwards, there was only slight pain in the wounded finger; and, in telling us about this the same evening, Yang brightly remarked that he expected that by this time, *all* pain had gone. We did praise GOD for this, connecting it with the promise in Mark xvi. to those who *believe*, that "they shall lay hands on the sick, and they shall recover."

Last Saturday a dear woman from 60 or 70 *li* off, came for a few days. We are teaching her every day, but, like ourselves, she cannot take in more than a certain amount at one time. So she has begged to help us with some needlework, and has been as busy as a bee, and so happy.

Most of the city people seem dreadfully indifferent to the Gospel, except, perhaps, the chief mandarin, who still tries to persecute the Christians, whenever he can rake up or invent the least excuse. Only a few days ago he caused a young scholar to be cruelly beaten on the hand, for no fault of his own, but on the pretext that some distant relations could not pay their taxes! Well, it would be grand, indeed, if the LORD turned him into a Paul, and there is *nothing* too hard for the LORD.

A PAVILION FOR PICNICS AT WAN-SHOW-SHAN, PEKIN.

Tidings from T'ai-chau.

FROM MR. RUDLAND.

SHANGHAI, *Nov.* 22*nd*.—Mrs. Rudland has been here since the end of July, and is much better for the change and medical care she has had. I arrived last Saturday, and we leave (D.V.) on Tuesday for T'ai-chau.

Last Sunday the chapel was full morning and afternoon, and after the afternoon service three gentlemen, two graduates and the head of the university from T'a-bing, came to see me, and we spent over three hours speaking about the doctrine. They had evidently read many Christian books, as well as much of both Old and New Testaments, and had heard it explained by Sing-ze, who, they told me, often visited them. I have never had such an interesting conversation with literary men before. Scholars have often come and talked about science, etc., but generally when one began to speak of the Gospel they had to go. But these came on purpose to inquire about the truth. We have so many evidences now that the SPIRIT is working in the hearts of some. There are many who have a good knowledge of the Gospel, and it seems as if only the SPIRIT'S power is needed to arouse their conscience, and to bring

* On again questioning Yang, to verify the accuracy of this statement, I find that after prayer the woman *immediately* recovered, and was able to go on with her preparations for the meal.

home the truth to their hearts. Only He can do this. May we during the winter's work see many convicted of sin and converted to CHRIST.

While I was here in the summer there was a terrible flood in T'ai-chau, the worst that can be remembered. There were three feet of water in our downstair rooms, and from fourteen to fifteen feet outside the city. In some places between T'ai-chau and T'in-t'ai, hamlets and large houses were swept down the mountain-sides. At T'a-bing the city was flooded, and about a third of the city wall gave way, crushing in the houses near, so that about 400 persons were either crushed in the ruins or drowned, it being night, and there being no way of escape. Praise GOD, none of our native Christians lost their lives, or suffered seriously in any way.

After the flood rain set in, and lasted almost continuously for nearly forty days, a thing I have never seen before at that season of the year. On the Saturday evening we had a special prayer-meeting for fine weather, but on Sunday it was still pouring, so instead of our usual service we had another special prayer-meeting. Prayer after prayer went up for over an hour, and before we concluded the rain ceased, and we all went home in the sunshine. On the Tuesday evening we had a praise-meeting.

Back at Nan-k'ang Fu.

FROM MISS HARDING.

DEC. 20th.—I know you will be glad to see that I am writing from Nan-k'ang again. I cannot tell you how glad I am. I feel full of praise to our blessed MASTER for so soon allowing us to return. We arrived on Monday afternoon with Mr. McCarthy, and found all quiet and peaceful. Since then we have been out a good deal, and some seem pleased to see us. We are expecting that many souls will be saved here.

We were visiting an old Christian woman this morning who is sick, and we also saw her nephew who has been ill for years: he asked us to pray with him there that GOD would heal him. Miss McFarlane spoke to him about his soul, and how far more important that was, and pointed him to the SAVIOUR; he was much interested, and we invited him to come and see the Evangelist, so this afternoon he came and stayed over an hour. He says he believes, but of course as yet he only understands a very little. I need not ask you to pray for us.

For the Young.

FROM MR. R. GRAY OWEN.

Chen-tu, Oct. 26th, 1889.

DEAR YOUNG FRIENDS,—

When this letter will reach you possibly 1889 will have given place to 1890, so I wish you all a Happy New Year. I pray it will be to all of you a new year of new joys and blessings, of new prayers and efforts on behalf of China's perishing millions. The grace of our LORD JESUS be with you all.

To us the sweetest of all names is the sweet Name of JESUS. He to us is the "chiefest among ten thousand." Alas! in heathen China there are millions who know not JESUS; to them the sweetest of names is "O-mi-t'o-fuh"—viz., Amida Buddha. The mere repetition of this name is supposed to be a safeguard against ills and dangers in this life, and to secure a place in the next life in Buddha's Western Paradise, the home of immortal bliss. Thus the evil one has sown his tares in dark China, while the Church of GOD slept, heedless of the LORD's command, "Go ye into all the world, and preach the Gospel to every creature." Thousands in this benighted land live and die believing and trusting in this lie of the evil one—viz., "O-mi-t'o-fuh." May the reading of these simple verses lead some of you to pray more earnestly and to do more for the salvation of China's perishing millions.

"O-MI-TO-FUH."
The shaven monk in lonely cell,
While others dig and spin and sell,
Loves to recite the " magic spell "—
O-mi-t'o-fuh.

Pilgrims toiling from day to day
Along the rough-worn merit way,
Heavy of heart, they ceaseless pray—
O-mi-t'o-fuh.

Bookworms, buyers let others be,
This name is everything to me,
Repeats the faithful devotee—
O-mi-t'o-fuh.

A SHAVEN MONK.

Amidst the busy cares of life,
Oppresséd by the daily strife,
Cry of the broken-hearted wife—
　　O-mi-t'o-fuh.

Climbing the path so steep, so high,
The burdened, footsore coolies sigh :
The resting-place in view is nigh—
　　O-mi-t'o- fuh.

SI-CH'UEN MOUNTAIN COOLIES CARRYING BRICK TEA.

Counting her beads, the aged dame,
Seeking merit and holy fame,
Repeats aloud the precious name—
　　O-mi-t'o-fuh.
E'en little ones are taught to know
The road to merit here below,
Repeating high, repeating low—
　　O-mi-t'o-fuh.
Pathway for all to peace, to rest,
To the home of the ever blest—
Joyous Paradise of the West—
　　O-mi-t'o-fuh.

Land of the birds with golden wing,
Land of beauty, eternal spring,
Land of delight, of bliss the king—
　　O mi-t'o-fuh.
Twenty-four thousand daily die ;
Alas ! how vain they pray, they cry—
The truth of GOD changed to a lie—
　　O-mi-t'o-fuh.
Soldiers of CHRIST, while yet 'tis day,
Come, tell these millions in dark Cathay,*
To Truth, to Life, the Only Way—
　　JESUS, the Sinner's Friend.

Letter from an Evangelist at Kwei-yang Fu.

THE disciple Ts'en Tsi-kwang respectfully salutes Chief Pastor Hudson Taylor, wishing him happiness and peace.

The disciple blesses the grace of the HEAVENLY FATHER and the love of the LORD JESUS, in sending their servants to form a Church and spread abroad the teachings of the LORD. Teachers, their wives, and single ladies, each in service to the LORD and love to men, have declined no hardship, danger, or journey, and have come to Kwei-yang. At that time the disciple was in the mists of ignorance and darkness ; but through the transforming power of the HOLY GHOST, and the instructions of various teachers, the LORD gave repentance and pardon, faith and regeneration. He has further bestowed the work of an evangelist, and the disciple has had the privilege of much service in the chapel ; thanks to the LORD, the supreme source of all grace, and to Mr. Taylor and the missionaries for each act of love. If Mr. Taylor would be pleased and should have opportunity to come to Kwei-yang, the disciple and all the members of the Church desire to see him face to face.

For several years the disciple has wished to go to Shang-hai to see Mr. Taylor and also other churches, to learn their methods and to see the good books they read and use, so as to know what books would be most helpful at Kwei-yang. Should a suitable opportunity arise to come, he will at once embrace it. The disciple has many opportunities of preaching and teaching, few of receiving instruction, hence he fears falling into repetitions and tasteless teaching. But he prays for the help of the HOLY

---

* A name for China.

SPIRIT and listens to the instructions of the missionaries hoping to obtain deeper insight into the teaching of the Holy Word for his own profit, and through the help of the LORD to serve Him to His pleasure.

Last year the LORD called the disciple's eldest daughter home to Himself. Through Mr. Andrews' kindness in writing to Mr. Taylor, the disciple obtained from Mr. Taylor much consolation. Thanks also for sympathy when Mr. Windsor wrote of the illness of the second daughter and the disciple's deep affliction. Now, praise GOD, she is well again. Thanks to GOD for marvellous grace; since the death of the eldest daughter her aunt has censed chanting the Buddhist Classics and relying on vegetarianism. Mr. and Mrs. Andrew and Mr. Windsor with the disciple have prayed for her, and the LORD has saved her and brought her into the Church.

The disciple prays the LORD to send many more teachers with their wives and single ladies, with a medical missionary, to work and reopen the Opium Refuge, or to go to distant prefectures and cities and open up stations. If the LORD permit, pray Mr. Taylor send such workers.

The LORD in His goodness has spared the disciple two sons and three daughters. The two sons and one daughter are at school; the other daughters are still young. His hope is that GOD will early give them faith that they may become disciples.

Missionary Methods.

FROM MR. SAUNDERS.

I SUPPOSE you saw in *The Christian* some time ago a letter by the late Rev. G. Bowen, of India. I think it is the best I have read on the subject now before Christian people, missionary methods, etc.; best because he brings forward a real difficulty, and also I think a solution for it—that is, that the average missionary in most heathen lands is so far above the people that although he may command their respect, yet I question very much if he commends the gospel to them by his life. Another real practical difficulty which we find here in China, and which I think may be solved in the same way, is the people clinging to the foreign missionary for what they can get either in employment or other ways.

The native Christian sees what to him seems a large sum of money being spent by the foreigner, and he thinks of course that the money is given for the church, and that he might as well have some of it, and in this way he begins to covet the foreigner's money. This subject was much on my mind for months before Mr. Bowen's letter in *The Christian* came, and you may be sure I was glad to receive and read such a valuable letter. I desire to know GOD'S will on the matter, and then to follow Him: to that end I am now searching the Scriptures and praying daily that GOD would give light, and I am sure He will. Praise be to His Name, He never allows his children to go blindfolded, but is at all times willing to lead and direct if we are only willing to be led of Him. The more I study GOD'S Word the more convinced I feel that to live in the simple native style is GOD'S way for me; of course I cannot say for other people, as I have no sympathy with those who have one view and think that every one else must be wrong. Let every man be fully persuaded in his own mind, but when persuaded let him act. Now do not let what I have written lead you to think that the average missionary in China lives on a high scale. I can assure you that, compared with what most of us have been used to at home, it is quite a descent in the scale; but, after all, it is far above the ordinary people of China. There is no doubt if we are among the people as they are, GOD will bless. Oh for apostolic days to return! If the LORD tarry we hope to see them in China. GOD will work if we are faithful.

Tidings from Scattered Workers.

Kan-suh Province.
FROM MR. GRAHAM BROWN.

Lan-chau, Sept. 14th.—Mr. Parker expects to leave soon for home, and that will leave us more than ever with GOD alone to look to. Praise Him, He is all-sufficient! Do pray that we may get some to go to the Hien and villages in this prefecture. Is it too much to ask for men to come and preach the Gospel here? The Roman Catholics are occupying new ground steadily, but we cannot for lack of numbers. My heart is sore because of the need.

FROM MISS M. GRAHAM BROWN.

Lan-chau, Oct. 4th.—We have been allowed to settle quietly and comfortably in this new house, and find its suitability for the work most evident. We have a few visitors, and feel that many doors are open round us; the sad thing is that some who, a little while ago, showed interest have become quite cold. We are coming more closely into contact with the unspeakable wickedness of this place, but we are not discouraged; the Lord has shown us His hand in granting this house so marvellously, and we know He has a mighty blessing for this people. Oh, to be fit channels for it to flow down in fulness! We shall miss Mr. and Mrs Parker very much; the Lord soon supply their place. I suppose the need of other provinces is just as great, and He knows it all; but we shall soon feel very short-handed. Our eyes are unto Him, whose resources *never* fail.

FROM MR. HOROBIN.

Ning-hsia, Sept. 19th.—Since the baptisms Satan has been most busily at work; three of the four who were baptised have had misfortunes; the tailor was bitten by a dog while coming to the service one evening; another has fallen from a building, but escaped with a severe shaking; and the third has been seriously ill; but so far we are united in the Lord. Those who professed to be inquirers have since manifested a different spirit, but our faith and hope are in GOD for the future.

A few weeks ago I paid a visit to the places north of us. At Ting-lo I was on the street from 7 a.m. till 3 p.m., and then went on thirty *li* for the next day. I visited Tao-feng Hien for the first time, and was sorry I had not a better supply of Arabic books, as there were many Mohammedans. At Ting-lo they were very urgent for an opium refuge. Mr. Belcher and I are working together exceedingly well, but I must plead with you to send more help to this district; I long to spend a little time in other places. Please continue to pray for us; the contest is no sham fight, but we mean to believe and go forward and that victory must come.

FROM MR. BELCHER.

Ning-hsia, Oct. 1st.—You must excuse me if I do not get on with Chinese study as quickly as I should, but what is one to do? With Pao-t'eo 300 miles distant, and Lan-chau 250, and all these poor dying souls between us, why, I could not rest if I

Shan-si Province.

From Mr. Beynon.

Kwei-hwa-ch'eng, Oct. 25th.—We are having meetings every evening, Saturdays excepted. We have had quite large gatherings, and the men stay for some considerable time. Some of them come regularly every night, and sit from beginning to end. One or two are quite well instructed in the great outlines of the truth. This is the most encouraging work I have seen in this place. Pray for us.

From Mr. Burnett.

Pao-t'eo, Sept. 2nd.—My wife finds no difficulty in getting into the houses amongst the women. I trust she will be able to carry this on through the winter. House visitation makes a great difference to the work, and is also a good means of getting people in to services on Sunday.

Lately I have been for a short journey into the mountains at our back. My books sold well. I hope to make another tour in that direction before long, and follow up the seed sown. A spirit of inquiry is almost sure to spring up, and when one goes for the second time, it is to find enlightenment where all was dark. I trust you will continue to pray for us and the northern stations; the work requires patient endurance, prayer, and indefatigable effort.

K'wei-hwa-ch'eng, Oct. 25th.—I arrived here two days ago, and am returning as soon as possible. You will be glad to hear of the very happy time I had at the two market towns on the bank of the Yellow River, and at the various places *en route*. I took with me Mr. K'en, our first earnest inquirer at Pao-t'eo, as I thought it would do him good and give me further opportunities of finding out where his difficulties were, and of leading him into a deeper knowledge of the truth. Suffice it to say I was thankful to God for allowing me to see such progress in the heart and life of one who has for only a month or two manifested an interest in spiritual things.

At Ho-k'eo the people listened with remarkable attention, and not a little haste was made to buy up my remaining portions of Scriptures and tracts. We stopped at every available place along the road, preached and sold books, and I was cheered and encouraged at the reception I met with.

I had the extreme pleasure of meeting with the Mongol lama, who continued with me for three days, and, notwithstanding the gibes and contempt, gave quite a testimony. My companion and the lama had quite a good time comparing notes. The meeting was helpful to both.

From Mr. Stewart McKee.

Ta-t'ung, Sept. 20th.—I am sure you were glad to hear of the first baptism in Ta-t'ung. Praise God our brother is going on well. I am glad to say we are having good times in the villages; prejudice is being broken down. In the last village I visited, I met a man who had been seeking a way for the remission of sins for over ten years, and admitted he was no wiser now than before. I often wish more was being done for the women by visitation; my wife has little time for that, so many come to see us; but she has managed to go out two afternoons this week, and always finds the women friendly.

From Mr. Hoste.

Hung-t'ung, Nov. 15th.—Mr. Hsi read me two or three exceedingly interesting letters from Si-gan. You may recollect that some time ago they were helped in getting premises by a Mahommedan military M.A., who broke off his opium with them. Well, at the recent examination two young scholars who were trying for the degree met their old friend, this Mahommedan, and were at once surprised to see how well he looked; they found out that he had given up his opium pipe, and on asking how this was, were told of the Refuge. Accordingly, at the close of the examination, they entered as patients, made rapid progress towards being freed from the habit, and in about two weeks left the Refuge full of gratitude. At first, being wealthy men, sons of a retired official, they pressed twenty taels on the man in charge as a token of gratitude; but on this being absolutely refused, they insisted, in spite of all remonstrances, in putting up a tablet on the front door, on which the account of their deliverance from the opium habit, together with a statement that this was due to the power of heaven, was briefly written out. In a city where the official classes have hitherto been so hostile the above is certainly very encouraging.

The policy which the brethren there have pursued by Mr. Hsi's direction has been to avoid, by public preaching and praying, exciting the prejudice and opposition of neighbours, whilst seeking by private prayer, gentleness and honesty towards all men, to disarm suspicion, and looking to God to give them acceptance with the people, and establish them in the place.

At Lu-ch'eng Hien there has been much trial by false brethren recently, who seem to have acted very outrageously; it was, therefore, a cause of thankfulness to receive the following:—

From Mr. Stanley Smith.

Lu-ch'eng Hien, Nov. 15th.—Thank God, the clouds seem to have dispersed, and the sunshine has come. Already some ninety and more men and women have been in and through the refuges here. I believe, too, a real spiritual work is going on. In fact, I am full of hope. I have been going about to market towns and villages and festivals. At one festival last week with a native we sold some hundreds of books. Our refuge is rapidly getting known far and wide; to-day two men came in from over 120 *li* away. I hope the Lord will greatly magnify His Name here. We have been through fire and through water, and He will assuredly bring us out into a wealthy place. To-morrow (D.V.) I go off to a market town to preach and sell books.

Chih-li Province.

From Mr. Bridge.

Ying-tseng, Sept. 18th.—I start to-morrow for Shun-teh Fu, probably to work alone; the exigencies of the work seem to be such that if many more workers are not forthcoming we cannot go "two-and-two," and the servant of Christ must be content to follow his Master in paths of loneliness. The Lord has been very good to me during the four months I have lived alone here. He has taught me many valuable lessons. In going forward to unknown work and untried paths, I lay hold upon the precious promise which has been uppermost in my mind of late, viz., Ps. xxix. 11: "The Lord will give strength unto His people; the Lord will bless His people with peace."

The work here has been rather encouraging of late; though none have taken a definite stand for Christ, there is a spirit of inquiry abroad. Many have expressed regret at my leaving, and two, an elderly man and a youth, actually shed tears. Praise God for this, but I am not satisfied; to get the people attached to me *only* and not led to Christ falls far short of my mission. I am thankful to say that I enjoy the best of health.

Oct. 12th to 25th.—The journey into the north of Ho-nan and to some cities further south in this province took me a fortnight. At U-an, 110 *li* from here, I spent two days, and and was very well received; while on the streets selling books and preaching many of the tradespeople invited me into their shops to speak. U-an is a large and busy Hien city, boasting two strongly-built walls and a pagoda; being situated upon the hills, it is the healthiest city I have yet seen in China. I was offered two rooms in a house if I would stay, and others asked if I would not rent a house.

Leaving Ts'i-chau, I went to P'eng-ch'eng, a pottery-manufacturing place situated in a very beautiful valley, large and crowded with visitors from all parts of the north. Of the inhabitants, seven-tenths are addicted to opium-smoking. Bookselling and preaching on the streets drew too large crowds, and I was obliged to return to the inn and sell and preach in the courtyard. They bought all the books I could let them have.

The next morning wended my way towards Lin-hien; the scenery was beautiful—sublime in places—passed mountains which put to shame the hills at home in Wales, which I once thought grand. Several large and fertile valleys are passed, of which that of the Chang River is the finest, and will probably be the richest in years to come when its immense strata of coal are worked. Descending from a very high mountain, 35 *li* north of Lin-hien, into a beautiful valley, the road becomes level. Lin-hien is a nicely-situated, quiet city, with 360 villages. A range of hills rise to a great height, and for miles are almost as perpendicular as cliffs on the seashore.

On Oct. 30th Mr. Pigott and I left for a large fair at Kenhien, 35 *li* north-east of this. Mr. Pigott returned the same day. The first day I only sold 216 cash-worth of books, but the following day I sold 500 cash-worth of books, and had some of the best opportunities for street preaching that I have had in China. Several tradesmen invited me to sit down in their stalls on the street, and I preached to the crowds that gathered round. It being the last day of the fair, business was not so brisk, hence their kindness and leisure to listen.

FROM MRS. SIMPSON.

Ying-tseng, Oct. 15th.—When we know people pray for us I think it is only right that when we receive an answer to prayer we should say so, that friends may join in praise. We have had not a few things to try us since coming north, but we have also had many blessings, and seen more of the LORD'S hand and more evidence of His answering our prayers than we had seen before. Since writing last, our teacher from Hwuy-luh has paid us a visit, and we expect him to pay us another on the 1st of next month. He came here in order to be absent from home, because it was the day for worshipping his father, and he did not want to do that. He told us that after I paid my last visit to his third wife's house, and had talked to both of them for a long time, she shut the door and said she wanted to pray, and asked him to kneel down with her; this he did, and she prayed that GOD would help her not to quarrel nor be angry, but would teach her about JESUS, and make her like Him, and help her to help her husband not to be afraid of men. He is teaching her to read, and they pray every night. I am expecting that he will bring her with him to stay with us for a week or two, so that we may teach her more. I intend going into Hwuy-luh to stay in his mother's home, and visit amongst those who were interested, and am looking forward to it with real pleasure.

My woman is still pressing on, and so is her little girl. For a week after we came here the little girl would not kneel down with her mother and me to pray, but made a noise, and laughed, and tried to divert her mother's attention. After that she gradually quieted down, until one night she asked if I would teach her to pray. I was surprised; she said her mother was always speaking of heaven and going there, and she was afraid her mother would go and that she would not, so she wanted to be JESUS'S disciple too. She prays every night with us now, and really knows a good deal of the Gospel; it surprises me the intelligence she manifests. My woman is of the same family as the teacher, and does seem to be very ready to teach others to pray. Not a few women has she taught, and in reference to their prayers about the healing of diseases it is wonderful the answers GOD gives them.

The people here still come in large numbers daily, but in many cases, especially among the men, the seed seems to fall on stony ground; the women seem far more teachable.

Shan-tung Province.

FROM MR. STOOKE.

Chefoo Sanitarium, Dec. 13th.—My dear wife and I desire to raise our Ebenezer for so many during the year having received lasting benefit during the weeks or months they remained at our home; in many cases restoration from extreme weakness seemed remarkably sudden. Dr. Douthwaite, our beloved superintendent, spared no pains to get at the real cause of a brother or sister's ailment, and his kind help, good sea-air, daily hill-climbing, etc., all tended to make the sick ones quickly pick up, as they could not possibly do while struggling on at their stations.

FROM MR. JUDD.

Ning-hai Chau, Nov. 23rd.—Since I wrote on September 26th, four women have been baptised on September 29th, and two men on the 18th of this month. One man is to be baptised this afternoon, and three or four women to-morrow. We have just heard that one of the women who was to be baptised to-morrow is likely to be hindered by her husband, who has heard evil reports about us, and forbids his wife to come. Another woman, whose name is Nan, suffers severely from a wicked, gambling husband. He not only spends his own earnings in gambling and leaves his wife to beg for herself and four little ones, but comes home at times, takes the best of what she begs, and, leaving his wife and children hungry, departs. Yesterday she came here heart-broken; he had been home, taken their food, together with her only cooking pan and the only garment which covered the legs of one of her children. When the mother told him he ought to be ashamed, she received a beating in reply. The poor woman, a few days ago, had been overjoyed because she had been latterly able to earn a little money instead of going out to beg, and then this rascal comes home to get it all. Thank GOD, she has a treasure which he cannot take away—life and peace with GOD. Another woman has been kept away for several weeks by her husband.

One of the men baptised last Monday is a poor blind beggar, who preaches the Gospel to many persons in his begging journeys. I expect some day he will go and join Lazarus. It does indeed rejoice my heart to win the poor for CHRIST. My dear wife has frequently from twenty to thirty poor women at her classes. Some of their happy faces show that there is life and light within; yet it would be more than we could expect if some of them did not come because they eat of the loaves, though certainly not of the fishes. The MASTER gave better food to the poor than we do. He did not give them mere leavings, as many do, and then think they have cared for the poor.

The other man baptised last Monday is the one who kept the opium shop, and gave it up, and opium-smoking, too, last New Year's day. He has been kept clear ever since. His present conduct, quiet and orderly, is a great contrast to his past life of opium, profligacy, gambling, fighting, etc., though he still has much to do to meet difficulties which his past life has brought upon him. However, GOD has wonderfully helped him. He needs our prayers.

My former teacher has again caused much trouble by going to law with his cousin, a Christian here. With great sorrow we have put him out of the Church till his amended conduct shall show the repentance he professes.

Nov. 24th.—Five women were baptised to-day. We had united prayer last night for the woman whose husband forbad her coming, and her Christian mother went and interceded with her husband, who has allowed her to come to-day, to her great joy.

Ho-nan Province.

FROM MR. COULTHARD.

Chau-kia-k'eo, Nov. 21st.—Yesterday's mail brought the good news of reinforcements. We shall be very glad of them. I am just on the eve of starting for our village station 145 *li* (between forty and fifty miles) away. I have been wishing to go for months. I was never happier in my life. Preaching the glad tidings every day in the name of the LORD JESUS, and with His power, is a very blessed and happy task, and not without encouragement, so many listen with deep attention, and give as a reason for coming often, that "it does them good inside."

FROM MRS. COULTHARD.

Dec. 3rd.—We have had another visit from Cheo Ta-sao and her friend; she continues so bright; she has a firm faith in the power of prayer, and gave us several instances of the way in which her prayers had been answered. When she was here in the summer she learnt the text, "Whatsoever ye shall ask the FATHER in My Name He will give it you," and she quotes this when she prays. Her youngest daughter (about my own age), who has often heard her pray, had a bad sore throat the day before the old lady started to come here, so at night she said, "O LORD, I want to go with my mother to-morrow to Chaukia-k'eo to worship Thee, and I cannot go unless my throat is well. Thou hast said, 'Whatsoever ye shall ask of the FATHER in My Name He will give it you;' please make my throat well." The next morning she was quite well and ready to come; but her mother decided that she should stay at home, as there were seventeen or eighteen wanting to come to see us, and she knew that we had neither beds nor bedding for such a large company this cold weather; as these women walk here they cannot bring their own.

FROM MISS GUINNESS.

She-k'i-tien, Nov. 7th.—There is much to tell you of the work of the LORD in this dear place. In some ways our hearts are very much encouraged. Six precious women, the first, were baptised last week, praise the LORD; and several more will soon follow, I believe. One of these, dear Tuan Sao-sao, is suffering much persecution at home; her faith has almost wavered, but we are clinging on her behalf to Him who is able to keep. The little weekly meeting we were having in her house has had to be discontinued for the present, in consequence of her husband's opposition. He will not allow her to come here either, but we hope his heart may soon be changed. Our four other little weekly meetings continue; two here on Sunday and Wednesday, one on the north side and one on the south side of the city. These are principally intended for the Christian women and the enquirers; strangers we meet at other times; indeed, all the day long and every day they seem to come. Many come for medicine, and if you could only know of the wonderful cures that seem to be wrought, I think you would not altogether scorn our small efforts in that direction.

We are out a good deal, going quite freely in and out all over the city, and many seem to welcome us warmly. Our own dear Christian women are growing, I believe, in grace as well as in knowledge; the two we have in the house with us are very bright. I cannot tell you how I love the HO-NAN people! My whole heart seems to be twining around them, and the blessed sphere to which the MASTER has called me in His marvellous grace. The language is coming, too, in answer to much prayer. I am greatly helped with speaking, especially at times, and in understanding what the people say.

Si-ch'uen Province.

FROM MR. W. HOPE GILL.

Pao-ning, Sept. 29th.—Preached to a yardful of people who looked on. Oh the gross darkness in which these poor things live!

The last day of the quarter I spent in prayer and fasting, waiting upon the LORD for more power for service in our up-hill work. One was feeling so weak and foolish : constantly preaching to crowds the whole Gospel of a full salvation from present sin as well as from future punishment ; and not only to large numbers, but also to the few, and yet with what results ? Ah ! tell the truth I must, for it is the present experience of all my brethren and sisters here also, scarcely one seems in any way interested, not to say convicted of sin. Not only is this the case in the city and towns, but also in the country ; the power of the prince of this world is something so terrible. One has to see these people and their superstitious practices to believe the awful sway the devil has over them. They only regard us as ordinary good people, exhorting them to do good deeds, etc. Oh, would to GOD we were different from all other men, charged with the power of the HOLY GHOST, living lives of such power and love as should win these benighted people to the risen REDEEMER'S feet ! We are useless in China, and oh ! how false, too, without being filled with the "fulness of Him," seeing that we are His witnesses, and that we are just "where Satan's seat is." May we not well cry to GOD to cause His face to shine upon us, as did Daniel ; yea, pray the whole prayer—" O LORD, hear ; O LORD, forgive ; O LORD, hearken and do ;" for He willeth not the death of *one* of these poor heathen, and *all* are dying ! Pray, oh cry to GOD for souls to be saved in East SI-CH'UEN.

Gan-hwuy Province.

FROM MR. EYRES,

Ning-kwoh Fu, Nov. 26th.—On Saturday last I returned from a three weeks' evangelistic tour through a number of towns, cities, and villages lying to the west of this city. I used the magic-lantern every evening to illustrate the truths of CHRIST'S life, death, resurrection, and ascension. I had with me two native Christians, one of whom is a B.A. and a born speaker ; he is a favourite in the villages of the west district, and, being able to speak the local dialect, has good attention. The church members in their second church meeting, chose him to be their evangelist, they agreeing to pay half his salary. Since he has been set apart for this work he has manifested a somewhat proud spirit. Please pray for him.

Cheh-kiang Province.

FROM MRS. THOMPSON.

K'iu-chau, Sept. 17th.—In this city a good number come to hear the Gospel, but so few really decide, though they understand and assent. Will the LORD'S dear children pray that these many poor souls may hear GOD'S voice and live ? One cannot but love some of the dear old women, and long for them to come out boldly. One day, when out visiting, I noticed how one old woman listened. She followed us, and then led us to her home, and understood so well for the first time of hearing. She promised to come to the service, but did not, so I got some women to go and visit her, and they found that she had been frightened by her neighbours against coming ; but she came the next LORD'S day with her daughter, and has been every Sunday since. The LORD has given me the assurance that she is His. Last Sunday I asked her if she prayed, and she said, "Yes ; every day twice." Before she opens her door in the morning they kneel down and pray, and at night, beside thanking GOD for their food. She does not fear her neighbours.

Kiang-su Province.

FROM MRS. LEWIS.

Shanghai, Dec. 6th.—We have been very much interested in your thought concerning 1000 more missionaries for China. The morning after hearing about it the following paragraph occurred in our daily reading, and we were both so struck with it in connexion with your thought : " The building of the tabernacle made very good dispatch. It was not much more than five months from the beginning to the finishing of it. Though there was a great deal of fine work about it, such as is usually the work of time, embroidering and engraving not only in gold, but in precious stones, yet they went through with it in little time. Church work is usually slow work, but they made quick work of this, and yet did it with the greatest exactness imaginable. For first, many hands were employed, all unanimous, and not striving with each other. This expedited the business and made it easy. Second, the workmen were *taught of* GOD, and so kept from making blunders which would have retarded them. Third, the people were hearty and zealous in the work, and impatient till it was finished. GOD had prepared their hearts, and then the thing was done suddenly. (2 Chron. xxix, 36). Resolution and industry and a cheerful application of mind will by the grace of God bring a great deal of good work to pass in less time than one would expect."—MATTHEW HENRY.

FROM MISS WILLIAMSON.

Shanghai, Dec. 27th.—We have been having a happy time of blessing ; all have felt the influence of the HOLY SPIRIT. We praise the LORD for all His goodness and loving-kindness. As of course you know, Mr. E. J. Cooper has been with us for some time helping with the building ; he has been made a blessing in the home. I do long more and more that all who come here may indeed find it good to be here, because CHRIST is here. May the new year bring blessing and help to all. Miss Sanderson came here from Chefoo, last Friday, and has gone on to Yokohama for a real change and rest. Mr. and Mrs. Nicoll and the five ladies have arrived to-day, all well and having had a good journey.

Departures for China.

On Jan. 13th, from Toronto, Canada, per C.P.R. for China, Misses MAUD FAIRBANK, THERESA MILLER, ISABELLA ROSS, ROSE POWER, and MARGARET and CHRISTINA SCOTT.

On Feb. 5th, from Toronto, per C.P.R. for China, Miss L. J. KAY and Messrs. E. M. McBRIER, C. J. STEVENS and R. RANDALL. Leaving for China per first French mail in March, Rev. J. HUDSON TAYLOR.

Table of the Roman Catholic Missions of China.

From The Chinese Recorder.

Vicariate	Population	Order	Founded	Europeans	Chinese	Catholics	Catechumens	Churches and Chapels	Schools	Pupils	Seminaries	Students
FUH-KIEN and FORMOSA	22,000,000	Dominicans	1696	24	16	36,090	2,420	51	71	1,290	2	20
SHAN-SI	14,000,000	Franciscans	1696	7	9	14,980	2,500	10	29	200	1	18
SHAN-TUNG, N.	29,000,000	"	1839	12	11	16,020	4,970	300	36	—	2	27
" S.		Belgian Sem.	1885	4	—	830	2,150	39	1	80	—	15
SHEN-SI	10,000,000	Franciscans	1844	15	14	21,300	—	105	15	100	2	35
HO-NAN, N.	23,000,000	"	1843	3	7	1,210	—	6	8	120	1	10
" S.		Mail'd Sem.	1880	6	3	5,000	—	45	20	1,000	—	17
HONG-KONG			1874	7	4	6,800	—	26	9	—	1	12
HU-NAN, N.	18,000,000	Augustines	1879	4	5	100	—	6	1	10	—	—
" S.		Franciscans	1856	8	1	5,000	—	33	7	85	2	24
HU-PEH, N.W.	27,300,000	"	1839	16	—	6,300	—	27	10	530	1	15
" W.		"	1870	6	8	13,000	—	42	16	1,065	1	20
" S.W.		"	1870	5	10	4,120	—	21	6	80	2	10
KAN-SUH	9,200,000	Belgian Sem.	1878	5	2	1,500	—	9	3	35	1	12
KIANG-NAN	76,000,000	Jesuits	1660	85	13	105,000	2,660	650	743	13,300	2	93
KIANG-SI, N.	23,000,000	Lazarists	1696	10	29	10,870	750	24	24	660	—	12
" W.		"	1858	5	6	3,230	510	43	22	140	—	—
" S.		"	1879	8	4	3,560	1,440	25	16	70	2	—
KWANG-SI	7,300,000	Parisian Sem.	1875	7	5	1,020	—	7	3	1,620	—	—
KWANG-TUNG	19,000,000	"	1850	39	7	28,670	—	121	117	1,090	1	40
KWEI-CHAU	5,300,000	"	1847	26	5	16,900	3,000	73	84	2,670	1	20
SI-CH'UEN, N.	35,000,000	"	1696	24	7	38,800	2,000	46	186	1,390	2	94
" S.		"	1556	31	49	26,080	—	64	123	4,150	1	85
" W.		"	1860	23	33	18,000	—	36	62	500	2	26
CHEH-KIANG	18,000,000	Lazarists	1883	9	9	7,480	560	39	37	1,540	2	36
CHIH-LI, N.	28,000,000	Jesuits	1690	19	7	33,770	1,520	121	66	1,710	2	46
" S.E.		Lazarists	1856	37	27	34,530	420	462	148	260	1	14
" S.W.		Parisian Sem.	1840	10	11	26,250	—	81	5	300	—	15
YÜN-NAN	5,300,000	"	1831	21	20	11,210	—	53	30	—	—	18
KOREA	9,000,000	"	1838	18	8	13,650	—	—	—	—	—	—
MANCHURIA	6,000,000	"	1840	44	—	12,530	—	140	—	—	—	—
MONGOLIA, W.		Belgian Sem.	1883	21	7	5,500	—	76	—	—	—	—
" Central	7,000,000	"	1853	41	3	9,000	—	115	—	—	—	—
" S.W.		"	1883	20	5	3,500	—	30	—	—	—	—
THIBET	4,000,000	Parisian Sem.	1857	9	—	1,000	—	18	—	—	—	—
Total	**390,700,000**	35		628	335	541,720	24,900	2,942	1,879	31,625	36	744

Blessed Prosperity.

MEDITATIONS ON THE FIRST PSALM.—I.

HERE is a prosperity which is not blessed: it comes not from above but from beneath, and it leads away from, not towards heaven. This prosperity of the wicked is often a sore perplexity to the servants of GOD; they need to be reminded of the exhortation, "Fret not thyself because of him who prospereth in his way, because of the man who bringeth wicked devices to pass." Many besides the Psalmist have been envious at the foolish when seeing the prosperity of the wicked, and have been tempted to ask, "Is there knowledge in the MOST HIGH?" While Satan remains the god of this world, and has it in his power to prosper his votaries, this source of perplexity will always continue to those who do not enter into the sanctuary and consider the latter end of the worldling.

Nor is it the godless only who are tempted by the offer of a prosperity which comes from beneath. Our SAVIOUR Himself was tempted by the arch-enemy in this way. CHRIST was told that all that He desired to accomplish for the kingdoms of this world might be effected by an easier path than the cross—a little compromise with him who held the power and was able to bestow the kingdoms, and all should be His own. The lying wiles of the seducer were instantly rejected by our LORD; not so ineffective are such wiles to many of His people; a little policy rather than the course for which conscience pleads; a little want of integrity in business dealings; a little compromise with the ways of the world, followed by a prosperity which brings no blessing—these prove often that the enemy's arts are still the same.

But, thank GOD, there is a true prosperity which comes from Him and leads towards Him. It is not only consistent with perfect integrity and uncompromising holiness of heart and life, but it cannot be attained without them, and its enjoyment tends to deepen them. This divine prosperity is GOD'S purpose for every believer in *all* that he undertakes; in things temporal and in things spiritual, in all the relations and affairs of this life, as well as in all work for CHRIST and for eternity; it is GOD'S will for each child of His that "whatsoever he doeth shall prosper." Yet many of His children evidently do not enjoy this uniform blessing; some find failure rather than success the rule of their life, while others, sometimes prospered and sometimes discouraged, live lives of uncertainty, in which anxiety and even fear are not infrequent. Shall we not each one at the outset ask, How is it with me? Is this blessed prosperity my experience? Am I so led by the SPIRIT in my doings, and so prospered by GOD in their issues, that as His witness I can bear testimony to His faithfulness to this promise? If it be not so with me, what is the reason? Which of the necessary conditions have I failed to fulfil? May our meditations on the first Psalm make these conditions more clear to our minds, and enable us with faith to claim definitely all that is included in this wonderful promise.

"*Blessed is the man that walketh not in the counsel of the ungodly.*"

More literally, O the blessings, the manifold happinesses of the man whose character is described in the first and second verses of this Psalm: he is happy in what he avoids and escapes, and happy in what he undertakes and is prospered in. The first characteristic given us is that he walks not in the counsel of the ungodly, the wicked. Notice, it does not merely say that he walks not in wicked counsel: a man of GOD clearly would not do this; but what is said is that he " walketh not in the counsel of the wicked." Now the wicked have often much worldly wisdom, and become noted for their prosperity and their prudence, but the child of GOD should always be on his guard against their counsel; however good it may appear, it is full of danger. One of the principal characteristics of the wicked is that GOD is not in all his thoughts; he sees everything from the standpoint of self, or, at the highest, from the standpoint of humanity; his maxim "Take care of number one," would be very good if it were meant that GOD is first and should always be put first; but he means it not so; self and not GOD is number one to the ungodly. The wicked will often counsel to honesty, not on the ground that honesty is pleasing to GOD, but that it is the best policy; if in any particular business transaction a more profitable policy appears quite safe, those who have simply been honest because it pays best, will be very apt to cease to be so. Now the child of God has no need of the counsel of the ungodly; if he love and study GOD'S Word it will make him wiser than all such counsellors. If he seek for and observe all the counsel of GOD, through the guidance of the HOLY SPIRIT, he will not walk in darkness even as to worldly things. The directions of GOD's Word may often seem strange and impolitic, but in the measure in which he has faith to obey the directions he finds in the Scripture, turning not to the right hand nor to the left, will he make his way prosperous, will he find good success. The history of the early Friends in America who would not take a weapon to protect themselves against the savage Indian tribes shows how safe it is to follow the Word of GOD and not to resist evil. And their later experience in the recent Civil War, in which no one of them lost his life, though exposed to the greatest dangers and hardships because they would not fight, further confirms the wisdom as well as blessedness of literally obeying the Scripture. The eyes of the LORD still run to and fro throughout the whole earth to show Himself strong in behalf of those who put their trust in Him before the sons of men. The enlightened believer has so much better counsel that he no more needs than condescends to accept the counsel of the ungodly.

And, more than this, the wise child of GOD will carefully ascertain the standpoint of a fellow-believer before he will value his counsel; for he learns from Scripture and experience that Satan too frequently makes handles of the people of GOD, as, for instance, in Peter's case. Little did the astonished Peter know whence his exhortation to the LORD to pity Himself came; "Get thee behind me, Satan," showed that our LORD had traced this counsel, which did not seek first the Kingdom of GOD, to its true source. Alas, the counsel of worldly-minded Christians does far more harm than that of the openly wicked. Whenever the supposed interests of self, or family, or country, or even of church or mission come first, we may be quite sure of the true source of that counsel; it is at least earthly or sensual, if not devilish. Further, the truly blessed man

"*Standeth not in the way of sinners.*"

Birds of a feather flock together; the way of the sinner no more suits a true believer than the way of the believer suits the sinner. As a witness for his MASTER in the hope of saving the lost, he may go to them, but he will not, like Lot, set his tent towards Sodom, lest he be ensnared as Lot was, who only escaped himself with the loss of all his possessions and of those he loved best. Ah, how many parents who have fluttered moth-like near the flame, have seen their children destroyed by it, while they themselves have not escaped unscathed. And how many churches and Christian institutions in the attempt to attract the unconverted by worldly inducements or amusements have themselves forfeited the blessing of GOD, and have so lost spiritual power, that those whom they have thus attracted have been nothing benefited; instead of seeing the dead quickened, a state of torpor and death has crept over themselves. There is no need of, nor room for, any other attraction than that which CHRIST Himself gave when He said, "I, if I be lifted up, will draw all men unto Me." Our MASTER was ever "separate from sinners," and the HOLY SPIRIT speaks unmistakeably in 2 Cor. vi.: "What fellowship hath righteousness with unrighteousness, and what communion hath light with darkness? . . . for ye are the temple of the living GOD; as GOD hath said, I will dwell in them and walk in them; and I will be their GOD, and they shall be my people. Wherefore come out from among them, and be ye separate, and touch not the unclean; and I will receive you, and will be a FATHER unto you, and ye shall be my sons and daughters, saith the LORD Almighty."

"*Nor sitteth in the seat of the scornful.*"

The seat of the scornful is one of the special dangers of this age. Pride, presumption, and scorn are closely linked together, and are far indeed from the mind which was in CHRIST JESUS. This spirit often shews itself in the present day in the form of irreverent criticism; those who are least qualified for it are to be found sitting in the seat of judgment, rather than taking the place of the inquirer and the learner. The Bereans of old did not scornfully reject the, to them, strange teachings of the Apostle Paul, but searched the Scriptures daily to see whether these things were so. Now, forsooth, the Scriptures themselves are called in question, and the very foundations of Christian faith are abandoned by men who would fain be looked upon as the apostles of modern thought. May GOD preserve His people from abandoning the faith once delivered to the saints for the baseless, ephemeral fancies of the present day!   J. H. T.

(*To be continued.*)

Items of Interest.

FROM REV. J. W. STEVENSON.

SHANGHAI, *Jan.* 10*th*.—Since I last wrote I have heard of the following baptisms :—

Dec. 16th at Hwuy-chau, GAN-HWUY ... 3
" 31st " Gan-k'ing " ... 4

I am happy to report the return to Ta-ku-t'ang of Mr. Steven and the five Canadian brethren, who went to the south of KIANG-SI; they report most favourably of their visit, and hope to return soon to take up permanent work. I hear very satisfactory accounts of the work at Kweiyang, from Mr. Samuel Clarke and others. Mr. Bagnall, who has been visiting the stations in the north of SHAN-SI, Ta-tung, P'ao-t'eo, and Kwei-hwa-ch'eng, reports very favourably; he was particularly pleased with the evening meetings at the two latter places, and speaks of the workers as all getting on very happily and labouring earnestly. Mr. Hoddle, in Hwuy-luh, CHIII-LI, who is abundant in labours, speaks of the friendliness of the people.

Jan. 14*th*.—Yesterday we had the pleasure of welcoming Mrs. Stott and six sisters, all well and bright. I hear good accounts generally from the workers in the interior. We are looking forward to the coming Conference with great interest.

Jan. 24*th*.—Yesterday we had the pleasure of welcoming Mr. and Mrs. Hunter, and Messrs. Evans, Sharp and Willett. Mr. and Mrs. Nicoll are going to Fan-ch'eng, to take up the work there. I have to report the following baptisms :—

Dec. 4th, Chen-tu, SI CH'UEN 2
" 21st, Chung-k'ing " 8
" 23rd, Kwei-k'i, KIANG-SI 7

Mr. and Mrs. Hogg, and Mr. and Mrs. Gracie have safely arrived at Chau-kia-k'eo in HO-NAN. I have heard from Messrs. Lambert and Selkirk from Bhamo; both were in good health. They speak of the Christians as a devoted band.

"To Every Creature."

THE articles in the December and February numbers of CHINA'S MILLIONS are, we are thankful to find, leading to thought and prayer in many quarters. We have been requested to publish them separately for circulation by letter, etc., so they have been thrown into a booklet, which can be had from the offices of the Mission, or from our publishers, Messrs. Morgan and Scott, at 6d. a dozen. We earnestly hope that our friends will not only give themselves to definite prayer that the Gospel may speedily be given "to every creature," but by circulating this appeal as widely as possible will seek to stir their own circle of friends also to prayer and effort.

Progress at Chen-tu, Si-ch'uen.

FROM MR. GRAY OWEN.

NOV. 2*nd*.—In the evening we had the joy of receiving two men into the Church, one a young man of twenty odd, the other an old cloth-seller of about sixty years of age; they had been inquirers for many months, both having a very clear knowledge of the truth. The clothseller's wife is an inquirer; her knowledge of the Gospel, as yet, very limited. We have other applicants for Baptism, whom we hope to receive before the year runs out.

I had the pleasure to-day of sending out our first local preacher, viz., Elder *Li*, to preach to-morrow at a hamlet two miles outside the south gate of the city, where the Chen-tu Church has rented premises to preach in. It is encouraging to see the native Christians thus willing to spend their contributions to the Church funds in spreading the Gospel amongst their own people. It will be a great joy to me when our native Church here will be able to send forth a preacher to some of the outcast nonChinese tribes in the west of this great province. For the Chinese there is a Bible translated and an extensive Christian literature written; but for these aborigines not a page of the Bible has been translated, not a Gospel tract has been printed, not *one* amongst them knows the way of Salvation. They number tens of thousands in the western part of this province.

Nov. 3*rd*.—Reading the other day in one of the Confucian classics, there was a beautiful piece about how to attain to the highest virtue—reforming the body, correcting the thoughts, and so on, until perfection was attained. Questioning an audience afterwards as to why, with all this fine teaching, none of the people were practising the virtue taught in the classics, the answer was—no one *could* follow the precepts of the Sage. Having gained this point, it was a delight to point out how CHRIST had come to save sinners, to make the immoral virtuous, the thief an honest man, and the bad good. An old gentleman, a member of an official family, comes almost every Sunday morning. Oh, how one longs to see the SPIRIT being poured on these people! Many around us know the Gospel theoretically. Oh, that they knew it experimentally! Now, we glean *before* the harvest, but the harvest is coming. Praise the LORD!

FROM DR. PARRY.

CHEN-TU, *Nov. 20th.*—Your last reached me while still at Tan-lin with my wife; now we have, by our FATHER'S good hand upon us, reached our home once more, after a three months' absence.

Our visit to the work in Tan-lin was a happy, though uneventful one. We found the Christians on the whole attending the services well, and we had many opportunities for teaching and upbuilding. There are a good number of inquirers and cured smokers who have given in their names as candidates, but we have felt it better to let them wait longer. We still have to pray and hope for the one or two who did run well but are turned aside. A good number of the inquirers are in and about a village fifteen *li* from Tan-lin, called Ho-kia-ts'ang, a name which we trust will yet become more familiar as a centre of blessing. Old Kwoh of that village, the once earnest Buddhist, promises to be a leader of others. I made it one object of a visit to his home with Brother Ririe to establish a Wednesday prayer and Bible-reading meeting in his home.

On our way home my wife and I stayed two days at Mei-chau, having, of course, crowds of visitors, and a good sale of books. We have taken this city as a special charge upon our hearts before the mercy-seat, and I fully believe GOD has good things in store for it.

Dec. 13th.—I have been away for a short visit to Ta-i Hien at the urgent request of the Hien mandarin, who was suffering blindness in both eyes from cataract. For the first time I was a guest in a *ya-men* for two days, and had good opportunities of witnessing for CHRIST.

I am able this week to report a new departure in our station-work: last Monday our teacher, Mr. Cheng, left us with his family to work as an evangelist in Mei-chau, in which city a small house has been rented. He enters upon his work with the full confidence and sympathy of all of us who have watched his course for the past two and a half years as an inquirer, a Christian, and a worker. He goes with gladness fully purposed to preach CHRIST, and we are equally glad that GOD has given us such a man to send forth, another offshoot from the church here. You will be pleased, I think, to know that as far as the house-rent and deposit go, this will not appear as a mission expense—at any rate for the first year.

You will be glad to know, too, that the village out-station at Hung-p'ai-lo is now fairly set on foot. The church pays the rent and keeps up the supply of preachers. The blacksmith, Liu, rents one half of the rooms, paying a proportion of the rent and taking charge. A second Christian lives not far away, and these two are, we trust, the nucleus of a future church. The preaching members go in turns, leaving on Saturday in time for an evening meeting, and returning on Monday.

On the 2nd inst. two men were received here by baptism in the presence of a larger congregation of men than usual. One is an old patient who has attended Dr. Pruen's services very regularly, and the younger is employed in a *ya-men*.

Praise GOD for these tokens for good, which lead us, in spite of other things the reverse of joyful, to thank Him and take courage.

Visiting Villages in Si-ch'uen.

FROM MR. WELLWOOD.

SUI-FU, *Nov. 6th.*—Since writing last, I have been away on a preaching and book-selling tour. I had determined to be only one Sunday away, so took a short trip, intending to go to the village of Su-nao-ch'eng by a by-road, and to return by the great road, taking the villages in order. I had only gone 70 or 80 *li*, when I found the road so bad that my coolie went knee-deep in some places in the wet clay road, and could not carry my things, so I decided to give up that road until the season was dry, and crossed over to Fuh-shun Hien. It was raining almost the whole time. The first evening I stayed at a place 40 *li* from the city, sold a good number of books, had a good time of preaching, and found the people very nice indeed. Next morning I left early for Ko-lu-k'iao, some 30 *li* distant, over a bad road. As it was market-day here, sales were good, and I had a splendid opportunity of preaching. I stood on rising ground, where I had a good view of the people, and with all the voice I could command told out the glorious message of salvation. The people were most attentive, and I found by questioning them that they understood very well, though there were. I should think, hundreds present. I had some straight talks to a few, and I pray that they may remember the word spoken.

Next morning I walked 30 *li* before breakfast, for fifteen of them going through mud up to the ankles; took breakfast, gave away a few tracts, and started again, and, 30 *li* further, came to Shih-k'iao-p'u, where I had some sales, and talked to a few at a tea-shop. The people were very nice and kind, and if the work can be followed up, results may be expected. Arrived at Kwan-in-p'u tired and footsore, and stayed overnight in an inn owned by a Roman Catholic. There did not seem to be much religion about him. . . . . In all, seventeen villages have been visited in the ten days and the Word scattered and preached. It was a joy to go amongst the people and find them everywhere willing to listen. Would that these places could be visited regularly, but with our present staff it is impossible; in fact, there are hundreds of villages and thousands of people willing to hear who have not yet had a chance. This is a most promising field. I question if in any part of China there are more open doors or a more willing people. It is a grief to me that I cannot do more. I trust that as long as GOD gives me health and strength I shall work with all my might, knowing that my labour is not in vain in the LORD. Pray for this city and district, and may your prayers have a practical outcome in sending us more workers.

DR. PIERSON is reported to have said: "If GOD will show me anything I can do for the evangelisation of the world that I have not yet done, by His grace I will do it at once."

Dear reader, will you put down this paper and think whether *you* are ready to say to the LORD, "If Thou wilt show *me* anything that I can do that I have not yet done, by Thy grace I will do it at once." Would that all our readers would say daily, "LORD, show me all that I may do for this perishing world, and for Thee."

Stations and Missionaries of the China Inland Mission.
JANUARY 1st, 1890.

(The Out-Stations of the Mission are not given in this table. The names of Associates are printed in Italics.)

I.—Province of Kan-suh. 1876.

Population* of Province, 3 Millions; Area,† 86,608 square miles.

1. Lan-chau, 1885.
GEORGE PARKER (*absent*)	1876
Mrs. PARKER (*absent*)	1880
GEO. GRAHAM BROWN	1886
Mrs. G. G. BROWN (*née* Fenton)	1886
Miss G. MUIR	1887
Miss MAY GRAHAM BROWN	1887

2. Si-ning, 1885.
CECIL H. POLHILL-TURNER	1885
Mrs. C. POLHILL-TURNER (*née* Marston)	1884

3. Liang-chau, 1888.
WILLIAM FYFE LAUGHTON	1884
Mrs. LAUGHTON (*née* Brown)	1885

4. Ning-hsia, 1885.
CHARLES HOROBIN	1884
W. T. BELCHER	1888

5. Tsin-chau, 1878.
HENRY W. HUNT	1879
Mrs. HUNT (*née* Smalley)	1878
Miss KINAHAN	1886
Miss FLORENCE ELLIS	1887
Miss CLARA ELLIS	1887
Miss SUTHERLAND	1887
Miss SMALLEY	1888

II.—Province of Shen-si. 1876.

Population* of Province, 7 Millions; Area,† 67,400 square miles.

6. Han-chung, 1879.
G. F. EASTON	1875
Mrs. EASTON (*née* Gardner)	1881
W. WILSON, M.B., C.M.	1882
Mrs. WILSON (*née* Goodman)	1883
Miss JOHNSON	1887

7. Cheng-ku, 1887.
EDWARD PEARSE (*absent*)	1876
Mrs. PEARSE(*née*Goodman)(*absent*)	1875

Miss FRYER	1887
Miss HOLME	1887
Miss STEDMAN	1888

8. Si-gan Plain, 1888.
A. H. HUNTLEY	1887
T. F. S. BOTHAM	1885
Mrs. BOTHAM (*née* Barclay)	1883
F. A. REDFERN	1887
A. BLAND	1887

III.—Province of Shan-si. 1876.

Population* of Province, 9 Millions; Area,† 55,268 square miles.

9. K'wei-hwa-ch'eng, 1886.
W. T. BEYNON	1885
Mrs. BEYNON (*née* E. Taylor)	1886
J. C. STEWART, M.D. (U.S.A.)	1886
ARCHIBALD EWING	1887

10. Pao-t'eo, 1888.
W. E. BURNETT	1883
Mrs. BURNETT (*née* Jones)	1881

11. Ta-t'ung, 1886.
STEWART MCKEE	1884
Mrs. MCKEE (*née* McWatters)	1887
C. S. I'ANSON	1887

12. T'ai-yuen, 1877.
B. BAGNALL	1873
Mrs. BAGNALL (*née* Kingsbury)	1880
E. H. EDWARDS,M.B.,C.M.(*absent*)	1882
Mrs. EDWARDS (*née*Kemp)(*absent*)	1882
A. HUDSON BROOMHALL	1884
D. M. ROBERTSON	1885
ALEX. R. SAUNDERS	1887

Mrs. ELLISTON (*née* Groom)	1882
Miss A. G. BROOMHALL	1884
Miss EDITH BROOMHALL	1888
Miss J. STEVENS	1885

13. Hiao-i, 1887.
Miss SEED	1883
Miss WHITCHURCH	1884

14. Sih-chau, 1885.
WM. KEY	1884
Mrs. KEY (*née* Symon)	1884
A. LUTLEY	1887

15. Ta-ning, 1885.
Miss M. E. SCOTT	1887
Miss ALICE A. MILES	1887

16. P'ing-yao, 1888.
ARCHIBALD ORR EWING	1886
W. G. PEAT	1888

17. Hoh-chau, 1886.
Miss JAKOBSEN	1886

Miss L. M. FORTH	1887

18. Hung-t'ung, 1886.
D. E. HOSTE	1885

19. P'ing-yang, 1879.
WILLIAM RUSSELL	1887

20. K'üh-wu, 1885.
DUNCAN KAY	1884
Mrs. KAY (*née* Mathewson)	1884

21. Lu-gan, 1887.
C. T. STUDD, B.A.	1885
Mrs. Studd (née Stewart)	1887
Miss BURROUGHES	1887

22. Lu-ch'eng, 1889.
STANLEY P. SMITH, B.A.	1885
Mrs. STANLEY SMITH (*née* Reuter)	1889

23. Yuen-ch'eng, 1888.
Erik Folke	1887
Mrs. Folke (née Grann)	1888
O. S. Nestigaard	1888

IV.—Province of Chih-li. 1887.

Population* of Province, 20 millions; Area,† 58,919 square miles.

24. Tien-tsin, 1888.
G. W. CLARKE	1875
Mrs. CLARKE (*née* Lancaster)	1880

25. Hwuy-luh, 1887.
A. HODDLE	1887

26. Ying-tseng, 1889.
JAS. SIMPSON	1888
Mrs. SIMPSON	1888

27. Shun-teh Fu, 1888.
T. W. PIGOTT, B.A.	1879
Mrs. PIGOTT (*née* Kemp)	1882
A. H. BRIDGE	1888
Miss KERR	1880

---

* The estimates of population are those given in the last edition of "China's Spiritual Need and Claims."
† For comparison, the following particulars are given:—

Population of England, 24,613,926; Scotland, 3,735,573; Wales, 1,360,513; Ireland, 5,174,836.
Area " 50,823 sq. mls.; " 29,820 sq. mls.; " 7,363 sq. mls. " 32,531 sq. mls

V.—Province of Shan-tung. 1879.

Population of Province, 19 millions; Area,† 65,104 square miles.

28. Chefoo, 1879.
- A. W. DOUTHWAITE, M.D.(U.S.A.) 1874
- Mrs. SCHOFIELD 1880
- Miss MILLER 1887
- Miss BAKER 1888

T'ung-shin, 1880.
- H. A. RANDLE, M.D. (U.S.A.) 1876
- Mrs. RANDLE (née Boyd) .. 1878
- Mrs. CHENEY 1884
- Miss OLDING.. .. 1889

Boys' School.
- ALEX. ARMSTRONG, F.E.I.S. .. 1887

- Mrs. ARMSTRONG 1887
- FRANK MCCARTHY (absent) .. 1887
- E. MURRAY 1888
- H. J. ALTY 1889
- Miss MALIN 1887

Girls' School.
- Miss HIBBERD 1886
- Miss KNIGHT 1887
- Miss L. K. ELLIS 1887
- Miss SANDERSON 1888
- Miss ESAM 1889

Sanitarium.
- J. A. STOOKE 1887
- Mrs. STOOKE.. .. 1887

29. Fuh-shan, 1885.
- E. TOMALIN 1879
- Mrs. TOMALIN (née Desgraz) .. 1866

30. Ning-hai, 1886.
- C. H. JUDD 1868
- Mrs. JUDD 1868

VI.—Province of Ho-nan. 1875.

Population of Province, 15 millions; Area,† 65,104 square miles.

31. Chau-kia-k'eo, 1884, and Out-Stations.
- J. J. COULTHARD 1879
- Mrs. COULTHARD(née M. H. Taylor)1884
- CHAS. F. HOGG 1884
- Mrs. HOGG (née S. Muir) .. 1883
- T. H. KING 1884

- J. A. SLIMMON 1884
- W. S. JOHNSTON 1887
- D. J. MILLS 1887
- ARCH. GRACIE 1887
- Mrs. GRACIE (née Waldie) .. 1887
- W. E. SHEARER 1888
- F. E. LUND 1888

- Miss A. CREWDSON.. .. 1888
- Miss CHILTON 1888

32. She-k'i-tien, 1886.
- H. H. TAYLOR 1881
- Mrs. H. H. TAYLOR (née Gray) .. 1884
- Miss GUINNESS 1888

VII.—Province of Si-ch'uen. 1877.

Population of Province, 20 millions; Area,† 166,800 square miles.

33. Chen-tu, 1881.
- HERBERT PARRY, L.R.C.P., M.R.C.S. 1884
- Mrs. PARRY (née Broman) .. 1884
- R. GRAY OWEN 1885
- Mrs. GRAY OWEN (née Butland).. 1885
- Miss BROMAN (designated) .. 1889

34. Tan-lin Hien, 1888.
- Miss ELIZABETH WEBB .. 1884

35. K'wan-hien, 1889.
- Miss FOSBERY 1884

36. Kia-ting, 1888.
- B. RIRIE 1887
- Jos. VALE 1887

37. Sui-fu (Su-chau), 1888.
- J. MCMULLAN 1884
- Mrs. MCMULLAN (née Davis) .. 1886
- R. WELLWOOD 1887

- Miss BANGERT 1888
- T. JAMES 1885
- Mrs. JAMES (Mrs. Riley) .. 1882

38. Chung-k'ing, 1877.
- J. CAMERON, M.D. (U.S.A.) .. 1875
- Mrs. CAMERON (Mrs. Kendall) .. 1883
- Miss WEBBER 1887
- Miss J. W. RAMSAY .. 1887
- Miss A. K. HOOK 1887
- A. H. FAERS.. .. 1887

39. Pao-ning, 1886, and Out-Stations.
- W. W. CASSELS, B.A. .. 1885
- Mrs. CASSELS (née Legg) .. 1886
- MONTAGU BEAUCHAMP, B.A. .. 1885
- EDWARD HUGHESDON .. 1884
- E. O. WILLIAMS, M.A. .. 1889
- Mrs. WILLIAMS 1889

- Miss S. F. JONES 1886
- Miss HANBURY 1887
- Miss F. M. WILLIAMS .. 1887
- Miss P. A. BARCLAY .. 1889
- Miss F. BARCLAY 1889
- Miss MARTIN 1889
- Miss F. H. CULVERWELL.. 1889

40. Kwang-yuen, 1889.
- Miss E. CULVERWELL .. 1887
- Miss BASTONE 1887

41. Pa-chau, 1887.
- A. T. POLHILL-TURNER, B.A. .. 1885
- Mrs. POLHILL-TURNER (née Drake) 1884
- W. HOPE GILL 1885

42. Wan-hien, 1888.
- ALBERT PHELPS 1884
- J. N. HAYWARD 1889

VIII.—Province of Hu-peh. 1874.

Population of Province, 20½ millions; Area, 70,450 square miles.

43. Wu-ch'ang, 1874.
- J. F. BROUMTON 1875
- Mrs. BROUMTON 1879

44. Han-kow, 1889.
- MAURICE J. WALKER .. 1885

45. Fan-ch'eng, 1878.
- GEO. NICOLL (designated) .. 1875
- Mrs. NICOLL (née Howland) .. 1879

- Miss MARY BLACK 1884
- Miss GATES 1887
- Miss MCQUILLAN 1887

46. Lao-ho-k'eo, 1887.
- GEORGE KING 1875
- Mrs. KING (née H. Black) .. 1883
- Miss JANE BLACK 1883
- Miss EMILY BLACK 1884

47. I-ch'ang, 1889.
- F. W. K. GULSTON 1885
- Mrs. GULSTON (née Evans) .. 1882

48. Sha-shi, 1884 (for Hu-nan).
- M. MCNAIR 1889

49. Shih-sheo, 1888.
- D. LAWSON 1887
- Mrs. LAWSON (née Arthur) .. 1888

---

* The estimates of population are those given in the last edition of "China's Spiritual Need and Claims."
† For comparison, the following particulars are given:—

Population of **England**, 24,613,926; **Scotland**, 3,735,573; **Wales**, 1,360,513; **Ireland**, 5,174,836.
Area   „   50,823 sq. mls.;   „   29,820 sq. mls.   „   7,363 sq. mls.   „   32,531 sq. mls.

IX.—Province of Gan-hwuy. 1869.

Population* of Province, 9 millions; Area,† 48,461 square miles.

50. Cheng-yang-kwan, 1887.
JOHN REID 1884
JOHN BROCK.. 1887
I. F. DRYSDALE 1887

51. Lai-gan, 1887.
J. DARROCH 1887
A. DUFFY 1889

52. Gan-k'ing, 1869.
WILLIAM COOPER 1881
Mrs. COOPER 1889
I' MARCUS WOOD 1883

Mrs. WOON (née Williams) .. 1883
G. A. CON, L.R.C.P. & S. 1887
H. N. LACHLAN, M.A. 1889
E. J. HUNT 1889
E. J. COOPER .. ..
THOS. MACOUN .. ..

Training Home.
F. W. BALLER (absent) .. 1873
Mrs. BALLER (née Bowyer) .. 1866

53. N'ing-kwoh, 1874.
GEORGE MILLER 1884

Mrs. MILLER (née Mitchell) .. 1887
H. N. MACGREGOR 1887
THOS. EYRES 1888

54. Ch'i-chau, 1874.
Miss ROBERTSON 1886
Miss UNDERWOOD 1888

55. Hwuy-chau, 1875.
T. D. BEGG 1888
C. A. EWBANK 1887

X.—Province of Kiang-su. 1854.

Population* of Province, 23 millions; Area,† 44,500 square miles.

56. Shanghai, 1854.
J. HUDSON TAYLOR (absent) .. 1853
J. W. STEVENSON 1866
J. E. CARDWELL 1868
Mrs. CARDWELL 1868
W. J. LEWIS 1885
Mrs. LEWIS (née Kings) 1886
Miss WILLIAMSON 1887
Miss PALMER 1887

57. Chin-kiang, 1889.
THOMAS HUTTON 1884

Mrs. HUTTON (née Le Brun) .. 1885
Miss IRVIN 1888
Miss THOMAS 1888

58. Yang-chau, 1868.
JOHN MCCARTHY 1867
Mrs. MCCARTHY 1867
Miss C. K. MURRAY 1884
Miss M. MURRAY 1884
Miss C. P. CLARK 1886
Miss FERRIMAN 1887

Miss R. CREWDSON 1888

59. Kao-yiu, 1889.
Miss MARY REED (absent) .. 1888
Miss KENTFIELD 1888
Miss OAKESHOTT 1889

60. Ts'ing-kiang-fu, 1869.
Miss JENNIE WEBB 1885
Miss C. L. WILLIAMS 1888
Miss M. STEWART 1888

XI.—Province of Yun-nan. 1877.

Population* of Province, 5 millions; Area,† 107,969 square miles.

61. Bhamô (Upper Burmah), 1875.
C. W. LAMBERT 1889
THOS. SELKIRK 1889

62. Ta-li Fu, 1881.
F. T. FOUCAR 1885
JOHN SMITH 1885
Mrs. SMITH (née CUTT) 1887

63. Yun-nan Fu, 1882.
T. G. VANSTONE 1885
Mrs. VANSTONE (née Stewartson) .. 1887
S. Pollard 1887
ED. TOMKINSON 1887
Mrs. TOMKINSON 1887
Miss ELAND 1887
Miss HAINOR 1887

64. Chau-tung Fu, 1887.
S. T. THORNE 1885
Mrs. THORNE (née Malpas) .. 1885
F. DYMOND 1887

65. K'üh-tsing Fu, 1889.
OWEN STEVENSON 1883
J. O. CURNOW 1887

XII.—Province of Kwei-chau. 1877.

Population* of Province, 4 millions; Area,† 64,554 square miles.

66. K'wei-yang, 1877.
GEORGE ANDREW (absent) .. 1881
Mrs. ANDREW (née Findlay) (absent) 1882
S. R. CLARKE 1878

Mrs. CLARKE (née Fausset) .. 1878
WM. PRUEN, L.R.C.P. & S. .. 1880
Mrs. PRUEN (née Hughes) .. 1876
B. CURTIS WATERS 1887

67. Gan-shun Fu, 1888.
THOMAS WINDSOR 1884
JAMES ADAM 1887

XIII.—Province of Hu-nan. 1875.

Population* of Province, 16 millions; Area,† 74,320 square miles.

This province is worked from Sha-shï and Shih-sheo, HU-PEH, which see.

---

* The estimates of population are those given in the last edition of "China's Spiritual Need and Claims."
† For comparison, the following particulars are given:—
Population of England, 24,818,920; Scotland, 3,735,573; Wales, 1,360,513; Ireland, 5,174,836.
Area „ 50,823 sq. mls.; „ 29,820 sq. mls.; „ 7,363 sq. mls. „ 32,531 sq. mls.

XIV.—Province of Kiang-si. 1869.

Population of Province, 15 millions; Area,† 72,126 square miles.

68. *Kiu-kiang*, 1889.			71. *Nan-k'ang Fu*, 1887.			Miss GARDINER	..	..	1888
A. EASON	..	1881	Miss MCFARLANE	..	1881	Miss R. MCKENZIE	..	..	1888
Mrs. EASON (*née* Southall)	..	1881	Miss ORD	..	1887	Miss GRABHAM	..	..	1889
69. *Ta-ku-t'ang*, 1873.			Miss BRADFIELD	..	1888	75. *Yüh-shan*, 1877.			
J. T. REID	..	1887	Miss HARDING	..	1888	Miss MACKINTOSH	..	..	1884
Mrs. REID	..	1887	72. *K'wei-k'i*, 1878.			Miss MARCHBANK	..	..	1887
F. A. STEVEN	..	1883	Miss ANNIE SAY	..	1886	Miss BUCHAN	..	..	1884
Mrs. STEVEN (*née* Tapscott)	..	1880	Miss J. MUNRO	..	1888	Miss GUEX	..	..	1889
W. M. SOUTER	..	1888	Miss HORSBURGH	..	1889	*Itinerating.*			
Miss LUCAS	..	1888	73. *Gau-sven*, 1889.			W. S. HORNE	..	..	1888
Miss ROGERS	..	1888	Miss H. MCKENZIE	..	1889	JOHN MEIKLE	..	..	1885
Miss S. M. BLACK	..	1889	74. *Ho-k'eo*, 1878.			GEO. H. DUFF	..	..	1884
70. *Kwang-feng*, 1889.			Miss GIBSON	..	1884	JAS. LAWSON	..	..	1885
Miss FITZSIMONS	..	1888				J. S. ROUGH	..	..	1889
Miss H. TURNER	..	1888							

XV.—Province of Cheh-kiang. 1857.

Population of Province, 12 millions; Area,† 39,150 square miles.

Hang-chau, 1866.			79. *Ning-hai*, 1868.			83. *Yung-k'ang*, 1882.			
(Pastor *Wáng La-djün*.)			N. HARRISON	..	1885	A. WRIGHT	..	..	1886
(„ *Nying Tsi-ky'ing*.)			80. *T'ai-chau*, 1867.			84. *Kin-hwa*, 1875.			
76. *Shao-hing*, 1866.			W. D. RUDLAND	..	1866	A. LANGMAN	..	..	1884
JAMES MEADOWS	..	1862	Mrs. RUDLAND (*née* Knight)	..	1875	Mrs. LANGMAN (*née* M. Williams)	..	1887
Mrs. MEADOWS (*née* Rose)	..	1866	81. *Wun-chau*, 1867.			Miss VOAK	..	..	1888
Miss CARPENTER (*absent*)	..	1883	Mrs. STOTT (*née* Ciggie)	..	1870	85. *K'iu-chau*, 1872.			
77. *Sin-ch'ang*, 1870.			Miss H. A. JUDD	..	1887	DAVID THOMPSON	..	..	1871
J. A. HEAL	..	1885	Miss BARDSLEY (*designated*)	..	1889	Mrs. THOMPSON (*née* Dowman)	..	1883
Mrs. HEAL (*née* M. Carpenter)	..	1883	Miss WHITFORD (*designated*)	..	1889	Miss F. BOYD	..	..	1878
Ning-po, 1857.			82. *Bing-yae*, 1874.			86. *Ch'ang-shan*, 1878.			
J. *Williamson*, Superintended from *Fung-hwa*.			R. GRIERSON	..	1885	Miss BYRON	..	..	1884
			Mrs. GRIERSON (*née* Oliver)	..	1886	87. *Peh-shih-kiai*, 1879.			
78. *Fung-hwa*, 1866.			Miss BRITTON	..	1887	Miss LITTLER	..	..	1886
J. WILLIAMSON	..	1866	*Ch'u-chau*, 1875.						
Mrs. WILLIAMSON	..	1875	*Superintended from Bing-yae.*						

Missionaries At Home or Undesignated.

Mrs. J. HUDSON TAYLOR	..	1866	Miss HORNE	..	1876	Miss TODD	..	1884
Mrs. J. W. STEVENSON	..	1860	FRANK TRENCH	..	1878	Miss CAMPBELL	..	1888
Miss E. TURNER	..	1872	Miss ANNIE R. TAYLOR	..	1884	J. H. RACEY	..	1888

Missionaries recently arrived in China‡—Engaged in Study.

At Yang-chau.			Miss COWLEY	..	1889	J. S. DONALD	..	1889
Miss CROSSTHWAITE	..	1889	Miss MAY LANE	..	1889	M. L. GRIFFITH	..	1889
Miss DUNN	..	1889	Miss E. RAMSAY	..	1889	C. H. Tjäder	..	1889
Miss HALIN	..	1889	Miss HOSKYN (*en route*)	..	1889	G. N. Hunter	..	1889
Miss ANDERSON	..	1889	Miss L. A. SMITH (*en route*)	..	1889	H. A. C. ALLEN	..	1889
Miss E. E. CLARE	..	1889	Miss THIRGOOD (*en route*)	..	1889	JNO. ANDERSON	..	1889
Miss F. E. DOGGETT	..	1889				J. DICKIE	..	1889
Miss ALICE GILLIAM	..	1889	*At Gan-k'ing.*			A. GRAINGER	..	1889
Miss KOLKENBECK	..	1889	M. HARDMAN	..	1889	J. C. HALL	..	1889
Miss L. A. YOUNG	..	1889	J. J. P. EGERTON	..	1889	J. STARK	..	1889
Miss L. Carlyle	..	1889	G. A. HUNTLEY	..	1889			

* The estimates of population are those given in the last edition of "China's Spiritual Need and Claims."
† For comparison, the following particulars are given :—
Population of England, 24,613,926 ; Scotland, 3,735,573 Wales, 1,360,513 ; Ireland, 5,174,836.
Area „ 50,823, sq. mls. ; „ 29,820 sq. mls. ; „ 7,333 sq. mls. ; „ 32,531 sq. mls.
‡ Since Dec. 12th twenty-five missionaries have left for China, making a total of 383.

Tidings from Kao-yiu.

FROM THE DIARY OF MISS KENTFIELD.

PRAISE God for giving us a house in Kao-yiu; it is an answer to many prayers. We have a nice large hall in front, which makes a splendid chapel, and at the back we have a good guest-hall and rooms at each side; now we want the glory of the LORD to fill the house and souls to be born again. We are just two sisters here, Miss Oakeshott and myself, besides a native evangelist and his aged father are the only representatives in this city of CHRIST and the Resurrection. Praise GOD, there are now two inquirers, an old man of seventy and his wife, sixty-four—such a dear old couple. The old woman is so bright; she comes constantly to morning and evening prayers, and on Sundays is with us nearly all day; they have two grandsons, who are dear children, and will, I trust, make bright Christians. Then our woman, who was dear Miss MacKee's woman, is, I believe, trusting the LORD. We have a few who look upon us as their friends, and often come to see us. This morning an old woman came alone, and listened so attentively; she asked several intelligent questions, and seemed to grasp the plan of substitution; she spoke of coming to worship with us, and as she was going out, remarked to our woman that she "was going to heaven with us." May the LORD truly save her!

November 6th.—On Sunday we had a very good day, beginning with our usual prayer-meeting, followed by a service in the chapel. In the afternoon numbers came, and JESUS was in our midst. Last evening I commenced a special class for boys, and had five, which I thought was very good for the first time. I should like to ask special prayer for this class. I think it is so important to try and reach the lads before they form bad habits; one longs to save them from that dreadful opium-smoking. To-day we have had a great many women to see us, and some who came this afternoon came to prayers in the evening. I never had a more attentive audience. One dear girl said she should not worship her idols to-morrow morning, and to-morrow is the 15th of the Chinese month, and the great worship day. We are sure that the LORD has many souls in Kao-yiu, and we want Him to save them. "Except the LORD build the house, they labour in vain that build it"; we want to remember this, and not to try to do the LORD'S part, but simply to abide in Him and let Him do what He will with us for the building of His house in Kao-yiu. Will our dear friends at home ask for us that the MASTER will thoroughly "purge His floor," that there may be nothing of our own intruding itself, but that we may forego anything and everything that the name of JESUS may be magnified.

November 8th.—I am *so* glad I came to China. I should never have seen half the goodness and wisdom and working of the LORD if I had not come at His call.

An Evangelistic Journey in Hu-nan.

FROM MR. McNAIR.

SHA-SHI, *Nov. 25th.*—It is now more than a week since Mr. James and I returned from a short journey of sixteen days into the still closed province of HU-NAN. We left Sha-shi on Saturday morning, Nov. 2nd, and got as far as Shih-sheo that night. We passed a quiet, but I hope profitable, LORD'S Day there. Several people visited us, and among them some who seemed to be sincere seekers after the Way of Life. On Monday Mr. James set about trying to get some business settled that had to do with the house that was destroyed and rebuilt. Early Tuesday morning it was very satisfactorily settled, and we proceeded on our journey by boat. That day we called at a village and spent about an hour in selling books and speaking.

We got as far as Gan-siang Hien about mid-day, and spent a very busy afternoon on the streets; the people bought gospels pretty freely, and, on the whole, work on that day was a pleasure. Shortly before we retired to rest, and pretty late at night, we had a visit from a man who was interested in what he had heard during the day. As our boat was too small to accommodate him while the truth was being explained, he invited us to his house, which was not far away. Here we found half a dozen or so gathered evidently for the purpose of hearing more about the new doctrine. They listened most attentively while Mr. James preached CHRIST to them. After exhorting them to repentance and trust in JESUS, the SON of GOD and only SAVIOUR of mankind, and declaring to them the fallacy of idols, and the eternal consequences that depended upon their decision, we took leave of them with thankful hearts, not a little encouraged by this token of the LORD'S confirming His Word by the signs we saw. Our interview lasted about an hour.

We would fain have spent more time in this city, but according to arrangements already made, which we believe to be of the LORD, we left at daybreak on Thursday. That day we visited two little villages, spending about an hour in each. By Friday night we were within ten *li* of Chang-teh, and rather reluctantly stopped for the night. Early next day, having got our beds and box of books brought to an inn, we were soon on the streets. It seemed quite incredible to the people that we could be foreigners, so they kept asking if we were not Ning-po men. Curiosity regarding our nationality and the size and shape of our noses seemed to occupy them more than an interest in our message. In order to accomplish more in the short time that we had arranged to stay in that city, Mr. James and I separated. We met with great indifference from the people.

On LORD'S Day we took a few books up our sleeves in the hope that we might be able to give them away, but we rarely found opportunity which we thought safe to attempt distribution. We visited a family who had at one time been members of one of the churches at Wu-chang. We did not find them bearing a bright testimony for the Gospel as they did at one time. Their medicine shop was open, and in this they did not differ from their neighbours. The deadening influences of heathenism around them are certainly most trying. I think few of us realise at all adequately the need of the native Christians of the help and prayers of the church at large. Their temptations are countless.

Shortly after we returned to our inn we had a visitor from the *ya-men*, who asked us a few polite questions regarding ourselves and our business, and then left. No sooner had our visitor gone than the landlord sent us a

CHAPEL IN CONNECTION WITH THE PROPOSED SCHOFIELD MEMORIAL HOSPITAL AT TAI-YUEN FU.

message, informing us that the officials wished us to leave the city, as they feared they would not be able to protect us from the students, 30,000 of whom were up for examination at the time, and would be out on Monday. We decided to call on the magistrate ourselves, and he received us very kindly.

At eight o'clock on Monday morning we were on our way to Tsin-shih. Nothing of much interest took place until Thursday, when we stopped early for a few hours at the flourishing town of Hsing-tseo. Here we had a busy time, and scattered a good number of gospels.

An hour's sailing brought us in sight of Tsin-shih, when we went ashore with an armful each of gospels and tracts, in the hope of being able to scatter them in the outskirts, but we were only partially successful. We entered the town itself a little before noon, and at once began to declare our message. The people were rude, and cursed us on every side. Crowds gathered round us of such as had nothing much to do, and before we had gone very far we could see that it would not take much to get us a beating. Towards evening the crowds got very rough; we tried not to lose sight of one another, but found that sometimes difficult. At last I lost sight of Mr. James, and soon discovered that I had fallen near to his mob together with my own. I tried to humour the crowd as best I could, but they seemed bent on mischief. Occasional pieces of broken tiles were being thrown, and my cue got a pull or two. I felt sure that Mr. James was not on the street, and began to think how I could get back to our boat. I knew it would not do to run, so I walked steadily towards the riverside among showers of missiles, without sustaining the slightest injury. The LORD preserved my head from being once struck, although I was struck on the back several times. On sighting the boat I saw Mr. James looking out for me. I descended the steep embankment without a single stone being thrown, but no sooner was I on the boat than a regular storm of missiles came battering against it. The boatmen put out from the shore as speedily as possible, and soon we were lost amongst the hundreds of boats that line the riverside. The fast-falling darkness helped us considerably to cover our retreat. We passed a quiet night at the riverside some distance down.

Next morning we spent a short time on the streets again, and met with much the same spirit; but, notwithstanding interruptions, we sold a good number of gospels, and had not a few opportunities of preaching. May the LORD bless His own Word.

We left there by road about eleven a.m. along with the postman whom we got to carry our box and bedding. We only stopped to sell books at one other town on the way home, and arrived late on Saturday night.

Schofield Memorial Hospital Chapel at T'ai-yuen Fu.

READERS of the "Memorials of R. Harold A. Schofield" will remember that at the end of the book it is stated :

"The friends of the late Dr. Schofield are anxious to erect a hospital to his memory at T'ai-yuen Fu, in the province of SHAN-SI, where he laboured as a medical missionary so successfully during the last three years of his life."

In 1885, an agreement was entered into for the purchase of a house and land for the above purpose, but it was not until 1887 that the matter was finally settled, and possession obtained of the premises. At that time the most pressing need was a chapel, as the small room used as such was overcrowded with men, and the women had to be accommodated in another part of the house. Building operations were commenced the same year, and the accompanying reproduction of a photograph shows the front view of the chapel. Behind it is a small ante-room, dispensary and drug store, and a large piece of vacant ground where buildings can be erected for the accommodation of male patients whenever funds will allow. An adjoining house, purchased for an opium-refuge, has meanwhile served as a hospital for men, there being no one to take charge of a refuge. A house for the use of the resident physician and a small court for female patients were on the plot when purchased, and only needed altering and cleaning to make them fit for immediate use. Towards the expenses connected with the above £178 0s. 1d. was contributed in England, and about £800 in T'ai-yuen Fu.

Prepared Hearts in Ho-nan.

FROM MISS CHILTON.

CHAU-KIA-K'EO, *Nov. 25th.*—You will have heard before this, very likely, that I am settled in our little house amongst the women. Since coming here, though only a week ago, I have very much to praise and bless GOD for, both for the way He has kept me from fear in this rough part of HO-NAN, and for the way He has helped me, both in speaking and understanding these people. I have had good numbers to see me, with whom I have had good times, and have been very conscious of the LORD'S help and presence. I do indeed praise Him for all the encouragement He has given me. I am expecting Him to do much here in Ho-si, as I have been long asking for the souls of these women, and it does seem as though He has begun to work in their hearts.

I have had three most interesting cases amongst those who have come to hear the story of JESUS' love, one a sister to a woman who has attended my Ho-Si weekly meeting about six times. She had heard from her sister just enough to make her want to know more, so came to pay me a visit in my new home, and to hear more for herself. She was not full of other questions, but listened so well, and seemed so sorry if she could not understand what I said to her. I was talking to her for about an hour and a half. When I commenced, my little room was full of women, but as it was getting far on in the afternoon, they went, leaving just these two sisters and another woman who was equally anxious to hear GOD'S way of putting away sins. When I had made the way quite clear to her as to how to come to JESUS, she said, "Could you not give me a book that tells of JESUS' plan, as my husband and son can read, and I do want them to know too?" You may imagine I gladly gave them a tract and Gospel, for which she seemed very grateful. The other woman was equally anxious, and I gave her a tract. My heart, indeed, was rejoiced at this ; I felt they were prepared hearts sent of GOD. He will not leave His work until He has perfected it ; I am believing for them. The sister of this woman who has been to my meetings week by week, although not at all a bright, quick woman, I have always had hope of, as she continued to come and always listened so well. I do feel the LORD is helping me so much, and I do want to spend and be spent for these people whom He has sent me amongst, and whom He has taught me to love.

Yesterday, although a wet day, I had my third interesting case among a number of women who had come to listen, their homes being close by. They had heard me teaching the little boy who is living here with his parents (our servants) to sing "JESUS loves me." We had been singing some time when the women came, saying they wanted also to listen. I very gladly let them in, and for some time they listened to my singing and talking to them, after which another woman came in, who at first did not seem inclined to listen. However, after a while she became very interested, and before she went away, having heard that JESUS would listen to her prayer if she asked Him to forgive her sins, she said, "I do want JESUS to wash my heart and make it clean." I had been teaching them to repeat a text of Scripture, as I always think GOD'S Word can do its own work. She had seemed to open up so well and learn so quickly that I just said " Praise GOD, another prepared heart come to listen." I was with her a long time. She did not seem in the least inclined to go. She told me her husband had heard the Gospel on the north side of the river, and was willing to listen; he believed it was true. I again said " Praise GOD." I inquired if her husband could read, and was told he could. She asked me for a book like that I had been reading to her, so that her husband might read it again to her, and might learn how JESUS had died to redeem them from sin, as they two did want to go on one road to heaven. I was greatly encouraged again by this to go forward, trusting the LORD who can influence all hearts. She said she was my neighbour, and would often come in if she might for me to teach her about JESUS. Being alone, I am kept very busy; but these are very happy days just now. I am sure this is a good place for women's work, as we are right amongst them.

PASSENGER-BOAT, KIANG-SU.   GUN-BOAT.

An Interesting Visit.

FROM MRS. SIMPSON.

YING-TSENG, CHIH-LI, Nov. 23rd.—In a previous letter I think I intimated my intention of paying a visit to some of our friends in Hwuy-luh. Accordingly my woman and I left here on 8th November for a nine days' stay in the city. Though it was very late before we arrived, our friends were expecting us, and I am sure accorded to us as hearty a welcome as ever we received from our own relations in Scotland. The time passed away all too quickly, and I am afraid I shall be unable to put on paper the many manifestations of the LORD'S presence and the workings of His SPIRIT in the family we visited. The old people of the home were unusually kind and very considerate.

My woman, who is a distant relative of the family, was a little afraid of the displeasure of the old people when told of her intention of becoming a Christian, so we had made it a special matter of prayer for some time, and as usual the LORD exceeded our expectations. I told them again and again of the Gospel glad tidings, and then the head of the family said to my woman, " I am sure this is a good Gospel ; you are constantly with them and can hear and learn a little every day. I would advise you and your little girl to learn all you can, and follow this religion ;" and she added, " I am old and cannot remember much at a time, and I have no one here constantly with me to tell me again and again ; if I had I think I would follow them too." I could hardly believe my ears when I heard this. We receive little because we ask little.

Our former teacher's first wife was away from home, and only returned the day before we left. I had daily talks with the second wife, and feel little hesitation in saying that she is walking the heavenly road. She knows a good deal of the Gospel, and is a most intelligent woman. She daily prays, and only needs a little wise counsel and help. The third wife I visited several times. She lives outside and seems to be making fair progress with her reading, and as far as one can know, she is living in accordance with what she professes. There seems to be some jealousy between the two first wives and herself. They think their husband gives her more attention than them. It is not easy to say anything, for this system of plurality of wives is certainly one of the devil's ways of trapping poor souls. I had a long talk with Mr. Liu himself on several evenings, and he said he was still trusting and praying, but felt a little cooled down, having no one to continually speak to him of these things. One evening he came in and joined us in worship. I prayed, then my woman, and then I asked him to do so. He hesitated, but commenced, and poured out his soul in prayer in simple language, words which I doubt not were the real breathings of his heart. He feels that it is a great difficulty having three wives, but can see no way out of it. He asked me to tell his friends that he was anxious to follow JESUS, because he said it will then be easier for him to confess CHRIST before them.

On two occasions his brother, who is also a B.A., came

in and spent the most of the evening in our room. The first evening he was inclined to laugh and dispute the divinity of CHRIST; I knew I could not convince him by argument, so just tried to speak words straight to his heart, and after a time I saw I was gaining ground, and if ever I spoke personally to any man, I did to him. He sat for a long time, and on going away I said I would pray for him. He was much surprised, and thanked me, and said he had enjoyed the talk very much. Two nights after he again came in, but this time he showed much more of the enquirer's spirit, and said he admired this doctrine and was anxious to know more about it. He read four chapters in Matthew, and what he did not fully understand, he asked me the meaning of. I do indeed trust he may be fully convinced, and accept this truth. He is of a very retiring disposition, and I feel sure GOD'S SPIRIT was working with him, or else he would not have repeated his visit.

My woman's eldest daughter came to spend four days with us when there. The first two, one would have thought she was possessed by an evil spirit. In every possible way she tried to hinder us from having worship. She laughed at her mother and sister for praying, and would not join us in anything. On the third night, however, after her mother and sister were asleep, she took hold of my hand and asked if I would teach her about JESUS. I was afraid she was not in earnest and told her so, but she said she was, and wanted to repent and go to heaven. I explained to her the outlines of the Gospel, and taught her one verse of "JESUS loves me," and then engaged in prayer and asked her to repeat the words after me, which she did. She seemed a good deal broken down, and next morning she woke me up early to tell her a line which she had forgotten.

I have still another item of interest, which has encouraged us not a little. When staying in Hwuy-luh, Mr. Simpson visited a village five *li* distant several times. At this time my woman and I visited it to see some of her friends. The village was in a great stir, all anxious to see me, and unfortunately I had one of the severe headaches which have troubled me so much recently. I felt quite unable to speak, and the room and courtyard were crowded. My headache increased with the noise of the people, and at last I felt, Well, if the LORD does not interfere I must return to get a little quiet. I therefore prayed earnestly about it, and in spite of the noise of the people I fell into a sort of doze for ten minutes, woke up and found it gone, and also a great many of the people gone too. Then one woman came in and said she had come purposely to get me to read and explain to her this doctrine. She said on one of Mr. Simpson's visits he had been telling some people there about this Gospel, and a friend in passing heard it, and came and told her that we spoke words that they could understand, which, if believed, would lead them to heaven. The woman said, "I have often thought about that, and been longing for some of you to come, so that I might hear these words myself." Some of the others laughed at the possibility of her understanding, but she was firm and went on asking again and again to make sure she knew the right meaning. I think she had a fair idea of the plan of salvation before I left, and we can only pray that He who implanted that desire will watch over and water the words—His own words—and lead this seeking soul to a seeking SAVIOUR.

One cannot tell what the real feelings are towards the Gospel of the family we visited, but as they are not a poor family, I do not think they could expect to gain anything by becoming Christians. The kindness I received, and the willingness to listen and seemingly to accept the Gospel, which I saw during my nine days' stay, has well repaid me for coming to China. I only hope that they may be real gems in the SAVIOUR'S crown, and not put their hand to the plough and then look back. They certainly need our prayers, patience, and sympathy.

I may say my woman and her little girl of nine, both let their lights shine brightly when on this visit to their friends' home. We promised to pay them another visit after the new year, so may it please GOD to use the weak things to confound the mighty.

There are a few about here who seem to be enquirers, but the great majority will talk of everything else, but they have "no time" when the Gospel is spoken of.

Tidings from Scattered Workers.

Kan-suh Province.
FROM MR. HOROBIN.
Ning-hsia, Oct. 17th.—It is now twelve months since I saw any European but Mr. Belcher, but if I had attended a Conference each day my cup would not be more full; the LORD is a satisfying portion. He is teaching me to glory in my infirmities, that the power of CHRIST may rest upon me.

Shan-si Province.
FROM DR. STEWART.
K'wei-hwa-ch'eng, Nov. 26th.—During the last month we have, of course, been working with all our might, but I cannot tell you of any results. The LORD has been with us personally, and has manifested His loving care and protection in many ways. He has enabled us to preach the Gospel to hundreds of people who came to us from many villages, and have, I believe, carried news of the Gospel back to many homes where it will yet bring forth precious fruit.

Our dispensary work is going on, the cold weather sending many more patients to us than usual. The sick have been restored, the blind received their sight, the Gospel has been preached, and confidence and friendship have been gained, which the LORD in His own good time will turn to account for His own glory. The meetings in Mr. Beynon's chapel continue to be well attended and much interest shown.

Mr. Ewing arrived some time ago, much refreshed and blessed by fellowship at the T'ai-yüen Conference. Mr. Bagnall arrived last Saturday from Ta-t'ung, and is going on to Pao-t'eo on the 29th. We are all gladdened by his presence.

Shan-tung Province.
Work in Che-foo, as in other free ports, is specially difficult and discouraging. The following extract will, we trust, call forth special prayer:—

FROM DR. DOUTHWAITE.
Che-foo, Dec. 16th.—I hope and pray that the coming year may be a time of great blessing to us all, and that GOD may be pleased to use us more in winning souls. I am not satisfied to go on year after year as I have done, seeing only a dozen or so converted each year as the result of my hard work. I have treated over 5,000 patients this year, and only three or four of them have—as far as I know—been led to Christ. This ought not to be, and yet I cannot see how to get more at the hearts of these people.

Ho-nan Province.
FROM MR. LUND.
Hwuy-k'ing Fu, Oct. 29th.—I am very glad to be able to tell you of a happy time in SHAN-SI. Both on the road, in company with Messrs. Hoste and Russell, and in T'ai-yüen, with all the dear brethren, I had a time of real joy and blessing.

Praise GOD for all the love and power manifested in the work and workers of SHAN-SI! Everywhere there are traces of a living SAVIOUR to be found; the darkness is dispersing and the light of our Gospel is spreading far and wide. Mr. Hsi is without doubt a great blessing to South SHAN-SI. I must say that I was pleasantly disappointed to find him so simple and warm-hearted; I had expected to see in him more of the Chinese gentleman—self-contentedness, superiority, etc.; but he has, indeed, a humble and CHRIST-like spirit. Would to GOD that China had many such men!

At the Conference I learned many useful lessons, and was stirred to more zeal for the salvation of souls and for a holy life. I do trust that the effect of that Conference may be felt widely, and that even Hwuy k'ing Fu may have its share.

FROM MR. D. J. MILLS.

Chu-sien-chen, November 17th.—Since arriving here in the beginning of October, I have been on a journey to the principal places immediately south and south-west from this. I do not think that any of these places had been visited previously, except by the agent of the British and Foreign Bible Society. However, along the whole route I was fairly well received, and succeeded in selling a good number of tracts, books and gospels. Suspicion and fear as to the result of buying these were evidently not wanting in many hearts; I trust that by GOD's grace something was done to break down these prejudices, and that the next time this journey is taken the ready welcome given by so many will be even more generally accorded. Some decidedly interesting cases occurred, and one can only hope that the truth, understood to some extent, was indeed received to the salvation of the soul.

This place is celebrated for the sale of paper gods; we are still resident in an inn, and apparently likely to be so. The people seem increasingly friendly, and when we have been bookselling or preaching at the theatrical shows or upon the streets, and in the tea-shops no sign of opposition has appeared; so we thank GOD and take courage. Mahommedans probably form two-thirds of the population here, and of course think it impossible that CHRIST can be superior to Mahomet. GOD give them an opened heart to receive the truth.

Mr. Johnston will probably be starting in a day or two on a journey to the east, taking in the capital again. Praise GOD, there are no difficulties that our Leader cannot overcome.

The advent of the iron-horse [the railway] is being eagerly spoken of by many here, when everyone will grow sick, and there will be little to do!

Si-ch'uen Probince.

FROM MRS. PRUEN.

Chen-tu, Oct. 9th.—Our house is made for three families, and is part of a compound of at least thirteen families, if not more, and until I lived in this place so close to the people, I had no idea how idolatry forms a part of their every-day life. The longer I live amongst the people the more convinced I am that through their wicked priests they talk with the dead and with devils. Poor people, how firmly Satan has got them! Oh, that it were easier for them to believe!

DR. PRUEN sends a report from Chen-tu, on Nov. 18th, of 621 dispensary patients, including 52 visited in their own homes, besides the restoration of 19 would-be opium suicides, 4 maternity cases, 1 of harelip, etc. An old man and a young one had confessed their faith in CHRIST by baptism, and a woman had professed conversion. Dr. and Mrs. Pruen were starting on Nov. 26th, to take up work in Kwei-yang Fu.

FROM MR. FAERS.

Chung-'ing, Nov. 9th.—I have started a boys' day school here, and have an attendance of fifteen daily. You may perhaps wonder why I did so, having my hands so full already. We have now forty-three church members, and I felt that all the home influence on their children would be lost without Christian instruction. Now all our converts' children attend, as well as some outsiders. I love children dearly; may I ask your prayers that all my life may so show forth CHRIST that many of these dear boys may be jewels in our SAVIOUR's crown. Dr. Cameron has kindly offered to pay the expenses of this school from the overplus made at the opium-refuge.

Our two street chapels are in full work, one supported entirely by the church, who contribute systematically every week, even the poorest; truly we ought to praise GOD, for this, being all their own doing, is practical Christianity, which really shows life. Some of our Christians are becoming good preachers. We have much here to cause us to cry Hallelujah; yet, on the other hand, we, too, have our disappointments, which send us to our MASTER's feet for help and strength.

Hu-peh Probince.

FROM MISS F. H. CULVERWELL.

Wu-chang, Nov. 20th.—I had intended to have written from Yang-chau, for I wanted to tell you how very thankful I am to have had so long a stay there. It has been a time of strengthening and building up in many ways, and of knowing more of the LORD. I do want to keep this one thing before me, "that I may know Him and the power of His resurrection and the fellowship of His sufferings," and so be ready to be or endure anything, if by any means some may be saved.

It was so nice to be able to make a little beginning at Yang-chau. The work in the old city is very interesting; such numbers have been coming. I do not know whether among the women there are yet any really convicted of sin; many have come very often, and seem to be getting the truth into their heads. I do trust that we shall soon hear that some have got it into their hearts.

I am rejoicing in going on to my sister at Kwang-yuen, but am so glad that I have had the opportunity of getting a wider knowledge of the work in China and much information that makes me understand my standing and responsibility as a member of the Mission. I think I grasp more deeply what one weak link in the chain means. For great kindness received from Mr. McCarthy and Miss Murray and many other dear friends I am deeply indebted, so that I shall ever keep a very sweet recollection of the nine months spent in Yang-chau.

Gan-hwuy Probince.

FROM MRS. COOPER.

Gan-K'in , Dec. 16th.—Owing to our long time of sickness, I have been kept back a good deal with the language; but I am now trying to prepare for the second examination, and the LORD is helping me wonderfully. On Sundays and Thursdays I have a meeting for women here, and on Tuesdays I go to the Westgate house and gather in the women of that locality, and with Mrs. U's help, speak to them. Mrs. U is almost blind, but as she was trained in the girls' school, she knows many hymns, and being a good singer, is a great help.

The other days of the week I go out to visit the houses in this neighbourhood, and as I take Willie with me, I get plenty of invitations to sit down. I soon get a crowd round me, anxious to see "the little foreign devil." His fair hair and bright blue eyes seem a mystery to them. As soon as their curiosity is a little satisfied, I try to speak a word for my MASTER. Some listen attentively, but the majority pay little heed. Many have heard the Gospel from other lips, and these seem hardened, and laugh at everything. Do remember me in prayer, that I may soon be able to understand, and to express myself better. The Christians here are being revived.

Arrivals from China.

Rev. E. and Mrs. PEARSE and two children reached England on furlough on March 5th; and on March 11th Mr. and Mrs. GEO PARKER and children and Miss ROBINA CREWDSON arrived.

Blessed Prosperity.

MEDITATIONS ON THE FIRST PSALM. II.

WE considered last month the things which are avoided by the truly blessed man. O, the miseries and the losses of those who fail to avoid them! We have now to dwell upon the special characteristic of the man of GOD, one which is at once the source of his strength and his shield of protection.

"*His delight is in the law of the LORD;*
"*And in His law doth he meditate day and night.*"

The unregenerate *cannot* delight in the Law of the LORD; they may be very religious, and may read the Bible as one of their religious duties; they may admire much that is in the Bible, and be loud in its praise—for as a mere book it is the most wonderful in the world—nay, they may go much further than this, and may imagine, as did Saul the persecutor, that their life is ordered by its teachings, while still they are far from GOD. But when such become converted they discover that they had been blind; and among the all things that become new they find that they have got a new Bible, and as new-born babes they desire the unadulterated milk of the Word that they may grow thereby. Well is it when young Christians are properly fed from the Word of GOD, and have not their taste corrupted and their spiritual constitution destroyed by feeding on the imaginations of men rather than on the verities of GOD.

It is not difficult to discover what a man delights in. "Out of the abundance of the heart the mouth speaketh." The mother delights to speak of her babe, the politician loves to talk of politics, the scientific man of his favourite science, and the athlete of his sport. In the same way the earnest, happy Christian manifests his delight in the Word of GOD; it is his food and comfort; it is his study and his guide; and as the HOLY SPIRIT throws fresh light on its precious truths he finds in it a joy and pleasure beyond compare. Naturally and spontaneously he will often speak of that which is so precious to his heart. By regeneration the believer having become the child of GOD finds new interest and instruction in all the works of GOD. His FATHER designed and created them, upholds and uses them, and for His glory they exist. But this is peculiarly true of the Word of GOD. Possessing the mind of CHRIST, instructed by the Spirit of CHRIST, he finds in every part of GOD's Word testimony to the person and work of his adorable MASTER and FRIEND; the Bible in a thousand ways endears itself to him, while unfolding the mind and ways of GOD, His past dealings with His people, and His wonderful revelations of the future.

While thus studying GOD's Word the believer becomes conscious of a new source of delight; not only is that which is revealed precious, but the beauty and perfection of the revelation itself grows upon him. He has now no need of external evidence to prove its inspiration, it everywhere bears the impress of Divinity. And as the microscope which reveals the coarseness and blemishes of the works of man only shows more fully the perfectness of GOD's works, and brings to light new and unimagined beauties, so it is with the Word of GOD when closely scanned. In what remarkable contrast does this book stand to the works of men! The science of yesterday is worthless to-day; but history and the discoveries of our own times only confirm the reliability of these ancient sacred records. The stronger our faith in the plenary, verbal inspiration of GOD's Holy Word, the more fully we make it our guide, and the more implicitly we follow its teachings, the deeper will be our peace and the more fruitful our

MAY, 1890.

service. "Great peace have they which love Thy law: and nothing shall offend them." Becoming more and more convinced of the divine wisdom of the directions and commands of Scripture, and of the reliability of the promises, the life of the believer will become increasingly one of obedience and trust; and thus he will prove for himself how good, acceptable, and perfect is the will of GOD, and that Bible which reveals it.

The words, "the Law of the LORD," which we understand to mean the whole Word of GOD, are very suggestive. They indicate that the Bible is intended to teach us what GOD would have us to *do*: that we should not merely seek for the promises, and try to get all we can from GOD; but should much more earnestly desire to know what He wants us to be and to do for Him. It is recorded of Ezra, that he prepared his heart to seek the law of the LORD, in order that he might do it, and teach in Israel statutes and judgments. The result was that the hand of his GOD was upon him for good, the desires of his heart were largely granted, and he became the channel of blessing to his whole people. Every one who searches the Scriptures in the same spirit will receive and communicate the blessing of GOD: he will find in it the guidance he needs for his own service, and ofttimes a word in season for those with whom he is associated.

But not only will the Bible become the Law of the LORD to him as teaching and illustrating what GOD would have *him* to be and to do, but still more as revealing what GOD Himself is and does. As the law of gravitation gives us to know how a power on which we may ever depend will act under given circumstances; so the Law of the LORD gives us to know Him, and the principles of His government, on which we may rely with implicit confidence. The man of GOD will also delight to trace GOD in the Word as the great Worker, and rejoice in the privilege of being a fellow-worker with Him—a glad, voluntary agent in doing the will of GOD, yet rejoicing in the grace that has made him willing, and in the mighty, divine power that works through him. The Bible will also teach him to view himself as but an atom, as it were, in GOD's great universe, and to see GOD's great work as a magnificent whole, carried on by ten thousand agencies, carried on through all spheres, in all time, and without possibility of ultimate failure—a glorious manifestation of the perfections of the great Worker! He himself, and a thousand more of his fellow-servants, may pass away; but this thought will not paralyse his efforts; for he knows that whatever has been wrought in GOD will abide, and that whatever is incomplete when his work is done the great Worker will in His own time and way bring to completion. He does not expect to understand all about the grand work in which he is privileged to take a blessed but infinitesimal part; he can afford to await its completion, and can already by faith rejoice in the certainty that the whole will be found in every respect worthy of the great Designer and Executor. Well may his delight be in the Law of the LORD, and well may he meditate in it day and night. J. H. T.

(*To be continued.*)

Items of Interest.

FROM REV. J. W. STEVENSON.

SHANGHAI, *Feb. 21st.*—I have heard of the following baptisms: Han-chung, Dec. 15th, four; Yang-chau, Jan. 29th, four. On Jan. 25th Miss Jones arrived from SI-CH'UEN, and gave a very interesting account of her experiences, especially in Chao-hwa; she has now gone up to Yang-chau to assist in the work there, and will probably in time return to SI-CH'UEN.

On Monday, Jan 27th, I left Shang-hai with Mr. and and Mrs. Hunter, and Messrs. Willett, Sharp, and Evans for up the river. Mr. Lund escorted the three brethren to Gan-k'ing, and I had the pleasure of taking Mr. and Mrs. Hunter and Miss Jones to Yang-chau. After rather an eventful journey from Chin-kiang in a native boat we reached Yang-chau on Jan. 30th. I was glad to find the friends there all well, and delighted with the new wing which has recently been put up, giving eleven more bed-rooms and a large dining-room and other small rooms downstairs. I only remained one night, and leaving Mr. and Mrs. Hunter to spend a week, Mr. McCarthy and I started at once for Kiu-kiang and Ta-ku-t'ang. At Ta-ku-t'ang we had a long conference with Mr. Steven and the five Canadian brethren, and settled on plans for working the south of the KIANG-SI province. The five brethren have gone forward, and I shall be glad of prayer on their behalf.

At Kiu-kiang we were glad to meet Miss McFarlane, who came from Nan-k'ang Fu to see us. Things have now settled down, and I trust that we shall yet have greater victories there in the ingathering of souls. I reached Gan-k'ing on Feb. 7th, and Mr. and Mrs. Hunter, escorted by Mr. Hutton, arrived the following day. I found the Brethren all well, and realising not a little of the LORD's presence while preparing for His service. We had one or two good meetings, and I left on Saturday evening, reaching Shang-hai on the 11th, and having been away just a fortnight.

While at Gan-k'ing I was sorry to receive a telegram announcing that Mr. Armstrong was ill, and asking that Mr. George Huntley might be sent back to the school. Mr. Huntley has gone to Che-foo, and I am glad to hear that Mr. Armstrong is recovering from the small-pox, and will be going to Japan for a short time. We are still in difficulties with regard to the girls' school on account of the weak health of Miss Knight and Miss Ellis. We trust that GOD in His goodness will raise up suitable teachers for it.

On the 13th inst. we had the pleasure of welcoming five ladies from Toronto: Misses Miller, Ross, Fairbank, and M. and C. Scott. On the 18th inst. we moved into our new premises, and with the help of the five Canadian Sisters were able to get in very comfortably. I think they will be most convenient.

I have heard of the safe arrival of Mr. and Mrs. James, the Misses Barclay, and others, at Chung-k'ing, and that Mr. Cassels had arrived to escort his party to Pao-ning.

Mr. Hoste sends me good news from the opium refuge at Si-gan, SHEN-SI; some fifty patients have been through it, and now daily worship can be held there without fear of interruption. He also reports that the various opium refuge centres from Hung-t'ung SHAN-SI have been closed for the Chinese New Year, and tells me that a refuge has been opened in Chung-yuan Hien.

Feb. 28th.—Last Saturday (22nd) we had our first prayer-meeting in our new premises; a splendid meeting —over sixty present. Our sisters, Misses Britton, Forster, Legerton, Leggatt, and Burt, arrived from England on the same day. These buildings are most suitable; they are a witness to a prayer-hearing GOD.

ENTRANCE TO THE I-CHANG GORGE.

A Visit to Scattered Converts in Gan-hwuy.

FROM MR. MARCUS WOOD.

GAN-K'ING, *Dec. 12th.*—It may interest you to hear about a journey I recently took into the country, some sixty English miles to the south of this city, in order to visit some native Christians who were baptised here a little more than a year ago. They had been visited once before by Mr. J. Reid and Mr. Simpson, and, as far as my memory serves me, there were only three Christians then—two were members of this Church and one an inquirer.

I had intended visiting them for some time, but had not been able to do so—partly because the time of the year was not a convenient one for them, as the country people are generally busy in the fields during the months of August and September; and also because, being in the Training Home, it is not always easy for me to be away ten days or so at once, for a journey of sixty miles here is a very different thing from one of the same distance in England; by rail it would only take an hour or so, whereas in China, where we have to walk, it takes two or three days.

I had made arrangements for leaving on Monday, Nov. 25th, but on the Saturday previous two Christians and two inquirers arrived from the district. They had come for the Sunday services, and also to do some business in the city before returning; consequently, instead of leaving on Monday, I waited for them, and on Wednesday morning, the 27th, we all started off together, the party consisting of the four men from the country, my own coolie, and myself.

It was past mid-day before we could get fairly away, and as our first day's journey was by boat, we only travelled thirty *li*, or ten English miles. The next day the rain came on at daylight, and owing to this we were only able to finish the boat journey of twenty *li*, and then put up in an inn, as it was too wet to walk.

The following morning it was still raining, but not nearly so heavily as the previous day; so after breakfast we made preparations for the road. I bought a Chinese umbrella for about threepence, and put on some straw sandals, and we then started out on our journey to try and get to the house of one of the Christians by Saturday night. On Friday we walked about fifty *li*, and the next day eighty, arriving at the first village where there are any Christians, about 6.15 p.m.; it was raining a little the whole of the way, and the roads were very bad in consequence. Two of the men who travelled with me live in this place, so we spent the Sunday with them—had worship in the morning at 11 o'clock, and in the evening a number of people came in and listened to the Gospel.

As far as I could find out, no foreigner had been to this village before. It is an out-of-the-way place, about twenty *li* from the high road to Hwuy-chau, and quite away amongst the hills; there are only about forty or fifty inhabitants. Among those who came in to listen were two men who seemed very interested and remained to evening worship, after which we had a long conversation with them, and gave them some books and tracts to take away. One was a native of the village, and the other belongs to the north of this province, and was only staying there for a few days on business.

One of the Christians in this place seemed very much in earnest; he is a farmer, and quite alone in the world. Before his conversion he could not read a single character, but now he can read his New Testament fairly well. He is very industrious, and spends most of his spare time in learning to read; his name is Ch'en.

The other man, named Iao, seems also very anxious to follow the SAVIOUR. He can read his New Testament without much difficulty; he also is a farmer. There are others who are persuaded of the truth of the Gospel, but they are afraid to make an open confession on account of the persecution it would involve.

On Sunday afternoon the weather began to clear, so on Monday, after breakfast, we set off for the home of Li Peh-fuh, in the village of Nan-ts'uen, twenty li from Kao-t'ien, still further in among the mountains. The two inquirers, Ch'en and Iao, came on with us for a few days. The weather became fine, and we enjoyed our walk very much, the road winding in and out amongst the high hills on either side of us. We had frequently to wade through mountain-streams, and this was very refreshing, as the water was so beautifully cool and clear. The scenery all round reminded one very much of the Highlands of Scotland.

We arrived at Li's house in the afternoon, and after partaking of some refreshment, which his good wife had prepared, quite a number of people came in from the neighbouring houses, and we preached to them for some time. When they had gone, we had our evening meal, and spent the rest of the day in Bible study with the Christians. I think there were six or seven present. Our subject was mainly

THE SECOND COMING OF OUR LORD.

As these Christians are quite young in the faith and have not yet very much knowledge of the Word, they were exceedingly interested, and seemed much encouraged by the passages referred to. Li's wife is a Christian, and also a nephew and his mother. Li and his nephew have suffered severe persecution for the sake of the Gospel, for since they learned that it is sin against GOD to worship idols they feel they cannot any longer give money to support the priests and keep up the temples, etc., and it is chiefly through their refusing to do this that the persecution has come upon them. A B.A., who is the leading man in the village, is so opposed to them that he threatens to have them driven out of the village if they do not conform to the customs of the place; but the Christians seem very bright notwithstanding, especially Li, who says that if necessary he is prepared to lay down his life for the MASTER rather than yield an inch to idolatry. The only thing he is sorry for is that this persecution hinders a good many who before seemed interested from coming out boldly and confessing CHRIST.

This man Li was, I believe, converted some two or three years ago in the city of Ch'u-chau in this province, when Mr. J. Reid, now of Cheng-yang-kwan, was living there. Li went up to this Prefecture, engaged in a lawsuit, and while there he visited Mr. Reid, heard the Gospel, and after a time became interested, and ultimately gave up the law case, yielded to his opponent, and went back to his village to witness for CHRIST. Before his conversion he was inclined towards vegetarianism—that is to say, he used to abstain from animal food twice a month—and it must be noted here that vegetarianism in China is connected with Buddhism, and is one of the strictest forms of idolatry. His chief persecutor, the B.A., told me that if Li did not worship idols, and would keep his doctrine to himself, no one would object ; " but," he said, "he is always preaching to others to give up idolatry," and that this could not be allowed, for he was afraid that at this rate very soon none of the people in that district would worship the idols. To which I added, " And would not that be splendid?" I had the opportunity of an interview with this B.A. on two different occasions, and put the Gospel before him as faithfully as I could—I might almost say, pleaded with him in tears, as he is a man of sixty-one years of age, and a miserable opium-smoker. He is exceedingly proud because he happens to have a literary degree, and was very vexed with me for speaking to him about the Gospel, evidently thinking that he knew a great deal more than myself ; but I told him my responsibility was to preach the Gospel, and it was his to either receive or reject it.

On the Tuesday evening we had another long Bible-reading from the Acts on the persecution of the early Christians, and I tried to prove to them, both from Scripture and the history of GOD's children generally, that those who will live godly in CHRIST JESUS shall suffer persecution. After this they all seemed cheered and comforted, and, I believe, felt that, though hard for the flesh, yet they were *privileged* in being allowed to endure hardship for CHRIST. In the afternoon of Wednesday some elderly men came to see me in Li's house ; this gave me a splendid opportunity of speaking to them about the Gospel. They were much more reasonable than the B.A., and acknowledged the truth of what was said. There are only about 100 inhabitants in this village, and my opinion is that many know the truth, only they are afraid to come out and join the Christians on account of the persecution. This same afternoon the two men Ch'en and Iao returned to their homes in Kao-hien, as they cou'd not afford to be any longer away from their work ; and later on Li went round with me to the house of a man named T'ang, in a village about fifteen li distant on the other side of a large mountain. In the evening quite a number of people came in and listened while we told them the Gospel. T'ang and his wife are both Christians ; thus in these three villages there are at present eight Christians. They need our constant prayers, for some of them—in fact most—have to bear severe persecution. The leaders in one of the villages have even threatened

TO BREAK THE LIMBS

of one young man if he comes home ; he is now working at his trade in another village, and is afraid to return to his family. At other times, when the Christians have refused to worship the idols and take part in the heathen festivals, the people have come to their house, burst open the door, and actually stolen articles of clothing out of their boxes in order to get money for idolatry. When one remembers that these young Christians are very poor and have to work hard to support themselves and their families, it will be seen that such treatment must be very trying. In other cases the village communities have threatened to turn them out of house and home, to drive them out of the district, and not to allow them to return unless they are willing to listen to the voice of the people and conform to the customs of the village. Up to the present nothing serious has taken place, but the petty persecution continues, and it is hard to say how things will go when the Chinese New Year comes round, in about five or six weeks. They will need much grace to stand firm then. My hope is that the friends who read these lines will take an interest in those who are being persecuted in these districts, as well as in other places in China, and pray that they may be kept from the power of the enemy, and used to bring others to the SAVIOUR.

On the Thursday morning I started for home. Li came 15 li on the road with me ; we were both sorry to part, and as long as we were able to see one another turned round for another wave of the hand I felt very much for this poor man going back to suffer persecution, almost alone, humanly speaking ; but we comfort ourselves in the fact that the almighty power of GOD is on the side of these tried ones, and we can trust Him to protect His own.

What shall be the Result of the Conference?

FROM MISS. C. P. CLARK.

YANG-CHAU, *Jan. 7th.*—I feel that the paper, "TO EVERY CREATURE,"* will be made a mighty blessing. I feel, too, that it lays upon each one of us out here, as well as upon those at home, added responsibility, and that if we only rise to meet it, and if the large number to whom the LORD is now speaking on this point will at once yield and obey, the whole Church of GOD will soon be aroused and shaken through and through, and great changes will be brought about. I fully believe that the result would be a more complete fulfilment of Joel ii. 28-32 than was seen at Pentecost, and that is what we are warranted to look for, and ought to expect. Is there *any* reason why "the glorious possibilities," so often talked about, should not become to *us* blessed *realities?* Surely not, if we are prepared to receive all that our GOD is ready to give. My great hope for

THE SHANGHAI CONFERENCE,

and for our own meetings, is that differences of opinion and the discussion of methods will be swallowed up in the one overwhelming desire of all who are there for a rich outpouring of the HOLY SPIRIT; and that each one will go back to the work so filled that there shall, indeed, be a "new thing"—blessing *far* beyond that of any past experience. Is not this the only thing that would justify such long absence from the stations as will be involved in many cases, and so much expenditure of various kinds?

[The Conference is to be held from May 7th to 17th. Will our friends remember it in daily prayer?]

Happy Service.

FROM MISS J. MUNRO.

KWEI-K'I, KIANG SI, *Nov. 2nd.*—I feel that I should like to tell you how the LORD led me to China, and a little of my past life, so that you may know me better.

I was born in the Highlands of Scotland and brought up in a Christian home, but not until four years ago had I the assurance that I was a child of GOD. I went out to Canada to friends, and while on a visit to Mrs. Merry's Home at Stratford, I was brought to accept JESUS as mine. From the time when I was three years old I had the wish to be a missionary, and four years ago it came back with renewed longings. I then understood what my dear father meant when he said, "You must first be called." The call meant to give myself to JESUS. I prayed now to my FATHER to lead me to the foreign field, and He heard and answered that prayer in His own good time. How I do praise Him to-night, that I am here in China. I will heartily join you in prayer that the LORD will lead your dear children to serve Him in the foreign field. Who would not like to be ambassadors for the KING of Kings! The more I think of it the more I get lost in wonder, love and praise. What condescension!

Yesterday I returned from a visit with the Bible woman into the country. We had a glorious time. The LORD was with us. We went to one little village where a man had just died, and they were wailing, burning incense, and beating gongs. The sight was sickening. No one invited us into their houses, so we sat on a bank and asked the LORD to lead people to hear. Presently we had a crowd of between thirty and forty. They listened very attentively, but gradually dwindled away, and only one man remained. He said, "Well, I do want to serve this true GOD, but I don't know how." The woman said to him, "Get down on your knees and ask the LORD to have mercy upon you," and he did so. Presently another man joined us, and he said, "I, too, want to know the true GOD," so we four knelt on the grass, and there these men gave themselves to the LORD, I believe there was joy in heaven. My heart was full to think that we should be so used. To GOD be the glory. All along the journey we had blessing. The people were so eager to hear, and we sold a few books. My words as yet are few, and in those country villages they speak different dialects, and consequently they did not understand me very well. But the dear woman was so earnest. The house which we stayed in all night was crowded with people until bed-time; indeed, we were so tired that we invited them to go away and come in the morning. This they did, for with the first streak of daylight they began to arrive. Pray that the Word spoken, and the books sold, may bring forth fruit, and for me, too, that utterance may be given me, and that I may have power for service.

Our message is not always received; in many cases they come to see the foreigner, and when their curiosity is satisfied they go away. These words from "Thoughts on the Spiritual Life" have been such a stay to me, I will pass them on, trusting they may be blessed to you too. "We must live upon JESUS CHRIST, not upon energy, upon success, upon notice, upon praise. And to live upon Him in service, we must, in the rule and habit of our lives, watch over times of solemn, sacred, blessed intercourse with Him in secret. Our part is to keep in touch with the blessed MASTER, to lose no opportunity of witnessing for Him, and to leave the results with 'GOD who giveth the increase.'"

Miss Say, who is in charge of this station, has kindly lent me a room, where I have the children's service twice a week. I send the son of our Bible-woman out on the street to invite them in, and then we have a hymn (they already know "Jesus loves me"), and I tell them the old, old story. Dear little things, I do want them to know and trust our loving SAVIOUR.

The weather now is beautifully cool, and studying is easier than in the hot days. My teacher is very bright, and suffers much persecution in his home because he will not burn incense. He said to me the other day with tears in his eyes, "JESUS said, if they persecute Me they will persecute you also."

---

* To be had as a booklet from the offices of the Mission, or from Messrs. Morgan and Scott, price 6d. a dozen; post free, 8d. How many of our readers will send for a dozen, and distribute them prayerfully where they think they may do the most good?

Key to the Group.

1. Mr Ho.
2. Hong, labourer.
3. Lin, woodman, chant.
4. Mr. Li.
5. Han, Yam-merchant.
6. Mr. Fu, lawyer.
7. La-chu, pedlar.
8. Mr. Lu, teacher.
9. Lao Li, labourer.
10. Mrs. Fu.
11. Kiang Ma-ma.
12. Mrs. Fan.
13. Mr. Kiang, colporteur.
14. Mr. Hong, pastor.
15. Mrs. Wang.
16. Wang Lao-pan.
17. Lao Wang.
18. Mrs. Wang, newly baptised, future Bible-woman.
19. Wang Sao-sao.
20. Mrs. Wang.
21. Mr. Fan.
22. Mrs. Ing, Bible-woman.
23. Mrs. Lu, servant.
24. Mrs. Wang.
25. Mrs. Hong.
26. Mrs. Tong.
27. Mrs. Kiang.
28. Lin Ling-ing.
29. Mrs. Tong.
30. Old Mrs. Wang.
31. Mrs. Ning, newly baptised.
32. Mrs. Hong, newly baptised.
33. Miss Munro.
34. Wang Shui-li.
35. Mrs. Chang.
36. Miss Horsburgh.
37. Mrs. Tsai.
38. Lin Pang-shi.
39. Mrs. Ing's daughter.
40. Miss Say.
41. Wang Hai-shu.
42. Mrs. Liu.
43. Miss Fan.
44. Ing Fah-shing.
45. Li Shu-li, Miss Say's boy.
46. Ning U-li, Miss Parker's boy.
47. Miss Wang.

The Kwei-k'i Converts.

FROM MISS ANNIE SAY.

KWEI-K'I, KIANG-SI, *January* 13*th*.—We have had an exceptionally fine autumn, and have been very busy. The LORD has given me such good health ever since I had the small-pox; and Miss Horsburgh says she has never been so well before. She is working hard at the language. Miss Munro has already been out several times to villages with the Bible-woman, and she has a very interesting class of children coming twice a week. I have been able to get about among the villages these last few months a good deal, and have had some very encouraging experiences—sometimes two or three women themselves asking to be taught to pray, and kneeling with us to seek pardon in JESU'S name. The last time that two dear women kneeled with us, and asked GOD to forgive their sins, a girl came up to me and said, " Is He willing to save me too?" Of course I told her He would save all who truly desired to be saved. So she joined those already praying, and I felt there was a work of grace begun in some of their hearts. "His sheep hear His voice and follow Him."

The LORD has graciously doubled the number of Church members in Kwei-k'i in 1889; nineteen were baptised by Mr. McCarthy in the summer. One of these has within the last few weeks gone to be with the LORD. He was a dear old man of over seventy, who truly loved JESUS, and it is nice to feel that he is safe home out of the reach of poverty and pain. His old wife, who was baptised at the same time, is very frail and weak, and we expect she will ere long join him. On December 23rd seven more were baptised, three men and four women. One was the brother of one of our members, another the boatman who took Miss Tapscott and the American sisters up the river in the spring. He was converted on that journey, and since then has been coming constantly to the services when at Kwei-k'i. I would ask prayer for him, that he may be a great blessing on the river. He does witness for CHRIST, and sometimes brings other boatmen with him to the chapel. The third man used to sell opium, and was otherwise bad; the LORD has done great things for him, and now, sooner than sin, he sells nuts and sugar-cane in the streets. The four women were all very bright, and gave us much cause for praise. One has been kept back twice because we feared she had not given up opium, but I have had her staying with us for some time, and she has proved herself worthy by her earnest, consistent life. She has been a great help to us in telling the Gospel, and I am thinking of training her for a Bible-woman. GOD used her for the salvation of *three* dear women previous to her baptism. One of these was her sister, a country woman, who was baptised with her. I do trust she will be used to bring in many more. One of the others baptised is a Kwei-k'i woman, the other from a village. It is such a joy to see the LORD'S children being gathered in one by one; they are so very precious. One feels the native Christians become part of one's self.

I want to ask prayer that the LORD will give us a house in one of two cities 120 *li* to the south. Native brethren have visited one of them twice, selling books, and I hope to go myself next time, and to spend a few days. There is so much to be done, and the time seems to fly along, leaving so little accomplished. May the LORD stir up the hearts of His people more and more to come and help gather in His harvest.

Just now I am in Ho-k'eo. It is a year and four months since I left here, and I see such real growth in the Christians. Some of them especially are very much advanced in the Christian life, and of course there are additions too. On the 31st of December we spent a very nice day in waiting on the LORD. Since then Miss Gibson and I have been up to Yoh-shan together, and spent a few days with our dear friends there. They are all well, and have a most commodious house now, which will no doubt be much more healthy than the old one.

The photographer has lately paid us a visit, so I am able to send you a group of our Kwei-k'i Christians, but it is not complete, for Mr. Tsai has lately gone to try and open Wu-chang on the Po-yang Lake. My cook and his brother were away preaching and selling books, and some of the country Christians could not come. The children in the front are not yet Church members, but I hope

"A GROUP OF OUR KWEI-K'I CHRISTIANS."

they soon will be. I know you will feel interested in these dear people.

January 24th.—Since I last wrote I have returned to Kwei-k'i, and we have passed the first few days of the new year. It has been a very happy time this year; the dear Christians are all so united, and in such a nice spirit. On the 1st they were with us nearly all day. We sat down to an early tea together, after which we had a capital meeting, a sort of conference which we could not get through in one evening, so we decided to meet again on the 2nd, and then we had quite a lively discussion on the best way to help each other to follow the LORD. I wi'l give you a brief statement of some of the propositions made and accepted:—

1. That twelve brethren and twelve sisters should be elected, one of each being responsible for one month during the year to visit absentees and inquire the cause of their absence. To have prayer with, and seek to strengthen each other's faith, and prevent backsliding.

2. Open-air work was undertaken as a direct command of the LORD, and also a benefit to our own souls, as well as to those to whom we go. Nine brethren volunteered for this work.

3. The brethren and sisters all agreed that it was their duty and privilege to bring others to the services, and to definitely seek the salvation of some souls; and they agreed by GOD's grace each to seek to lead at least one soul to JESUS this year.

4. It was agreed that the *whole* Sunday belonged to the LORD, and should be used in His worship and service.

5. All agreed that where both parents were Christians, their girls' feet should not be bound.

6. That it is the duty and privilege of GOD's children to give to His cause, and it was thought best to follow the injunction of the Apostle Paul in 1 Cor. xvi, and to put aside, as GOD prospered them, something each week, bringing monthly their contributions to the Church, when it would be duly registered to each name.

7. It was also agreed that family worship was a duty where the parents were Christians.

I do feel that with our FATHER'S blessing on these few simple rules, the work will become more solid. Please pray that all may seek the power of the HOLY SPIRIT to be His faithful servants. These dear Kwei-k'i Christians do really want to do His will. I do rejoice in some of them.

I am praying that the LORD may speedily answer your prayer for a thousand more messengers of his salvation.

The Little Flock at Gan-ren.

FROM MISS HELEN MACKENZIE.

GAN-REN, KIANG-SI, *December 31st.*—If I had been told, when I arrived in Shanghai a year ago to-day, that in nine months I should be living in a Chinese city alone, I should probably have said, "It cannot be possible!" I believe the wonderful help GOD has given me in acquiring the language, and otherwise, is largely in answer to the many prayers offered here and by praying friends at home. I have been here now three months, and never before did I realise the reality of the promise, "Lo, I am with you alway," as I do now. It is truly blessed to be alone with the LORD, and it is more blessed still to witness His working in the hearts of the people of this dark land, shedding abroad in them His glorious light.

I know you will be interested to hear a little about the blessing He has been giving here. When I first came I sought to make the acquaintance of the little flock, sixteen in number. I found that there were two missing, a tailor and his son. They had altogether ceased coming to worship. When the father came into the city, he would go a long way round to avoid passing the chapel door. I wanted to visit them in their own home, which is sixty *li* distant, but kept putting it off, feeling that I had not enough language to speak to them as was necessary under the circumstances. Meanwhile I could only pray, and the LORD knew how to help me. When I had been here two months, Miss Say came to see me quite unexpectedly. She had with her a Christian man and woman, and intended only to stay one night, going off next morning to do some village work. But I felt that the LORD had sent her, and with a little persuasion she consented to stay a few days. I at once made inquiry as to the tailor's whereabouts, and found he was working in the city. So I sent the evangelist with an invitation to him to come and see us, and in a short time, to our surprise and delight, he returned, bringing him with him. According to the tailor's way of looking at things, we had to listen to a rather sad account. From the time of their baptism, in the spring, everything had seemed to go against them;

and his son had been in ill-health, and not able to work. He could not stay long that evening, as he had business to attend to, but he promised to come on Sunday to worship, which he did, and seemed to get much blessing. He has come every Sunday since, and a'so on week-days for evening worship. I could think of no other way of helping his son except having him here, to give him some medicine and nurse him up. He is a bright, intelligent lad of eighteen, fairly educated. After three weeks' stay he left, feeling quite well. I found this lad a true disciple of the LORD JESUS CHRIST. He had not come to worship because of his weak health, and the distance of their home. I cannot but hope that if the LORD spare him he will become a bright star in the Church here.

Another case of interest is a family named Wang, three of whom were baptised at the same time in the spring. They have a shop here, and a farm in the country. At the time of their baptism they, of course, left off selling things for idol worship, and closed their shop-door on Sundays.

Because of doing this their business decreased somewhat, and a younger son—a worldly-wise man, who also professed to believe, but had not been baptised—thought the existing state of things would not pay. So the door was opened again on Sunday, and the idolatrous things were sold, the father and elder son seeming too weak to prevent it. They were all very unhappy, however. Conversation was had with the eldest son, and he said that if his father and mother were willing, he was ready to take a stand and have all put right. So we at once set out for their home in the country Mr. Fan (the son), Miss Say, and myself—and after conversation and prayer with the parents we were all of one mind. The father spontaneously gave us a commission to go to the shop, when we returned, and clear out everything idolatrous; but we did not feel this to be the right step, we wanted themselves to do it. We therefore refused to go except the father and mother would accompany us to the city, whereupon they both came. We had our evening meal together here, and afterwards sent for the younger son from the shop. The LORD triumphed gloriously. The young man listened quietly to all that was said, and heartily assented. We had prayer with them, and afterwards, at his own suggestion, although the hour was late—10 p.m.—we all proceeded to the shop, and had all the idolatrous things brought here to be destroyed. The crackers we could not burn, because of the display and noise they would make; so we drowned them in a tub of water, and the next morning the dear old boatman had the privilege of tumbling them into the river.

About a fortnight ago this same family was severely tested. As you know, at this time of the year it is customary to go round all the business houses collecting money to spend on idolatry. The Wangs, wanting to be true to their GOD, refused to give any, and, upon doing so, were severely threatened. The threats were repeated time after time, in the expectation that they would give in at last. But, praise the LORD, He kept them true. The evening previous to the day on which the threats were to be executed they called, giving them a last chance, but without effect. All the next day abuse was given vent to in the street against them, and in the evening three men arrived and carried off everything in the shop of eatables, tables, etc. After it was all over, the young son came to tell me, and to know what they were to do, as the people said if they stocked their shop again they would again come and take away everything, and in future prevent them from selling. I asked him what he himself thought of doing. He said, "Ask the mandarin's protection." I said, "Did he not think it better first to ask the LORD'S protection?" He said, "Yes, but his enemies were so strong and he was so weak." I tried to show him that GOD with him was far stronger than all who were against him; and after we had had prayer, pointing to a tall old tree outside the window, I said. "Do you know that every strong wind that comes sends the roots of that tree deeper into the ground?" He said, "Yes." I then tried to show him that the LORD had allowed this trial because He wanted him to be deeper rooted in Himself, and, turning to Heb. x. 34 ("Ye . . . took joyfully the spoiling of your goods, knowing in yourselves that ye have in heaven a better and an enduring substance"), I asked him to read it. After a pause he said, in such a triumphant tone, "Yes, now my heart is the same as that." He afterwards joined us in our evening worship, when I chose the hymn, "He leadeth me, oh blessed thought." The words seemed to give expression to his feelings of faith and confidence in GOD. It was lovely to see how his face lit up as we sung over and over, "He leadeth me."

The LORD has protected them. Two days after this happened they again furnished their shop with goods, and have since been able to carry on their business quietly. It is worth giving one's life a thousand times over to see the LORD so manifestly working in the hearts of the people of this land. I feel deeply my responsibility, and the need of continuous prayer. It is no light matter to be made a steward of the mysteries of GOD.

The people in the city as a whole are quiet and friendly. On Sundays our little chapel has been quite filled lately, and I believe a great many more would come if we had more room. This is now a felt need with us. Lately I have been sending several Christian men to preach in the streets on Sunday afternoons, and they have had quite a number of attentive listeners. I feel I shall never be able to praise the LORD enough for all His goodness to me.

God's Work at Wun-chau.

FROM MR. GRIERSON.

DEC. 21st.—This has been the most successful year, so far as baptisms and general work is concerned, since the opening of the station, over twenty years ago, by that true man of God, our late beloved brother, Mr. Stott. For this year, up till now there have been fifty-seven persons received into the Church by baptism, and "still there's more to follow"! A goodly number have been successfully helped to break off opium-smoking, and many of these are now earnest enquirers, whom we hope may be received into the Church soon.

I send you a few notes of interest which I trust will call forth much praise to the Giver of all good. "Whoso offereth praise glorifieth Me."

CONVERSION OF A NOTORIOUS CHARACTER.

At our Sunday evening service the other week, we had some remarkably bright and cheering testimonies. The meeting was held in our large open court facing the public street. About forty Christians and enquirers were present, in addition to a large crowd of outsiders.

In was a lovely star-lit evening, and all our friends seemed very happy as one after another of our native brethren rose to tell of GOD'S wondrous grace. One brother, who was baptised only a few months ago, rather startled some of us. "Look at me!" he said, "I have been a most dreadful character—a rebel and a recruit by turns. I have killed men. I have butchered men. I have eaten human flesh. My brother is here to-night, and he can bear testimony to the truth of what I say. When very young I ran away from home. I joined the stage, and in a short time became a ring-leader in evil, an opium-smoker, and gambler. In the City here many know me as the clown. About a year ago, the master shipbuilder introduced me to Mr. Grierson, who helped me to break off opium. Now by the grace of GOD 'I am what I am.' I have entirely left off my former evil ways and am working at ship-building. I have a peace and joy in my heart such as I never experienced before. Is not this worth having? Most people spurn me, and say I have 'joined the foreigners'; but that is not so. I have found out that my Heavenly FATHER loves me, and sent JESUS the SAVIOUR to rescue me from everlasting woe."

Several others also gave splendid testimony to the preciousness of CHRIST JESUS. One man from Dong-ling, formerly a professional boxer, told of the wonderful way in which he was led to the LORD. At first he was bitterly opposed to His "doctrine," but, like Paul of old, he was arrested in his course, and now goes about the whole country side, following his lawful occupation of cattle-dealer, and at the same time most earnestly preaches "CHRIST" to all who care to listen.

"FOUND AFTER MANY DAYS.'

'O-dzing is a mountain village 120 li (forty miles) from the port of Wun-chau. It is a romantic spot, entirely enclosed between mountain and stream, so that in time of heavy rains the inhabitants, consisting of about 300 families, are blockaded, communication being quite broken off from the outside world.

Over a year ago our colporteur, in the course of his journeying, had occasion to go through the village selling the WORD of GOD. As he passed one of the more respectable houses, a kind, motherly woman asked him, "What books are these?" He replied, "Heaven's book." She thereupon invited him to enter, and explain his message to herself and family. After listening attentively for some time, she interrupted him, saying, "A long time ago, when in Wun-chau, I heard an old gentleman at the 'Native Orphanage,' exhorting people not to worship idols, but to worship 'HEAVEN.' I had not time to hear much, but as it all seemed good and true, I determined, along with another woman of our place, to try how worshipping 'Heaven' would do. So, on returning home here. I used every day (when fair) to go out into the garden and reverently bow down several times to 'Heaven.'" But after several months so "worshipping," as she did not *feel* anything, the practice was given up. On hearing this strange story the colporteur broke out, "Why, I am that same old gentleman." And after carefully comparing notes, they found it was even so.

The colporteur spent several nights with the family, and had large crowds every evening to hear the "wonderful words of life." During the day he went into the surrounding district to sell scriptures, returning to 'O-dzing as his centre.

On his return to Wun-chau, he told of all his experiences. The result was that a preacher was sent up to 'O-dzing, to follow up his labours. About two months ago I spent a fortnight amongst the villages of the whole district.

When at 'O-dzing, I heard a remarkable testimony to

THE IDOLS LOSING THEIR EFFICACY.

Ever since the woman mentioned above, Mrs. Dzang, and her family, and others, numbering twenty to thirty persons, have received the "good tidings of salvation," the villagers complain that at their temple the idols have lost their power. Up till now, they say, our large idol was noted for power, now when we beseech him about anything, all seems to go wrong.

Four more men have come in to-day from 'O-dzing, and I hope to baptise them to-morrow. This will make nine of that place baptised - all within the last few months.

"According to their Ability."

GIFTS AND PROMISES AT A Y.W.C.A. MISSIONARY MEETING IN FEBRUARY.

I WILL give 2s. 2d. this year.
I will gladly give anything that may be required for the training of the first accepted candidate from the Institute.
I will make a blouse, and my friend will buy it.
I will do plain knitting, or work a few mottoes.
Order for six copies of a motto for walls, neatly written.
I will give £1.
I will knit a pair of stockings.
We will make a dress for any lady who will give us an order, and give the money for the making to the missionary. (Anglo-Parisian dressmakers.)
Order for six pairs of gentlemen's cuffs.
I will give all the coppers I get in change.
Order for six collars and six pairs of ladies' cuffs.
Order for underlinen.
I will be responsible for at least 10s.
I will take orders for gentlemen's collars and cuffs.
From a member interested in foreign mission work, 10s.—Paid.
I will make one pair of Macrame bracket drapes.
From a member, 12s.—Paid.
Order for four housemaid's aprons.
I will give £a towards the outfit of the first missionary who goes from the Institute.
I would do some sewing if I had the material, or sell some ladies' collars and cuffs if some one would make them.

From a member's mother, 5s.
From a member, 2s.
I will take orders for knitted petticoats, stockings, socks, or other similar articles.
Work sold at the close of meeting, 6s. 3d.
I will make ladies' underclothing.
I would like to bear all the expense of the visit to London o. the first missionary candidate from the Institute.
We will take orders for dresses and make them at the working party. (Anglo-Parisian dressmakers.)
Six self-denial boxes ordered.
I promise to give 2s.
I will save 10s. out of my summer's allowance for dress, and give it to the missionary fund.
£15 15s. advanced for the missionary service of song, "White unto Harvest," to be repaid if covered by sales, not unless. Profits to go to our own missionary.
We might, some of us, go without some luxuries, such as butter or sugar, and give the money to missions; also we might get up an hour earlier and work for missions.
I will make a dress; please order soon. (Scientific dress-maker)
My brother will give 1s. a week for washing his dog; I will give it to the missionary fund.
I will sell the last of my jewellery, and give the money for the missionary.

Tidings from Scattered Workers.

WILL our readers get their maps and note the locations of the twenty-two workers from whom the following tidings come. It will be seen that they write from twenty-one different stations in twelve of the fifteen provinces in which the Mission is working. Also please note the requests for prayer.

Kan-suh Province.

FROM MRS. CECIL POLHILL-TURNER.

Si-ning, Dec. 4th.— Miss Kinahan and I are alone just now; she arrived for a long-expected visit about the beginning of November. My husband is gone to pay a second visit to the Lamasary where we stayed together last summer. He hopes to spend two or three weeks there, getting more Thibetan lessons while preaching the Gospel to the Lamas. The work here is specially difficult just now, owing to the very cold weather, which not only keeps the women indoors, but seems also very much to destroy our own energies. It seems to affect one's head especially, and make it difficult to think or speak clearly—an experience which I have never had before. It is such a comfort that our LORD knows our circumstances exactly, and that He uses the weak things. I think that workers in the southern provinces have not any idea of the hardness of the work in

KAN-SUH. If they had I think there would be more prayer for this part of the field, that would result in more blessing. As to the Thibetans, we often feel inclined to ask, Does no one care for them? Are Christians quite unmindful of the multitudes in perfect bondage to Buddhism in Thibet and the neighbouring districts? We here so little of prayer for the work among them. The devil has immense power through the Lama system. Attacking him among Thibetans will be no child's play, but a tremendous struggle, and if the work is not of GOD, it will be an utter failure. Do pray that we may be fully equipped for any warfare to which our CAPTAIN may lead us, and for Si-ning that a harvest may be gathered in. There are droppings, but we are thirsting for the showers, and so, surely, is our MASTER.

FROM MRS. HUNT.

T'ien-chau, December 27th.—We always seem to be very busy here, though it is such a remote corner. In the work there is much to encourage us. We now have openings on all sides for visiting amongst the women. I often wish that we could manage more systematic visiting, for it gives a grand opportunity for taking the precious tidings to the homes of the people. So many of these poor women never leave the seclusion of their own yards; so unless we take the message to them it will be unknown. I believe a good deal of the nice feeling that exists is owing to the medicine that has been given away. It lets the people see that we are really their friends. The natives here are so different from those in SI-CH'UEN and the more southern provinces. They do not easily make friends with strangers.

Since the cold weather set in we have all put what money we could spare into a common fund and commenced a soup-kitchen which is open every other day; the number of tickets is limited to thirty, and each person holding a ticket is entitled to a saucepan full of good soup. The Christians all have tickets, and most of them are glad to avail themselves of the help thus afforded. They are almost without exception very poor, and we think this is a good plan of helping them a little all round equally.

Shen-si Province.

FROM MRS. BOTHAM.

Feng-tsiang Fu, Dec. 9th.—We did not expect to remain here, but since we arrived we have found many opportunities of work, which seem to indicate that we are to stay on for a while. The people have been listening well to the street-preaching, and I have had invitations to people's houses. I am able to get about the city without any crowding, although I do not think a foreign lady has been seen here before. Our rooms are down one side of the front court of an inn, just opposite the Hien Yamen, about the busiest part of the city. It is a very poor inn; there are no good ones in the place, I believe. Feng-tsiang is just off the high road, so there is not much traffic. A week or two ago we went over to Si-tien, one of the stopping places on the high road, and the fresh air and the large dry room in the inn quite freshened us up. It was just at the foot of some mountains, too, which look grand now with the snow on their peaks. I do not think I have been better all the time I have been in China than I am now.

Dec. 16th.—I went last week to stay two days in a village ten *li* away. I think this is the first visit that has been paid in a village on the Si-gan plain, so we were very pleased to have the invitation, and hope it will lead to further work in the country. There must be a large population living in the walled villages which are scattered all over the plain. The people were very kind to me, and I had a most pleasant visit. The work is full of interest, but we long to see some souls saved.

Shan-si Province.

FROM MR. BURNETT.

Pao-t'eo, Nov. 27th.—We are getting on splendidly. I have taken the small yard leading from our big one, and turned the room which opens into the street into a comfortable little chapel. Here we have preaching every evening except Saturday. My wife and I are there to the sound of the watchman's gong, and we sing a hymn, during which time the people assemble. I take a subject and go on till the watchman again comes round,

after which the congregation separate. I am thoroughly in love with my new work, and look forward with delight to the evening. Already there are one or two regular attendants, and I am sure that conversions will soon follow. The HOLY SPIRIT helps me wonderfully, and assists the people to understand in a way that I have not seen here previously. I doubt not but that a shower of blessing will soon fall in North SHAN-SI. I do not know from what quarter the cloud will appear, but I am at the top of the hill, expecting to see a sign shortly.

One inquirer is at the present time in a critical position; he is opening a shop. The great enemy will do all he can, but I am hoping to see him come out boldly for CHRIST. He has many against him; his wife especially tries to hinder him. Pray for him and for others who are interested. He is going to put up a large tract in his shop, so that customers may learn something of the Gospel when they come to purchase goods.

If you could send us another helper I should be so glad.

FROM MRS. ELLISTON.

T'ai-yuen, Dec. 18th.—I am now able to visit in the city. You have heard of the Christian mason; he has recently married a young wife who had had no Christian teaching, but she seems so glad to learn. They are really an interesting household, consisting of the mason and his younger brother and their two wives. The brother has a ten-months-old boy, the pride of the family. They have family prayers regularly, and we have been surprised to find how much these two young women have learnt already. I am teaching them Dr. Blodgett's Catechism, and they ask me to go and help them with it every day. We are so hoping to see these and another brother come out fearlessly on the LORD's side. The mason himself is a very bright Christian. There is a great deal of want among the people just now, and the weather being so cold adds to it.

FROM MISS WHITCHURCH.

Hiao-i, Dec. 3rd.—No doubt you will have heard that several of our dear converts have been causing us much sorrow, proving very plainly that they are but "babes" in the truth, causing us also to fear that some have not yet experienced the "new birth." But our SAVIOUR has been with us in the fire, and now I am beginning to see that these trials are but the outcome of our prayer that GOD would give us a pure Church; it came to me with such cheer a few days ago that these severe testing times are but the LORD coming "to purge His floor," to purify the true and bring the false ones to light; since then it has been far easier to rejoice and to wait patiently till the LORD shall make the crooked things straight. I know we have your prayers that GOD may make us wise, patient, loving "nurses" to these "babes" in CHRIST, that by our *example* and teaching they may be led to follow CHRIST fully, and grow "unto a perfect man, into the measure of the stature of the fulness of CHRIST." We cannot aim too high, can we?

You will be glad to hear that the LORD has been giving us a happy, busy time in the villages during the past month. Pastor Chü, four of the Christians, and I have gone five days in the week into the surrounding villages, carrying our banner and books. The people have given us a good reception, and we have sold 411 books within the month. All the villages not more than fifteen *li* away have been visited, and we have lately had the joy of taking down idols in two homes, one in a village five *li* away, the other in the east suburb.

FROM MR. HOSTE.

Hoh-chau, Jan. 7th.—Yesterday I reached here from a tour of five days in the Yo-yang district, having spent the LORD's Day at Yo-yang, and then visited Tang-ch'eng. There have been encouraging numbers in both these small centres during the past months, and it was a great pleasure to visit the district. Yesterday I came over the Ho-shan, the mountain range lying 40 *li* to the east of here, having passed the previous night in a truly outlandish little place, where we had to share our room with our donkey! After a fairly good night, we got off at daybreak, and had to toil up such an ascent! The hills, of solid dark rock, towered all round us, and I could not help thinking of that line—

"From crag to crag leaps the live thunder,"

as in imagination one pictured the scene which a storm in such surroundings would present. I was brought back to prose however, by suddenly seeing the donkey and man in charge fall in attempting to cross a path covered with ice, and go sliding away down a smooth steep slope, which looked as though it might end in a precipice. Happily, however, after about ten yards, they were landed in some long grass, without any hurt to speak of.

Chih-li Province.
FROM MR. SIMPSON.

Ying-tsing, Dec. 7th.—Two barbers in this place, and a son of our landlord, say now that they are following JESUS, and in their homes pray daily that He will help them and give them wisdom to know more, and to be able to tell others of this love of GOD and the forgiveness of sins.

Only last night one of the barbers was here, and when we asked him if he was still trusting JESUS, and praying in his home, he said most decidedly, "I am trusting JESUS." I then asked, "What do your family think; does your wife kneel down and pray with you?" "No," he said; "she will not pray nor kneel down. *I think I will give her a beating.*" This was a novel and amusing suggestion to us, and of course we said, "If you are JESUS' disciple you must not beat your wife, even if she should never believe in JESUS; pray for her daily, and tell her all you know, and we will also pray that GOD may save her." With this advice he was thoroughly satisfied, and went away rejoicing.

Shan-tung Province.
FROM MR. TOMALIN.

Fuh shan, Jan. 13th.—As to the work here, there is very little to report. There are no Christians except the servants we brought with us, and two women who, though not church members, are, we trust, believers in JESUS; they are the only ones who dare face the ridicule and scorn that is poured on those who attend worship. They are the fruit of Mrs. Cheney's efforts. The people are friendly as neighbours, but are strongly prejudiced against the Gospel. There is good scope for work in the many villages and market-towns that lie scattered thickly all around within easy distance.

A short time ago we had a cheering visit from an old man, a native of the place, but living at Ts'ing-chau. He seemed a bright, earnest Christian, and has been a believer more than twenty years. He came to preach the Gospel to his relatives. With much emotion he told us that he made mention before GOD on behalf of this place in all his prayers, longing for the salvation of his own people.

Ho-nan Province.
FROM MR. COULTHARD.

Chao-kia-K'eo, Jan. 27th.—Our oldest member here, and the first to be received, is passing again through deep waters. He suffered first from the Yellow River flood, then by the fire last year, and now just after the new year from robbers, who have taken all his stock-in-trade. Recently I received a contribution from the SI-CH'UEN native Christians for distressed families, and I think his case appropriate.

Our rich member rejoiced my heart on the second day of this year by giving me a contribution of 3,000 cash, saying that he had promised GOD the tenth of his income this year. Do pray that grace may enable him to fulfil his promise, and I am sure that his soul will be blessed and GOD's kingdom extended. We have weekly contributions, and hope that gradually the church will become entirely independent of foreign aid.

Si-ch'uen Province.
FROM REV. E. O. WILLIAMS.

Pao-ning, Dec. 25th.—Ere this happy day has passed away I want to give you an account of how we have spent it. [The diary goes on to tell of Christmas hymns and services, and of a Chinese feast, etc.] I have not much fresh news to tell you about ourselves. My dear wife and I are going on steadily with our studies day by day; we hope to finish St. John's Gospel in a few days. We have very blessed seasons of communion and fellowship with our dear fellow-labourers here. We always have a happy season of prayer on Saturday evening, joining with so many who remember poor China on that day; we also have a very good time when we meet each Friday afternoon from 2 till 4 or 4.30 for special prayer for this enormous province, and more particularly for eastern SI-CH'UEN, the district in which members of the Church of England are working. One special petition we continue to put up to our FATHER is for more labourers. I suppose this district is far larger than England and Wales, perhaps as large as Great Britain and Ireland, and the *only* Protestant missionaries are five men and four ladies here, one man and two ladies at Pa-chau, two ladies at Kwan-yuen, and one man at Wan-hien, fifteen in all. Thank GOD, we are expecting four ladies here in a few weeks, and one man for Wan-hien. But fancy twenty workers to carry the everlasting Gospel to a district the size of our United Kingdom! What can they do? May the LORD send us hundreds, and soon, for He is coming, and these poor souls are perishing. Oh, what a warm welcome we will give to any whom the LORD may send! I am sure if many of those labouring at home could only *see* the needs of these poor people as we are beginning to see them, they would cry, "Here am I, send me." And if they could only see the readiness of multitudes to listen to the Gospel, the story of GOD's love to them in CHRIST JESUS, they would be glad to come and tell out that story. I cannot but think that many are kept back by the difficulty of the language who need not be; it is *not* difficult to learn sufficient to be able to point poor souls to JESUS; souls who are seeking for satisfaction in all sorts of ways of their own devising. And after all, as at home, it is the life that influences those around us more than the words. May GOD send MANY to *live* CHRIST before these poor people. Brethren, pray for us.

FROM MISS F. M. WILLIAMS.

Pao ning, Dec. 30th. The days are more filled up with blessed service for the MASTER now; it is becoming daily a deeper joy to serve *such* a MASTER, *such* a FRIEND. I have just returned from spending a week at a village five *li* on the other side of the river, where we have a weekly class; it is good to live right among the women. They have a considerable knowledge of the truth; oh, that the HOLY SPIRIT may make it *saving* knowledge! I had a very interesting visit to a blind man while I was there. I trust he really found peace in JESUS.

Hu-peh Province.
FROM MR. GEO. KING.

Lao-ho-K'eo, Nov. 19th.—During the last few months the constant wet weather has brought an appalling amount of malarial disease in its train, and applicants for medicine have been very numerous. Among my patients was the Hien mandarin's second wife, who was much benefited; and the leading man in Lao-ho-k'eo, who was recommended to come to me by the mandarin after seeing the good his wife had gained. The mandarin, his wife, and daughter came in state at different times to give thanks.

We have been wonderfully preserved in GOD's mercy. Some of our employés were very ill, but all are now convalescent. Our youngest child, too, suffered from the miasms, but is now quite well, and Mrs. King, who had remittent fever severely, is recovering.

Being single handed, I have to go at each call to whatever needs to be done or seen to at the moment. I never have crowded audiences, usually but few at a time, and preaching is more like street-preaching to separate audiences every few minutes, and is consequently somewhat monotonous, the same truths having to be continually repeated. Few of our hearers are from our neighbours; I presume they suppose themselves to know, as indeed many of them do know, what is our principal line of teaching, and knowing it, do not care to follow it. A large proportion of our visitors are from HO-NAN, our house being close to the great HO-NAN highway, and the tracts received and the truths heard are thus, I hope, disseminated in far-off localities, and prepare the way for an ingathering some day. Many of our patients are from long distances, fifty and seventy *li*, but unfortunately to many of them there is little opportunity of preaching. A good Chinese evangelist would be a GOD-send, for he could converse with the people while I was engaged.

Gan-htwuy Probince.

FROM REV. W. COOPER.

Gan-k'ing, Jan. 7th.—I was greatly prospered on the journey round the stations, and had the joy of baptising three men at Hwuy-chau Fu. The women converts won to the LORD during the stay of our sisters in that city seem to be exceptionally bright. There is prospect of a good work around T'en-k'i; two of the converts baptised are from a village near there; one of them was for years the proprietor of an opium den. I returned *via* Ch'i-chau. Misses Robertson and Underwood have abundance of work there—open doors on every hand, and a goodly number of women to visit them daily.

FROM MR. MACGREGOR.

Ning-kwoh Fu, Jan 17th—Latterly I have been twice to Gan-ling Hien, and hope soon to return; it is a large city, and I earnestly desire that some half may be opened, and many souls saved. China is an excellent place to knock out all frothiness and false enthusiasm, and to drive one to the Source of true power. This city is in the hands of Satan at present. Mrs. Miller and and the native women visit, but few come here. I fear there must be scurrilous rumours about us; otherwise, why such general apathy? Circumstances seem to point to evangelizing, rather than working this city; there are open doors everywhere. Mr. Eyres and Wang the evangelist have been itinerating, and thousands have heard the Gospel.

Have been enjoying study the last week, during which, as you know, China is busy for their new year. Some of the Christians give one very great joy and encouragement, though I know Mr. Miller feels the backslidings of others. The two evangelists are true men and full of the HOLY GHOST, I believe; very zealous for souls, they are growing in grace. I have found the baptism of GOD'S HOLY SPIRIT to be a most humiliating thing; in my case now it does not bring great joy, but a sense of one's weakness and nothingness, a salvation from self-consciousness, an admiration of grace in believers, and a consciousness that GOD is with me. I believe missionaries need to be filled more and more with continual dissatisfaction with the present attainment, and never to rest in it or its joys. Oh, how one is apt to fret because one cannot do this or that, instead of trusting all simply though blindly to the loving LORD'S hands. To make our trials and difficulties ladders to heaven, instead of cages of doubt and despair, would be a far more profitable investment of time and thought, I never realized so much my glorious privilege of telling sinners of JESUS as when deprived of it; with GOD'S love impelling me to some act I could not perform, I then realized, " Communion is blessed, but I can afford to wait till I reach heaven for that: down here, save GOD'S will, what is worth living for but the salvation of souls?" You will rejoice to hear that " It is well with my soul," though only GOD knows what a barren fig-tree my plant has been; still, in mercy He leaves it some years more that He may glorify Himself by bringing forth in me much fruit. With regard to service, I must be a disappointment to the LORD as I am to myself, but I hope to make some progress; as yet I can lay no souls to my account, but the day is near I hope when I shall win some for my SAVIOUR.

I must draw to a close. What shall this year see? I know not, but we are full of hope—oh to be fuller and fuller, and that in darkest days—of seeing a glorious harvest this year. This hope only comes from GOD; there are no special indications in our circumstances, yet there is good ground by reason of the ready access, friendliness, and much seed already sown. What is needed is our prayers, as a body, unceasingly. I feel one does not know the A B C of intercessory prayer.

Yun-nan Probince.

FROM MISS HAINGE.

Yun-nan Fu, Nov. 19th. You will not wonder to hear that GOD is blessing us in our work. Many of the people living in the streets around, who once looked upon us with mistrust, now receive us warmly. In one street for which we had prayed, the LORD opened the way for work through saving a woman from opium-poisoning. Now, whenever we go to her house, she receives us quite gladly, and immediately brings out a form and places it in a shady part of her large yard.

I spent last Friday in visiting with Mrs. Tomkinson, and also Tuesday. We are making our way through less familiar parts of the city.

We still gather the little ones twice each week; they much enjoy singing the hymns, and work happily at the Kindergarten. We find that they remember what they are taught. Sometimes we meet them while visiting, and they take us to their homes and ask us to sing. Their parents are always pleased when the children can sing with us. I trust that I shall soon be able to tell you that our scholars number fifty.

On Thursday Miss Eland and I visited Ma-kiai and four villages, and at each had nice little groups of listeners. We sold a few gospels and tracts. Yesterday we took some tracts and started for an afternoon of visiting. We had not gone far when we were greeted by a woman who had attended the meetings at the chapel several times. She invited us to the house of some Chinese ladies, who entertained us in quite a sisterly way. We had a nice time with them, talking over the tracts which we gave them. Early in the evening another of our friends brought several relatives, who had come from a place sixty *li* away to hear the Gospel. Praise GOD, the work is His, and therefore not in vain. All the friends here are well and happy.

FROM MR. THORNE.

Chao-tung Fu, Oct. 10th.—Lately I have been out for two weeks visiting new ground. I find there are nine markets to the West, the farthest not more than 100 *li* (thirty miles), and all of them near each other. Indeed, in this field I calculate there are 100 to 150 markets, each with an average attendance of 500 people at least. Plenty of work to be done! Mrs. Thorne and I continue visiting over a dozen villages, and are generally well received.

Nov. 28th.—We have had sixty opium poisoning cases in eleven months, and have attended to 1,500 applications for medicine in nine months. We have spent sixty-nine days in visiting thirty markets and towns, and paid 107 visits to twenty villages within ten or fifteen *li* of home. Here we have done a good deal of visiting and street preaching, and have had a nightly service for fifteen months. But the best news is that one family have burnt their idols. Oh, for precious souls to be brought into the kingdom!

FROM MR. CURNOW.

K'üh-tsing Fu, Nov. 2nd.—When will GOD's people, clustered in Christian countries, rouse themselves to the desperate need of these dying millions? Upon arrival at Gan-ning-chau I stayed at a street corner and sold books very rapidly, interspersing sales with preaching. I continued selling until late in the afternoon, having several times gathered up my books and then reopened them to supply more. At the inn I had large numbers to see an I hear the foreigner; some were not without sympathy, and all were attentive. The landlord of the inn appears to know something of our doctrine, and I was struck with the earnestness of the man in all that he did.

Kiang-si Probince.

FROM MR. STEVEN.

In a Native Boat, Dec. 2nd.—I bless GOD that He is teaching me something more of the blessedness of bowing to His will and of agreeing with it. GOD is most distinctly opening up each step of the way before us on this journey, I never saw it half so clearly before. I think it is chiefly because so many good people in China, in Canada, and in England are praying for us on this expedition, and also, of course, because my eyes, by the grace of GOD, are more open to see His hand than they have been at some other times.

Only yesterday we came to T'ai-ho Hien, where we were to change boats. We had a most disagreeable boatman, and it was not at all convenient to wait on the boat until we could get another, yet there was no prospect of our getting another till the boats came in at night, if even then. We prayed to GOD, and we had hardly ceased, when a large and good boat came along. The boatman was willing to take us as passengers, and asked a fair price at once. We accepted his terms, got our goods on board, and sailed off before a fair wind, well within an hour of our stopping. I never had a quicker or pleasanter change. Our GOD does hold the hearts of all men in His hand. To Him be all praise, and in Him be all quiet, restful trust.

Dec. 6th.—Yesterday morning we arrived at the city of Wan-gan Hien, and are still detained by strong head winds. GOD has undoubtedly a wise purpose in this. Yesterday we saw it in the fact that we were able to go on shore and sell over 500 cash worth of books, half of which were Gospels, including two Testaments; for this witness left in the city we are very thankful.

Ta-ku-t'ang, Jan. 4th.—After giving up all hope of reaching here before the close of the year, GOD sped us on our way wonderfully. We arrived early on the 31st, and had a good day of united prayer.

FROM MISS HATTIE TURNER.

Kwang-feng, Nov. 2nd.—We are so happy in the work and so well in body, and GOD has so blessed us in our souls. It is now a year since we arrived in China, and I am sure we have all had the same experience. What a friend we have in JESUS! We have learnt more of Him; He is more precious. When we think of our loved ones in the home lands, such a great, great longing comes over us to see them and speak with them, but He makes up for it. Oh, it is sweet to work for Him! GOD is for us, He does so help us at all times. We feel our own weakness, but He has promised to use the weak things, He is our strength. We do praise Him for ever leading you to Canada, and for leading us to China.

We had a test this week in trusting GOD to supply our needs, and *we knew* He would. We had only a few cash left, and I gave them to get vegetables for dinner. Before we had finished eating our vegetables and rice, money came by a messenger! This is my first experience, and I praise GOD for it; for I *did* fully trust Him. I never had a test before.

FROM MISS GIBSON.

I-yang Hien, Nov. 14th.—The work seems to be opening up on all hands. Last week Miss Grabham and I visited Ien-shan Hien. We took a dear native woman to help us. It has been her earnest desire to accompany us for some time, but the LORD only now opened her way. Mrs. Wang, for that is her name, is a very bright Christian. She believes in prayer; prayer and her Bible are her daily delight. She says that sometimes after being occupied in household matters her heart is not perfectly at rest; she has prayer, and then she is full of joy and peace. She asked that some friends would specially pray for her husband, that he may be converted. We do praise GOD for this golden sheaf gathered in. Oh, that we had more of these consecrated ones in China, willing to go all lengths with JESUS!

I feel that Ien-shan Hien is quite ready for Gospel work. One woman has very kindly opened her house to us, so we expect to return shortly. A friend of Mrs. Wang's, an opium smoker, returned with us to Ho-k'eo. She professes faith in JESUS. I do trust she will be truly saved, and return to Ien-shan to shine brightly for JESUS.

You will be sorry to hear that two of our number have had to be suspended because of idolatrous worship in their house. For nearly two months they stood firm, but at last gave way. Their little child was seriously ill; prayer was offered for it, but it pleased God not to restore the child. The neighbours tried their very utmost to induce the parents to worship idols for the child's recovery. We believe that GOD will restore them both. This has been a warning to our little church.

An inquirer, Mrs. Yeh, has been bereaved of her two grand-children; her husband persecuted her, but, praise the LORD, she keeps faithful. We believe that the LORD is saving many souls in the district. Our Sunday services are well attended.

Last week Miss Gardiner and I came here from Ho-k'eo. From early in the morning until late in the evening we have had a great many visitors, who have listened most attentively while we told them of the love of JESUS. Our teacher and the native brother in charge of this house have had a great many more. We have received nothing but respect and kindness. One man from Lo-ping Hien inquired very earnestly regarding the truth. He asked us to visit his district. We were very much interested in him, and continue to pray for his conversion. He said he would return home and tell his friends and relations of JESUS. Lo-ping is about 100 *li* from here. We intend to go there soon.

We are all very happy. The LORD has been showing us the necessity of living a consecrated life. I do trust He will never let me live on the work, or on any other thing but Himself. It is sweet to find that as the days pass on JESUS is more real and more precious to one's own soul. What could we do without Him in this land so full of darkness?

Cheh-kiang Province.

FROM MR. WILLIAMSON.

Si-tiu, Nov. 29th.—I have just been spending five days at O-zi. Old Kyuo-yiao is still hale and able to walk sixty *li* a day with little apparent fatigue, but I am sorry to say the members are not in a lively spiritual state. We need to pray that they may be quickened. A great many people in the village and neighbourhood are like the people at home, they have heard and known something of the Gospel, but not having felt its power remain indifferent. The work is more encoura-ging here; three have been baptised recently, and there are several inquirers.

Mr. Harrison and Mr. Vaen went to Tin-tai about the begin-ning of the month. Two women were baptised there, and there were a few inquirers. We need continued prayer for awakening at all our stations. At Ning-po old Mrs. Tsiu is still active.

Dec. 2nd.—Had good meetings with the members on Satur-day and yesterday; one girl was baptised.

THE ANNUAL MEETINGS
In connection with the
TWENTY-FOURTH ANNIVERSARY,
will (D.V.) be held in the
CONFERENCE HALL, MILDMAY PARK,
ON WEDNESDAY, MAY 21st, 1890.

The Chair to be taken at 3 o'clock by
GEORGE WILLIAMS, Esq.,
President of the Young Men's Christian Association,

And at 7 o'clock by
JAMES E. MATHIESON, Esq.

MEETINGS for Prayer, in the *CONFERENCE HALL,* on Tuesday Evening (20th), at 7 o'clock; and on Wednesday Morning (21st), at 11 o'clock.

China's Millions.

Blessed Prosperity.

MEDITATIONS ON THE FIRST PSALM.—III.

LET us now proceed to notice the remarkable promise in the third verse of this Psalm—one of the most remarkable and inclusive contained in the Scriptures :—

"*And he shall be like a tree planted by the rivers of water,*
"*That bringeth forth his fruit in his season ;*
"*His leaf also shall not wither ;*
"*And whatsoever he doeth shall prosper.*"

If we could offer to the ungodly a worldly plan which would ensure their prospering in all that they undertake, how eagerly they would embrace it ! And yet when GOD Himself reveals so effectual a plan to His people how few avail themselves of it ! Many fail on the negative side and do not come clearly out from the world ; many fail on the positive side and allow other duties or indulgences to take the time that should be given to reading and meditation on GOD's Word. To some it is not at all easy to secure time for the morning watch, but nothing can make up for the loss of it. But is there not yet a third class of Christians whose failure lies largely in their not embracing the promise and claiming it by faith ; in each of these three ways failure may come in and covenant blessings may be lost.

Let us now consider what are the blessings, the manifold happinesses which faith is to claim when the conditions are fulfilled.

I. *Stability.* He shall be like a tree (not a mere annual plant), of steady progressive growth and increasing fruitfulness ; a tree planted and always to be found in its place, not blown about, the sport of circumstances ; the flowers may bloom and pass away, but the tree abides.

II. *Independent supplies.* Planted by the rivers of water. The ordinary supplies of rain and dew may fail, his deep and hidden supplies cannot. He shall not be careful in the year of drought, and in the days of famine he shall be satisfied. His supply is the living water—the SPIRIT of GOD, the same yesterday, to-day, and for ever ; hence he depends on no intermitting spring.

III. *Seasonable fruitfulness.* The careful student of Scripture will notice the parallelism between the teaching of the First Psalm and that of our LORD in the Gospel of John, where in the sixth chapter we are taught that he who feeds on CHRIST abides in Him, and in the fifteenth that he who abides brings forth much fruit. We feed upon CHRIST the incarnate WORD through the written Word. So in this Psalm he who delights in the law of the LORD and meditates upon it day and night, brings forth his fruit in his season.

There is something very beautiful in this. A word spoken in season how good it is ; how even a seasonable look will encourage or restrain, reprove or comfort. The promise reminds one of those in John about the living water thirsty ones drink, and are not only refreshed, but become channels through which rivers of living water are always flowing, so that other thirsty ones in their hour of need may find seasonable refreshment. But the figure in the Psalm is not that of water flowing through us as through a channel ; but that of fruit, the very outcome of our own transformed life—a life of union with CHRIST. It is so gracious of our GOD not to work through us in a mere mechanical way, but to make us branches of the true Vine, the very organs by which its fruit is produced. We are not, therefore, independent workers, for there is a fundamental difference between fruit and work. Work is the outcome of effort ; fruit, of life. A bad man may do good work, but a bad tree cannot bear good fruit. The result of work is not reproductive, but fruit has its seed in itself. The workman

JUNE, 1890.

has to seek his material and his tools, and often to set himself with painful perseverance to his task. The fruit of the Vine is the glad, free, spontaneous outcome of the life within, and it forms and grows and ripens in its proper season. And what is the fruit which the believer should bear? May it not be expressed by one word—Christliness? It is interesting to notice that the Scripture does not speak of the fruits of the SPIRIT in the plural, as though we might take our choice among the graces named, but of the fruit in the singular, which is a rich cluster composed of love, joy, peace, longsuffering, etc. How blessed to bring forth such fruit in its season!

IV. *Continuous vigour*. "His leaf shall not wither." In our own climate many trees are able to maintain their life through the winter, but unable to retain their leaves. The hardy evergreen, however, not only lives, but manifests its life, and all the more conspicuously because of the naked branches around. The life within is too strong to fear the shortened day, the cold blast, or the falling snow. So with the man of GOD whose life is maintained by hidden communion through the Word; adversity only brings out the strength and the reality of the life within.

The leaf of the tree is no mere adornment. If the root suggests to us receptive power in that it draws from the soil the stimulating sap, without which life could not be maintained, the leaves no less remind us of the grace of giving and of purifying; they impart to the atmosphere a grateful moisture; they provide for the traveller a refreshing shade, and they purify the air poisoned by the breathings of animal life. Well, too, is the tree repaid for all that it gives out through its leaves. The thin stimulating sap that comes from the root, which could not of itself build up the tree, thickens in giving out its moisture, and through the leaves possesses itself of carbon from the atmosphere. Thus enriched, the sap goes back through the tree, building it up until the tiniest rootlets are as much nourished by the leaves, as the latter are fed by the roots. Keep a tree despoiled of its leaves sufficiently long and it will surely die. So unless the believer is giving as well as receiving, purifying by his life and influence, he cannot grow nor properly maintain his vitality. But he who delights in the law of the LORD, and meditates in it day and night—his leaf shall *not* wither.

V. *Uniform prosperity*. "Whatsoever he doeth shall prosper." Could any promise go beyond this? It is the privilege of a child of GOD to see the hand of GOD in all his circumstances and surroundings, and to serve GOD in all his avocations and duties; whether he eat or drink, work or rest, speak or be silent; in all his occupations, spiritual, domestic, or secular, he is alike the servant of GOD. Nothing lawful to him is too small to afford an opportunity of glorifying GOD; duties in themselves trivial or wearisome become exalted and glorified when the believer recognises his power through them to gladden and satisfy the loving heart of his ever-observant MASTER. And he who in all things recognises himself as the servant *of* GOD, may count on a sufficiency *from* GOD for all manner of need, and look with confident expectation *to* GOD to *really* prosper him in whatever he does.

But this prosperity will not always be apparent, except to the eye of faith. When Chorazin and Bethsaida rejected our LORD's message it needed the eye of faith to rejoice in spirit and say, "Even so, FATHER, for so it seemed good in Thy sight." Doubtless the legions of hell rejoiced when they saw the LORD of Glory nailed to the accursed tree, yet *we* know that never was our blessed LORD more prospered than when, as our High Priest, He offered Himself as our atoning sacrifice, and bore our sins in His own body on the tree. As then, so now, the path of real prosperity will often lie through deepest suffering; followers of CHRIST may well be content with the path which He trod.

But though this prosperity may not always be immediately apparent, it will always be real, and should always be claimed by faith. The minister in his church, the missionary among the heathen, the merchant at his desk, the mother in her home, the workman in his labour, each may alike claim it. Not in vain is it written, "Whatsoever he doeth shall prosper."

VI. Finally, let us notice that these promises are all in the indicative mood, and, provided the conditions are fulfilled, are absolute. There is no "may be" about them. And further, they are made to individual believers. If other believers fail, he who accepts them will not; the word is "Whatsoever he doeth shall prosper."

"*The ungodly are not so.*"

Our space will not allow us to dwell at any length upon the contrast. The ungodly cannot enjoy the happinesses of the child of GOD, for they cannot carry out the conditions. They neither can nor desire to avoid the counsel, the society, or the ways of their own fellows; and they lack that spiritual insight which is essential to delighting in GOD's Word. Instead of being full of life, like the tender grain, they become hard and dry; and the same sun that ripens the one prepares the other for destruction. Instead of being "planted," the wind drives them away; and He who delights in the way of His people, causes the way of the ungodly to perish. J. H. T.

The Feast of Lanterns.

FROM MR. A. EWING.

KWEI-HWA-CH'ENG, N. SHAN-SI.—To-day there is a great hubbub in the city! This is the 15th of the first Chinese month, and is the feast of lanterns. The shops are all shut and the city is "*en fête*." Along with my teacher I wended my way down through the crowded streets to a large lama temple. Lamaism is the religion of the Mongols, and is a kind of watered Buddhism. Priests are called lamas, seldom wear caps, shave the whole head, and are supposed to live celibate lives, which is far from the case. In this city there are eyes the thing seemed imposing, but to mine it was ludicrous. The Mongol mandarins were there in state, much the same as a Lord Mayor goes to patronise a show. This was religion! If the light in them be darkness, how great is that darkness!

Being the feast of lanterns, great preparations were being made by all the shops for a suitable display when darkness set in. Lamps were being cleaned, candles placed in them, and everything got ready for the evening. Meanwhile, at the head of the Great South Street, the

LANTERN PROCESSION.

our sects, each having their distinctive names and temples. On great occasions they all meet in one large temple called the "Great Wu Temple." On the night of the 14th visiting and fraternising went on much the same as with us at the New Year in the northern part of Great Britain. About 6 a.m. on the 15th all the lamas gathered at this Great Wu Temple, and had a time of dancing and general merriment; at 10 a.m. they separated, and the sects returned to their respective temples, to the largest of which I now wended my way. In the temple court a vast concourse of people had assembled and formed into a ring, the inside of which the Mongols reserved for the players. On the north side of this ring was a temple from which emerged two lamas dressed in hideous costumes, and went into the centre of the ring. With wooden daggers and other harmless weapons they played at killing one another. On a given signal they retired amid the blowing of trumpets and the plaudits of children, while another two dashed into the ring to go through the same performance. This went on for three hours, and then all joined in one grand *finale*. To a Mongol's

main thoroughfare of the city, the assistants, apprentices and workmen of the various places of business were assembling, with banners flying and gongs beating. A wooden stand was erected, idols were placed in it, and a delegate from each place of business, with bread in his hand, kneeling, offered it to the lamas. All this time a tremendous noise was going on—drums beating, trumpets blowing, fireworks going off, anything, in fact, that would contribute to scare away the evil spirits. This finished, they formed into line and marched out to the gate of the city. In their absence the remaining assistants erected poles in the ground covered with fireworks from top to bottom, so that, when lighted at the bottom, they would go off without any more ado, the only duty of the people being to get out of the way as soon as possible. Chinese are adepts in making fireworks and in letting them off. In one year this town of about 100,000 inhabitants spend as much money on these trifles as would rebuild the city. Trifles they are to us, but to a superstitious Chinaman they are indispensable to his peace of mind, as, being regularly let off, they keep away evil influences.

Professing themselves to be wise, they became fools. After dark I went out to see the display of lamps, and a most uncomfortable time I had. The streets were literally one mass of living beings, and I had not yet baptized any such a squeezing as I never had before. In this Great South Street there must have been many thousands of people, and like all Chinese streets, being very narrow, the crush was great. To add to the general discomfort, carts, horses, mules, and donkeys, each with their complement of sight-seers, persisted in making their way through the crowd. There were at every few yards huge bonfires, and one was in danger of being pushed suddenly amongst the burning coals. The safest plan was to stand still, but as I wanted to see the whole affair, standing still did not suit me. The various shops, especially the wealthy ones, had really a fine display of lamps, with all sorts of devices to make them both attractive and amusing. The most noticeable and the most effective display, however, was a foreign chandelier with eight paraffin lamps burning brightly. Most Chinamen hitherto have known only their harmless candles, and these lamps were the cause of no small comment. I heard one Chinaman seriously tell another that they burnt for six months without intermission. After many obstacles and discomforts, I was glad to take refuge in a cash shop till the crowd should melt away. About 9 p.m. the streets were such that I managed to get safely home, wondering when shall light arise upon the darkness of this people, when, instead of lamps and other trifles to please false gods, they shall know the one true GOD, and the light shall lead them into purer, higher ways.

"Ring out the old, ring in the new."

Experiences at Lao-ho-k'eo, Hu-peh Province.

FROM MRS. GEO. KING.

FEB 18*th*.—We have been settled here now rather more than two years, and have not yet baptized any converts. Amid much to discourage and cast down, GOD has been very good to us, and now I trust we are beginning to see some tokens of His working; if His time has indeed come, soon we shall have "abundance of rain."

We have since coming to this place gone through in our experience pretty nearly all the usual stages, having been, by turns, wonders to be gazed at; beings, half human, half demoniac, to be dreaded; very clever people to be enquired of, and even now are regarded by most as rather good, inoffensive persons, who, having mounted a hobby, are riding it to death—said hobby being that our particular GOD is the only one to be worshipped, and that we only, and those who "follow" us, are on the way to Heaven's hall, while all others must assuredly perish everlastingly. How often does my heart sink within me as, when talking to a larger or smaller crowd, I see the incredulous shrug, the covert sneer, or worst of all, the vacant stare, as one turns from the colour of our hair, or the make of our dress, to speak of the never-dying soul and its infinite destinies! I have not found the Chinese women *en masse*, thirsting for the Gospel. Far from it ; they seem to me just as worldly, as indifferent as wrapped up in self as our unconverted sisters in Christian lands, and, until the SPIRIT begins to work, as utterly impervious, callous, and dead, as the infallible Word declares the unrenewed soul to be.

We have had our fair share of superstitious awe, though, on the whole, the Chinese around us shew a kind and friendly spirit. For long after we first came, multitudes feared us as beings *very uncanny*, not on any account to be offended, and still less on any account to be trusted. I have seen the shutting of the guest-room door on a cold day, when a crowd of women were in, cause as much alarm almost as if a bomb shell had burst at their feet, and the whole party, with one accord, rise and fly, rejoicing, when outside our outer gate, that the closing of the door had not, after all, meant the immediate and utter destruction of the unwary ones who had so foolishly put themselves into our power.

I have been applied to by owners of lost property to find it for them, as by my second sight I could not fail to detect the transgressor. Over and over again I have been asked when the rain would come, or the weather become fine, as I was in Heaven's secrets.

Many have supposed that we are living on the proceeds of the golden horses, ducks, etc., which, when we stand in need of funds, we dig at pleasure out of the grounds of the unsuspecting lords of the soil ; for if not supported by the treasures of the Flowery Land, how *do* we live? We don't trade, and we don't farm ; whence, then, comes our money? A few wiser than the rest know that these are but old wives' fables,—the foreigner is a spy of the worst type, and if not driven from the Empire, China will ere long be annexed by England, as India and Burmah have already been, and in that day these spies and traitors will be exalted to posts of high honour and dignity. Time, explanations, and the friendly words of those who have really got to know us and our errand have done much to dispel all these illusions, and now we have before us a pretty fair field. I would not willingly, and of my own accord, exchange our sphere here for any in the world. Of course, if GOD calls us elsewhere, I should be willing to go ; if He does not, I shall be quite content to live all my days amongst this people—aye, and to die among them too ; for if the LORD come soon, or if He tarry, I should like to go to Him *direct* from China.

Our visitors have always been very numerous, and those of us who were not engaged with these have gone to the villages around. Many hours daily have been spent in this delightful work. The plain there is very populous, *hundreds* of villages, larger or smaller, being within walking distance of our Mission-house. Into all the nearer villages some "beams of light" have shone, and in many a fair knowledge has been gained of the leading truths of the Gospel. This last winter has been exceptionally fine and mild, and we have made it our aim to push into the more distant villages,thus penetrating into our "regions beyond."

As a rule, *much* is not accomplished in the first visit, but some seeds of truth are always sown, and GOD will give the increase. The work which seems to *tell* most is that done in our various classes and meetings. These are usually well attended, and it is in these gatherings that we see the clearest traces of real interest—of *some*, we hope, that GOD is bringing them slowly into the Kingdom. It was but the other day, when in one of these classes, I was speaking of the heavenly home and our Omniscient Guide, several voices at once cried out, "We also will walk this heaven-ward road ; we also will follow this mighty Leader. *Teach us the way.*" Will you join with us in earnest prayer that many of these precious souls may soon come out into the light and liberty of

GOD's children. We do so want that any who enter the Church may be real, earnest, and out-and-out for CHRIST. Please ask that no wolf in sheep's clothing may be brought into the fold in this place, and yet that not one of CHRIST's sheep may be excluded.

Another feature of our work here is children's classes. I suppose it is partly because our home is almost in the country that such numbers of children gather round us. We try to take the children several times a week, and could have a large children's class daily if only we could spare time from other work. Some of these little ones have pretty clear views of the Gospel, but I do not think that any of them are really saved. I have never lived in any place where such numbers of children, boys and girls, of from seven or eight to perhaps fifteen or sixteen years of age, come so freely about the Mission-house and are so willing to learn.

Last, but not least, I must tell you of our night school, which we have now been carrying on for some months. It begins immediately after tea, and lasts for about an hour and a half. It is intended for young men and lads who are working during the day, and, though not largely attended, is by no means an unhopeful branch of our work.

One of our best pupils is a young man who seven or eight months ago did not know a single character, but can now read his New Testament fairly well, and, best of all, is, we trust, a disciple in CHRIST's school.

I have purposely abstained from speaking of my husband's work. I know he writes to you from time to time. I would only try to emphasize his appeal for helpers. The amount of work he gets through is wonderful, but with all his efforts much has to be left undone, and the work is greatly crippled for want of more labourers. Even *one* good brother worker, whether native or foreign, would be an immense help, and many things might be kept going which have now to be set aside. Most of all, a helper is needed to be in our chapel to preach to the guests who come in a never-ending stream from dawn till dark ; and Mr. King, with so many other duties pressing on him, cannot always be with them. And then there is all the outside work, so immense, so much requiring haste, and the *one* already over-worked messenger unable to touch more than the outer edge. Please think of sending *at least* one brother when the places *more* needy than ours have been supplied.

An Evangelistic Journey in Shen-si.

FROM MR. BLAND.

DEC. 10*th*.—To-day I left for the district to the north-west of Feng-tsiang, with the aim of making known the Gospel in some of the towns and villages to be found there. I scarcely knew how far I might go, but set out, looking to the LORD to go before and lead in everything.

Dec. 13th.—Remained at Yiu-liu-p'u until to-day, and in the meantime had many opportunities of telling out the Gospel; also posted up several large sheet-tracts and sold a fair number of books. To-day went on to the next village, a distance of 30 *li* ; the road led over a sharp range of hills, and then descended into a long, narrow valley, which stretched right away beyond Long-chau, 150 odd *li*. Either side is bounded by low, bare hills, which are pierced with caves, in which the majority of the people make their homes. Reached Hwang-nui-p'u by noon; on the way passed drove after drove of mules bearing loads of coal, and on arrival found the inns of the village nearly full. Had a good time in the afternoon speaking and bookselling, principally to the muleteers.

Saturday, 14*th*.—In the morning the place was crowded, for in nearly all the villages a market is held every other day. Later on left for a lively little city some 20 *li* further on. I had hoped to have remained at Hwang-nui-p'u over Sunday, but after spending a night in the best room to be found in the place I went on. This room had an open slit in the wall, which served as a window, and admitted far more cold air than light, whilst the door was some inches too narrow for the frame. Table, stool, and such things were not to be had.

On Monday made my way into the busy street of the town, and while posting up a street-tract a good number of people came round and listened with much attention ; many bought books and tracts.

On the following afternoon, as I was passing the same spot, a man greeted me, and, fetching a stool, invited me to be seated and tell him the Gospel. Many gathered to hear me, and if able I might have gone on for hours, they seemed so willing to hear. When I had finished I went into a barber's shop, and the first thing I saw was a sheet-tract pasted on the wall, which I had given to the barber the day before in the street.

On Wednesday had equally good times. I hope to revisit this city before long.

Dec. 20*th*.—My next halting-place was a very small village. Arrived during the morning, and found the market getting busy, so, securing a room for the night, I got out my books, and was occupied for some hours in preaching. Found I was not understood so readily as before. My night's lodging was in one of the many cave homes, and the place being somewhat lonely my horse had to share the room with us.

Saturday, 21*st*.—As the next day was Sunday, and Christmas followed a day or two later, I went on to the next city, Long-chau, a distance of 90 *li*; passed three villages on the way, at which I hoped to make a stay on my return. Found all the inns were occupied by soldiers for the time being, but after a while found a room in a HU-NAN inn. Made friends with some of the soldiers; several I had seen once or twice before when travelling. Spent a whole week at Long-chau, and found the people very friendly. I had a happy time with the LORD on Christmas Day. Perhaps for the first time songs of praise ascended to Him on this day from this city. May the time be hastened when others will join in singing them ! My recent experiences enabled me to picture the wondrous scene of the LORD of Glory a babe in a manger of an inn as never before.

As the following Tuesday was New Year's eve, I thought it better to return to Feng-tsiang, and to work the remaining villages later, as opportunity shall be given.

Tuesday morning I observed as the time of special waiting upon GOD. Reached Feng-tsiang late in the afternoon, and had the privilege of taking part with Mr. and Mrs. Botham and Brother Redfern in the Watch-night Service. It was both a happy and a solemn season to us all.

I do indeed praise GOD for the privilege of having been permitted to tell out the Gospel to these heathen, although so feebly spoken, and am looking forward for many happy days to come in His holy service to this people.

Idolatry.

FROM MR. GEORGE KING.
"*They that make them shall be like unto them.*"

THE Nemesis that GOD has ordained to follow idolatry may be seen in the state of all nations that have become idol-worshippers, whether in the fearfully gross cannibalism and savagery of Polynesians and Africans, or in the dead inertia of a black pall of ignorance weighing on and blinding the nations of Thibet, Korea, China, etc. It may be said that what a man worships, such he is or will be. Familiarity with devils will as surely degrade the man to their level, as communion with GOD will raise him to be an imitator of GOD as His beloved child. No whitewashing of the idolatrous religions can make them one whit other than they are—systems framed and furthered by the evil spirit. That rays of GOD'S primeval truth glint here and there through their thick darkness may well make us adore His goodness, who would not leave Himself without witness even when men would fain cast Him off; but they are in nowise part and parcel of the systems themselves. The Apostle to the Gentiles said truly, "The things which the Gentiles sacrifice, they sacrifice to devils," and the great systems of Satanic craft by which hundreds of millions are held down, not only in bondage to but in adoration of the evil spirits that enslave them, are a more convincing testimony to the awful reality of Satanic personality and power than would be the sight of men possessed by devils, writhing and foaming under their dread rage. A few instances of idolatry of various kinds may help to show what are the religions which the American Buddhist Olcott persuades these people to stand by.

A few miles east of Lao-ho-k'eo, by the highway to HO-NAN and the North-east, which leaves the Han river basin by a steep ascent to hilly country at this point, an aged aspen has for many generations flourished. Long dead at the heart, and its larger branches minus any sign of vitality, the outer rim of living wood still nourishes many smaller branches, and the old black stump bears a spreading plume of green, the leaves tremulous to every breeze. There is a touch of pathos in a slender shoot struggling into growth out of the gnarled old trunk, on which storms and lightnings have left their mark, and something solemn, albeit invigorating, in this life from the midst of death. Heathen minds have felt awed at the sight, but their expression of it has been so modified by superstition as to take the form of worshipping the aged tree. A thick plaster of earth forms a base for a censer, placed in front of the newest shoot, which might pass for a recent graft. Like other aged trees, and aged foxes, rats, weasels, frogs, etc., its longevity is held a proof that it has attained the high honour of a place among the immortals, and has become consequently endowed with supernatural powers.

Three instances of this kind of idolatry may be seen here within a few miles of each other, the trees bearing votive offerings attached to them, red silk scrolls, gold lettered tablets, and the like. None of them, however, come up in profuse decoration to a tree worshipped at Long-ku-chai, in south-east SHEN-SI, which is laden with testimonies to the efficacy, proved and tested, of prayer to the tree, or its sprite, in sickness, danger, difficulty, travelling, etc.

Nor is this belief in tree sprites confined to aged trees alone; a sudden calamity which befell a household in the Si-an plain (the death, I think, of the master of the house was attributed to having neglected, previous to felling a tree a few days before, the proper propitiation of its sprite.

Outside the east gate of Kwang-hwa Hien, by the same great highway to Peking and the North-east before mentioned, are some high stone tablets to the memory of worthies of a few hundred years back. These tablets are as usual resting on the back of a huge stone tortoise, and are built in strongly with brick. The stone tortoises at the base of these weird-looking, tall and narrow erections, are believed to have "attained completion," viz., reached by age the sentient and demoniac stage which enables them to place themselves (invisibly) as barriers across the road by the side of which they stand, and to form impassable hindrances in the way of unwary carts plying between Lao-ho-k'eo and HO-NAN. It is currently reported and firmly believed that the axles of many carts have been snapped by their foul means, and that the crops in the fields facing them have been impoverished and thinned to enrich them, while those at their backs are rich and luxuriant.

Another instance of the same kind is seen at a stone bridge a few miles further east. In this case, a stone dragon carved on the parapet at the entrance to the bridge is the wicked cause of the carts' misfortunes. To a prosaic Westerner, the ready and natural course would be to remove such ill-tempered stones to some place out of the carts' way, but who would dare ! A more congenial remedy is found in the paying of divine honours to the said tortoises and dragon, and following this by freely anointing them and the tablets with the oil carried to lubricate the cart wheels. Even the reverence for "written characters" does not prevent the sticky varnish stuff being smeared over the characters of the inscriptions, and the oil, having run over the tortoise's head, until eyes, nose, and mouth present a woful sight, falls finally to the ground beneath.

A stone lion of very ancient date at Han-chung Fu, who had reached the sentient stage, had his mouth daily plastered with opium by his devotees, and nasty enough he looked in consequence.

Again, on the left bank of the river Han, some thirty miles above Hsing-gan Fu, at the Cih-nu rapid, a rocky point some forty or fifty feet high, shoots up perpendicularly from a spur of the mountain, and viewed from some points much resembles a young lady. This came to be believed to have some occult connection with the Weaver constellation, and to have acquired power to work evil, which it appears to have done with a hearty ill-will to poor mariners. The Stone Lady's foot being in the rapid, she contrived (with her toe?) to upset unlucky boats, or she put her dainty rock foot so in their way that the current dashed their frail barks to pieces against it, or she made their tow ropes break, sending them backwards helter-skelter when in the most dangerous surf; in short, did all the harm her wicked stony heart was capable of. This same obstreperous stone lady appeared in a dream to the Hien of the district, tempting him to run riot with her, but he would have none of her, and by some means the unruly spirit was quelled.

The "Lady who escorts the infants" is a very important personage to the Chinese women, and, with some other female divinities, e.g., the "Goddess of Eyesight," "The Goddess of Small-pox," "The Goddess who steals new-born children," frequently, if not always, finds a place

Itinerant Needle Women

in the temples to the "Goddess of Mercy." It is embellished with a representation of the (unborn) infants' hill, where multitudes of tiny boys and girls, in unclothed simplicity, disport themselves merrily, awaiting their call to our cold world. Horses stand at the side caparisoned and waiting for the escortress of infants, but in her frequent journeyings she is presumed to wear out a good deal of "shoe leather," or is credited with the usual feminine Chinese fondness for new and gaudy shoes to adorn her "golden lilies." Those anxious for the blessing of motherhood take a shoe off her foot to serve as a pattern, and perhaps, also, that the missed shoe may serve as a reminder should the lady forget them (she, Chinese like, being unlikely to forget the whereabouts of her loaned property). The shoe is taken home and secreted carefully until the desired boon is obtained, when a pair of shoes after the pattern of the one borrowed must be made and returned with it to the goddess, with of course all the proper thanksgivings and observances. There was certainly a litter of shoes in a temple I visited a few miles west of this, but to judge from them, either the patterns taken home must have been of the poorest description, or "the staff was thrown away when the bridge was crossed," and they treated the goddess precisely as they would treat each other in like circumstances.

The Eyesight Goddess was adorned with strings of silk eyes (or what ought to have been silk, but was undeniably calico). Each ophthalmic sufferer cured by her potent spell has to bring a few pairs of eyes back (worked on silk), which besides the advertisement they form of her medical powers, are probably looked upon as serving to replenish her stock, being capable of transmutation in the same way as the paper images, etc., which do duty for holocausts at funerals.

The "goddess" to whom belongs the thankless task of stealing away the new-born children (by convulsions, etc.) gets few presents, but angry nudges, spiteful pinches, and rough pushes to express the detestation felt at her, in short "more kicks than halfpence." None, however, would dare to exclude her from a participation in the honours done to the more amiable goddesses. When an infant is ill, a female form may, it is believed, be seen entering the room, waving a towel wildly round her head, and the longer she whirls the more unconscious the little sufferer becomes. Heaps of paper are burnt in hopes of scorching her away, but guided by the high rate of infant mortality in China we may conclude that the plan is of doubtful efficacy.

The city god of Kwang-hwa was worshipped in the usual manner, his own and his wife or wives' images being placed in their niche and the customary candles, incense, and offerings presented. These attentions, however, proved insufficient, and it was ascertained (probably by some fortune-teller or priest), that the old god was a libertine, was quite dissatisfied with so small a harem, and that more concubines must be supplied if favours were to be granted. The petitioners hastening to win the god's favour by pandering to his imaginary lust, brought with them as suitable offerings to accompany their prayers, pretty little images of beautiful girls.

A god of Lao-ho-k'eo has been ascertained to have another predilection which must surely be of rather modern date, viz., his being addicted to opium smoking or eating. Opium accordingly forms a very acceptable offering, and his petitioners daub his mouth well with the extract. Were it suffered to accumulate it might prove inconvenient, but that difficulty is considerably guarded against by the beggars, who carefully relieve his idolship of the wholly superfluous narcotic. Scraping his august lips as clean as they can, they transfer the welcome opium to their own receptacles, to come in handy later on, when, their day's adventures over, they lie down for their brief intoxication in which to dream of comfort and plenty.

Time will not permit more than the passing mention of the disgusting obesity deified as the god of Riches, the lascivious half-nudity which represents the goddess of Mercy, or the chambers of horrors to be seen in the various municipal temples, representing the most ingenious forms of diabolical cruelty as being practised by the god of Hades—sawing asunder, frying in oil, grinding in mills, disembowelling alive, and other revolting atrocities.

Themselves the result of the darkest ages of GOD-abandoned superstition, when under the spell of the Egyptian darkness of idolatrous ignorance, man wreaked his hellish hate upon his fellow men, they tend to perpetuate the use of the horrid tortures still legal in China, at the trials, and capital and other punishments of unhappy criminals. The sanction given to covetousness by the universal worship of the Wealth god; to drunkenness by the worship of deified distillers and tipplers as the Wine god, both of whom "tumbled into the water whilst drunk and were drowned;" to bribery and corruption by the whole system of backstairs influence, exerted by money and presents through the priests to gain the god's favour, the degradation of women, and female infanticide, consequent on the deification of celibates, and an immoral male and female celibate priesthood—these are but a few of the instances producible, proving that China is no exception to GOD's rule that the judicial punishment of idolatry shall be mental and moral degradation. "They that make them shall be like unto them; yea, every one that trusteth in them" (Ps. cxv. 8, R. V.).

"Here am I; send me."
Isaiah vi. 8.

BOUND in chains of cruel bondage,
  Crushed by abject misery,
Multitudes of souls are groaning :
  "Who will go," and set them free?
Who, with willing heart, will answer,
  "Here am I; send me, send me"?

Groping amid heathen darkness,
  Not one heavenly ray they see ;
Who will show them how to enter
  Into light and liberty ?
Who, with willing heart, will answer,
  "Here am I; send me, send me"?

Lo ! they're bowing down to idols
  Which can neither hear nor see ;
Who will tell them of the SAVIOUR,
  Waiting to accept their plea ?
Who, with willing heart, will answer,
  "Here am I; send me, send me"?

Dreary is their earthly portion,
  Hopeless their eternity !
Who will by GOD's grace determine

That these souls shall rescued be ?
Who, with willing heart, will answer,
  "Here am I; send me, send me"?

Who with earnestness will tell them
  Of sin's curse and penalty ;
And declare the glorious message
  Of salvation full and free?
Who, with willing heart, will answer,
  "Here am I; send me, send me"?

Blessèd truth ! For their redemption
  JESUS died on Calvary's tree :
Who'll proclaim that through His merit
  They may live eternally ?
Who, with willing heart, will answer,
  "Here am I; send me, send me"?

Oh, my precious LORD and SAVIOUR,
  Thou whose stripes have healed me ;
Take the life which Thou hast purchased,
  Let it all be spent for Thee :
To Thy call I gladly answer,
  "Here am I; send me, send me."

C. P. CLARK.

A Visit to the Shan-tung Promontory.

FROM MR. STOOKE.

HAVING just returned from a visit to this neglected part of S.E. SHAN-TUNG, perhaps a few lines may be interesting. I started in company with a brother missionary on the last day in January, and we took three days to do the 300 li (or 100 miles) from Che-foo to Shih-tao.

On our way we locked up Brother and Sister Judd, and had two or three hours' fellowship with them. After leaving Ning-hai we came to the rough, mountainous part of the journey, but in answer to prayer the weather was exceptionally fine, and we were able to enjoy the fine scenery as we passed along.

We reached Wen-teng Hien late on the Saturday night, and rested there on LORD's Day. We found ample opportunity for tract-distribution, and preached, to the best of our ability, to two or three Chinamen on the hills overlooking the city. We thought it wise *not* to collect a crowd inside the walls, for the Chinese in this district are known to be anti-foreign. The last day's journey to Shih-tao was stiff work, the road was so mountainous ; the country round was very thinly populated—very different to the western portion of the province.

My friend has only just settled in this needy spot, and I was glad of the opportunity to help him. The house and preaching-room is in the midst of the Chinese quarters and close to the sea, and therefore each day, when the doors were opened, our congregation quickly appeared. To these we spoke about the ever-precious Name, and explained in our simple way the plan of salvation for lost sinners. At the close we retired to the little dispensary, and there my friend dealt with the many cases of sickness needing treatment, and whilst the medicines were being prepared I sought to drive home the truth.

I urge for earnest prayer to be made for this needy place; it is a very Sodom of wickedness, the majority of houses are "houses of ill-fame," and there can be no doubt that Satan will do his utmost to overthrow the work. Blessed be GOD! we have the CONQUEROR on our side, and we are therefore bound to win.

The return journey was far more difficult and dangerous; it took us five days in all to cover the same ground, owing to a heavy fall of snow. We were detained in Wenteng Hien for nearly two days, and had to content ourselves with reading and resting in the dirty inn. We were glad to have a visit from a few of the city men (all opium-smokers), and to these we distributed tracts, etc.

On the fourth day we travelled from before sunrise to long after sunset; several times the hind mule in my mule-litter fell, and the front animal ran away with the litter and myself. Once this occurred at a very dangerous spot, but we were all kept by the "mighty arm."

Late at night we reached Ning-hai, wet and weary. Two or three times we had to tramp through half-frozen slush in the shallow rivers; however, we did not catch cold, notwithstanding that we were obliged to walk ten miles with wet feet. To Him be all the praise!

Native Schools in Che-foo.

FROM MRS. SCHOFIELD.

IT is just two years since I re-opened a school, started by the late Mrs. Douthwaite a few months before her death, where, in the loving and faithful discharge of her duties amongst the pupils, she contracted the fever which proved fatal to her. I felt how important it was that the young should have the "Bread of Life" given to them, and that the work begun, at the sacrifice of her consecrated life, should not fall through.

Ten boys came at once, and within a few weeks the mother of one of the boys was converted, and has since then been my greatest help in visiting amongst the women; she is now learning to read, so that she may be more efficient in her work.

The school soon increased to twenty-five, most of them bright, intelligent lads from nine to fifteen. Some of them have committed to memory the whole of "Peep of Day," portions from the gospels, a book similar to "Great Truths," and one or two other small books.

Their power of memorising is wonderful; they repeat chapter after chapter without any mistakes. Some of the older boys are learning "Pilgrim's Progress." They gain a thorough knowledge of Bible truth, upon which the SPIRIT of GOD can work in their hearts now, or, in some cases, it may be, years hence.

In addition to the books I have named, they learn some of their own classics, and this year they will be taught geography and arithmetic. Their teacher is a Christian Chinaman. Every Sunday afternoon, at 2.30, they meet for a children's service, specially held for them. In the mornings they attend a service held by one of the missionaries.

In visiting amongst the women lately, I have been asked by some who have little ones if I had a day-school for girls, to which I had to reply in the negative. After thinking and praying about this matter, I felt led to open a school for girls—they are quite as capable of learning as the boys, and, as it has been truly said, "the hand that rocks the cradle—rules the world"; so we cannot estimate the future blessing that may follow the training of these little ones in the right way, while even now, through them, the parents will hear the "old, old story," which we hope may not only make them wise unto salvation, but help them in bearing the trials of life, in hope of the "rest that remaineth for the people of GOD." I ask for your sympathy and prayers in this work. The schools will not be supported by Mission funds, but carried on in dependence upon Him who has promised to supply all our need, "according to His riches in glory by CHRIST JESUS."

Visiting Old Opium Patients.

FROM MR. PEAT.

P'ING-YAO, *Dec. 31st.*—I send you an account of my visit to Wen-shui and district. A large door, and effectual, seems to have been opened there; we were everywhere pressed to stay longer or to come again soon, and splendid opportunities were afforded of preaching the Word. Pray much for this promising district. We had received pressing invitations through our opium patients to go and visit them in their homes at Wen-shui. So on Mr. Orr-Ewing's return from Ling-shih, on December 10th, we agreed that it would be a good opportunity for me to accept the invitation and to accompany Mr. Chang. On Monday morning early we set off, led by one of the Wen-shui men who had just broken off his opium. It was beautiful mild weather, often more like spring than winter. We walked, carrying all we needed in our shoulder bags. I had a selection of gospels and books for sale, and tracts for distribution. Although our friend Liu, who had recently broken off opium, at first thought he would not be equal to such a long walk, he got on bravely; the LORD renewing his strength. It was nice to see him so happy, singing as he went along the songs of Zion that he had learnt while breaking off his opium with us. It became dark before we reached his village home, so we took refuge for the night in another village, the home of another opium patient, a Buddhist priest, who was among the first cured from that district. He himself was not at home, but his brother priest made us heartily welcome, giving us ample refreshment and rest for the night, in return for which we preached to him the gospel of free salvation through CHRIST alone. I believe he would gladly give up Buddhism.

On Tuesday morning, after a pleasant walk of ten *li*, we reached Ma-si, the home of our friend Liu, beautifully situated at the foot of the hills. On our way to his house we went in to see the village teacher—another of our late opium patients—whom we found among his little scholars. Liu's mother and friends were very pleased to see him home again, and gave us, also, a very hearty welcome. How thankful they seemed that their son and brother had given up his opium and was looking so well and healthy. After a meal we went to visit other opium patients in two adjoining villages, intending to return and spend the night in Liu's home, but on getting to the next village there were so many friends to visit, and they were so gracious in their offers of hospitality, that we found it impossible to get back that night. Here there were five opium patients, whom we visited in their homes, having opportunities of coming in contact with other villagers and telling them of the saving love of JESUS. In one of these homes the family unanimously agreed, and while we were there took their paper idols and burnt them in the fire. We afterwards gathered the opium patients with others, in the house of one of their number, and had a nice little service. O how glad one was to hear their songs of praise rising to GOD from their own village home, where only recently the devil had had it all his own way. Before retiring to rest I went out for a little. It was a beautiful clear starry night, and everything was still; when suddenly the silence was broken by the sound of footsteps passing along the single street of which the village is composed, and a voice sounded loud and clear through the frosty air, singing, "JESUS loves me." It did seem sweet indeed to my ears, and I am sure it must have been as sweet incense to the LORD JESUS Himself. Can one help praying that very soon all over this vast empire there may be in every village such living witnesses to the fact that JESUS loves the sons of men.

On Wednesday morning, after a good night's rest, we were preparing to return to Ma-si, where we intended having our morning meal before proceeding on our way to Wen-shui city. However, the kind people out of whose homes the idols had been destroyed, had got up early and prepared their simple morning repast, and would take no refusal to have us breakfast with them. The kind hospitality we received at the hands of these simple country people was really very touching. We were accompanied by our friends to the outskirts of their village, and proceeded on our way to Ma-si. Here we visited two other opium-patients, one of whom destroyed his idols, and bought a complete New Testament.

After a pleasant walk at the base of rugged and barren hills, we reached Wen-shui after midday. This city is said to have a population of about 20,000 souls, and I found, in going through the shops with tracts, that most of its business people are natives of P'ing-yao. In this large city, surrounded as it is with many flourishing villages, it is a sad fact that there is at present no labourer for these fields, white to the harvest.

Our friend Liu, from Ma-si, still acting as our guide, took us first to the homes of two opium patients in the city, after which we made our way to the north suburb, where are the homes of the majority of our Wen-shui friends. We received a hearty welcome from an old man named Chang, who seemed very happy in soul, and continually asked us to join in singing hymns, of which he was very fond. We were not long in his home before one and another of the opium patients, hearing that we had arrived, came to welcome us. They all seemed bright and happy, and the fat faces and healthy looks of most of them showed that they were no longer slaves to the deadly pipe. The LORD gave me a good opportunity of pressing upon them all the necessity of true repentance, and I believe He blessed the message. I asked who among them were willing to destroy their false gods? They all expressed themselves as willing, but several of them said they were not in a position to do so, as their parents were unwilling. Old Chang, in whose house we were, set them a good example by there and then putting his old paper idol in the fire, and when we went to the home where we were to sleep, our host also took down his idols and burnt them, but not without first getting the rather reluctant permission of his old mother. This made four sets of idols within two days. Hallelujah!

In Memoriam.

MR. J. H. RACEY.

THE following lines from Canada tell of another consecrated life taken from the MASTER's service here to His service above. As yet we have no other tidings. Our brother, Mr. RACEY, went to China in 1888 with Mr. Taylor in the first C. I. M. party from Canada, and after studying in the training home at Gan-k'ing for a time, was sent to Che-foo on account of health. Dr. Douthwaite found him in rapid consumption, and as he did not benefit by treatment or the sea air, sent him to California as the only chance of prolonging his life. He endeared himself to all who came in contact with him.

EXTRACT FROM A LETTER FROM MR. H. W. FROST, OF TORONTO.

APRIL 21st.—We have received word this morning from Mr. Frank McCarthy, now at Los Angeles, California, of the falling asleep of our beloved brother, Mr. Racey. Recent letters had prepared us somewhat for this; and yet the sad news comes to us with a great shock. The dear friend was much beloved by us all. Although he was little known to us personally, his submissiveness and gentleness, and especially his self-forgetfulness, had manifested themselves through his letters so clearly that we had come to regard him with special fervency of spirit.

Mr. Racey has failed steadily ever since he has been in California. A few weeks ago he had a hemorrhage, and this left him weaker than ever, so weak, indeed, that he could not walk, and had to remain in his bed. Just recently a second hemorrhage came on, which was followed by rapidly increasing weakness, which finally produced unconsciousness, in which condition he fell quietly and gently to sleep. He is in the presence of the KING, and for his sake, as well as for the SAVIOUR's sake, we are glad. The little time of blessed service will soon be over for us all, when we shall know as not now, and be able to say, as not now, Surely "He *hath* done all things well."

On the Borders of Hu-nan.

FROM MRS. LAWSON.

SHIH-SHEO, *Feb. 17th.*—We arrived here on Jan. 3rd, and have been very busy since; large crowds are coming every day, many from HU-NAN. Many thousands have heard the Gospel in a very short time; one wonders where the people come from. The work is very trying to the flesh, but as our day so has our strength been, and every day we have had some new thing to praise the LORD for. He is working in many hearts, and with this the devil is very busy.

One woman has been coming every day for some time; she never thinks of talking about anything but the Gospel. For over ten years she has not worshipped idols, because of dissatisfaction. She is meeting with opposition at home already, but she tells her family decidedly that she intends to receive JESUS into her heart. A man came a few days ago, a distance of 200 *li*, from HU-NAN, and is now living with us. Two years ago he bought a Gospel; last year he came again to hear more; this time he has come believing. He will not take his food from us, but goes out for it, saying, "The doctrine is one thing and my food is another." A man who broke off his vegetarianism here is very earnest. An old farmer, who lives sixty *li* from here, has paid us two visits. My husband questioned him on fundamental truths, and he answered most correctly; he has been coming for a long time, and seems most sincere. We hope to see him and a few others join the church soon.

The people, on the whole, are friendly, although each day we have much to contend with. We like the place well, and can now get out for a short walk daily, and in this way let the people see that we are not afraid of them; they generally follow us in large crowds.

A Frequent Testimony.

EXTRACT FROM MR. A. H. HUNTLEY TO MR. BROOMHALL.

CHEN-KU, SHEN-SI, *January 21st.*—My coming to China has truly been a blessing to myself, and also, I am rejoiced to know, to the poor heathen. Among those whom the LORD has given me is my teacher. He found it hard to come out and be separate; but, by GOD'S grace, he *has* come out very decidedly, and now when I am not using him in study he, of his own free will, preaches in the chapel. For him and some others, I do truly rejoice; and praise the matchless wisdom and grace of GOD, first for having led me to Himself through Jesus; and secondly, for having led me to this, the noblest of all Christian work.

If you are brought at any time in connection with any of my fellow-colleagues at the Pastor's College, please impress upon them what *real*, solid joy is given to those who follow out the SAVIOUR'S last command.

You may also tell them that I am happy in this GOD-given privilege, and since my stay in China (over two years) have never either felt any regret for having come, or desired to return and become one of those who bring up the *rear* of CHRIST'S grand army.

Tidings from Scattered Workers.

Shen-si Province.

FROM REV. G. F. EASTON.

Han-chung, Jan. 9th.—We are toiling on, with joys and sorrows, encouragements and discouragements, all intertwining and weaving the fabric of our life-work; the pattern is not always what we would have it to be; there are many departures from the ideal, and yet in spite of all the broken threads and entanglings GOD works His own will into it, and we believe it brings some pleasure to Him.

Some few souls are turning to GOD and give us much joy, and we see more of CHRIST in some of the dear believers, for whom we greatly desire an extraordinary outpouring of the HOLY SPIRIT, that they may more clearly understand themselves to be a sacred and separated people, and may seek more heartily to win souls. I believe GOD is going to greatly use these people by-and-by.

We are a rather small company in Han-chung now; Dr. Wilson and family, Misses Johnson and Holme, and ourselves living in three separate houses in different parts of the city. Mr. Huntley is in charge at Cheng-ku, where the work is very encouraging. There is to be another bonfire of idolatrous things there to-morrow.

FROM MR. BOTHAM.

Feng-tsiang Fu, Feb. 11th.—We find our little shop is not much use for preaching in. We get crowds at the door who listen attentively, but they seem afraid to come in. Praise the LORD, this does not prevent their hearing the Gospel, for we can always get a congregation on the street, and after preaching we nearly always get a few visitors. I have recently taken an idea from a native, and had a tract written out on a piece of calico five feet square. I have only tried it twice, but found it answer very well indeed, so I hope to use it often. I leave it hanging on the shop door, or on a wall in some open place all day, and go several times to preach to the people who gather round. In this way many have a chance of reading it when I am not there, and, so far, no one has done anything to spoil it.

Last week we were much encouraged by seeing a SI-CH'UEN man and his wife brought to a knowledge of the truth. They were passing through this city, and stayed three days in the inn of which our shop is a part. Mrs. Botham got into conversation with the woman and told her of the SAVIOUR. She was greatly interested, and went and told her husband. Shortly afterwards I saw him, and tried to put the Gospel clearly to him. Next morning they came to our room to prayers, and said that they had been talking of what had been told them for a good part of the night. They were very attentive to the reading and explaining of God's Word, and after prayer they told us that they had been praying for years, and for some time had been vegetarians, but that they were not one whit the better, but rather worse. "Now," they said, "we have found the truth." It was a sign of their sincerity that, though exceedingly poor, they did not ask us to help them in any way, but seemed as though they would like to give us something to show their gratitude for the good news we had brought them. It was good to see how they realised that they were sinners, needing a SAVIOUR. On the second morning the woman said at prayers, "We are sinners; how can the LORD listen to us?" We think they understood the way to GOD before they left. Our last words to them were to tell them to remember JESUS as SAVIOUR and MEDIATOR. Their last words to us were to ask us to pray for them. May the HOLY SPIRIT go with them!

Our brothers Redfern and Bland are at a place twenty *li* from here. They have a good deal of travelling, and love to tell the story.

Shan-si Province.

FROM MISS JAKOBSEN.

Hoh-chau, Jan. 28th.—A man came to the services last Sunday, and asked if we would go to his home, forty *li* away, and pray for his child, who was ill. I could not well leave, so I asked two of the native Christians to go. After worship on Monday morning they went, and came back the next day full of praise, telling of the simple-hearted people they had met with amongst the hills, and their readiness to listen to the Gospel; also about the taking down of idols in three homes. It was suggested that we should have a praise meeting, and we all knelt down and mingled our praises with prayer that more light might be given to these poor souls who seemed so willing to receive it.

I went to a village one day to see a sick woman, and returned to the city next morning, after having had worship with the people. Three of the Christians came with me, and we had blessed conversation along the road; but some of them have funny ways in which they explain the Bible. One asked me what hidden meaning there was in the five loaves and two fishes. I asked what he thought, and after a good while, he said, "May not the two fishes mean the Old and New Testament, and the five loaves the five virtues or the five elements?"

Mr. Hsi arrived this evening. It is so good of the LORD to send him for to-morrow's services. He had no breakfast before he left Hung-t'ung, and all day on the road he had no food. When he arrived here, tired and weary, he still ate nothing, and led three meetings the next day without any food. His reason for thus fasting was partly this: It has always been the rule here for the men who came to the services on Sunday to have a meal in the middle of the day in the front of the house, and for the women to have a meal with us at the back. Mr. Hsi altered this rule lately, and this was his first visit to Hoh-chau since. In one of the meetings on Sunday he wept when he said, "As you have come a long way and all day have had no food, I did not wish to have any either," and he told them that this rule had to be altered because there are not a few who say, "You believe in GOD for the food you get." "I am glad to see that so many of you have come to the meetings, although you do not get any food; we have to step this evil speaking." Before he left Mr. Hsi comforted the dear Christians here, saying "There was a time when JESUS could not work. It was when He was in the grave. It is the same with Hoh-chau now, but look forward to the resurrection morning."

I have seven women staying with me just now and two girls. Some of the women are learning to read and to repeat the Ten Commandments and verses from Scripture. Some of them give me great joy. Last Sunday, after the noon service, I was called to an opium case. It was a young man of twenty years old in one of the richest families in Hoh-chau. He was very far gone, but he came round after a while.

Those whom I have written about who took down their idols have been here each Sunday since. They leave their homes before daybreak, and arrive here before any of the other village people, although they have to walk forty *li* (twelve miles). It is so nice to see them. It is a great joy to live among these people and to see them one after another turn to GOD.

Chih-li Province.

FROM MRS. SIMPSON.

Hwuy-luh, Feb. 8th.—You will no doubt have heard from Mr. Pigott of our return to Hwuy luh. This step was taken after much prayer and waiting upon GOD. We enjoyed Mr. Pigott's visits so much, and profited largely by it in many ways. He was very much pleased with the one young man (the landlord's son) at Ying-tseng and our two servants, who were following JESUS, and hoped to be able to return this way in two months' time and baptise them.

At the Chinese new year we had specially good times. For three or four days our courtyard was crowded from morning to night. We sang hymns, and spoke again and again, and repeatedly were asked to go on (no account was taken whether we had breath or not). A particularly good feeling was manifested during these days, and, as our increased numbers at evening prayers showed, there was an inquiring spirit which we had not seen before. When we came away, I am safe in saying that a crowd of several hundreds gathered in the streets—all friendly, just desiring to speak a few words, or to give us some little present. We hope to visit them once a month, if at all possible, until some one comes to settle there. The landlord's son is suffering much persecution at home. His father threatened to turn him out and to beat him. In a crowd before we left he said, "I am the only one here who openly follows JESUS; I am not afraid or ashamed to say so. Although the foreigners are going away, JESUS will not go; He will be with me, and if anyone wants to know more, I shall be so glad to tell them all I know." He accompanied us far outside the village, and again and again pressed Mr. Simpson's hand, and said, "I am so sorry to lose you, only I must just pray more to JESUS to give me wisdom, and to help me to understand His Word, even without any one to teach me." All the time large tears were rolling down his cheeks. He put up his rough, dirty hand to wipe them away, making his face a sad spectacle. He said, "I am longing for the time when I shall be baptised. I know it will be worse for me, for my father hates me, and may turn me out; but if he does, I will be like the sparrows, and trust in GOD to give me one meal at a time, and I will preach the Gospel." May GOD help him to be firm and steadfast!

Since our return to Hwuy-luh, the devil seems to have suddenly wakened up and found his kingdom interfered with. My woman and her little girl have been so outspoken in telling all that they follow JESUS, and hate idolatry, and hope to prove it by being baptised soon. This has set a good many of her friends and mine against us, but there are some who are still friendly. One old woman is considering the advisability of taking down the idols she has worshipped for half a century. My woman was seeking to rent a room, and the neighbours met and said if she would not follow JESUS she might have it, but they were frightened that they would be troubled by her always preaching to them. I do so rejoice to see her so firm and decided, and her little girl no less so. It is such an encouragement, and she is such a help to me in every way. I am sure you will all pray for them and us. I think the opposition is a good sign.

Shan-tung Province.

FROM DR. DOUTHWAITE.

Che-foo, Feb. 11th.—I presume you have heard that Misses Knight and Ellis have decided to leave us [on account of poor health]. We shall miss them very much, and their leaving will be a great loss to the school, which now has a high reputation through their untiring labours. The standard of education is equal to that of any first-class school at home.

You will be pleased to know that in the late famine district in SHAN-TUNG there are now over a thousand applicants for baptism.

Ho-nan Province.

FROM MRS. HERBERT TAYLOR.

She-K'i-tien, Feb. 18th.—Herbert and I saw Misses Guinness and Crewdson on to their boat bound for Han-kow this afternoon. They have a nice comfortable boat, and a warm-hearted Christian man to escort them. When we came home the place looked very desolate. I shall miss them both so much. To-day, as we passed through the town to the boat, we could not help contrasting it with a little over a year ago. What a difference! Then, such crowds, all curiosity to see the foreigners. To-day we passed along with very little notice, except now and again a friendly voice would call us by name, and ask where we were going. We do not feel like foreigners here now. When we go out we are always sure of a warm welcome somewhere. There was real, true sorrow to-day in many hearts because of our sisters' leaving. "To GOD be the glory; great things He hath done."

This afternoon was my class afternoon. Miss Guinness used to take the children, Miss Crewdson the outside women, and I the Christian women and inquirers. This afternoon I had them altogether. The LORD was near, and we had a real helpful time. I have a class of eleven women and some boys learning to read the Romanised letters; they are getting on splendidly. I wonder if you will send any sisters up to us before Miss Guinness comes back? I will do my very best to keep the work going that has been begun. I have old Mrs. Li to help me. She is one of our baptised Christian women, and *a real treasure*. We shall be very busy. May the work be all for JESUS; work that will stand. Pray for us.

Si-ch'uen Province.
FROM MR. A. POLHILL TURNER.

Pa-chau, Jan. 13*th.*—The last half-year the work has been uphill. The women's work here gives us cause for thankfulness; though two old women of last year have rather disappointed us, yet others have come forward, and seem zealous to walk the heavenly road. The Sabbath-closing is a difficulty with many. We get large numbers of men to the preaching daily, and some keep on coming, yet we cannot point to any during the year as really converted souls. May the LORD soon give us souls!

We had a very bright young man, a stonemason, down here on his way from Cheng-ku to his home, in a village seventy *li* from here; though not yet baptised, we all got quite stirred up by his visit. I hope to visit the village shortly. I have visited some twenty markets in the neighbourhood, preaching and distributing tracts at each.

Hu-peh Province.
FROM MISS MARY BLACK.

Fan-ch'eng, March 3*rd.*—Mr. and Mrs. Nicoll will find much to encourage as well as much to try them in the work here. Mr. Kiang has good audiences in the front of the chapel from day to day, and the hall is well filled every Sunday. The Wednesday class has grown to large proportions. There are a good many inquirers, and several are anxious for baptism. I trust Mr. and Mrs. Nicoll may have as much joy in reaping as others have had in sowing. At the great harvest-home sowers and reapers shall rejoice together.

Gan-hwuy Province.
FROM MR. DARROCH.

K'u-chen, Jan. 3*rd.*—We have paid a visit to Fuh-hsing-tsih. The old man named Ts'ii, who has for a long time been the main pillar in the Church there, is seriously ill. He desires to be with the LORD, and asked me to pray that GOD would quickly and painlessly remove him to Himself. I wish that it might please GOD to spare the old man: he has been a helper of many, and now that the love of some is waxing cold, it seems as if for him to remain were more needful for us.

Mr. Ts'ii, who has been the evangelist here during the past year, has gone home to Gan-k'ing, and will, perhaps, not return. He had a good deal of influence in this place, and was respected by every one. If these two brethren, beloved in JESUS, are taken from us, we shall be weak indeed. Please pray that we may learn more and more to trust wholly in GOD, knowing that He is able to do exceeding abundantly beyond what we ask or think, apart from all earthly helps, however valuable.

In our absence a family of Christians came here, who had been flooded out of their home in An-tong Hien. They were very poor, almost starving, and our brethren received and helped them in a very Christ-like spirit. The family were originally well-to-do, and although their land is now flooded, they have planted part of it with wheat, which will be ripe in the fifth moon. They will be able to pull along here until then; afterwards they will go back and bear witness to JESUS again in their own home.

FROM MR. BEGG.

Hwuy-chau, Jan. 26*th.*—A blessed Sunday, ending with a really home-like testimony meeting. Mr. Eyres told us how he was led to the SAVIOUR. Then followed dear Mrs. Chen with a warm word for her JESUS, and it made our hearts burn within us as she told of her past life, her love of gambling, etc., but how JESUS had saved her, and now she longed to devote all her time to telling of Him. Then came Chen Nai-nai with her equally interesting testimony, and I don't think I have heard any native Christian speak so clearly on salvation through His blood. Ieh Nai-nai followed, and then our brother Iao; thus a happy, helpful evening was spent, the memory of which will long abide.

Jan. 29*th.*—Went to Mei-ling this forenoon for the purpose of having an open-air service in the evening. Hundreds assembled; I spoke for about an hour, and the people not being in the mind to scatter, Mr. Eyres' coolie mounted the chair and continued the service for some time longer. This is the place where our brother Pih gave up his opium den, and his name seems to be in everybody's mouth.

Kiang-su Province.
FROM MISS DOGGETT.

Yang-chau, Feb. 25*th.*— I am going with four other sisters on the 27th into KIANG-SI, and before leaving this happy home I feel I must write and tell you what a blessed time it has been since landing at Shanghai on Nov. 29th. I do indeed thank GOD for bringing me here; it is almost like leaving home again to say good-bye to the dear sisters, yet it is a great joy to be getting more into work. I am going to Miss Say at Kwei-k'i, Miss Gillham to Nan-k'ang Fu, Miss E. Ramsay and Miss Cowley to Ho-k'eo, and Miss Carlyle to Gan-ren.

Kwei-chau Province.
FROM MR. S. R. CLARKE.

Kwei-yang, Jan. 5*th.*—May I ask you to make it a special request at the Saturday prayer-meeting that our Kwei-yang Christians, especially those who have been smokers, may be kept away from opium? I never was in such a place as this for opium-smoking and poisoning. About a fortnight ago we had six cases of opium-poisoning in twenty-four hours. Three or four a day is not an uncommon occurrence!

FROM MR. WINDSOR.

Kwei-yang, Feb. 12*th.*—The work at Gan-p'in is looking bright. Many have been cured of opium-smoking, several have destroyed their idols, and a few are desiring baptism.

Mr. Mao has come from T'ung-chau for baptism, and has brought three men with him—two to be cured of opium-smoking, who are now under treatment, and one to learn more of the Gospel. Two of these have put away idolatry from their houses, and the other will do so on his return. There are many people in the place expecting me, and wanting to be cured of opium-smoking; I hope, therefore, to take some medicines with me, and probably stay some time, making that the centre from which to work the Tu-shan district.

Kiang-si Province.
FROM MISS BUCHAN.

Yuh-shan, Dec. 27*th.*—It is now nearly a year since our party landed in China, and we can all say, "Hitherto hath the LORD helped us." The past year has been one of great blessing to me. My progress in the language is slow, but still I think it is steady. I have taken one or two small [women's] meetings, and Miss Mackintosh says my idiom and tones are good, but at present I have great difficulty in expressing myself.

The Church here seems to be very bright; some of the members are so nice and earnest, it is quite a pleasure to see their happy faces all so different from their idol-worshipping neighbours; the religion of JESUS CHRIST is to them a reality, enabling them to live worthy in some small measure of the love which redeemed them.

Miss Grabham and I spent two very happy months with Miss Say in Kwei-k'i. We went out once or twice a week with the Biblewoman, and did what we could with her help in speaking to the women in their homes; it was very enjoyable work; the women were not afraid of us, but as a rule welcomed us. In this way we used what Chinese we did know, and felt our store increasing every week. The people of China are very good; they seldom laugh at our broken words; neither do they take it amiss if we listen to what they say and repeat it after them.

It is very comforting to know that so many are praying for us.

From Miss Guex.

Yuh-shan, Feb. 24th.—I visit now regularly in and outside the city, and have also been to several villages. How many sad hearts, how many suffering from sin one meets with! How glad one is to go to such with such good news, to speak to them of the living and true God, a very present help in time of trouble, to tell them of a living Saviour, a man of sorrows and acquainted with grief, who died that they might live. Oh, to be all the time in the spirit of the Master when He thus poured out His life for the lost! Oh, for a heart *full to overflowing* with His constraining, unspeakable love for sinners! " Our sufficiency is of God." What a sweet rest for the labourers together with Him—we the instruments, He the perfect Builder. Pray much for the church in Yuh-shan and for the candidates waiting for baptism. I do love the dear Christians very much, and find a real deep joy in being right among the natives. For fifteen years I have longed for what is now my blessed privilege, and I do want to give my whole life to the Chinese till Jesus comes, and with the help of the Holy Ghost to magnify the God of love among them.

Cheh-kiang Province.

From Mr. Heal.

Sin-ch'ang, Feb. 25th.—During the Chinese first month we had a large number of country people and others in the city; whenever the chapel was opened we had it crowded. Some seemed glad to hear the Gospel, and I trust that now they have returned to their village homes they will remember it, and that the Holy Spirit will open their hearts to receive it. We shall be very glad to get a larger place of worship, but must wait the Lord's time. Two have asked for baptism, and one to be received back.

From Mr. Wright.

Ch'u-chau.—Gladly do I try to give you some little account of the Lord's marvellous goodness during my last journey. Every door was thrown open to us, and the general cry was—"Can you not stay longer?" We spent two days, a day, or half a day in a village, and often we felt it a pity that such a splendid field should be without workers. May the Lord bless the little that has been done. Our first night was spent in a village twenty *li* from Wu-i Hien. Crowds gathered round me, and listened to the old old story, and after it was dark some waited on, listening as long as I was able to speak. Next night we were twenty *li* further in a quiet village at the foot of the hills, and long shall I remember the happy time spent in the courtyards of some houses there. The people wanted to hear more and were sorry to see us go so soon. Our next stay was in the largest village in the district. The people seemed so kind and willing to listen to the doctrine, that we decided to spend the Saturday and Sabbath there. On Saturday we also visited four other villages, and how gladly the people received us. Even now the kind earnest faces of some of those dear old people, who so willingly listened to what I said, come up before me. O that some one was with them to lead them to the truth! Why should such an open and hopeful field be left without a worker?

On Saturday the landlord of the inn, hearing that we desired to preach, offered us the use of his ancestral hall and theatre platform. We gladly accepted his offer, and thanked God for thus opening the way before us. We invited the villagers to come and hear, and after singing a hymn, the place was pretty well crowded, holding I should say from 200 to 300 people.

The Gospel was preached for about an hour and a half, and many waited the whole time, and I talked with some afterwards who were delighted that we had preached to them, and seemed to have gathered the rudiments of the truth. In another village the people listened almost an hour, and bought up every book and gospel we had with us.

I find much cause for thankfulness in Ch'u-chau. The number of enquirers is increasing, and a few Mahommedans are seeking the truth. Praise God.

Yung-k'ang.—After I wrote from Ch'u-chau, I returned to Sung-yang Hien, spending three days there, which were days of blessing, especially in the villages; the people in the city did not receive us as the country people did. The people in Siu-ch'ang seemed like the Suan-p'iog people, and as willingly welcomed the doctrine of Jesus Christ. One afternoon was spent at their request in their largest temple, where the people came in large numbers to listen. After we had finished, one young man came forward, and said he wanted to buy a New Testament, that he might know more of that " light " and that " way " we had spoken of. I wonder *when* there will be some one to teach them. It seems such a pity that places so open should be left without any one to tell the way of salvation.

I returned to Yung-k'ang on the 2nd inst., and found that all had gone on as if I had been there. During my absence a small house had been rented in Hu-chen, a large market town sixty *li* distant from here; we have had two or three enquirers there for some time, and the church thought that we ought to open a little hall there, and it is done. Much success is following the effort to spread a knowledge of the Gospel in the various villages near the city. I was in one to-day, and was surprised at the knowledge of the truth they had.

From Miss Boyd.

Kiu-chau, Feb. 14th.—I started off with Choh-ma, my woman, at twelve. We made one halt at a little place about half way, where we got out of our chairs and spoke for a little. After two hours' travel, we reached a place where we had a good hearing, especially in one house. Then on again to another village, where the vegetarian woman lives. As she had particularly asked Choh-ma not to come again, saying, " None of their village believed this Gospel," etc., I had a little fight first of all to make Choh-ma see that *I* meant to go, and then it was curious how, step by step, I had to stand my ground.

When we reached Li-chia, where the woman lives, we had a good crowd, and spoke for some time to about fifty or so of all ages and both sexes. As she did not appear, I got Choh-ma to lead the way to her part of the village. There they were going to give us a stool in a small passage. " This will not do," I said; so they led the way to a large square, and there we held forth, the old vegetarian listening. I think God gave Choh-ma special strength at the point she had dreaded, for I never saw her stand up and speak more boldly or decidedly. There is no mincing matters when she declares the truth: The idols, vegetarianism, and the rest of such things are all empty and false, and lead to hell, while the Blood of Jesus will wash clean and give you peace now and happiness in heaven. Such is the burden of her talk, and she says it as one who believes every word, as one who has tasted and proved the Truth. I do thank God for her. She seems so strengthened physically, mentally, and spiritually since I came back this time. I hope she will live long to be a witness for God. I was never so attached to a Chinese, or felt so at one with any other. We had about two hours at the last village, and then home again.

Kan-suh Province.

From Miss Florence Ellis.

Ts'in-chau, Jan. 6th.—My sister and I are often able to be out together now. She and Miss Smalley have gone to-day to a village five *li* away to spend the day, and to bring back one of our old scholars to stay over the new year with us. Mr. Hunt will probably have told you that on the 19th of this month (native) three women and three men are going to confess Christ by public baptism. They need much prayer, especially at this season, when so much idolatry is practised. The attendance at the chapel is very good, both of men and women. On Sundays a good many women come to the class. Miss Kinahan is still at Si-ning.

Anniversary Meetings at the Conference Hall, Mildmay Park.

WEDNESDAY, MAY 21st, 1890.

Afternoon Meeting.

GEORGE WILLIAMS, Esq., Chairman.

The meeting was opened with the hymn:
"Onward, Christian soldiers."
Isaiah xii. was read by Rev. D. B. HANKIN, who then offered prayer.

The CHAIRMAN.

DEAR FRIENDS,—It is always a gratification to meet at the anniversary of the CHINA INLAND MISSION. Another year has passed; much good seed—the word of GOD, the truth of GOD—has been sown since our last gathering here; many hearts have been enlightened; many have been brought savingly to trust in the LORD JESUS. GOD in His great goodness, too, has preserved His servants. His shield has been over them, He has comforted and helped and strengthened them. We desire to-day to remember that we should praise the LORD, as we read in that 12th chapter of Isaiah, " Praise the LORD, call upon His Name, declare His doings among the people. . . . Cry out and shout thou inhabitant of Zion, for great is the HOLY ONE of Israel in the midst of thee." Great to provide the means, and we praise Him for the manner in which He has provided. But as the work extends, as extend it surely must, more means will be required, and may GOD who is in the midst of us, stir up our hearts and lead us to consecrate yet more and more to His blessed service.

"Praise the Lord, call upon His Name." That is one of the charms of this Mission—that there is so much prayer. And in answer to prayer the blessings come! Herein lies the strength of the missionary church. Weakness can do but little by itself. You will remember that saying of Luther, "If it is the Pope and Luther, well, then the Pope will have it; but if it is the Pope against Luther and Luther's GOD, woe be to the Pope!" And so it is with us, beloved friends, wherever we are labouring: if GOD is with us we have omnipotent power, power all-sufficient to supply every necessity; let us trust in Him and rejoice in Him in the future as in the past. "Declare His doings among the people." That is what the CHINA INLAND MISSION is doing.

The large Conference that they have just had in China cannot fail to have stimulated all the workers who were privileged to gather together, and I am told that they have adopted dear Mr. Hudson Taylor's suggestion—that of sending out a thousand more missionaries. What a large heart Hudson Taylor has, has he not? A thousand more missionaries, five hundred from Europe and five hundred from America and Canada! Now, if a thousand more could be sent out, and the money raised to support that thousand, Mr. Hudson Taylor and others think that every family in China might be visited in three years, and have the glad tidings of great joy spoken to them. Nothing is impossible with God. We have had wonderful things before in answer to prayer. You remember the hundred that were sent out as a Jubilee thankoffering. "All things are possible to him that believeth." Mountains are to be removed in answer to prayer. Now here is a mountain: who shall say that GOD will not raise up and send out this thousand? many going at their own costs, many delighting, not to sacrifice themselves, but to receive the honour and privilege of being ambassadors to declare to the heathen in China the unsearchable riches of CHRIST.

THEODORE HOWARD, Esq.

In the absence of our dear friend, Mr. Taylor, I have great pleasure in reading a letter which we have just received from him.

Letter from Rev. J. Hudson Taylor to the friends assembled at the Annual Meetings.

DEAR FRIENDS,

The mail from Singapore affords me an opportunity of posting a letter to you, of which I gladly avail myself. Though absent from the meetings in person, I shall be with you in spirit, as will many of our workers in China. May the earnest prayers for blessing which have gone up and will yet be offered for all those who attend the meetings, either as speakers or hearers, be abundantly answered. Your prayers for us we count on. As our numbers increase and the work grows we need all the more prayer. Each new station opened and each effort to open one brings its own record of difficulties; for our work is a warfare, and we are sure of opposition, at least, from those unseen but mighty powers, the wicked spirits in heavenly places, and not seldom, also, from opponents who make themselves both seen and felt. And the more successful we are in winning souls for our MASTER, the deeper antagonism we may expect from the powers of darkness. Where, then, is our strength or even our safety to be found, save in abiding in CHRIST?

We ask your fervent prayers that *all* our workers may be kept so abiding ; and beg for special remembrance for those who, as senior missionaries, superintendents, members of our councils and directors, are sure to be specially tried, and who need special guidance and support.

I regret that I cannot present to you a detailed account of the work of the past year. Having been detained in England till too late to reach China in time to post back for the annual meetings, and yet leaving England too early to receive full particulars from our more distant stations, a fuller report must appear in the columns of CHINA'S MILLIONS. At Colombo, of the letters from China which I received, three were dated December and one November, so that, even now, all last year's information has not been received. To a few of the general facts, however, I will briefly refer.

1. *The Number of Missionaries.*—Last year's report gave 332 as the number of workers in China and on furlough. A list published in the number of CHINA'S MILLIONS for April, 1890, gave 358 as in China or on furlough on January 1st. To them we may add the Rev. George Hunter, M.A., and Mrs. Hunter, late of Stranraer, and the three young men who sailed with them on December 12th, bringing the total number of workers for 1889 to 363 (including associates).

Though not among those to be reported for 1889, we may here mention that from England ten new workers sailed in January; and from America, also, ten left in January and on February 3rd. So in March, 1890, the total, including associates, was 383. It is no small joy to me that among the last party from England was my dear son Dr. F. Howard Taylor, the third of my children who has joined our work. May I here ask prayer for the children of all our missionaries, that they may all be converted and blessed, and that many of them may be called to missionary service?

II. *The Number of Stations.*—In 1888 there were 77 stations in which there were resident missionaries, besides 68 out-stations, worked principally by native helpers. A list received in England (if my memory serves me, in November) gave 87 as the number of stations, so that there is at least an increase of ten. This does not at all represent adequately the growth of the work in 1889, as additional out-stations have also been opened.

III. *Additions to the Number of Communicants by Baptism.*—In the absence of a complete list, I can only mention that letters already received have mentioned over 500 persons as baptised during the year. I do not yet know the number removed by death or discipline, so cannot state the nett increase of communicants.

Great care is now taken in most of the stations not to baptise candidates without a previous testing probation, in which the profession of each one of having passed from death unto life has been supported by the testimony of a consistent walk. We may therefore hope that there will be fewer subsequent disappointments than where this precaution has been neglected. As an evidence of growth in grace among the converts, we may add that the number of *unpaid* native preachers has considerably increased. For this we are profoundly thankful : no feature of the work is more cheering. The hope for the future lies, in no small measure, on the work of the HOLY SPIRIT through the spontaneous efforts of the native Church.

IV. *Our Funds.*—With a larger number of workers, there has not been a proportionate increase in the contributions in England for the general purposes of the Mission. The small remittances caused considerable exercise of faith to the workers in China, and led to much earnest prayer, especially during the autumn. But the LORD answered prayer in various ways. Some of the members of the mission in China received special gifts or legacies, and many contributed liberally to our funds. One donor at home, who had contributed a considerable sum to the Home Building Fund, finding that the operations could not at once commence, transferred the gift to the General Fund. The money contributed for the floods, etc., proved more than was needed, and the principal donors were consulted as to their wishes. Some left their gifts to be used in future distresses, some transferred them to the general funds, and some were transferred to our Medical Mission Fund. In China we received liberal gifts from friends who knew the work there. So in one way or another the needs were met. Truly it is *safe* to trust in the LORD, and it is most blessed too !

V. *Mission Premises.*—The LORD has graciously prospered us in erecting very suitable premises in Shanghai, into which our friends moved early in 1890. The funds were all contributed in China, though much of them passed through the home accounts. (We hope that in due time we may be warranted by the state of our Home Building Fund to build in London on the excellent freehold site which the LORD has given us near Pyrland Road, and that the home-work also may have the benefit of premises more adapted to our present and prospective needs.)

In Kiu-kiang also suitable premises have been acquired for mission use. But we are still greatly needing mission premises in Hankow and Chin-kiang—especially in the former port. Neither the requisite buildings, nor suitable sites, for our extending work have yet been obtainable, and we need the prayers of our friends for these objects.

VI. *Fund for Superannuated Missionaries.*—This is not, of course, a part of our China work ; but being intended for the benefit of the workers in China, it may be referred to here. The question has often been asked, "What will your missionaries do when they are superannuated?" and the reply has been, "Just what they are doing now—*rely* on the faithful promises of GOD, and *experience* their fulfilment." But *before* any of them *are* superannuated—our senior missionary, who went out in 1862, is still in vigorous service—GOD has put it into the heart of one of our oldest and most liberal friends to found a special fund for worn-out workers by a donation of £4,000, hoping that many others will sympathise with his desire to see such workers provided for independently of the current income of the Mission, and will add to the fund. May the LORD abundantly reward our kind friend and sustain him in his old age with every blessing !

Lastly, may I ask your earnest prayers that the whole Church shall be stirred up to quickly obey our SAVIOUR'S great command to "preach the Gospel to *every* creature," so far as China is concerned ? We have shown the possibility of speedily obeying this command in the pages of CHINA'S MILLIONS and in *The Christian*. A little reprint of this paper, called "To Every Creature," has been published by Messrs. Morgan and Scott at 6d. per dozen, and can be had, at the close of this meeting, by those who will help to circulate it. The force of the argument and the practicability of the plan have been recognised by many missionaries in China and by returned missionaries in America and Europe ; not a few are daily praying for its accomplishment. The question has been raised, Could not native Christians do the work? To which we may reply that there are few, if any, not now employed who are fit for such work *alone ;* but many who, *with* the foreign evangelist, would be of great service, and who would, *in the course of the work*, receive the same kind of training which CHRIST gave to His disciples and Paul to those who travelled with him. It would be a great blessing to the whole Church to do the work ; hence our desire to see many missions and countries engaged in it. We feel no doubt that the thing is of GOD, and hence are assured that it *will* be accomplished. It only remains to be seen *who* will come "to the help of the LORD, to the help of the LORD against the mighty." Let none of us be among those who will be ashamed before the LORD at His coming, on account of indifference to His last-expressed wish, His last emphatic command ere He ascended on high.

"Brethren, pray for us!" You are partners with us in this great work for the glory of CHRIST and the good of the perishing heathen. Soon we shall rejoice and share the spoil together; and in the meantime let us pray and work for one another as the LORD enables us.

Yours gratefully in CHRIST,

April 16th, 1890. J. HUDSON TAYLOR.

Mr. BROOMHALL.

MISSIONARIES.

AFTER the letter that you have just heard read from Mr. Taylor it will only be needful for me to make a very brief statement. During last year there left for China from this country thirty-five missionaries, besides two associates and two members of the Swedish Mission. Two also left from Canada, making an increase to the force working in connection with this Mission of forty-one. During the present year (though it does not come strictly within our report to-day) seven have left, also two belonging to the Bible Christian Mission, one to the Norwegian Mission, and ten from Canada, bringing, as you have heard, the entire number now in connection with the Mission, including the associates and the wives of the missionaries, up to 383.

INCOME.

The total amount of money received by the Mission during last year was £51,484 1s 8d, but of that amount £9,188 9s. 6d. was contributed for the famine fund, £3,255 4s. 2d. for the building fund, £4,046 1s. 3d. for the superannuated missionaries' fund; and other special accounts, £1,351 12s. 4d., leaving available for the general purposes of the Mission £33,642 14s. 5d., an increase upon the receipts for the general account for the previous year of £3,638 2s. 10d. But, though there has been this increase of £3,600, it is not, as you have just heard from the letter from China, in proportion to the increase of workers. The brethren and sisters from America have been provided for by funds sent from that land. We have joyfully in the past raised our "Ebenezers," and we must continue to count upon the faithfulness of GOD in providing for those of His servants who have gone out to do His will; but He will be inquired of for these things.

BAPTISMS.

You will be glad to know, from a report received a few days since, that the number of baptisms during 1889 was 538. And for this in-gathering of more than five hundred, received, as Mr. Taylor's letter has told you, with more caution than has sometimes been exercised, there is cause for profound thankfulness to-day.

PUBLICATIONS.

It only remains for me to mention the publications of the Mission. A new edition of "CHINA'S SPIRITUAL NEED AND CLAIMS" has been published during the last few days. That is a book well known to most of you. There has also been published a new edition of "DAYS OF BLESSING IN CHINA." The circulation of these books could not fail to be helpful to the work generally, and we commend them to you. There is also another little publication to which reference has just been made. The title is "TO EVERY CREATURE; or, Shall China have a Thousand Evangelists without Delay?" It is published through Messrs. Morgan and Scott, at the price of sixpence per dozen. I am not so sanguine as my brother-in-law, Mr. Taylor, as to the number of people who can be reached in a given time, but I trust that there is no one here who does not heartily sympathise with the desire that the Gospel shall be preached to every creature. This was our SAVIOUR'S last and most solemn command, and no limit less than this will satisfy the heart of Him who tasted death for every man, and who now waits that He may see of the travail of His soul and be satisfied. It is in accordance with apostolic teaching that the Gospel should be proclaimed to every creature, to every man and woman living; and when the Christian Church awakes to a sense of its duty and privilege this will be its watchword, "To every creature," as it should be the earnest prayer and the resolute purpose of every individual Christian.

We cannot doubt for a minute that if there was a right sense of responsibility the work could be done both as to men and means. I often, in a public meeting of this kind, ask myself, "What will be the result of this meeting? Who will be the better for it?" and the question arises now, "How many more in China will hear the Gospel because of our gathering in this hall to-day?" That depends upon the action of each one of us—upon how much we may make it a matter of special prayer and of special endeavour. I trust that we may have, through the days that are coming, abundant evidence that GOD is working with us, and that He is raising up a noble band from the natives themselves who shall help to carry on the glad work of preaching salvation throughout China.

Mrs. HUDSON TAYLOR.

DEAR friends, I do feel that our new motto, "To every creature," is our MASTER'S message to us to-day, and that it is to be a new inspiration for us each one. The LORD in all His resurrection power is waiting for us: *waiting for us*; *kept* waiting till we carry His message. He is with us here now: "Lo I am with you alway." He has given us a great and a glorious work to do, and His business requires haste, for He is waiting till it is done. "This gospel of the kingdom shall be preached in all the world for a witness unto all nations, and *then* shall the end come." "Ye shall be witnesses unto Me .... unto the uttermost part of the earth."

Our aim has been in the past to reach every province, every city, but this year the old message has come with new power, "Go ye into all the world, and preach the gospel *to every creature.*" It was last October, on a Sunday, my birthday, in my Father's house at Hastings that the words were given to my dear husband, which were printed in the December number of CHINA'S MILLIONS. I shall never forget the thrill I felt. Since then the LORD has been laying His message on many other hearts in different lands; I am so glad this afternoon because we have just heard by telegram that the Shanghai Conference has taken up the appeal; and now GOD is speaking to us here. Do *you* love Him? Do you *owe* Him anything? Then He wants to speak to *you*, and to ask you what you have that you can bring to Him. What can you bring? Have you health and youth? Bring these to Him now, and perhaps He will give to you the glorious privilege of going for Him with the message of life to those who have never yet been told of His death on Calvary. Are you older and have you long proved His power and His faithfulness? Then does He want your faith, your prayers, your influence, your time, your money? look and see what you can bring to Him to-day; ask Him to show you, and then come and bring Him *all*. You have brought Him all before? Ah, see if He has not been giving you fresh gifts to lay at His feet. Bring Him some fresh fruit to-day. You, who may not go to the heathen, will you not pass on the message, "To every creature"; will you not take some of the little booklets and ask GOD to speak by them to your friends?

But some have said, You must train natives ; *they* must do this work. Yes, by GOD'S help we will ; we *are* doing it ; we will put them to the front ; we will seek to let GOD use them to the uttermost ; we will pray GOD to raise up many more full of faith and of the HOLY GHOST. But, dear friend, *no* native, no number of natives can do *your* work ; you have had privileges that the native Christians have not ; what part are you taking in giving the gospel to every creature? Train natives ; yes, we will train natives by going with them throughout the land and sharing with them the opposition of the devil, the difficulties of the work, and the glorious reward.

"To every creature" in China means a vast, an inconceivable number. Yet, with the MASTER'S authority and the MASTER'S power, the Church is well able to reach them, as has been shewn in the little pamphlet ; but the LORD must have *all* our loaves and *all* our fishes if the multitudes are to be fed.

We thank GOD for what the native Christians are doing : they can speak to their countrymen from their own standpoint as we cannot ; but they cannot do the work alone ; they are too few and too young in the faith. For pioneering work, too, without us they would be at a disadvantage, for they could not command the attention of the people, as the interest in us as foreigners enables us to do. Again, the question of the support of a large number of native evangelists, if we had them, would bring in a twofold difficulty : the little native churches in their poverty could not sustain them ; and if foreign money is used, experience has abundantly proved, first that their countrymen discount their words because they put it down that preaching is their way of earning a good living ; and, second, that a number of men in foreign pay is a sure way of attracting to the Church false professors.

A thousand men and women are needed by the LORD for China to carry out His last command—a thousand filled with His divine compassion, ready for self-sacrifice and hardship and toil—a thousand who have learned to stand alone with GOD and to live as serving Him who is invisible—a thousand to go "everywhere preaching the Word." So many thousands in our own little isle, one thousand for that vast land ! In the apostolic days it needed a persecution to scatter them abroad ; shall that be needed now ? Or will glad volunteers covet the privilege and honour? Dear friends, the people there are perishing for utter lack of the knowledge that you possess ; not once have they heard the glad tidings that here are so freely proclaimed. So many workers here, so few hungry seekers ! The MASTER'S own last word was, "To every creature," and England is the loser day by day, for He cannot work here as He would because His command has not been obeyed. Shall we not *all* be of one heart to reach "every creature"?

Mr. GEORGE ANDREW
(of the China Inland Mission, Kwei-yang, Kwei-chau).

CALLED TO CHINA.

I AM specially glad to see Mr. Williams in the chair this afternoon, because it was when I was a member of the Y.M.C.A. in Manchester that I first became acquainted with the work of the CHINA INLAND MISSION. The call came to me to go to China in the year 1880, and I said, "Here am I, LORD, send me," and very soon I was on my way to China, which I reached in the early part of the year 1881.

Going from Shang-hai, up the river Yang-tse, to the city of Han-kow, it was my privilege to meet with a dear brother, Mr. Broumton, who was a great help and blessing to me and others. We took our journey from Hankow, in the centre of China, through HU-NAN to KWEI-CHAU ; it occupied more than two months, and we did not pass one single mission station. Arriving in the city of Kwei-yang, we found two Christians there. After studying the language for a few months, Brother Easton and I were asked to go forward, and it was our privilege to open a station in the provincial capital of YUN-NAN. After that I went on to the city of Ta-li Fu, farther west, and lived there alone for more than nine months, preaching to the Chinese, and also meeting with a number of Thibetans, who came to the great fair that is held once a year in the city ; although I could not preach to them, yet I had some text-cards which I distributed amongst them.

It has been a great joy to go to places in Western China, and preach the Gospel where CHRIST'S Name has never been mentioned ; but it brings a feeling of sadness when we think of the number who have passed away beyond recall ; and when one stands up in the streets of a city, or town, or village to preach to the people who gather round, one's heart is pained to think that, before another missionary comes, a number of the hearers will have passed into eternity.

OPIUM.

After my marriage I went again to the city of Kwei-yang, where we laboured for several years.

The opposition that is met with there is to be met with in every city throughout China. We found that the devil was opposed to the Gospel ; we found that idolatry was opposed to the Gospel ; but there is one thing to which the people at Kwei-chau are especially addicted—the sin of opium-smoking. Opium is so cheap that all classes smoke it, from officials down to beggars. We have a number of Christians who were opium-smokers before their conversion. It is a terrible evil. I recollect Mr. Broumton one day bringing in a book that he had met with in the streets. It was about opium-smoking and its cure. It was being circulated in the city, and in this book again and again we found ourselves described as "foreign devils"—"foreign devils who had brought the foreign smoke to China." We have often been called foreign devils, but that is the only book that I have seen in which we are written about as foreign devils, and it is in association with opium.

METHODS OF WORK.

In preaching the Gospel we use various methods, and when the people do not want to hear it in one way we try to get them to hear it in another. We preached in the streets ; we also opened a preaching shop. Day after day we proclaimed the glad news of salvation there, and the LORD gave us results. I recollect one young man who used to come often to the preaching shop, but he never told us that he had become a Christian. We heard, after his death, that while lying on his death-bed he turned to his mother, and said, "Mother, what time is it?" And when his mother told him, he turned his face to the wall, and just uttered the prayer, "O LORD JESUS, Thou SAVIOUR, save me," and passed away.

We preached the Gospel, too, by taking our sheet tracts and paste-pot and brush, and ornamenting the walls here and there with Christian tracts. We circulated a great deal of Christian literature through the province, selling books, which have found their way into many cities and towns and villages. At the time of the examinations we distributed a large number of Christian books and tracts to the *literati*.

We opened a refuge, and got a number of men to give up opium-smoking; but we found that unless a man was willing to repent of his sins and turn to JESUS CHRIST to find the needful strength, he was nearly sure to go back again to his opium.

The year before last I was called to some

SEVENTY-FOUR OPIUM-POISONING CASES.

People of all classes poison themselves with the opium. It is done on the slightest provocation. Children who have been beaten by their parents, slave-girls who have been beaten by their mistresses, wives who have been beaten by their husbands, and sometimes people who cannot get on in life, take the opium to get rid of their misery.

Then, too, we travelled about north, south, east, and west of the provinces, taking CHRIST'S Gospel to as many cities and towns and markets as we could reach.

On the LORD'S Day, at eight o'clock in the morning, we used to gather for a prayer-meeting, which lasted, perhaps, till half-past nine. A native evangelist once said, 'I think we ought to have a prayer-meeting on Sunday evening in which each person can pray for himself;" and so they started a prayer-meeting after the service every Sunday night, and the prayers which were uttered there were such as, "LORD, the other day I took some wine," or, "LORD, the other day I told a lie," or, "LORD, the other day I went to sleep during the meeting. O LORD, forgive me, and help me not to do so again."

Every evening throughout the year at dusk we had an evangelistic service. Two or three nights a week we had meetings and classes for the instruction of the native converts or for inquirers. We preached the Gospel, too, by opening two schools.

THE CONVERTS.

We do thank GOD for the blessing granted to us in that city of Kwei-yang Fu. Where, fifteen years ago, there was not a single Christian, now there are between forty-five and fifty saved and baptised.

I wish there was time to tell you about these converts; several of them—the evangelist, the colporteur, and others—are fine men. I should like to tell you about one whom it was my privilege to baptise in Yun-nan Fu. JESUS CHRIST had to wait more than eighteen hundred years after He died upon the cross before He saw one Christian baptised in the south-western province of YUN-NAN!

In preaching the Gospel we look for conversion not merely from idolatry to Christianity, but from sin to righteousness. We look for a change of heart and a change of life. One of the first things that the native converts do is to learn to read. Many who come to us know no characters, but when they get converted, they want to read the Word of GOD for themselves, and they take out their money and buy a New Testament or hymn-book. They sit down and get off John iii. 16 by heart, or learn some familiar hymn, and then they get a Christian to show them where John iii. 16 is in the book, or where the hymn is, and they begin to spell it out for themselves. And while they are learning their characters they are also learning something about GOD which is a blessing to their own souls.

We teach the Chinese Christians that they must confess JESUS CHRIST not only by talking, but by their lives. In Kwei-yang Fu the heathen themselves expect more from Christians than from others. We thank GOD that they do. A heathen prays to his idols, and when he has finished he may lie or he may steal, and it will not be thought to be very bad; but if a Christian is found telling a lie or doing anything wrong, we are pretty certain to hear about it. The last letter which I received from Kwei-yang told me of the death of an old man named Pen, and that his relatives would not allow him to be buried in our Christian cemetery, but got their Tauist priest to come and burn candles and incense and chant prayers over the body of that old Christian. When Pen was converted I said to him, "Now, you must be willing to preach JESUS CHRIST. You cannot preach a sermon, but you can confess Him somehow. You can learn that little hymn, 'JESUS loves me,' and go and sing it." By-and-by I saw him again, and I said, "Well, Pen, did you sing that hymn in the street?" He said, "Yes, I did." "What did the people do?" "Oh," he said, "they called me a fool." The people in China, when they become Christians, must be willing to be accounted fools.

We teach the Christians to give themselves first of all to the LORD, and then to give their time; we teach them to keep the LORD'S Day and to come together to worship. There was one Christian who will bear to the grave the marks of a scar received for the Name of JESUS. He was going home one morning after our prayer-meeting, when he met a friend who said to him, "You *are* a foolish man to give up one day's work in every seven to help these people to worship GOD, and they will not even give you your rice to eat."

Then we teach the Christians that they must be willing to suffer for the Name of JESUS—to suffer in their homes, and to suffer among their friends and the people with whom they work.

WHAT THERE IS YET TO BE DONE.

The Gospel has been spreading of late years, and a station has lately been opened in the city of Gan-shun. There are some Christians there, and there are also Christians in another town, and a Christian man living at a place in the country. But, while we thank GOD for what has been done, we should like to impress upon you what there is yet to be done. Why, in that province of KWEI-CHAU we have forty-eight walled cities, and there are only two of them yet with Christian mission-stations—only two out of forty-eight! And then, throughout the West of China, you meet with the Lo-lo and the Miau-tsi, and the Yin-ren and the Ming-kia, and other aborigines who are still waiting for the Gospel, still in dense darkness, to whom *not one* missionary has yet been sent. When shall the light come to these poor aborigines of Western China? Pray for them; pray for us; and ask GOD to bless His work abundantly in those western provinces of China.

The CHAIRMAN.

We have a Chinese lady with us, the wife of one of our missionaries, who will kindly say a few words.

Mrs. PARKER.

OPIUM SMOKING.

I AM very glad to-day to stand here to tell you something of my own country. Just now Mr. Andrew spoke about opium and the opium-smokers. I belong to a family of opium-smokers, and I am able to tell you something about it. About thirty years ago if any one had gone to our family he would have found them very different from what they are now. I am now twenty-eight, and I remember that when I was a child of three or four years of age our family used to live in the country in a large house. There were thirty or forty families together in a nice comfortable place such as in your English towns you would call a square. It was like a country gentleman's house. At that time opium had but recently come to China; but about twenty years ago my father and others, all of them young men, took to opium.

After a time grandfather died, and when he died all the people in the village began to be lazy because the opium overcame them; they could not get up in the morning, and they could not do as they would; and so they began to sell their property and to destroy their houses; they would even take up the boards from the floor and sell them, and divide the money between them. Well, after that, my father became very poor. He was doing work for some of the mandarins. That was good work in China in those times. When he began to be dirty and lazy people would not employ him; so he has been out of business for the last twenty years, and now no one who saw him before would recognise him.

I was rescued when I was young, and sent to the missionaries, who are so kind to the children; so I have been brought into the fold of JESUS, and in later years GOD gave me a marriage which I could not have counted upon. But I believe it is all of GOD's grace to me and to my family. I may be able to help them in some way or other. I am living a different life to theirs. For the last ten years I have been travelling in different parts of China away from my native place. I was engaged in the service of GOD, but I have not done as much as I could wish, as I have been so often required to stay and keep the house and do other sorts of work.

OPIUM SUICIDES.

As to the opium suicides, they are dreadful. I have often seen with my own eyes people dying through taking opium. I knew one case of a woman with a daughter thirteen years old; the child was doing something wrong, and the mother gave her two or three smacks. The mother then went out to the fields to work, and when she came back in the afternoon her daughter was dying. She had taken opium while the mother was away.

We had a servant-woman who was not far from the kingdom of GOD. One day I missed her about dinner-time, and two hours afterwards I was called. I went directly to her, but she died in a few minutes; we could not save her.

There is much opium-smoking, especially in some parts where opium grows, and so is very cheap. Of course I put the blame on the foreigners, because my father's house was ruined by the English people, and not by the native opium. Even girls of nine and seven years old smoke opium. A father and mother smoke, and the children smell the opium, and smoke too.

In a good many cases it is not people's wish to smoke, but in those parts there are very few Chinese doctors, and if they have any pain or illness, they have only one cure, and that is opium; and by-and-by, when they are cured of the pain, they cannot leave off the opium. The children are left to do the home duties, and the home becomes no better than a pig-sty. I hope that friends will pray to GOD to send some doctors who will cure diseases and cause less opium to be smoked; and I hope also that more ladies will go and teach the people, and especially the women, that they may not poison themselves, and that they may pray to JESUS instead. I hope that you will excuse me, I am not a very good speaker

The meeting then sang the hymn commencing,

"LORD, speak to me that I may speak."

The Rev. A. T. PIERSON, D.D., of Philadelphia.

DEAR friends, if the great work of evangelising the world is ever to be done, we must penetrate the deceptive halo of mere enthusiasm, and come down to the bald, hard facts of a world's condition. Zeal is a good thing, but zeal according to knowledge is better. I confess to you that my heart is oppressed on the subject of missions. When we attend some missionary gatherings, one would suppose that the work not only of evangelisation, but of conversion, was going on so rapidly that we should not be surprised, at almost any time, to read in the morning papers that the whole population of the world was now brought to CHRIST.

Suppose we get past this rose-coloured cloud, and look at those great bald facts that rear themselves up like petrified shafts of eternity. Fifteen hundred millions of human beings—enough people, if they went by a given point, at the rate of one a second, to consume fifty years, day and night, in passing—fifteen hundred millions of human beings, going down to the grave at the rate of one a second; death, in from thirty to forty years, sweeping away the entire population of the globe, and giving room for another generation; and this going on for nineteen centuries, uninterruptedly, so that since CHRIST was born nearly sixty generations have lived and died, and the greater proportion of them never heard of Him. If that august procession, embracing all who have lived since CHRIST came, might be supposed to pass by any given point, it would take not only fifty years, but more than a thousand years, day and night, without interruption. And while we are talking about the world's evangelisation, and some enthusiastic people are talking even about the world's conversion, there are more unsaved people to-day than there were in the last century, or during the last decade, or even last year. Our missionary work is going forward so slowly that the world's population is advancing more rapidly than the membership of the Christian Churches.

It is time that the Church of GOD should awake to her responsibility. We have been acting as though we had an eternity in which to do the work, and the people whom we seek to reach had an eternity on earth in which to be reached; whereas the fact is that our term of service and their term of life must both very soon expire.

The CHINA INLAND MISSION found the stimulus and the impulse for its creation in the fact that there were eleven provinces in China into which no missionary had yet gone to reside. In *ten* of those eleven provinces missionaries are now working.

If you look abroad on the face of the earth in this year 1890, what do you find? Look a few facts in the face and let us not shrink. Let us at once be glad and be sorry to know the truth. 700 missionaries in China among 350 millions of people—one missionary to 500,000 souls; about the same number in India, where are from 250 millions to 300 millions—one missionary to somewhere about 400,000 souls; in Siam, from eight to ten millions, the whole missionary band labouring among the Siamese and Laos people numbering only thirteen men and women, and that means more than one million of souls as the average parish of every male missionary.

THE NEED OF AFRICA.

I read, a few weeks ago, in a missionary journal, that Africa might now be considered "tolerably well supplied with missionaries," because there were thirty-five missionary societies labouring in that dark continent. Now, there never was a more absolute falsehood than is contained in that statement about Africa. If you will go to Liberia, cross that narrow strip of country on the western coast, and descend the eastern slope of the Kong Mountains, go through the Soudan of the Niger and of Lake Tchad, and of the Nile, and if you should be able from some lofty point, as you went along, to survey the country 400 miles north and 400 miles south of that line of journey, 3,000 miles long, you would not be able to find a missionary or mission-station among ninety millions of people. You might go south of that to the Congo Free State, and start at Equatorville on the west, and go directly east to the great Lake stations, where the beloved Mackay has recently fallen (and I think that no more serious blow has come to missions in half a century than in the death of that marvellous man), and you would have passed over one thousand miles east and west, and five hundred miles north, and five hundred miles south of that line of travel, there was not, a few years ago, one missionary or mission-station among forty millions of people. And here is Africa, with at least one hundred and eighty millions of people that probably never saw a missionary, never saw a copy of the Bible, and have never heard the first proclamation of redemption; and yet it is said, that Africa is "tolerably well supplied with missionaries."

Am I not justified in saying that we must get above all this deceptive glamour? We must get beyond the passing of resolutions, beyond the evanescent touches of mere sympathy. We must even get beyond mere praying; and something must be *done* for men that are dying without CHRIST.

I have heard a great deal said about

THE GENEROUS GIVING OF THE CHRISTIAN CHURCH.

There are thirty millions of Protestant Church-members to-day, and two and a half millions of pounds is the aggregate sum that is given to foreign missions by these Christians; whereas, if every one of them gave one penny a day, it would amount to forty-five millions, and if every one of them gave threepence a day, it would give us one hundred and thirty-five millions a year.

We have six or seven thousand missionaries, and thirty millions of Church-members—one of five thousand members; four thousand nine hundred and ninety-nine staying at home for every one that goes abroad; whereas, if the Church of GOD gave, out of her membership, one in three hundred, we should have a hundred thousand missionaries in the field, not to speak of the native helpers which, by the way, have always outnumbered, four or fivefold, the missionaries sent from Christian lands. You are, perhaps, not ignorant of these facts. Many of you have heard them before, and some of you have heard them from me. Sydney Smith says that, for the purpose of impressing an audience, the only figure of speech that is worth a farthing is the figure of *repetition*; and I thank GOD that I can repeat, and I do. We have to beat these facts in. We have not only to strike while the iron is hot, but to keep striking till the iron is hot. The people of GOD will never take up the work of missions as they ough until they understand the extremity of the emergency of a dying world, and their own opportunity and obligation with reference to it.

A GRAND DAY OF OPPORTUNITY.

There never was such an opportunity. We are living in days that are more augustly awful than any in previous human history. I say, deliberately, that I would rather live in the year 1890 than have lived in the time of CHRIST Himself, not because it would not have been a transcendent privilege to see the LORD in the flesh, and to be among the number of those who were closely associated with His life, but because this is a grander day of opportunity and a more magnificent day of privilege.

Look at the world open before the children of GOD. When I was a little boy and first heard prayer in public for Christian missions, the burden of the prayers was that GOD would *open the doors of the nations* to the preaching of the Gospel. In those days Japan seemed hermetically sealed; China was walled about with a wall fifteen hundred miles in length, shutting out the foreigner; India was held under the control of the East India Company; Africa was not even explored; the South Sea Islands were inhabited by cannibals. It seemed as though there was no chance of reaching the world with the Gospel a hundred years ago. Here and there were one or two breaks in this great wall of idolatry, prejudice, superstition, and exclusion, which surrounded the nations; but now, instead of that great wall of exclusion, with here and there a breach, the wall itself is down, with the exception of here and there a fragment that remains to oppose the advance of Christian missions. Now, I say that no human being, no combination of human elements, could ever have brought about changes as colossal as these inside of a century, and, in fact, "one day is with the LORD as a thousand years," and there have been single years in the course of this century in which GOD has done mightier things in the way of opening up access for His Church than in centuries or millenniums which preceded.

THE YEARS 1858 AND 1878.

Let me repeat what I said on a previous occasion about the year 1858—that, during that year alone, the way was opened by which the Church of GOD might carry the Gospel to *eight hundred millions of the human race*. England, in 1858, made her Treaty with Japan after over two hundred years of exclusion. In that same year China, enlarging the previous Treaty of 1842 by the Treaty of Tien-tsin, opened her ports, and even gave permission to travel into the interior upon passport. India transferred the possession that had belonged to the East India Company to the control of the English Crown. David Livingstone, in 1858, sailed on his second voyage for South Africa, to complete his wonderful explorations, little knowing that the man that was born in the same year, 1841, in which he first went to Africa, was to meet him, in 1871, in Ujiji, and was to feel the mighty impression of his humble but marvellous heroism, and, as he saw his body laid in the open grave in Westminster Abbey, in 1873, was to take up the work which he had laid down. In the same year, 1858, Benito Juarez, in Mexico, overthrew the monastic system, confiscated the revenues and the estates of the Romish Church, and opened the way for the missionary to go into Central America. And in that same year, 1858, the first successful opening was made into the Zenanas of India by Mrs. Elizabeth Sale.

Now, dear friends, look at what GOD did in that one year! Why, when Paul and Barnabas came back from their first missionary tour, and gathered the Church at Antioch together, they rehearsed all that GOD had done with them, and how He had opened the door of faith to the Gentiles ; but did GOD ever open such doors of faith in apostolic days as He has opened in your day and in mine ? Shall we say that the days of miracles are past, when GOD performs such miracles as those before our very eyes ? I am alarmed at the apathy and the lethargy of the Church of JESUS CHRIST. The fact is that we are like people that walk in the midst of a blare and glare and flare, and whose eyes and ears are dazed and dulled by the glory of the things in the midst of which they are moving. How many of us have ever put together those marvellous events of 1858, which constituted it the *annus mirabilis*, the wonderful year of modern missionary history? And how many of us have ever noticed that, passing over the intervening twenty years, we come to 1878, another *annus mirabilis*, when sixty thousand people in Southern India turned their backs upon idolatry and superstition, through the grace of JESUS CHRIST? In that one year there was given to the LORD, on the altar of missions, by less than twenty individuals in the United States and in Great Britain, nearly one million pounds sterling! Thus GOD showed us, in 1858, what wonders He can do in opening the way before His Church. And then, in 1878, He showed what wonders He can do in giving large harvests from the seed sown, and what other wonders He can do in moving His people to come forward, like Barnabas at Cyprus, to lay the proceeds of their estates on the altars of Christian missions.

SOMETHING WRONG.

It seems to me that we have to get down on our faces before GOD, before the great pentecostal baptism of missions comes on the Church. All our efforts now are practically sporadic and scattered. Many a time on the field of missions there are a dozen different denominations labouring in one comparatively small district, when, beyond, there are regions where millions of other people dwell without an evangelist or a missionary. I have been through Scotland on a tour of missions, and I went into one town or village where there were about twelve hundred people and five handsome stone churches, with five educated Christian ministers. One of those ministers could have accommodated in his own church the entire church-going population of the place, and the other four ministers, with the money that these four churches cost to build, might have been put into the Soudan or the Congo Free State, to carry the Gospel to the millions that never saw the face of a Christian missionary. There is something wrong in the Christian Church when denominational zeal outstrips our zeal for the evangelisation of the world. There is something wrong when, in the coffers of the American and British Christians, there lie ten thousand millions of pounds while I am speaking, and GOD cannot get for the whole work of foreign evangelisation more than 2½ millions of that immense sum. There is something wrong in the basis of missions when the Church of God can calmly look on eight hundred million of human souls on the face of the earth going down to the grave that never yet, after nineteen centuries, have even so much as heard whether there be a CHRIST.

When Chamberlain, my personal friend, first went to Brazil, he penetrated the interior and found ten millions of people in that nominally Papal country who scarcely knew what a Bible was. He met one old patriarch, with a long white beard and long white hair meeting at his waist, eighty-four years of age, and when he gave him a Portuguese New Testament, and explained the simple way of salvation from John iii. 16, tears ran down the old man's face, and he said, "Young man, this is what I have been waiting for for eighty-four years. But," said he, "young man, I want to ask you one question. Where was your father when my father was alive, that, having this Bible, he never came to tell my father before he died that 'GOD so loved the world that He gave His only begotten Son, that whosoever believeth in Him should not perish, but should have everlasting life'?" My brother, my sister, we must answer some such question as that, if not before we die, then at the judgment-seat of CHRIST!

A portion of the hymn, " Far, far away, in heathen darkness dwelling," was sung, and the meeting closed with prayer.

Evening Meeting.

J. E. MATHIESON, Esq., Chairman.

The meeting was opened with Heber's hymn, "From Greenland's icy mountain," and prayer was offered by WM. SHARP, Esq.

The CHAIRMAN.

I COUNT it a great privilege to be permitted to take part in meetings concerning this blessed mission to China. From the catholic character of the CHINA INLAND MISSION, it is very proper that it should hold its gatherings in this hall. Our platform is a widely open one. "Grace be with all them that love our LORD JESUS CHRIST in sincerity," are the words which I see opposite me on the wall, and long may it continue so. The dear founder of the Mission and his fellow-workers in China have found a *modus vivendi* by which members from various Churches in this land going out to China can co-operate in the most brotherly way without jar or friction. Even our dear friends of the Church Missionary Society adopt this plan. The beloved Mackay, of Uganda, was really a son of the Free Church of Scotland, and, as far as I know, he remained a Free Churchman to his death ; but the doors of the C.M.S. were opened widely enough to let him in as one of their workers. What a blessing it would be if this could be carried out far more widely in connection with all the societies !

Now, China, as a mission-field, presents very remarkable attractions. It is a wonderful empire, the most ancient and the most populous in the world. The Chinese have more muscle and larger brains than any other people to be found upon the vast Asiatic Continent, and we thank GOD that not only are they physically strong men, but that they make strong Christians when they are brought to the feet of the LORD JESUS. They are meeting us on many fields of labour. I mean that the Anglo-Saxon is confronted by the Chinaman in the labour-market in many places; and this will prevail more and more as the years roll on. They can hold their own, and they can live more frugally than others. They can do many things which we are unable to do in consequence of the manner in which we have been brought up, and we may find them very tough antagonists in some future day. It may be that GOD may bring a day of reckoning with England for the opium curse which she has inflicted upon China. They are strong men; they are wise men; they are clever men; and if they had unity of purpose and good leaders, who knows that they might not turn the tables on us in some future conflict? Therefore, for the sake of our self-defence, if for no other reason, let us bring the Gospel of the grace of GOD within the reach of the Chinese.

THEODORE HOWARD, Esq.

MR. HOWARD read extracts from Mr. Taylor's letter, for the benefit of those who were not present in the afternoon, and added: In writing to me Mr. Taylor says—

"I shall be glad if you will say a little on the privilege and duty of obeying the MASTER's command, which we have never yet taken up seriously—as practicable and intended to be obeyed. The more I think of it and pray about it, the more convinced I am that it *can* and *ought* to be done. I have never had a burden laid on me as this is, which I have not found the LORD sufficient for and ready to help in. Each mail brings me more letters from China, from those well able to judge, in full sympathy with the proposition, and who are daily praying for its accomplishment. My paper has been reprinted in America by the Secretary of one of the Presbyterian missionary societies, himself for many years a missionary in China, with an approving note. And a German returned missionary writes me that he hopes he will go from Germany to join in the movement, and that he has already secured funds for sending out ten of them. I am firmly convinced that the thing is of GOD, and will consequently be accomplished. Many important details remain to be worked out, and providential guidance will have to be carefully followed; this will be given as needed, and, following Him, we shall not walk in darkness."

I feel that this meeting has occurred at a very solemn time. Some—yea, very many—of GOD's dear children have been thinking of the ascension of their blessed LORD to the right hand of the FATHER, of why He came down to earth, and why He ascended up again to GOD's right hand; and they are, in thought, looking forward to the coming and the power of the HOLY GHOST. I have felt that this is just the time for such a meeting as this; for what those of us who are in some measure engaged in this work never felt the need of, as much as we feel it now, is the power of the HOLY GHOST. If we look merely to human agency we shall fail utterly; but if we are willing to put ourselves into the LORD's hands, and let Him work, then in the power of the HOLY GHOST the work shall be done, and His servants shall be witnesses for Him right through that mighty land of China.

I want to say to any dear young brethren in CHRIST here, who know not yet exactly what the LORD has called them to, Will you wait before the LORD to know His will? May it not be that He calls you to be of that thousand who shall go forth? Have you learned yet what a blessed thing it is to yield yourself to Him in whole-hearted service? Before the LORD says, "Go ye into all the world," He has something else to say; He says, "Come unto Me." And if we are brought into living fellowship and union with Him, then, and then only, can He say to us, "Go." Ah! and we go in company with Him who bids us go, for He says, "Lo, I am with you all the days." Right through China in its length and breadth, right away, if it be His will, to every family there, the LORD Himself shall go with His servants. Do you know what a blessed and happy thing it is to be a missionary? Some of us feel sometimes that we may have missed blessing by staying at home. I want to read you a few lines from a dear brother who is in China now, and I think that if you go and speak with your friends at home—those who are living for themselves, or living for the world, or living a half-hearted life—you will find that they have not one tithe of the joy that this dear brother speaks of. He writes from Cheng-ku, in SHEN-SI, on January 21st. Mr. Huntley says—

"My coming to China has truly been a blessing to myself, and also, I am rejoiced to know, to the poor heathen. Among those whom the LORD has given me is my teacher. . . . . If you are brought at any time in connection with any of my colleagues at the Pastors' College, please impress upon them what *real* solid joy is given to those who follow out the SAVIOUR's last command. You may also tell them that I am happy in this God-given privilege; and since my stay in China (over two years) have never felt any regret for having come, or desire to return to and become one of those who bring up the rear of CHRIST's grand army."

Now, one thing, and I will sit down. When you leave this hall, will you all take with you the burden of the millions who are perishing? It is a burden that you cannot bear alone, but will you take it, each one individually, to Him who is the great Burden-bearer, and cast it on Him? And then, will you abide in Him and with Him, that you may see how He bears the burden and how He fulfils His promises? May we each one feel the responsibility that, as believers in CHRIST and partakers of His precious promises, we have in making them known to these perishing millions. And may He whose work it is, and into whose kingdom we seek to bring them, fill our hearts with His love and with His power, that we may go forth in this coming year with more zeal, and earnestness, and love than we have ever known before.

The CHAIRMAN.

THE next name on the programme is that of my beloved successor in the superintendence of the Conference Hall—Colonel Morton.

Colonel MORTON.

I AM paraded here by the orders of Mr. Broomhall—I suppose, on the principle that "he who is a friend should show himself friendly." As you are interested in the CHINA INLAND MISSION you will like to know what the views of the new Superintendent are. I suppose Mr. Broomhall's object has been that I should say to you how my heart is with you in this work. I hope that, as years go by, I may prove myself to be as friendly as I now show myself to be. I think that I have now made a very long and satisfactory speech, and I should certainly sit down, but in the interests of the writer of this postcard, and also to excite your prayers, I will read it. It is from

Dr. Baedeker, a true soldier of the Cross, who heard some one (I believe it was Lord Radstock) say, "Come," and he came. And then he heard the LORD say, "Go," and where do you think he has gone? Why, to Siberia, to preach the Gospel to the poor captives. It is a most wonderful work, and I know that you who are interested in the CHINA INLAND MISSION have such large hearts that you can give a little corner of them to Dr. Baedeker. He writes from Nijni Novgorod, May 14th:—

"I write this postcard to tell you that hitherto the LORD has helped, yea, carried us in the hollow of His hand. By the time this will reach you I shall be nearing the borders of Siberia.

"The prisons are full in every place, and hitherto the LORD has kept the door open for His precious Gospel to the poor captives. I would ask you to praise Him for His goodness hitherto, and to pray for further journeying mercies."

It is a noble bit of self-sacrifice to go there with his life in his hand to preach the Gospel to poor captives doubly imprisoned—imprisoned actually in such prisons as we read about as having existed in England two or three hundred years ago, but about which we know nothing now ; and imprisoned in sin and in ignorance of GOD. Will you pray for him and hold up his hands? And when he comes back again we will get him here to tell you, if he will, what he has been through and what he has done.

The CHAIRMAN.

We shall make mention in prayer of Dr. Baedeker at a further stage of the meeting.

Rev. E. PEARSE
(*of the China Inland Mission, Chen-ku, Shen-si*).

I FEEL intensely the responsibility of addressing such an audience of Christian people as is here to-night, and I do ask GOD that He may enable me to say the right things in the short time I have. Who knows but that here, amongst this audience, there may be some to whom GOD may speak through us! I would not care to speak here at all unless I believed that GOD, by His SPIRIT, would use any words which I may say to add to the burdens that may be laid upon your hearts on behalf of China. The Apostle Paul and his companion, on returning from their first missionary journey, assembled the Church at Antioch and told them what GOD had wrought through them. And their report no doubt called forth much praise and prayer. In the hope that anything we may say may also call forth praise to GOD'S glory and prayer for the workers, I want to tell you a little of what GOD has wrought through us. GOD forbid that I should say what *we* have done ; we desire to give *Him* all the glory.

BEGINNING WORK IN CHENG-KU.

I have been in China over fourteen years, but I propose to speak only of the last two. Six years ago my wife and I went to Han-chung in SHEN-SI. We were there for four years, and then Mr. and Mrs. Easton, who had been home, returned to the work in that station, and we felt free to go elsewhere. Not that there were too many workers there ! Far from it ; but there were many, many places where there were no workers at all, so we waited upon GOD, and, after much prayer, we determined to try to open the next city, that of Cheng-ku. I went and lived in an inn for two or three months before attempting to rent a house. It quite defeats one's object to be too hasty in trying to secure premises.

We rented a house, and after putting it a little in repair I took my wife and family into it. I suppose that it is hardly possible for you, dear friends, to conceive what it is to go into a strange city ; not one hand held out to welcome us, not one word of greeting, not one Christian man or woman in the whole place, no one to care in the least degree whether we lived or died. That was the state of things when we went there a little over two years ago. I am thankful, and I say it to GOD'S praise, that the case was different when we left to return home some five or six months back. Then we had a little church of thirty-four baptised believers, and those thirty-four Christians had not been hastily received into the Church, for our rule is to keep them at least six or seven, sometimes twelve, months, as probationers, before they are baptised. Not only were there thirty-four baptised believers, but there were also some five and twenty others who desired baptism ; and I have since heard from Mr. Huntley that that number is now increased to forty-six ; so that the city which was opened only about two years ago has now about eighty professing Christians meeting together on the LORD'S Day. On the first Sunday our worship was a very cold affair. We sent our woman-servant to ask some women, who had been to see my wife during the week, if they would come and see our worship. A few came from curiosity, but that was all. Before we left fifty or sixty attended the LORD'S Day services regularly. The first Sunday the service was in a little room in our own house. After a few months we had to adjourn to a larger room. A few months later we had to take down a partition and throw two rooms into one. And now I hear from Mr. Huntley that that is too small, even with chairs and forms placed outside for late-comers, so he has bought a large tent, and proposes in the summer weather to have services in the court-yard.

When my wife left there was no lady missionary there, but I am thankful to hear that the women have been carrying on the services themselves, and holding weekly meetings for prayer. Not one of them is able to read, though one is learning. Now, I am glad to say, a lady has gone to them. When we came away there were many willing hands to carry our bundles and other belongings to the river side. I think that fifteen or twenty women went down to the boat to see us off, and we could not but thank GOD and contrast our leaving with our arrival.

DAILY PREACHING.

Now, how was the difference brought about ? There are various ways, and Mr. Andrew told you this afternoon some of the methods adopted for reaching people. We adopted all the methods we could that he has spoken of, but the one thing which we depended upon was the daily morning preaching in the hall on the street. We wear the native dress, and adapt ourselves to the customs of the people, and we determined that we would make ourselves as accessible to them as it was possible. Consequently, we took a house in the busiest street in the place, and every day after breakfast I preached for two, three, or four hours to those who came. I never failed during the time I was there to get an audience. Some would always come in and listen, and many would come again and again. When they had heard for some time and shown any interest, we would ask them to come on the LORD'S Day; the meeting then was not held in the front chapel because many people would have come in from the street and have spoiled the meeting for worship, so we had it in the back part of the premises, always, however, keeping the front door open, so that any who desired to join us might do so.

When any had been coming for several Sundays, we

appealed to them to decide for GOD, and sometimes they would give us their names, and then and there we would go down on our knees, ask GOD's blessing, and pray that He would enlighten and teach them and make them His children; many, I believe, have decided at those meetings to give themselves to GOD.

On the morning that we were riding into that city GOD gave me the message, "Ye have not chosen Me, but I have chosen you, and ordained you, that ye should go and bring forth fruit, and that your fruit should remain." We took it as a message from GOD, and we pleaded it as a promise over and over again, and expected the people to be converted. We preached the simple Gospel of the LORD JESUS CHRIST; the blood of JESUS shed for our redemption; and the risen CHRIST living for us to save us from sinning. We preached these two things, and kept at it.

We have no paid agents, and the work does not cost the Mission anything except for the missionaries and the house. We teach the Christians that as soon as they are converted, it is their privilege to do all they can to bring others to the knowledge of the LORD, and very often those who themselves have received the Gospel come to the chapel whenever they have spare time, and help us to preach, telling what GOD has done for them. Otherwise the work has been entirely in our own hands.

We have had no medical work, no school work, simply because we were there alone, and we were not able to do it. We could only give our strength to the simple, direct preaching of the Gospel, and GOD has blessed that.

THE GREAT NEED.

This is only one spot, and I am thankful to know that similar work is going on in different parts of China. No doubt there have been many Churches gathered together within the last two or three years. But we must remember that the little company of believers is but as a little garden in a vast desert—a little stream of the living water in a wide, arid wilderness. The needs are great—greater than I can express. I have often written from that city, asking for help. My wife and I were there alone, and there were a great many things which we wanted to do, but could not. Often when she went into the street a number of women would stand at their doors, and ask her to go in; houses were opened to her, but she had not the strength to do half the work that might have been done. She commenced meetings in the country, and got the women together, and then had not physical strength to carry them on. I was asked to go and preach the Gospel to persons was had heard something of it and were interested; and I was unable to go. I very much desired to preach in all the surrounding villages within ten or fifteen miles. There were a large number of market-towns, and thousands of people meeting together in the streets; and you could put up your little tent, and stand all day, and get crowds of people round to preach to. But I was unable to go to those places, simply because, if I went, people came to my own place and found the door shut and went away.

THE CONDITION OF THE PROVINCES.

In going down the river from that station to the coast we have to travel a distance of from 600 to 800 miles before we come to another station. With the exception of Han-chung, twenty-five miles from us, there is no other station within ten days' journey in any direction; and there are hundreds of towns in that province, which is as large, I suppose, as all England. There are some sixty walled cities, and only two are occupied. We have some brethren in the provincial capital living in an inn, but they have not yet succeeded in securing premises. The condition of that province is similar to that of almost all. Oh, the harvest is plenteous; and, although I do not mean to give the impression that the people are hungering for the Bread of Life—for they do not know anything about it—yet I do mean to say that the people are willing to listen to the message; and, what is more, that you do frequently come across those who are hungering for something better than what they have. You come across those who have heard something of the Gospel, and do not know where to go to hear more. In preaching once in the country I met an old man, who sat listening to me for a very long time, and at the end of the preaching he said, "I bought one of your books some years ago, and I have read it, and, as well as I know how, I am praying to GOD, but I do not know how to pray." I took the old man to my inn, and together we knelt down and prayed, and the old man followed me, giving himself to GOD and asking GOD's blessing. On our way down the river my wife went up to a house at a place where we stopped for about half a day, and preached to the women there, and when she had done a woman said, "Who will tell me about this when you are gone? How am I to pray to GOD? and how is it that I have not heard of this before?" We could not say, and we could not tell her who would come and teach here when we were gone.

PRAY FOR LABOURERS.

Now, my time has gone, but I should like to repeat this passage of Scripture: "Pray ye, therefore, the LORD of the harvest, that He will therefore send forth labourers into His harvest." When I was coming home before, I met a young man at Singapore who said to me, "It is through an address you gave that I am here to-day." I was very thankful, and I asked him about it. He said, "You were speaking in such-and-such a place, and you asked us to pray to GOD to send labourers, and I went home and began to pray that the LORD would send labourers. I prayed on, and I seemed to get into sympathy with the LORD JESUS in the matter; and by-and-by the thought came to me, 'I am asking GOD to send out labourers; perhaps He would have me to go.'" And this thought became impressed upon his mind until he was obliged to say, "LORD, not only send labourers, but, if it be Thy will, send me." Now, I trust that you, dear friends, will obey this command, and it may be that by-and-by the thought will come home to you, "I am praying the LORD to send forth labourers; perhaps the LORD wants me to release my son or my daughter, and to let them go, or perhaps the LORD would have me to go." If so, do not do as Saul did—hide yourself amongst the stuff—but do as Abraham did, when God called, "Abraham, Abraham," and he answered, "Here am I;" or as Mary did, when she answered, "Behold the handmaid of the LORD." It may be that GOD will choose many from this hall.

Prayer was then offered by the Rev. J. D. KILBURN, of St. Petersburg, and the short hymn was sung.

"There shall be showers of blessing,"

The Rev. A. T. PIERSON, D.D.

I AM always glad to have anything that I say on this great missionary subject centre about some word of the LORD. The words that the Apostle Paul used in 2 Cor. x. 16 have acquired, after much prayerful study, a very new meaning to me. I trust that it is of the SPIRIT —"To preach the Gospel *in the regions beyond* you, and not to boast in another man's line of things made ready to our hand." That might be translated a little differently—

"Unto those things which are beyond you, to evangelise, and not to boast ourselves in another man's canon or measure as to things already attained."

If you will examine the whole passage you will see that the Apostle seems to be referring to a *general law* of life. Here is a territory of things *already attained*. Here is a territory of things that *lie beyond* and that are *not yet attained*. Now, he says, "GOD forbid that I should accept any man's method of measurement, or be satisfied with any man's circumference in preaching and living. I ought to reach to something beyond." There is a magnificent conception there. It affects the whole question of missions; it affects the whole question of living. He says, "We dare not make ourselves of the number that measure themselves by themselves and compare themselves among themselves." It is a spirit like that which breathes in the Epistle to the Philippians when he says, "Forgetting those things which are behind, and reaching forth unto those things which are before, I press toward the mark for the prize of the high calling of GOD in CHRIST JESUS." Spinosa was by no means a Christian writer, but he said a great many wise things. He said, for instance, that nothing is a greater foe to all progressive movement than self-complacency and the laziness which self-complacency begets. In the Olympic games the Greeks manifested peculiar sagacity in the race-course, which was a furlong or stadium long. There were three pillars—one at the beginning (the starting-point), one at the goal, and one midway. On the first, at the starting-point, was a Greek word which meant "*Show yourself a man*," *i.e.*, do your best. At the end was a word which might be translated, "Stop! Arrest your steps!" In the middle there stood a pillar that contained the word Σπεύδε, from which comes our word speed—"*make haste;*" because the danger was that, when one racer had outstripped the rest, and at the middle of the course found the others behind him, he would *relax his efforts*, and so some man that had been reserving his strength for the supreme effort at the end would pass him and get first to the goal. Now, we have begun in the work of missions, and the LORD says "make speed." The danger is that we shall have self-complacency, and grow lazy, and lie back on past successes, instead of considering that nothing we have done is to be mentioned.

I.—"THE REGIONS BEYOND."

That is the motto of missions.

First, the regions beyond, literally, *in territory hitherto unclaimed and unoccupied for Christ*, I spoke on this subject this afternoon indirectly, and the whole evening might be taken up in speaking upon the duty and the privilege of occupying unoccupied places for the MASTER, but I tarry just to say one word about it.

CONCENTRATION ON THE MISSIONARY FIELD UNSCRIPTURAL.

CHRIST'S policy indicated for His Church was not concentration, but *diffusion;* and I pray GOD to impress this thought upon missionary workers. It is said, for instance, that it would be a wise thing for the A.B.C.F.M. to concentrate the greater part of its forces in Turkey, and then, when Turkey is thoroughly evangelised, let those people become evangelists to their neighbours. The Presbyterian Board in New York has been pressed with appeals from Churches and individuals to concentrate largely the missionary force upon Japan, under the idea that, when those thirty or forty millions of people are Christianised, they will become the evangelists to China and India, and Siam and Burmah. It looks well on paper; it sounds well in public meetings; but it is unscriptural, and the Church of GOD makes a mistake whenever she departs from the clear line laid down for her in the MASTER'S final commission, "Go ye into all the world, and preach the Gospel to every creature."

The policy of concentration more or less limits the area of the work of the Church. She does not go into the regions beyond. She chooses a field comparatively near by, or a field of comparatively highly-civilised people—a field apparently attractive and promising and offering large and rapid harvests—and the consequence is that distant, degraded, destitute, or dangerous fields are doomed to be neglected. While we are concentrating on Turkey or Japan, what is to become of the other millions of the human race that have only the lifetime of a generation in which to live?

The Church of GOD is to take whatever money she has, whatever men she has, whatever resources she has, and go into all the world, just as her MASTER said, and preach the Gospel to every creature. And what will happen when this is done? She will find that the miracle of the loaves and fishes will be repeated, on a larger scale, in human history; and the five loaves and the two fishes that are nothing amid a multitude of five thousand men, beside women and children, will, when brought to the MASTER and used along the lines of His command, multiply as they are divided, and increase for distribution as they are decreased by distribution. I believe, with all my heart, that the blessing of GOD to the largest extent will never come upon the work of Christian missions until the Church of GOD ceases her policy of concentration and adopts the LORD'S policy of diffusion, until she emphasises evangelisation and not conversion, until she bears the witness among all nations and leaves the LORD to take care of the results.

Now, leaving this point—the literal application of the words "regions beyond"—I want to call attention to some other regions beyond that are to be taken possession of by the disciple, and by the Church of God.

II.—REGIONS BEYOND OF PROMISE.

I mention next the unclaimed, untrodden, territory of *Divine promise*. What did GOD say to Joshua in chap. i. v. 3? "Every place that the sole of your foot shall tread upon, that have I given unto you," and then He gives the outlines of the Land of Promise—all theirs on one condition: that they shall *march through the length and breadth of it*, and measure it off by their feet. They never did that to more than one-third of the property, and they never had more than one-third. They had just what they measured off and no more. Now go to the New Testament, turn to the Second Epistle of Peter, read about that other "Land of Promise" that is opened up to us, "Whereby are given unto us *exceeding great and precious promises*, that by these ye might be partakers of the Divine nature, having escaped the corruption that is in the world through lust." Why, there is a close analogy between those two passages. Here is GOD'S Land of promise, "exceeding great," "exceeding precious"; and it is GOD'S will that we should, as it were, measure off that territory by the feet of believing obedience, thus claiming it for our own, becoming partakers of the Divine nature, and escaping the corruption which is in the world through lust, and which was typified by the Canaanites that had to be expelled before the Land of Promise could be possessed.

FAITH VERSUS SIGHT.

Now look at these promises. They are marvellous! How many of us have ever imagined the wealth and the extent of that land? And how many of us have ever taken possession of the promises of GOD in the Name of JESUS CHRIST? It is a territory for faith to lay hold on and march through the length and breadth of, and faith has never done it yet. The faith of the Church has taken possession of a very small portion of this exceeding great and precious land, and the rest lies in "the regions beyond." We are limited by sight; sight makes a great deal of the *visible*, and unbelieving disciples prefer that which is tangible to that which is unseen and eternal.

Sight emphasises *numbers*. Hear what GOD says : "One of you shall chase a thousand, and two put ten thousand to flight." That is GOD'S arithmetic. Twice one thousand is two thousand, but in GOD'S arithmetic twice one thousand is ten thousand. GOD is sublimely indifferent to numbers. It is not quantity but quality for which GOD cares; He would rather have one consecrated man or woman than a thousand who are half-hearted in His service; so He keeps sifting down, and down, and down, just as He did Gideon's great multitude, till He gets the choice three hundred with whom He can do mighty works.

Sight emphasises *power*. See how sublimely indifferent GOD is to power. While we are seeking the patronage of great, or rich, or mighty men, GOD is taking up the poor and the weak, and the despised and the base, and the things that are nothing, and with them bringing to nought the things that are something.

Now, my dear friends, we have to take possession of this region of unclaimed promise; and before I leave this department of the thought, inasmuch as I am speaking especially in the interest of missions, I want to call your attention to a most important distinction. CHRIST says, in Matthew : "Go, ... make disciples of all nations. All power is given unto Me in heaven and in earth. Lo, I am with you alway, even unto the end of the age." Then, in Luke, He says : " Behold, I send the promise of My FATHER upon you but tarry ye in the city of Jerusalem until ye be endued with power from on high." Is

THE PROMISE OF CHRIST AND THE PROMISE OF THE FATHER

the same thing? I trow not. CHRIST'S promise is the promise of personal presence, and the exercise of omnipotent power in behalf of His missionary band. The promise of the FATHER is the promise of a descending HOLY SPIRIT to break down internal barriers in the minds and the hearts of men, and endue His own disciples with the wondrous unction from above. Now, these are two promises—not to speak of any others. Think of them in their bearing on Christian missions.

When Joshua saw a man standing in the neighbourhood of the city of Jericho, he said, challenging him, "Art thou for us or against us?". This strange personage said, "Nay, but as Captain of the host of the LORD am I now come;" and Joshua perceived that it was the Angel of the LORD. He took off his shoes in reverence, and waited for commands; and in accordance with the precise directions that he gave, Joshua moved round that city once a day for six days, and seven times on the seventh day, and then, without a blow being struck, the walls fell, and they went into Jericho and took captive all that were within it. What is that but an allegory in the Old Testament illustrating the facts of the New? When the Acts of the Apostles opens, which corresponds in the New Testament to Joshua in the Old, we have there the hosts of GOD on the Day of Pentecost simply surrounding the fortress of prejudice, Jewish superstition, and alienation from GOD with the trumpet-blast, the preaching of the Gospel, and on that day also without a carnal blow being struck, without any human philosophy to account for it, three thousand souls were pricked in their hearts, and said, "What shall we do?" What is this? The Captain of the LORD'S host is going before the missionary band, and He repeats the miracle of Jericho. Walls fall at once that might have stood for a thousand years but for His presence. All human calculation is disappointed when the Captain of the LORD'S host appears on the scene.

The promise of the HOLY GHOST is a special grace from above on teachers and preachers; and then on those that hear the Word ; as in the house of Cornelius, it becomes converting grace to them, as it has been anointing grace to those that speak.

Now, dear friends, look at this territory of promise. Suppose that the Church should pass all that has been attained, overleap all barriers, disregard the measure of human attainment, and simply march over the length and breadth of these promises, claim the presence of the Captain of the LORD'S host, claim His intervention, the fulfilment of His word, "Lo, I am with you alway, even unto the end of the age," claim the prostration of barriers that no man could prostrate without the power of His presence and influence. Suppose that the Christian Church should get down on her face before GOD to-day, and pray the Captain of the LORD'S host to remove the obstacles that prevent our going into Thibet, that has stood there on her heights, walled about by her mountains, and thus far defied even the Moravians to obtain access to the shrine of the grand Lama worship,— what might we not see in the year 1890, if we believed that this Jericho that could not be taken by the power of man could be taken by the simple fiat of the Captain of the LORD'S host?

And suppose that there was this prayer for the HOLY SPIRIT in anointing power on teachers and preachers, and in converting power on audiences that hear the Word in the communities in the midst of which these men are labouring, what new things we might see! I want you to remember that Peter did not say on the Day of Pentecost that this was the fulfilment of what had been spoken by the prophet Joel. The more I study the Scriptures the more I believe in the inspiration of the *words* of Holy Scripture. There is no mistaking the words he uses here. He does not say, "This is the fulfilment of what Joel said." He simply says, "This is *that* which was spoken by the prophet Joel. This is not spirituous intoxication, but spiritual exhilaration. It is not new wine, but it is the new wine of the kingdom, even as Joel foretold." The fulfilment of Joel's word is *yet to come*. There is to be a greater Pentecost, to which that was only like the first few drops that indicate the mighty rain that is to come down on the mown grass and refresh the earth ; and we ought to pray to-day for a Pentecost so much greater than the first Pentecost, that it should at last begin to fill up to the full the language that Joel uses in that remarkable prophecy.

III.—REGIONS BEYOND OF PRAYER.

And this leads me to say that, as there are regions beyond in the promises that faith has not taken possession of, so there are regions beyond that *prayer is yet to tread*. Ah, my dear friends, faith and prayer are so intimately associated that we cannot speak of one without at least implying the other. I beg you to notice that there are *different levels of prayer*. As our blessed LORD teaches His disciples, He goes from one rung in the ladder to another, and lifts them with Him, higher and higher, to a sublimer level of prayer.

Our LORD'S first lesson on prayer was, "Ask, and it shall be given you ; seek, and ye shall find ; knock, and it shall be opened unto you." But then, as you go on in Matthew and come to chapters xvii. and xxi., a new element is emphasised : "Whatsoever ye shall ask in prayer, *believing*, ye shall receive." Now, it is not simply asking, but asking in faith and receiving according to faith. But when we come to the Gospel of John, we read, in chapter xvi., I think, the most marvellous words our LORD spoke on prayer in the New Testament: "Hitherto have ye asked nothing *in My Name*: ask, and ye shall receive, that your joy may be full. Whatsoever ye shall ask the FATHER *in My Name* He will give it you." Now, this is beyond asking; beyond asking *in faith*. This is asking by virtue of, and because of, *our identification* with the LORD JESUS CHRIST. His *Name* is His *person*. To ask in His Name is to ask by virtue of my identity with Him being merged into His personality in the sight of GOD, so that God does not look on me as I am, but looks on me as I am *in Christ Jesus*. Why, my dear friends, here is a "region beyond," in the matter of prayer, that one man or woman in a thousand has scarce dreamt of. When I go to the FATHER in JESUS'S Name—reverently let me say it—CHRIST is the suppliant rather than myself; and because the FATHER can deny the SON nothing that He wants, it is certain that what I ask in His Name I shall receive—nay, I have already received it; and it is my privilege to believe that I have received that which I ask.

Now, suppose the Christian Church gets hold of this power of prayer, and gets above the level of simply asking, or even of asking in faith, and realises her identity with her LORD and the privilege of praying in the Name of JESUS; then keeping in fellowship with CHRIST, nourishing and cherishing this daily walk with Him, and therefore having within the motions that His SPIRIT creates, the groanings unutterable awakened by the HOLY GHOST—these presented in the golden censer of CHRIST before the throne shall certainly be heard and heeded by the FATHER. And so I believe that the greatest need of missions to-day is new prayer—prayer on the highest level of prayer.

IV.—REGIONS BEYOND OF GIVING.

Then I want to call attention to another "region beyond" that has not been taken possession of, and that is the region of *giving*. We are coming to a very practical matter. There is a whole world of promise and of power to be taken possession of in the matter of consecrated means. The Church of GOD is doing nothing to-day in comparison to what she might do and ought to do. I am ashamed, however, to speak of giving as a duty, because it grows on me more and more that we ought to lose sight of it as a duty, and only think of it as a transcendent privilege. There is something in love that takes off the asperities of duty. "I delight to do thy will, O my GOD." That is the atmosphere of service—not the *law* atmosphere—"I *ought* to do this thing," but the *love* atmosphere, "My meat is to do the will of Him that sent me, and to finish His work." Now, in this unclaimed and untrodden region with regard to giving, there are three or four things to which I want to call especial attention.

In the first place, *individual* giving is something yet to be reached by the Church of GOD. "Let *every one* of you lay by him in store." GOD'S principle is not that the rich should give, not that the poor should give, but that rich and poor should alike give; and every man, woman, and child have part in this consecration of substance.

Then we want *systematic* giving. "*Upon the first day of the week* let every one of you lay by in store;" at stated times, with regularity, as a matter of habit, so that, just as regularly as the week comes round, there should be an account with GOD that is audited, corrected, adjusted, to see that there be no failure in this part of our duty. Just as we are to bring a certain portion of our time and set it entirely apart to GOD, so we are to bring a certain portion of our substance, statedly and habitually offering it to the LORD.

Then there must be *proportionate* giving. We must give, first, according to our means, and, second, "as GOD hath prospered us." And this law of proportion must never be overlooked. I hold that the difficulty with the Church to-day is that, too often, we are calculating how little we can give to satisfy the claims of conscience, whereas we ought to ask, "How much can I give to GOD? and how little can I reserve for myself, and yet satisfy the absolute necessities of my own reasonable wants?" We ought to turn the rule of our giving entirely round. Give to the LORD the first portion, not the last. Give to the Lord the largest portion, not the least.

Then there ought to be *self-denying* giving, which lies still further beyond in this untrodden territory. A woman went round my church to get offerings from the women of the congregation for foreign missions, and her uniform plea was, "You can give this, and you will *not feel it a bit*." That was the damaging recommendation. That is the trouble in the Church of CHRIST. We give and we do *not* feel it; neither does the world feel it very much! I cannot conceive how GOD can take much pleasure in a gift that costs us nothing; and I pray GOD never to let me use such an argument as that rather give until you do feel it.

EXAMPLES OF GIVING.

There was Sarah Hosmer, a poor woman living in an attic, and working with her needle. She saved, on six different occasions, the equivalent of £10, and sent it to educate a native preacher in Oriental countries; and when she was borne to her rest six men were preaching in foreign lands whom she had helped into the ministry.

I passed by in Scotland the estates formerly owned by Robert Haldane, in the neighbourhood of the Bridge of Allan, and I felt a degree of reverence that inclined me to take off my hat, for it seemed that I was standing on holy ground. The fragrance of the act of that godly man who sold those estates, and offered the £35,000 that they yielded to establish in Benares, the centre of Hindoo idolatry, a mission for the LORD JESUS CHRIST, is still shed abroad all through that country, and people pass those estates not without a reverent thought of Robert Haldane, and a grateful recognition of the power of a consecrated life.

Then, in Alloa, when I was delivering the closing words of one of my addresses, I saw an old man sitting there and leaning on his staff. He was over ninety years of age, and I was told by the chairman, "That is David Paton. He has given his entire fortune—£200,000—to missions, and he is living now on a little annuity which has been purchased for him that he may not come to absolute want." And yet, when that man heard me plead for missions, he managed to get out of the little that was left him £250 more, which he gave the next day.

There was Mr. Hamilton, a mere clerk in a surveyor's office in Glasgow, and all the income that he had was 25s. or 30s. a week—say £75 a year—yet he annually gave to the U. P. Church £20, nearly one-third of his entire income. And when, in 1887, there was a special call made by the Synod for £20,000 for missions, that man furnished a one-hundredth part of the amount. He sent £200, one-half of the savings that he had made all through his life-time. And after his death his cash account was found with the LORD'S offering indicated there, and it was discovered that he only spent one shilling a day on his own needs, besides the three shillings a week for lodging—ten shillings a week in all—that he might give the more to the cause of the LORD JESUS CHRIST. My friends, I feel as if I had never denied myself anything for my MASTER when I read the story of such a man as that, living seventy-one years with slender income, and in that slender fashion, that he might be one of the noblest givers in all Scotland, giving unobtrusively and quietly "as to the LORD, and not unto men."

V.—THE REGION BEYOND OF HOLY LIVING.

Now I must close; but I want you to notice one more region that lies beyond, if you will give me your attention for a few moments longer; and that is the region of *holy living*. That is the most important region of all. We must not measure ourselves by ourselves, or compare ourselves among ourselves, or stop where others have stopped, or stop where we have now attained; but we must go on, if this world is to be evangelised, to a life of which very few people know much. I want to compress all that I have to say on this point in just this one maxim: "A holy life is a life in a supernatural realm—in a walk with GOD." That is strong language, but the New Testament is stronger: "He that dwelleth in love dwelleth in GOD, and GOD in him." Did you ever notice the expression that Jude uses—" praying *in* the HOLY GHOST"—as though the HOLY GHOST were a divine atmosphere in which the praying disciple moves, which he breathes, which exhilarates him, which nerves him to duty, which vitalises him, and which strengthens him? And that is exactly the truth. A man that is a truly holy man is breathing the HOLY GHOST as a sacred atmosphere. That is the atmosphere of missions.

The thing that, more than anything else, has led me to devote myself to the advocacy of missions has been that I have recognised in the working of missions the nearest approach to repetition of all the supernatural occurrences of the Old Testament and of the time of the Acts of the Apostles. There is the pillar of cloud and fire going before GOD'S people, causing Red Seas to present a passage on dry ground, causing fortress walls to fall instantaneously without a blow being struck, causing the enemy-like Amalek to be defeated as long as the arm of faith and prayer is extended. When CHRIST says, "I am with you," He means omnipotent power; He means guidance, guardianship, government. JESUS CHRIST is with us in every sense that is most precious, when we seek to proclaim the Gospel to a dying world.

DIVINE INTERPOSITION.

In Psalm ii. the kings of the earth are represented as conspiring together to break the bands of JEHOVAH, and cast away the cords of His dear SON; what does GOD say to them? Yet have I set My KING upon My holy hill of Zion;" and He says to His KING, "Ask of Me, and I shall give thee the heathen for thine inheritance and the uttermost parts of the earth for thy possession." That text has been preached from a great many times as a missionary text, as though it meant that the whole world is to be converted. But notice the next verse: "Thou shalt break them with a rod of iron: thou shalt dash them in pieces like a potter's vessel." Psalm ii. is the encouragement of the Church of GOD, not in the direction of the harvests that are to come from the sowing. There are abundant such encouragements elsewhere; but here the encouragement is given that, although the kings of the earth conspire and rulers take counsel to obstruct the work of missions, to defeat the plans of the great KING Himself, He who has sent His enemies as His inheritance, and the hostile territories of conspiring kings to do with as He wills, shall dash them in pieces like a potter's vessel, and break them with the iron rod of His just rule.

Missionaries of the Cross have seen many such interpositions of GOD.

In Turkey, in 1839, at the crisis of missions, the Sultan Mahmoud said, "There shall not a representative of the Christian religion remain in the empire." And Dr. Hamlin came into the house to Dr. Goodall, and said, "Doctor, it is all over with us—we have to leave; the American Consul and the British Ambassador both say that it is no use to meet with antagonism, this violent and vindictive monarch." Dr. Goodall, sitting in his chair, moved to and fro with undisturbed serenity. Dr. Hamlin said, "Well, you do not seem to give yourself much anxiety." That devout and godly man looked up to heaven and said, "Dr. Hamlin, the SULTAN of the Universe, in answer to prayer, can change that decree." And they gave themselves to prayer, and the next day the Sultan Mahmoud *died*, and the decree has never since been mentioned, and is only a matter of history. There the ruler conspired against the KING of Zion to defeat the plan of evangelising His empire and to expel His missionaries; and He stretched forth His rod of iron and instantly "dashed him in pieces, like a potter's vessel."

And in Siam, in the crisis of missions, in 1851, when another hostile king would not even allow the missionaries to get premises in which to live, or ground upon which to build, and would scarcely suffer them to obtain a lodging, they were only waiting for a vessel to bear them away from the harbour of Bankok, believing that their work was all in vain; but meanwhile they called upon Almighty GOD to interpose, and again the KING of Zion stretched forth His rod and smote that monarch, and broke him in pieces, "like a potter's vessel." And when his corpse was borne to burial, the question came up, "Who is to be his successor?" and again they besought GOD to interpose. The man that was selected was the only man in the empire that had ever *been trained by a Christian missionary*. He was not himself a Christian, but in studying language and philosophy and history and political economy with the missionaries, he had imbibed tolerant and catholic impulses, and he inaugurated in the Empire of Siam the most aggressive and the most liberal policy in all Asia, and his successor, Chulalangkern, is to-day the most enlightened sovereign on that continent. He and his wife are nursing father and nursing mother of Christian missions. Only two years ago they made munificent presents to our American missionaries to enlarge the borders of their hospital and dispensary work.

A NEW STANDARD NEEDED.

My dear friends, I am impelled to say to you that we must have these "regions beyond" entered. Faith must enter the unclaimed territory of promise. Prayer must enter the unclaimed territory of divine power in the divine presence. We must get a new standard of giving, that shall be individual, that shall be systematic, that shall be proportionate, that shall be cheerful, and that shall be self-denying. And we must get a new standard of living, that shall dare to invade the supernatural, that shall walk with GOD, and dwell in GOD, and pray in the HOLY GHOST, and shall recognise the word of our MASTER, "Lo, I am with you alway, even unto the end of the world," and the word of the FATHER that the HOLY GHOST shall come down to anoint disciples, and bring the unconverted to the knowledge of CHRIST. Oh! we must enter this unclaimed and untrodden territory, and then it may be permitted to some of us to see the glorious day come when the Gospel, having been preached as a witness among all nations, the KING himself shall come in His beauty, and those that have looked long for Him, with fainting desire, shall be permitted to share in the glory of His coronation.

Rev. J. HEYWOOD HORSBURGH
(of the Church Missionary Society).

AS a member of another Society who has received much kindness from the CHINA INLAND MISSION, I should like to tell you the reasons why I love the C.I.M.; but as there are other missionaries here to-night it would simply be unkind if I were to take up much of your time. What I will say is that if any of you want to go where you will be thoroughly at home, and where you will be in a kind, simple, brotherly, Christian household, you should go to Shang-hai, and ask Mr. Stevenson, and Miss Williamson, and Miss Palmer to put you up for a few days. And if any of you ever itinerate in China, and you want to have your arrangements nicely made for you, and have nice Christian companionship, ask the C.I. missionaries to let you come under their wing, as I did myself. And if in the midst of your itinerating you want a little refreshment and inspiration and a warm-hearted welcome, why, just call at the nearest C.I.M. station, and there, as I can tell you from experience, you will get it.

There is only one thing more which I will say about the CHINA INLAND MISSION, or rather, about the work of GOD in that Mission. The other day I was in the province of KIANG-SI, and I tell you the honest truth when I say that I believe that there, on the borders of the Kwang-sin River, is one of the most beautiful sights to be seen on GOD'S earth. And what is it? Just a little band of Christian sisters living entirely alone, far out of the reach of human aid—living simple, devoted, happy lives, and witnessing for JESUS CHRIST in those needy districts. Perhaps some of you are inclined to shout, "What an outrageous thing to allow those innocent, helpless ladies to go and live in that country far away from human aid!" Well, if that is what you say, the simple answer is this: Why do you let them? Why do you not go to them? If there is any shame about it, and I believe that there is in that sense, it is for you dear Christian friends at home to remedy it. But putting that aside, I believe that it is one of the most beautiful sights on GOD'S earth. I quite agree with certain people who think that to allow that kind of thing is an utterly wrong and almost cruel and wicked thing to do, *supposing that there were no GOD in the world*. But there is a GOD, and GOD has led those sisters just to go on, step by step, till they have found themselves there. And I believe that one reason why He has permitted it is to show people that there is a GOD who can do without man, and who Himself can protect His servants, and keep them in safety and in peace far removed from all human aid. And if He does permit a riot, as He did the other day in the city of Nan-k'ang Fu, surely it is just to show that even in the midst of a howling mob, when the house has been torn to pieces and everything stolen, GOD Himself is still able to keep defenceless Christian ladies in perfect peace and unharmed, and to take them back again in increasing power and blessing.

And now, dear friends, one last word. It is this : do pray for us. I should like to tell you what to pray for, but I will not do that to-night ; but add one further word : live for us. It is no good to pray for us unless you live for us. Now, what do I mean? Why, that if you dear Christian people at home are living out of communion with the LORD JESUS CHRIST, and do not love Him very much, if you have cold hearts, and do not love the souls of the people around you, if you are living in ease and comfort, just pleasing yourselves and thinking but little of others or of the glory of GOD, what sort of lives will your missionaries in China be living? We sometimes hear people speak of missionaries as if they were the most wicked people on earth—sheer hypocrites and humbugs. We know that that is not true. We sometimes hear people speak of missionaries as if they were little short of angels, and that is just as little true as the other. The fact is simply that what you Christian people are at home your missionaries will be in China or Africa or India; or if you want your missionaries abroad really to be living lives of power, really to be pleasing the LORD JESUS, really to be bearing witness by their lives as well as by their words, for the MASTER, in whose Name they go, do mind that you yourselves are living in communion with JESUS. If there is a thing that makes the heart of GOD sad it is to see a lukewarm missionary, a man or woman, who is discouraged and living a miserable, coldhearted, lazy life amongst these perishing heathen. See to it that you pray for us ; but far, far more important than that, see to it that you live for us. Do not forget it. Do it. Live for us; live for us ; *live for us!*

The CHAIRMAN.

I have now pleasure in calling upon a former dear fellow-worker at Mildmay, Miss Florence Campbell.

Miss FLORENCE CAMPBELL.

IT is just three years since I stood here to tell the friends who had gathered that I was very shortly to go to China, and since then the LORD, in His goodness, has taken me there and brought me back again. I have not come back because I was dissatisfied with the mission-work, or because the country disagreed with me, or anything of the sort. Every report that I could give about the country, about the climate suiting, about the Mission, would be most favourable. I have simply come back, constrained by GOD to seek to tell those who are at home that the LORD has need of them. The LORD has need of trained workers in China. He is calling in unmistakable tones. He has spoken to many, as we passed through America, and there are those who are ready to go, and some who have already gone, who have heard GOD'S message through the meetings that we had there. And there are those in this country whom GOD intends to go, and He longs that they would yield themselves up to Him. And why not? I expect that there are some here now whose hearts are in deep sympathy with the foreign work. GOD is speaking to some young men here to-night and to some of the sisters. Do let His voice be heard. Do not let the impression of this meeting pass away. This afternoon and this evening GOD has been speaking unmistakably to His redeemed ones. The LORD JESUS says, "If ye love Me keep My commandments," and then He says that His commandment is that we should love one another as He loved us. Shall we not think over those words more than we ever have done? As we go home let us take them with us and pray about them. As He loved us meant a complete denial of Himself, a yielding up everything that was precious and glorious in the home above, it meant leaving the presence of the FATHER to come down here and be despised and rejected, a Man of sorrows and acquainted with grief ; and He calls us from that which is dear to us in the home-land that we may give it up for Him, to go out with Him, that His power may be used through us in bringing the Gospel-message to those who have it not. There is no time to-night to talk more about it, but this message must be an important one, because GOD has brought me all the way back from China to give it, for nothing else but to go up and down the length and breadth of the land, and tell you brethren and sisters that the LORD has need of you, and need of you quickly. If you love Him keep His commandment, and be one of those who shall have the joy and privilege and blessing of going out with Him to tell the Gospel-message to some of "the every creature" that we have heard so much about. Every one here is responsible in some way for the Gospel being carried, and carried quickly, to those who know it not.

The CHAIRMAN.

MR. BROOMHALL wishes me to mention what was mentioned in the afternoon meeting—that a telegram was received to-day to the effect that the Conference in Shanghai appeals for 1,000 missionaries.

Mr. GEORGE PARKER

(of the China Inland Mission, Lan-chau, Kan-suh).

I HAD no intention to occupy any minutes to-night in speaking to you. It is the first time that I have been on a platform since I came from the East; during ten years, I suppose I have not seen more than a dozen European faces, and I do not feel, in regard to health, capable of addressing you. Therefore I pray you to excuse me. But there are some words which were very much impressed on my mind while I was travelling in the north-west of China, and those words are in the first chapter of Acts—"unto the uttermost part of the earth." Endeavour for a moment to imagine a young servant of the LORD JESUS CHRIST getting to one of the innermost parts of the earth, getting far beyond points hitherto reached by other missionaries, and then realising the immense extent of territory that lies right before him for hundreds and thousands of miles; and then imagine whether he would be capable of settling down in a little town, just one of the first towns that he came to. It is almost an impossibility. So during fourteen years I have just been rambling through the north-west of China, over two and a half provinces, and visiting every town, and village, and highway, and byway, over one hundred and twenty counties. I have a number of stories that I could tell you of the state of individual souls in those parts who have heard the Gospel once, and got interested in it, and came and sought me out to hear more about it, and we have parted, and I have gone on my way, and have not been able to visit the district again, and no one else has gone. I do not know how many years it will be before any one else can go, because the country is of such vast extent. What I should like to see, and what I hope the LORD will bring about, and that very soon, is that two of His servants will be able to go here and there, and only have a parish as big as different railways occupy—for instance, the Midland Railway. You can have a parish as big as that if any of you would go.

Mrs. PARKER.

I SHOULD like, dear friends, to turn to one or two verses in the Romans—the tenth chapter, at the twelfth verse: "For there is no difference between the Jew and the Greek: for the same LORD over all is rich unto all that call upon Him. For whosoever shall call upon the Name of the LORD shall be saved. How, then, shall they call on Him in whom they have not believed? and how shall they believe in Him of whom they have not heard? and how shall they hear without a preacher? And how shall they preach except they be sent? as it is written, How beautiful are the feet of them that preach the Gospel of peace, and bring glad tidings of good things."

Dear friends, I am here to-night to represent my own country people, and to thank all the Christian friends in England. I suppose that many of them, if they could, would be glad to thank you themselves; but they are far away, and I am sure would like me to thank you for them for sending the glad tidings to them. I am not satisfied to say, "I am saved; I am all right. It does not matter about others." Far be it from me to do that. I have come to thank you for the vast trouble that you have taken, and to ask on behalf of the places that have not had the Gospel. I cannot tell you how many thousands or millions have not heard anything about it yet. Will the Christian friends of England send it to them? That is my intention—to thank you, and to beg for more. May GOD fulfil the desire of my heart!

The Doxology was then sung, and Dr. PIERSON closed the meeting with prayer.

Items of Interest.

FROM REV. J. W. STEVENSON.

SHANG-HAI, *March 20th.*—Yesterday we had the pleasure of welcoming a Canadian party—two ladies and three young men. We are very much cheered by the way the LORD is guiding and helping our friends in Toronto. I am glad to say that Miss Legerton is willing to go to the Che-foo school and render temporary assistance until permanent help can come from home. You will be sorry to hear that Mrs. Cardwell is ill with a slight attack of small-pox.

We are praying earnestly that GOD will guide in the selection of teachers; they are wanted for both schools.

Shanghai, April 4th.—Mr. Nestigaard arrived from SHAN-SI on March 21st, and left us again on April 2nd, to return to Yuin-ch'eng, escorting Mr. Tjader and Mrs. and Miss Hattrem. Miss Clare and Miss Leggat, who go on to She-ki-tien, will accompany them as far as Fan-ch'eng.

Mr. Griffith, who has done remarkably well in the language at Gan-k'ing, left us on March 26th for Tien-tsin *en route* for Shun-teh Fu to join Mr. Bridge. Messrs. McBrier, Stephens, and Randall, from Canada, left us on March 24th for Gan-k'ing.

I have heard of the following baptisms: at Ts'in-chau, KAN-SUH, on January 9th, five; in the Kuch'eng district, GAN-HWUY, ten, during the recent tour of Mr. Cooper.

Mr. George King reports troubles at Lao-ho-k'eo, caused by a large number of destitute people who are wandering about begging in that neighbourhood; he tells me that between 800 and 1,000 people came round his house one day demanding help; and that with the assistance of the magistrate he was able to distribute some relief, when they were quietly dispersed

FROM REV. J. HUDSON TAYLOR.

Shanghai, May 1st.—We reached the new Mission house about 6 p.m. last Sunday, where I found a large gathering awaiting us. Howard arrived from Gan-k'ing on Monday, and the Rev. Charles Parsons from Melbourne on Tuesday. On Wednesday our new prayer-meeting room was opened, and to-day we have had the first of a series of consecration meetings, which will be continued each evening until the general conference begins. We are a very happy band, and there is sure to be a shower of blessing. The LORD is with us, He *will* bless us, and we shall be blessed indeed.

[A telegram on May 31st states that Mr. Taylor and Mr. Beauchamp were proposing to pay a visit to Australia. Will friends pray that it may result in much blessing.]

Christians in Prison at Chu-ki, Cheh-kiang.

FROM PASTOR NYING.

HANG-CHAU, *March 4th.*—According to the preacher of the C.M.S., our six brethren are "firm and joyful, reading their Bibles and singing hymns; every day they have prayers in the prison. Neither are they impatient, only hoping to be released in time to plant their fields, if it is our FATHER'S will; and, if not, the LORD'S will be done," they say. When I received such news I was exceedingly pleased, and I thank my Heavenly FATHER for it. Of their six families there are two where neither the wives nor sons are Christians, and when the men were first seized, they were very bitter against the Gospel; now they willingly are keeping the Sabbath. That is something we did not hope for, and also there are more inquirers, which is a cause of wonder to the outsiders. I send you this news that you may praise our FATHER that He has heard the prayers of many. This is a proof of the grace of the LORD, for the six have already been in the prison over a hundred days, poor fellows. What should I have done if I had been shut up? When I think of them I am grieved, but this good news has comforted me much. If our brethren had been at all bitter in spirit, and their wives and children lamenting, I should have not known what to do. I thank GOD for His unsearchable grace that those who once were weak now are strong.

I have sent a man to tell our brethren of the five dollars which the Sin-ch'ang brethren and sisters have sent. Will you please write to Mr. Heal, and ask him to thank the brethren and sisters for us?

Brief Notes.

Kan-suh Province.

FROM REV. H. W. HUNT.

T'sin-chau, Jan., 1890.—Writing of opium, I hope dear friends will do all they can at home to help the Christian Union in its efforts to stop the British traffic in the drug, which is, in deed and in truth, a traffic also in the bodies and souls of the Chinese. In suicides alone by opium-poisoning our Government is responsible for the deaths of thousands of Chinese every month, not to speak of the millions of besotted smokers. Alas! that revenue should be derived by a Christian (?) nation from the vice and misery of the poor Chinese. Can a heavy judgment from GOD on England be possibly averted? Time will show.

FROM MISS MUIR.

Lan-chau, Jan. 29th.—We have just been called out to an opium case. The whole scene was most ghastly. We were called too late, alas! Though we did what we could, we could not save the woman. These things make one quite heart-sick. What an awful reckoning-day must be in store for the English nation as regards these opium suicides, as well as the smoking This is the second death from opium in our immediate neighbourhood within the past few days. Very little is cultivated for miles round but opium. The people themselves say that nine-tenths of the adult population, men and women, are opium-smokers, and in a large proportion of cases smoking was commenced in order to soothe the pain caused by some trifling ailment.

Ho-nan Province.

FROM MR. HOGG.

Chau-kia-k'eo, Jan. 27th.—You may have heard of our arrival here on Christmas Eve after a rather tedious journey. Mr. and Mrs. Coulthard gave us a very hearty welcome, and soon made us quite comfortable; we are enjoying our stay with them. We were glad to find both in excellent health and spirits. The work is, as you no doubt learnt from them, in a very prosperous condition; deep, I judge, and real. The services are well attended by attentive people, to whom it is a pleasure to speak. I am happy to be able to relieve Mr. Coulthard a little during my stay.

Si-ch'uen Province.

FROM MR. BEAUCHAMP.

Pao-ning, Jan. 4th.—I should like to draw out prayer for a man I came across on my last journey. I can tell but part of his story. His name is Chao; he is a scholar of good degree, the head man of a large district. Before I got to his home I heard in some neighbouring markets that he had gone to Pao-ning to join the Gospel Hall people; so, you see, whatever his intentions were, it was not his wish to come by night. My informants were chiefly his disciples; he has a great following, being much looked up to by all. His visit to Pao-ning had been a very short one, and he had not, I gathered, met with quite the reception he expected. He went home a little huffed, so I am the more thankful to have met him and had his testimony in the presence of some of his friends in his own market town. He bought a New Testament from me here more than two years ago. He went home and studied it, but for the first year held out against the truth. He both wrote and spoke against the Gospel, but the two characters "happy sound," which is the literal rendering in English of the word Gospel, would always turn up and haunted him, until he was so convinced that it was GOD teaching him that this was the truth that he called his baby-boy, just born, "Happy Sound." He now writes and speaks in favour of the Gospel, but I would have you know there is not the least sign of conversion; yet we may surely see the finger of GOD, as he himself does, in thus turning a man of influence from antipathy to sympathy with the truth.

Arrival in China.

On April 29th the Rev. Charles Parsons arrived from Melbourne to join the Mission.

CHINA'S MILLIONS.

Report for the Year 1889.

HE following brief report shows the progress made as far as it can be tabulated, yet gives little idea of long journeyings, of seed scattered, of mercies received, or of the results of faithful labour that eternity alone can show. As mentioned in the report of our annual meetings last month, forty-one foreign workers in all were added to our number during the year, and 536 converts were received into the churches by baptism. The year will be remembered by us all as that in which Sweden was visited; the American Training Home opened; the home-work strengthened by the addition of the Council for Scotland, and of the London Ladies' Council, and the Training Home under the care of Miss Soltau; the large new premises erected in Shanghai; and the removals to service above of Miss MAGGIE MACKEE on January 10th, of Mr. STOTT on April 21st, and of Miss SUSIE PARKER on July 8th. In the joys and the sorrows alike we have seen the LORD's hand, and we trust Him for the future.

Statistics of the China Inland Mission for January, 1890.

PROVINCES. (ranged in three lines West to East for reference to Map. Italics in this column (many cases are of 'ations begun.)	STATIONS. (Capitals of Provinces in capitals, of Prefectures in small capitals, and of Counties in romans: Market towns in italics.)	Work Begun.	Stations and Missionaries.					Paid Native Helpers.							Unpaid Native Helpers.	Communicants in Fellowship.				Baptised in 1889.	Baptised from commencement.	Organised Churches.	Schools.				
			Stations.	Out-Stations.	Chapels.	Missionaries & Wives, Associates, and those absent.	Ordnd. Pastors.	Asst. Preachers.	School Teachers.	Colporteurs, Chapel Keepers.	Bible Women.			Male Communicants.	Female Communicants.	Total.				Boarding.			Day.	
																				Schools.	Native Pupils.	Schools.	Native Pupils.
KAN-SUH, 1876...	1 LAN-CHAU	1885	1	...	1	6	...	...	...	...	...	...	...	...	...	...	3	...	1	...	...	...	...
	2 SI-NING ...	1885	1	...	1	2	...	...	...	...	...	...	...	...	...	...	1	...	1	...	...	...	...
	3 LIANG-CHAU	1888	1	...	1	2	...	...	...	...	...	...	...	...	...	...	...	...	...	...	...	...	...
	4 NING-HSIA	1885	1	...	1	2	...	...	...	...	...	...	4	...	4	...	...	...	1	...	...	...	...
	5 TS'IN-CHAU	1876	1	...	1	7	...	1	...	...	...	...	8	19	27	...	34	1	...	...	2	10(G)
SHEN-SI, 1876...	6 HAN-CHUNG	1879	1	1	2	8	...	1	...	...	...	1el.	62	47	109	13	172	2	1	...	1	16G.
	7 Cheng-ku	1885	1	...	1	3	...	...	...	...	...	...	19	15	34	34	34	1	...	...	...	...
	8 Si-gan P'lain	1888	1	...	...	4	...	...	3	...	...	...	...	...	...	...	...	1	...	...	...	...
SHAN-SI, 1876 ...	9 Kwei-hwa-ch'eng	1886	1	...	1	4	...	...	...	...	...	...	...	...	...	...	...	...	...	...	...	...
	10 Pao-t'eo	1888	1	...	1	2	...	...	...	...	...	...	...	...	...	...	...	...	...	...	...	...
	11 TA-T'UNG	1886	1	...	1	3	...	...	...	...	...	...	1	...	1	1	39	1	...	...	...	...
	12 T'AI-YUEN	1877	1	1	2	11	...	1	2	...	...	...	9	10	19	...	39	1	...	...	...	...
	13 Hiao-i	1885	1	2	1	2	...	...	...	1	...	...	11	19	30	5	41	1	...	...	...	...
	14 SIH-CHAU	1885	1	3	2	3	...	...	3	2	...	...	16	12	28	5	35	1	...	...	...	...
	15 Ta-ning ...	1885	1	2	1	2	1	...	3	...	...	...	33	15	48	15	51	1	...	1	...	5B.
	16 P'ing-yao	1885	1	4	5	2	...	...	...	12	...	...	...	...	...	...	5	1	...	...	...	...
	17 HOH-CHAU	1881	1	...	1	2	...	...	...	...	1	...	28	14	42	10	...	1	...	...	...	...
	18 Hung-t'ung	1886	1	15	10	1	1	...	...	...	...	1el.8d	359	9	44	51	597	1	...	...	...	...
	19 P'ING-YANG	1879	1	...	1	1	...	...	...	...	...	1el.2d	47	20	7	...	82	1	...	...	...	...
	20 K'üh-wu ...	1885	1	...	1	2	...	1	...	1	...	1el.	9	...	9	6	12	1	...	...	...	...
	21 LU-GAN ...	1887	1	...	...	3	...	...	...	...	...	...	...	...	...	...	...	1	...	...	...	...
	22 Lu-ch'eng	1886	1	...	1	2	...	...	...	...	...	...	...	...	...	...	...	1	...	...	...	...
	23 Yuen-ch'eng	1885	1	...	...	3	...	...	...	...	...	1el.	1	3	4	...	...	1	...	...	...	...
CHIH-LI, 1887 ...	24 TIEN-TSIN	1888	1	...	...	2	...	...	...	...	...	...	...	...	...	...	...	1	...	...	...	...
	25 Hwuy-luh	1887	1	1	...	2	...	...	...	...	...	...	...	...	...	...	...	1	...	...	...	...
	26 Ying-tseng	...	1	...	...	2	...	...	...	...	...	...	...	...	...	...	...	1	...	...	...	...
	27 SHUN-TEH FU	1888	1	2	2	4	...	2	...	...	...	...	...	...	...	...	...	1	...	...	...	...
SHAN-TUNG, 1879	28 Che-foo	1879	1	...	1	2	...	1	...	...	...	...	...	...	43	9	62	1	2E	...	1	25B.
	29 Fuh-shan	1885	1	...	...	2	...	1	...	...	...	...	...	...	...	...	...	1	...	...	...	...
	30 Ning-hai ...	1886	1	...	1	2	...	1	...	...	...	...	16	23	39	27	41	1	...	...	1	12B.
HO-NAN, 1875 ...	31 Chau-kia-k'eo	1884	1	1	3	14	...	1	...	...	1d.	...	23	1	24	8	24	1	...	...	...	...
	32 She-k'i-tien	1886	1	...	1	3	...	...	...	...	1	...	9	6	15	8	15	1	...	...	...	...

AUGUST, 1890.

STATISTICS OF THE CHINA INLAND MISSION FOR JANUARY, 1890.—*Continued.*

PROVINCES. (Arranged in three lines from West to East for easy reference to Map. The dates in this column in many cases are of itinerations begun.)	STATIONS. (Capitals of Provinces in capitals, of Prefectures in small capitals, and of Counties in romans; Market towns in italics.)		Work Begun.	Stations and Missionaries.			Paid Native Helpers.					Unpaid Native Helpers.	Communicants in Fellowship.			Baptised Persons.		Organised Churches.	Schools.				Hospitals, Dispensaries, and Refuges.
				Stations.	Out-Stations.	Chapels.	Missionaries & Wives, Associates, and those absent.	Ordnd. Pastors.	Asst. Preachers. School Teachers.	Colporteurs, Chapel Keepers.	Bible Women.		Male Communicants.	Female Communicants.	Total.	Baptised in 1889.	Baptised from commencement.		Boarding.		Day.		
																			Schools.	Native Pupils.	Schools.	Native Pupils.	
VII. SI-CH'UEN, 1877	33 CHEN-TU	1881	1	1	2	5		2	1	1	2	2c.	29	15	44	10	84	1			1	6B.	1D.
	34 Tan-liu	1888	1	...	1	1			1				14	12	26	21							1
	35 Kwan-hien	1889	1	...	...	1																	
	36 KIA-TING	1888	1		1	2							2					1					
	37 SUI-FU	1888	1		1	6			1				1	2	3		1						
	38 CH'UNG-K'ING	1877	1	1	2	6		2	2	1	2	2d.	32	19	51	30	53	1	1	8G.	1	16B.	1D.
	39 PAO-NING	1886	1		2	13		1	1				5	3	8		13	1			1	10B.	
	40 Kwang-yuen	1889	1	...	1	2																	
	41 Pa-chau	1887	1		1	3		1					4	2	6		4				1	18B.	
	42 Wan-hien	1887	1		1	2																	
VIII. HU-PEH, 1874	43 WU-CH'ANG	1874	1	...	...	2							6	5	11		44						
	44 Han kow	1886	1			1																	
	45 Fan-ch'eng	1878	1		1	5							14	11	30		35				1	10G.	
	46 Lao-ho-k'eo	1887	1		1	4							1		1								
	47 I-CH'ANG	1880	1			2							1	1		1	1						
	48 Sha-shi	1884	1			1									2								
	49 Shih-sheo	1888	1		1	2							1										
IX. GAN-HWUY, 1869	50 Cheng-yang-kwan	1887	1		1	3							5	1	6	3	3	1					
	51 Lai-gan	1887	3	3	2	1		1	3		2		3										
	52 GAN-K'ING	1869	1	2	1	11						3	100	50	165	4	226	2					
	53 NING-KWOH	1874	1	4	5	4		1	1			1	32	18	50	9	61	1	1	2G	1	6B.	
	54 Ch'i-chau Fu	1886	1			2																	
	55 HWUY-CHAU	1875	1	2	2	2							1	4	10	7	7						
X. KIANG-SU, 1854	56 Shang-hai	1854	1	...	...	8													1				
	57 CHIN-KIANG	1888	1		1	4																	
	58 YANG-CHAU	1868	1			7		1	1	1	3		5	45	101	13	101	1		19G.			
	59 Kao-yiu	1888	1		1	3																	
	60 Ts'ing-kiang-p'u	1869	1	1	1	3																	
	... Former work																	98						
XI. YUN-NAN, 1877	61 Bhamô (Burmah)	1875	1	...	1	2						2	14	1	11		7	1					
	62 TA-LI FU	1881	1			3							1		1		1	1	1	12B.			
	63 YUN-NAN FU	1882	1		2	7																	
	64 CHAU-T'UNG	1887	1		1	3																	
	65 K'UH-TS'ING	1888	1		1	2																	
XII. KWEI-CHAU, 1877	66 KWEI-YANG	1877	1	1	1	7						1	21	16	37	10	48	1	1	3G	1	15B.	
	67 GAN-SHUN	1888	1		1	2							2	1	4	1	1						
XIII. HU-NAN, 1875	...																							
XIV. KIANG-SI, 1869	68 KIU-KIANG	1889	1			2																	
	69 Ta-ku-t'ang	1887	1		1	8							2	1	3		10	1					
	70 Kwang-feng	1889	1			2									1	12	1							
	71 NAN-K'ANG	1887	1		1	4							2	2	4	7	1	1					
	72 Kwei-k'i	1878	1	1	1	3		2								37	15	5	1				
	73 Gan-ren	1889	1			1																	
	74 Ho-k'eo and I yang	1878	1	1	1	4									2	4	31	1					
	75 Yuh-shan	1877	1		1	4		1					46	46	9	24	95	1					
	... Itinerating					5																		
XV. CHEH-KIANG, 1857	HANG-CHAU	1866		6	7			2	5			1	75	44	119	16	264	6					
	76 SHAO-HING	1866	1	5	6	3		1	7	1	2	1	114	77	191	18	271	5	1	9G.			
	77 Sin-ch'ang	1866	1	1	2	2			2				9	8	17		25						
	... NING-PO	1857		2	2																			
	78 Fung-hwa	1866	1	2	3	2		1	4		1	2	48	63	111	9	336	7					
	79 Ning-hai	1868	1	1	2																			
	80 T'AI-CHAU	1867	1	6	7	2		...	5	...	3		131	63	191	8	271	7					
	81 WU'S-CHAU	1867	1	...	1	2		2	3	1	4		26	27| 121	34	64	444	5	1	24G	1	6B.	
	82 Bing-yae	1870	1			3																		
	... CH'U-CHAU	1875							3		1		26	9	38	15	33	2					
	83 Vung-k'ang	1887	1	...		1			1	2	1		17	13	30	7	60	1					
	84 KIN-HWA	1875	1	1	1	2		1	2		1													
	85 KIU-CHAU	1872	1	1	2	3		2	3	2	1		29	25	54	17	146	3					
	86 Ch'ang-shan	1878	1		1	1																		
	87 Pch-shih-kiai	1879	1		1	1																		
			87	71	132	320*		14	64	18	50	26	60	1737	989	2839	530	4113.	88	8	65G	14	163B	
																					2E. 12B.		30G	

* Missionaries absent, location undetermined, 9; Undesignated Missionary Students, 29; Jan.-April, 1890, 25. Total, 383.

The Six Northern Provinces.

I.—KAN-SUH.

Population of Province, 3 millions; Area, 86,608 square miles.
MISSIONARY SUPERINTENDENT—REV. G. F. EASTON.
Stations, 5; Missionaries, 19; Native Helpers, 1; Baptised in 1889, 4 Converts; Communicants, 31.

FROM the table of statistics it will be seen that the stations in this Province remain as last year. The missionaries reckon one less, Mrs. Botham having gone into SHEN-SI with her husband. The only station from which baptisms are reported is *Ning-hsia*, and these are the first converts. At *Ts'in-chau*, when the year closed, our friends had a number of inquirers, five of whom were baptised in January, so will come into next year's report.

At *Lan-chau* a suitable house has been secured inside the city, not without considerable difficulty. The work in this important capital has been greatly weakened by the necessary leaving for home on furlough of Mr. and Mrs. Parker.

Mr. and Mrs. Cecil Polhill-Turner, of *Si-ning*, have been devoting most of their time to the study of the Tibetan language, and have made several important journeys to the Tibetans on the border. The Misses Ellis have removed from Si-ning to Ts'in-chau.

Mr. and Mrs. Laughton have been enabled to remain in *Liang-chau*, and the people seem very friendly. During the year there was a slight disturbance, but the magistrate showed a kindly spirit, and the trouble soon passed away. It is unquestionably a most important centre.

At *Ning-hsia* the work has been prosecuted with great vigour and earnestness, not in the city only, for a good deal of itinerating has been accomplished; our friends have been rejoiced by four persons having openly professed faith in CHRIST. Mr. Horobin was laid aside with illness for some time, but GOD graciously raised him up. Both Mr. Horobin and Mr. Belcher are asking very urgently for reinforcements for the vast district around them.

At *Ts'in-chau*, Mr. Hunt writes that the meetings are well attended; many have come very near to the Kingdom, giving much encouragement, and then have drawn back through lack of courage. Mr. and Mrs. Hunt have spent some time in the villages around, and found the people very accessible. He does a great deal of dispensing, and hopes to enlarge this work, and also to open an opium refuge. We ask earnest prayer for all our friends in KAN-SUH.

II.—SHEN-SI.

Population of Province, 7 millions; Area, 67,400 square miles.
MISSIONARY SUPERINTENDENT—REV. G. F. EASTON.
Stations, 3; Missionaries, 15; Native Helpers, 4; Baptised during 1889, 47 Converts; Communicants, 143.

We are thankful to report forty-seven baptisms, as against thirteen the previous year. The stations remain as before.

In *Han-chung* the work has gone on steadily during the year, and thirteen baptisms are reported. The work has been particularly interesting in the out-station, Shih-pa-li-p'u. Elder Liu has been fully recognised as Church evangelist, and is supported by a Local Evangelistic Fund, to which both natives and foreigners contribute. He is generally accompanied on his journeys by a native or foreign volunteer. Mr. Easton reports that he lately spent three days with Elder Liu at Shih-pa-li-p'u. The Christians on the spot provided them with an awning, table, and stools. He wrote :—

"We were able to keep the preaching going nearly all day, sometimes assisted by passing members of the Shih-pa-li-p'u Church. The evangelist and myself, accompanied by a catechumen volunteer, have since spent a week in the south country, enjoying much two days' preaching at a busy market town; a friend provided table and stools, and for *four cash* (one-fifth of a penny) we rented an excellent site; we had most attentive audiences. The work is extending very encouragingly in the country, and a native of Yang-hien, who has been a patient in the hospital for some time, has given much encouragement. Miss Holmes spent a few days there, but had to leave on account of the great crowds."

We are sorry that no report of the Han-chung medical work has reached us, but we are quite sure that it has been carried on with encouraging results.

In *Cheng-ku*, where Mr. and Mrs. Pearse have laboured so faithfully, there has been considerable encouragement. No less than thirty-four persons were baptised during the year, for which we do praise GOD. Mr. and Mrs. Pearse having gone home, Mr. Huntley has taken charge. We ask prayer that the good work begun so hopefully may continue.

Our brethren at *Feng-tsiang Fu* have been joined by Mrs. Botham. They have not yet rented a house, but are living in an inn, and spending most of their time itinerating on the Plain, waiting for the time when GOD shall open the door for permanent residence.

At *Wei-nan Hien*, Mr. Folke has been able to keep an opium refuge, though the place is hardly ready for foreign occupation.

Pastor Hsi has been successful in placing an opium refuge in *Si-gan*, the capital, and not without success, as several scholars of high rank have been cured of the habit. We would ask special prayer that all wisdom and grace may be given to our native brethren at this most difficult station.

III.—SHAN-SI.

Population of Province, 9 millions; Area, 55,268 square miles.
MISSIONARY SUPERINTENDENT—REV. B. BAGNALL.
Stations, 15; Missionaries, 43; Native Helpers, 30, and many unpaid; Baptised in 1889, 97 Converts; Communicants, 702.

We are thankful to report two new stations opened in this Province during the year, viz., *Lu-ch'eng Hien* by Mr. Stanley Smith, and *Yuen-ch'eng* by Mr. Folke. We also report two more missionaries—Mr. and Mrs. Duncan Kay. The number of converts baptised is ninety-seven, as against 116 last year. These are distributed as follows :—

Ta-tung District	...	...	...	...	1
Sih-chau	,,	...	...	...	29
Hung-t'ung	,,	...	...	...	61
K'üh-wu	,,	...	...	...	6

To adopt the division of last year, we will begin with:—

I. *The North.*

In *Kwei-hwa-ch'eng*, Mr. and Mrs. Beynon have been much encouraged by the large numbers who come regularly to the services. Dr. Stewart has had many patients, and we pray that GOD'S blessing may rest upon his efforts.

Mr. A. Ewing has made visits to the country, besides visiting the other stations, Ta-t'ung and Pao-t'eo, as also the capital during the year.

Mr. and Mrs. Burnett continue to be encouraged in their work in *Pao-t'eo*, though as yet no baptisms have been reported.

At *Ta-t'ung* more suitable premises have been secured. Mrs. McKee has had interesting openings among the women. It will be noted that the first convert has been baptised there.

II. *The Capital (T'ai-yuen Fu).*

The station has been weakened by the departure of Dr. and Mrs. Edwards for home on furlough. While much earnest work has been done both in the city and country, no baptisms have been reported. We would ask for special prayer for the workers in this city. A good deal of Mr. Bagnall's time has been spent in visiting the various stations and superintending generally, so that he has not been able to do much direct work in the capital. We are sorry that the medical work in the Schofield Memorial Hospital is at a standstill for lack of a medical missionary.

III. *West of the River Fen.*

In this district twenty-nine baptisms are reported. The work is particularly interesting in *Hiao-i* and *Ta-ning*. Our sisters, Miss Seed and Miss Whitchurch, have been indefatigable in their labours, as also Miss Scott and Miss Miles. Mr. Key and Mr. Lutley, at *Sih-chau*, have both done a good deal of itinerating work, and there is room in this large field for many more labourers.

IV. *East of the River Fen.*

At *P'ing-yao*, Mr. Orr Ewing and Mr. P'eat have been encouraged in their large district, although they have not been without their discouragements. The five Hien cities take quite a long time to visit. Through the opium refuges our friends are reaching a large number. No baptisms are reported for the year, though it closed with several inquirers.

At *Hoh-chau*, Miss Jakobsen and Miss Forth have laboured very zealously amid a good many discouragements.

Mr. Hoste and Pastor Hsi have worked most harmoniously in the large district of *Hung-t'ung*, and GOD has owned their labours. Sixty-one baptisms have been reported. They have also had to exercise discipline in not a few cases. We trust that the rules they have lately brought into force will tend greatly to the purity and extension of the Church. GOD has helped in some very difficult matters, and some who were causing trial the year before show signs of repentance.

Mr. Russell labours on faithfully in *P'ing-yang*, and not without encouragement, especially in the country.

Mr. and Mrs. D. Kay have commenced their work in *K'üh-wu* under encouraging circumstances, and write most hopefully.

Mr. and Mrs. Folke and Mr. Nœstigaard have their headquarters at Yuen-ch'eng, where several have been baptised during the year. They superintend a large district over the border in SHEN-SI. We ask prayer for their work, as Mr. Folke has recently had sore trials.

At *Lu-gan*, Mr. Studd has been greatly encouraged in the number of opium smokers who have passed through the refuge. Though no baptisms have been reported, still there is every reason to believe that GOD has blessed the efforts of His servants to not a few, for which we give GOD praise.

Mr. S. P. Smith has opened a Hien city, called *Lu-ch'eng*, where he is also having encouragement; though at the beginning he had great trials and difficulties through false brethren, which have happily been removed. The work in the whole Province is going forward steadily. We are quite sure that the precious seed committed to the ground will in due time bring forth fruit to the praise and glory of GOD.

IV.—CHIH-LI.

Population of Province, 20 millions; Area, 58,919 square miles.
MISSIONARY SUPERINTENDENT—T. W. PIGOTT, B.A.
Stations, 4; Missionaries, 9; Native Helpers, 4; Communicant, 1.

During the year Mr. and Mrs. G. Clarke have removed to *Tien-tsin*, and taken up the business work there, while Mr. and Mrs. Tomalin gone to Fuh-shan, SHAN-TUNG. Mr. and Mrs. Pigott were joined by Miss Kerr.

We are thankful to say that Mr. Pigott has succeeded in securing a most suitable house in *Hwuy-luh*, after a long period of waiting, though this was not in the year under review.

Mr. and Mrs. Simpson have spent some months in Ying-tseng, a village station fourteen miles from Hwuy-luh, and report much encouragement. The work, however, in the whole district is still in its initial stage, and we ask for earnest prayer that soon many souls may be gathered in.

There is a good deal of encouragement at *Shun-teh Fu*. Mr. Pigott reports over ten inquirers in the neighbourhood. Several extensive journeys have been made into North HO-NAN.

V.—SHAN-TUNG.

Population of Province, 19 millions; Area, 65,104 square miles.
MISSIONARY SUPERINTENDENT—A. W. DOUTHWAITE, M.D.
Stations, 3; Missionaries, 25; Native Helpers, 4; Baptised in 1889, 36 Converts; Communicants, 82.

In the *Che-foo* station nine baptisms are reported for the year, and eight for the previous year. Dr. Douthwaite reports that the medical work has been more satisfactory than in previous years, owing to the increase of in-patients, among whom we look for the greatest success in treatment, and, above all, in spiritual enlightenment. At the Tung-shan hospital 130 patients were admitted, including 131 surgical cases. Most of these required prolonged and careful treatment. With three or four exceptions, all the operations were successful. The Lily Douthwaite Memorial Hospital has been a great blessing to many poor folk. Over 5,000 cases have been treated in the dispensary connected with it. It is impossible to give the exact number, for the hospital was entered by burglars in May, and every portable thing was carried off, including the register of out-patients. Since the beginning of May 4,000 patients have been registered, and sixty-seven minor operations, exclusive of dental surgery.

In the T'ung-shin Hospital, under the care of Dr. Randle, thirty patients have been admitted during the eight months it has been opened. Of these, five were surgical cases. In the out-patient department, 1,874 cases were attended, and thirty-three minor operations performed. This brings the total number of out-patients for the year to over 7,000 (two-thirds of them were new cases), and of in-patients to 169. Many professed to believe in CHRIST. The importance of this work is increased by the fact that men from all parts of the empire are found among the in-patients, and as they return to their distant homes they must carry with them some knowledge of the Gospel. 129 patients at Tung-shan Hospital were from twelve different provinces!

Mrs. Schofield and Miss Miller have rendered valuable assistance in the Lily Douthwaite Memorial Hospital, and by regular visitation of the female patients, whose acquaintance they make at the dispensary. Owing to our having to furnish and supply things for the new hospital at T'ung-shin, the expenditure this year has been much greater than usual, viz., 921 dols. 66 cts. Of this amount, only 378 dols. was received from Mission funds, 592 dols. having been received during the year in fees and donations from foreign patients.

The Sanatorium has been a great boon to our sick missionaries; seventeen members of the C.I.M., with five children, have been entertained there during the year, also two ladies, with two children, not connected with the Mission. Mr. and Mrs. Stooke have been indefatigable in their efforts to make our friends comfortable and happy. As we have intimated, there have been nine baptisms during the year. Dr. Douthwaite reports an average attendance on the LORD'S Day of about sixty. The work is going on hopefully. No natives are employed in connection with this work, but 'sometimes one of the members assists in conducting services held every morning. The chief part of the work devolves on the superintendent, Dr. Douthwaite. Mrs. Schofield has opened a day school and reports twenty-five pupils.

Our English schools for boys and girls have grown to the fullest extent of their present capacity, and many children have been refused for want of accommodation. The pupils have made marked progress in their studies during the last year, but, best of all, many of them have learned to trust in CHRIST as their SAVIOUR. Forty-three pupils are reported in the boys' school and thirty in the girls' school; total, seventy-three.

Dr. and Mrs. Randle, at *T'ung-shin*, have a fine field and many opportunities, which are fully taken advantage of, and we trust soon to hear of fruit to their labour.

We have already mentioned that Mr. and Mrs. Tomalin have taken up work at *Fuh-shan*, Mrs. Cheney having gone to T'ung-shin.

In *Ning-hai* Mr. Judd reports twenty-seven baptisms. The people are much more friendly than they used to be.

VI.—HO-NAN.

Population of Province, 15 *millions; Area,* 65,104 *square miles.*

DEPUTY SUPERINTENDENT—REV. J. J. COULTHARD.

Stations, 2; *Missionaries,* 17; *Native Helpers,* 2; *Baptised in* 1889, 16 *Converts; Communicants,* 30.

Eight have been baptised in the *Chau-kia-k'eo* district, and eight in *She-ki-tien*. The work is going forward with a good deal of encouragement in these two new centres. We have been unsuccessful in attempts to open stations in Ho-nan Fu, Hwui-ching Fu, and Chu-sien-ch'eng. We ask prayer for our brethren who have had these serious reverses, and that GOD will graciously overrule and grant that we may be enabled to begin permanent work in these places before long.

There has been considerable advance in the women's work at both stations. At first there was a good deal of excitement and curiosity, which has happily passed away, and now our sisters are welcome in the houses of the people. We look forward in the near future to a time of great blessing in HO-NAN. Mr. Coulthard has been greatly encouraged in some of the native Christians.

Mr. and Mrs. Hogg removed to Chau-kia-k'eo, and hope in time, with Mr. Slimmon, to open up work in a fresh centre. We would ask prayer for them.

Several visits to the capital have been made during the year, and we are glad to know that the province is fast recovering from the inundations. There is still much land to be possessed in this province for the LORD.

The Four Central Provinces.

VII.—SI-CH'UEN.

Population of Province, 20 *millions; Area,* 166,800 *square miles.*

MISSIONARY SUPERINTENDENT—REV. J. W. STEVENSON.

Stations, 10; *Missionaries,* 41; *Paid Native Helpers,* 20; *Baptised in* 1889, 61 *Converts; Communicants,* 143.

We have to report in this province the opening of two new stations; *Kwang-yuen*, north of Pao-ning, has been occupied by Miss Emma Culverwell and Miss Dastone; and Miss Fosbery has taken up her abode in *Kwan-hien*, a city 120 *li* to the north-west of Chen-tu. In the capital, *Chen-tu*, ten have been baptised, and twenty-one at *Tan-liu Hien*. Dr. Parry reports that a small house has been taken in Mei-chau. The staff at the capital has been reduced during the year by the leaving of Mrs. Riley (now Mrs. James), and that of Dr. and Mrs. Pruen, the latter having gone to Kwei-yang. During the examinations Mr. Owen arranged and carried out a weekly special meeting, which was attended by large numbers of men. He was assisted by several of the native brethren. Mr. Owen has also started a small preaching out-station at Hong-p'ai-leo. He has been able to do a good deal of itinerant work round Chen-tu. Evening classes and the general work, both among the men and women, have been carried on systematically during the year with great encouragement. Dr. Parry has visited *Tan-liu* four times, and has been altogether about six months away from the capital on evangelistic and medical tours. He has registered 681 separate cases at the dispensary, and had thirty opium-curing cases. Four of the men baptised in the year in Chen-tu may be regarded as fruit of the dispensary work, and of a few in-patients who have been received for a time two are now enrolled as inquirers. One of the patients baptised is a HU-NAN man, a mandarin's servant. During the year much progress has been made in the church, in spite of some times of serious trouble. Of the thirty-one persons baptised in Chen-tu and Tan-lin, thirteen are women and eighteen men. As last year, four of the natives have regularly taken in turn the services on the week-days, and sometimes on the Sundays, both in the station and outstations. All the services have been carried on regularly, one change being that the evening daily meetings for men and women are now held separately, this giving our sisters better opportunities of getting at the women.

We have had times of trouble and sorrow as well as of encouragement. At Tan-lin one trouble in the church resulted in the suspension of a prominent member. We have also sorrow over a few who are not running well, though, on the whole, the members give cause for joy and gratitude. The church contributions towards local expenses and outside aggressive work have been during the year 20,000 cash (tls. 13), this being a common fund to which all contribute.

At *Kia-ting* our brethren, Ririe and Vale, are hopefully and joyfully going forward in the work, both in the city and in the country ; and Mr. and Mrs. McMullan, with Mr. Wellwood, have been preserved in peace in *Sui-fu*. They find many open doors in both city and country.

At *Chung-K'ing* thirty baptisms are reported, and Dr. Cameron has been much encouraged and has been full of labours in both the medical and spiritual work. Our sisters, Miss Ramsay and Miss Hook, have also been encouraged in their work. Dr. Cameron reports an interesting work in Yoh-chi Hien district, to the north of Chung-k'ing, but for lack of workers was unable to develop it.

At *Pao-ning* our friends have had trial in some of the baptised church members, but have to rejoice in one station opened during the year, and in a vast amount of itinerant work done in the surrounding districts. Mr. Hughesdon has given almost his whole time to this latter blessed work, and Mr. Beauchamp has given as much as possible consistent with the claims of the work in Pao-ning ; he has also visited Pa-chau. Our friends have had reverses in their attempts to open new stations, but are not thereby discouraged; rather are seeking to know the LORD'S mind with regard to extensions.

Mr. and Mrs. A. T. Polhill-Turner, at *Pa-chau*, have been joined by Miss Fryer from Han-chung, and they report friendliness of the people and many open doors.

Mr. Phelps has laboured faithfully at *Wan-hien*, and has been joined by Mr. Hayward ; the work here is still in an initial stage. We are thankful to GOD for ten stations in SI-CH'UEN, and forty-one foreign workers. Mr. James has, since the year closed, been successful in opening a most important city on the Yang-tsi, Lu-chau Fu, which will (D.V.) be mentioned in next year's report. We ask continued and earnest prayer for this large province.

VIII.—HU-PEH.

Population of Province, 20½ millions ; Area, 70,450 square miles.

MISSIONARY SUPERINTENDENT—REV. F. W. BALLER.

Stations, 7 ; Missionaries, 17 ; Native Helpers, 1 ; Baptised in 1889, 1 Convert ; Communicants, 45.

The one baptism reported from this province is from I-chang, which, with Hankow, was added during the year to our stations, chiefly for business purposes, though Mr. and Mrs. Gulston have also been able to do missionary work. They have had great difficulties with regard to premises.

At *Han-kow* and *Wu-ch'ang*, our work is entirely of a business character.

At *Fan-ch'eng*, owing to Mr. Hutton's illness and subsequent removal, the staff has been weakened and the work retarded ; but our three sisters, Miss Gates, Miss McQuillan, and Miss Mary Black, have been indefatigable in carrying on the work. Since the close of the year, Mr. and Mrs. Nicoll have taken charge there.

Mr. G. King has been able to send us interesting accounts of his work in *Lao-ho-k'eo* and neighbourhood ; large numbers have visited him for medicine ; Mrs. King, Miss Jane and Miss Emily Black have found many open doors.

The work in *She-shi* has been weakened by the removal of Mr. James to SI-CH'UEN. In this station we have only Mr. McNair working.

It will be remembered that at *Shih-sheo* there was a riot, and the house was partly destroyed in the early part of the year, but the place has since been quietly reoccupied by Mr. and Mrs. Lawson.

We would ask prayer that GOD would raise up reinforcements for these important and needy fields.

IX.—GAN-HWUY.

Population of Province, 9 millions ; Area, 48,461 square miles.

MISSIONARY SUPERINTENDENT—REV. W. COOPER.

Stations, 6 ; Missionaries, 24 ; Paid Native Helpers, 14 ; Baptised in 1889, 23 ; Communicants, 231.

Miss Robertson and Miss Underwood have re-occupied *Ch'i-chau Fu*, and thus added one station to those of last year. The work in the province is progressing very hopefully, and Mr. Cooper is looking forward to large advances in the near future. Attempts are being made to open several new places ; we hope that in the next year's report we may have still better news to tell of the older stations, as well as of new ones opened up. The direct mission work in the capital *Gan-k'ing* has been somewhat retarded by the claims of the Training Home, but we are thankful to hear that things are improving. The services of Mr. and Mrs. Wood have been greatly appreciated by the young men passing through the Training Home, and the work of the province has been substantially advanced by Mr. Cooper's able superintendence ; the workers have been greatly cheered by his return from England.

X.—KIANG-SU.

Population of Province, 20 millions; Area, 44,500 square miles.
MISSIONARY SUPERINTENDENT—REV. J. MCCARTHY.
Stations 5; *Missionaries*, 25; *Native Helpers*, 6; *Baptised in* 1889, 13; *Communicants*, 100.

In *Shanghai* much attention has been absorbed during the year in the erection of new premises, which at the time of writing (April, 1890) are completed.

At *Chin-kiang* Mr. Hutton has been able to resume the work in the city, and Miss Irvin and Miss Thomas are now there. Besides carrying on the business department, Mr. Hutton has also done work among natives and foreigners. We are praying for permanent premises in Chin-kiang, and shall be glad of fellowship in prayer.

At *Yang-chau* much work has been done during the year, though, as at Gan-k'ing, the Training Home has largely taxed the energies of the workers. Work has been begun in the old city in Yang-chau, where our sisters live for days together with the people, generally going in twos.

At *Kao-yiu* we have secured more suitable premises, and Miss Kentfield and Miss Oakeshott have taken up their residence there.

The work in *Tsing-kiang-pu* goes on steadily and hopefully. Miss J. Webb, who was so remarkably restored to health in the early part of the year, has charge of the work at present in that place, assisted by Miss Stewart and Miss Williams. We would ask special prayer for the many cities on the Grand Canal that are without the Gospel.

The More Southerly Provinces.

XI.—YUN-NAN.

Population of Province, 5 millions; Area, 107,969 square miles.
MISSIONARY SUPERINTENDENT—REV. J. W. STEVENSON.
Stations, 5; *Missionaries*, 17; *Native Helpers*, 1; *Baptised in* 1889, 7 *Converts; Communicants*, 18.

The additions have been in *Bhamo*; we have much to praise GOD for in the work there. Mr. Steven left during the year, and his place has been taken by Messrs. Lambert and Selkirk. The work is progressing very hopefully.

In *Ta-li Fu* we have nothing much to report; Mr. Foucar has been some months alone, and has had special difficulties with regard to a house. We are looking to GOD that soon fruit may appear in that distant station.

The work in the capital, *Yun-nan Fu*, has been prosecuted with vigour and earnestness, both among the men and women. Our friends have been greatly helped and supported by our brethren of the BIBLE CHRISTIAN MISSION.

We have, by GOD'S goodness, been enabled to open a new station to the east of the capital, *K'uh-ts'ing Fu*, where Mr. Owen Stevenson and Mr. Curnow are labouring; they report abundant opportunities for work.

At *Chao-tung Fu* Mr. and Mrs. Thorne and Mr. Dymond have been toiling on in faith, and have had some encouragement, though no baptisms are reported.

We would ask special prayer for YUN-NAN, that GOD would pour out HIS HOLY SPIRIT, and bring many souls to Himself.

XII.—KWEI-CHAU.

Population of Province, 4 millions; Area, 64,554 square miles.
MISSIONARY SUPERINTENDENT—REV. J. W. STEVENSON.
Stations, 2; *Missionaries*, 9; *Native Helpers*, 4; *Baptised in* 1889, 11 *Converts; Communicants*, 41.

Mr. Samuel Clarke has been very much encouraged by the condition of the work in the capital, *Kwei-yang*, and reports a very interesting work in the country. Mr. Windsor has been indefatigable in his labours, as also Mr. Waters.

Mr. Adam has been able to quietly reside in *Gan-shun Fu*, not without encouragement.

Though not within the year, we may refer to the fact that Dr. and Mrs. Pruen have removed to Kwei-yang, to take up medical work.

XIII.—HU-NAN.

Population of Province, 16 millions; Area, 74,320 square miles.

In this province several journeys have been taken during the year. Our earnest prayers still ascend for reinforcements for HU-NAN, and for an open door for permanent residence, as also in KWANG-SI.

XIV.—KIANG-SI.

Population of Province, 15 millions; Area, 72,176 square miles.
MISSIONARY SUPERINTENDENT—REV. J. MCCARTHY.
Stations, 8; *Missionaries*, 33; *Native Helpers*, 14; *Baptized in* 1889, 66 *Converts; Communicants*, 169.

In this province we have added two stations during the year, where our missionaries are now resident—*Gan-ren* and *Kwang-feng*. As will be observed, there is a good deal of encouragement in KIANG-SI, and considerable advances have been made. Besides strengthening the old work, we are evangelising in the south of the province. Six Canadian brethren have been specially designated for this work, under the superintendence of Mr. Steven, and we are hoping to open up several important centres.

At *Kiu-kiang* a very suitable house has been secured, which has already been of great service to the workers and the work in the province.

At *Nan-k'ang* there was a riot, and the houses partially destroyed, but we are thankful to say that our sisters have now resumed work in that city. We ask prayer that great blessing may follow the efforts of GOD'S servants in this province.

At *Kwei-k'i* we had the great sorrow of losing a promising worker in our dear sister, Miss Susie Parker. Though she lived but a short time in China, her life will tell for many days.

XV.—CHEH-KIANG.

Population of Province, 12 millions; *Area*, 39,150 *square miles*.

MISSIONARY SUPERINTENDENT—REV. J. MEADOWS.

Stations, 13; *Missionaries*, 26; *Native Helpers*, 67, *and many Unpaid*; *Baptized in* 1889, 154 *Converts*; *Communicants*, 1,097.

We are thankful to have a larger number of baptisms reported this year than last. The work has been carried on steadily, and we are praying earnestly for larger ingatherings. Much earnest work has been done in this province, and seed sown through many years. We ask special prayer for the 1,097 communicants, reported that they may all be filled with the HOLY GHOST, and with power, and that our brethren and sisters may be more and more encouraged in their service for the MASTER.

A SAMPAN

The Shanghai Conference.

THE Missionary Conference, long looked forward to and much prayed about, is now looked back upon with thankfulness by the 430 missionaries who attended it, and early reports are to hand, which call for grateful praise. Shanghai papers, *The Celestial Empire* and *The Shanghai Mercury*, give long accounts of each day's meetings, from which we cull most of the following:—

Never before in the history of Shanghai has such a concourse of missionaries been seen here. Long before the hour fixed for the opening services the seats in the pit and dress circle [of the Lyceum Theatre], which are generally seen under very different circumstances, began to fill up with an audience dressed partly in Chinese and partly in foreign clothes. There were amongst the audience many grey heads of the pioneers in the mission-field, but the majority were men and women of middle age. The sexes were about equally divided in point of numbers. Eighty-two members of the C.I.M. attended the Conference. One wrote:—

". . . That evening did me more good than many a sermon. It was the outcome of lives whose home, whose dwelling-place was in GOD. It was not only in our own C.I.M. house that I felt this; nothing impressed me more during the whole Conference. To look at these men and some women whose hair had grown white in the work in China, to see them full of faith in GOD and confidence for the future of the work, and to know that in spite of many years of discouragements and difficulties, that some of us know little about, they had been kept faithful, was indeed an inspiration to a young missionary."

The conference began with a prayer-meeting, conducted by the Rev. H. Blodget, D.D., of Pekin. In prayer the Rev. H. C. Du Bose, of Su-chau, referred to the fact that they were met where prayer was *not* wont to be made.

At 11 o'clock the Rev. J. Hudson Taylor preached the opening sermon, taking as his subject, "Christ Feeding the Multitude." Before commencing his discourse, he alluded to the annual meeting of the British and Foreign Bible Society being held that day in Exeter Hall, and offered prayer on behalf of that meeting, and all the meetings of GOD's people.

The business of the meeting at 2.30 was the organization of the Conference and the election of officers. A list of the members of the Conference was read, from which it appeared that missionaries had come from a great variety of places. Two Chairmen were elected, the Rev. Dr. Nevius, of the U.S.A., and the Rev. D. Hill, of Great Britain. Dr. Allen then read a paper on "The Changed Aspect of China."

In the evening the paper by the Venerable Archdeacon Moule on "The Relation of Foreign Missions to the Foreign Communities" was read, and addresses were given by Professor Thwing and Dr. Ashmore.

On May 8th the proceedings were led by Dr. Wright, of the British and Foreign Bible Society, the subject being the diffusion of the Scriptures throughout the Empire. In the course of the day Dr. Williamson read a resumé on "The Need of Brief Introductions, Headings, Maps, and Philological, Historical, Geographical, and Theological Notes;" and Rev. S. Dyer read one on "Bible Distribution in China, its Methods and Results."

On Friday, May 9th, the Rev. J. Hudson Taylor read his paper on "The Missionary," and the Rev. D. Hill read one on "Lay Agency." Dr. Ashmore spoke most earnestly in favour of lay agency, and especially of woman's agency. In the afternoon, Dr. Nevius read his "Historical Review of Missionary

Methods," and Dr. Henry a paper on "Preaching to the Heathen in Chapels, in the Open-air, and during Itineration." The Rev. Y. K. Yen, a native minister, was listened to with great attention, as he urged that missionaries should adopt Chinese modes of life, and that none should be brought out from home who were over-bearing in manner. The Rev. A. Elwin said that denominational differences were not of much consequence so long as they all had the work of GOD at heart; that in Hang-chau all the missionaries worked heartily together. The Rev. W. Muirhead said that the men who were wanted were those who had acted as missionaries at home. On Friday evening the Rev. A. H. Smith gave an address on "The Relation of Christianity to Universal Progress."

On Saturday, 10th, it was proposed and carried that the members of the Conference about to go to the home-lands be appointed to appeal to the churches of Europe and America for an increase of missionaries to China. A paper by Miss Safford was read, entitled "A General View of Women's Work in China, and its Results." Miss Hattie Noyes and Miss Haygood read papers on "Girls' Schools." Papers by Miss Cushman and Miss Ricketts were also read on "The Best Method of Reaching the Women." In the afternoon Miss M. Murray read an essay on "The Feasibility of Unmarried Ladies Engaging in Evangelistic Work." The next essay was that of Miss Fielde on "The Training of Native Female Evangelists," and then Mrs. A. Smith read her paper on "The Training of the Women of the Church." Dr. Williamson said that the women of China could only be reached by women, and that the permanent Christianisation of China depends on the women; that their work is root work, and can only be done by their going through the country reading and teaching. Mr. Taylor believed we should find in ladies efficient pioneers in cities to which male missionaries had no access, the people not fearing them as political agents. He cited an instance in which a lady succeeded in getting a house where a male missionary had been unable to get inside the city walls, and said that when she went home a married missionary was enabled by her influence to carry on the work.

On Monday, 12th, Dr. Douthwaite read his paper on "Medical Work as an Evangelising Agency"; another was read on "The Value of Lady Physicians in China," and an interesting discussion on medical work followed. In the afternoon the Rev. F. Hartman and Rev. W. H. Murray read papers on "Work for the Blind and the Deaf and Dumb." Dr. Whitney read one on "The Value and Methods of Opium Refuges," and it was followed by Dr. Dudgeon's on "Statistics and Resolutions on the Evils of the Use of Opium."

On the 13th the subject was "Methods of Dealing with Inquirers, Conditions of Admission to Church Fellowship, and the Best Methods of Discipline"; and in the afternoon papers were read on "Deepening the Spiritual Life and Stimulating the Church to Aggressive Work," on "The Service of Song in China," "The Relation of Christian Missions to the Chinese Government," and "The Best Methods of Developing Self-support and Voluntary Effort."

Wednesday, the 14th, was given to the subject of education, and May 15th to that of literature. "The Division of the Field" and "Ancestral Worship" were the subjects taken up on Friday, and on Saturday, 17th, the tenth day of Conference, papers were read on the "Aboriginal Tribes," and on "The Results and Statistics of Missionary Work." The following interesting statistics were given: Foreign missionaries—men, 589; wives, 390; single women, 316; total, 1,295. Native helpers: ordained, 209; ur ordained, 1,260; female helpers, 180. Medical work—hospitals, 61; dispensaries, 43; patients during 1889, 348,439. Organised churches, 520; wholly self-supporting, 94; half ditto, 22; quarter, 27. Bible distribution, 1889—Bibles, 1,454; New Testaments, 22,402; portions, 642,131. Communicants, 37,287; pupils in schools, 16,816; Contributions by native Christians, 36,884 dollars, little less than one dollar for each member.

One of the results of the Conference, which was a cause of great thankfulness, was the agreement to use one version of the Scriptures, instead of several as heretofore. Upon this decision being come to, all rose and sang the doxology.

The daily united prayer, the exchange of views on so many important points, and the happy social intercourse, were *most* helpful to those present; and we trust that the appeals issued to the home churches will be nobly responded to, and that the full report when published may be largely used in deepening interest and enlarging the views of Friends and Helpers at home on missionary subjects.

A special note of praise must be added for the signal preservation of the precious lives of the missionaries: arranged on a platform to be photographed in a group, the platform, the upper tiers of which were 18 or 20 ft. high, gave way, and they were thrown down in heaps; those underneath remained still until those uppermost could rise, and most mercifully no one was seriously injured, though many were much shaken, and scratches and bruises were numerous. The collar-bone and two ribs of one lady were broken, but she was progressing favourably towards recovery by last accounts.

We have indeed to praise GOD for His help given all through the Conference, and look forward with bright hopes for the near future. We append appeals made by the Conference, reserving that for lady-missionaries until next month.

An Appeal for Ordained Missionaries.

To all our Home Churches.

GREETING:—

Realising as never before the magnitude of China and the utter inadequacy of our present numbers for the speedy carrying into execution of our LORD'S command, "Go ye into all the world and preach the Gospel to every creature"; therefore,

Resolved, that we, the four hundred and thirty members of the Missionary Conference, now in session in Shanghai, earnestly and unanimously appeal to you to send out speedily *as many hundreds as can possibly be secured of well qualified ordained men.*

The whole of China is now open to missionary effort and needs a large number of men of prayer, and patient endurance and of common sense,—men full of the HOLY GHOST, and of faith in the Gospel as "the power of GOD unto salvation."

The missionary here encounters hoary and subtle superstitions, a most difficult language, a people of vigorous intellect, with a vast literature and an elaborate educational system. There is need, therefore, of men of commanding practical and intellectual as well as spiritual endowments,—men who shall be able to engage in and direct the work of evangelization, to educate, train, and induct into their work a native pastorate, to found and conduct educational institutions and to provide a general theological, scientific and periodical literature.

Seeing, as we do, the utter destitution and helplessness of these millions still " having no hope and without GOD in the world," we appeal to young men to give themselves to this work. We believe that the great question with each of you should be, not, "Why should I go?" but, "Why should I *not* go?"

We recommend that the men be sent under the regularly constituted missionary societies of the various denominations, and that these societies search out suitable men before they are committed to the home work.

With the highest appreciation of the claims of the home churches, we still urge young pastors to consider whether the places of some of them might not be filled by men who cannot come to the mission field, while they might bring their experience to spheres of work in China which must otherwise be left wholly unoccupied.

We call upon individual congregations to greatly increase their contributions for the support of one or more of these men.

We urge Christian men of wealth to prayerfully consider the duty and privilege of giving themselves personally to this work, or of supporting their representatives.

Finally, we shall not cease to pray the LORD of the harvest to move you mightily by HIS HOLY SPIRIT in behalf of this vast and ripening field.

Yours in CHRIST,

(Signed) J. L. NEVIUS, } Chairmen.
DAVID HILL,

Shanghai, *May*, 1890.

An Appeal for Lay Missionaries.

THE Conference unanimously resolved that the accompanying Appeal for additional Lay Agents be sent to the Home Churches from the present Conference:—

That this Conference, whilst strongly urging upon the Home Churches the sustentation and continued increase of the staff of thoroughly trained and fully qualified ordained missionaries, and the further development of native agencies in every branch of Christian work, is still so profoundly impressed with the manifold need of this vast country, that it would present a direct appeal to the laity of the Home Churches for lay missionaries; and in doing so would place before them some of the departments of service in which their help is more especially needed.

Beginning with the highest service, and touching the deepest need of the country, they would point to the many millions of our fellow men who have never heard the Gospel of the grace of GOD; and to some millions more, who, though they have possessed themselves of some portion of His Word, still fail to comprehend its meaning for want of some one to guide them in their study of it; and they would urge the claims of these unevangelised millions on the youth of the Home Churches, and would emphasise the nobility of the service which a Christian evangelist may thus render to the LORD in China.

The country long closed is open. The people, if not decidedly friendly, are not hostile. The work of the Bible colporteur has prepared the way. The promise of ingathering is yearly brightening, but the labourers are few; and with the abundance of Christian workers in the Home lands, surely hundreds or even thousands might be found to hasten on the evangelisation of this empire by their personal effort and consecration.

Passing now to the intellectual requirements of China, we rejoice to record the progress of missionary education in the East during recent years; but are admonished by the fact that purely secular instruction so largely tinges the educational movements both of Christian and heathen governments; and in this fact we hear a loud call to the Christian Church to supply in larger numbers Christian educationalists for China. The intellectual renaissance of the empire is just commencing, there is an incipient cry for Western culture; and the response which the Christian Church may make to this cry will, to no inconsiderable extent, decide the course which the education of the country will take in the future.

With Christian men in the chairs of the colleges of China, what may we not expect from so powerful an auxiliary in the evangelisation of the empire? University men may find here at no distant period some of the most influential posts in the mission field; and we would earnestly invite all such Christian co-workers to weigh over with all seriousness the question whether they may not more effectively serve their generation in China than in the Home lands.

But besides the intellectual need of the country, there is also the chronic and often dire necessity of physical distress.

The masses of the people are poor. Physical suffering meets us at every turn. Medical science is almost unknown. Charitable institutions, though established both by the government and by private effort, fail to compass the need of the masses. Flood and famine slay their thousands; and yet the wealth of the world is in Christian hands, and might by judicious distribution both save the lives of thousands yearly, and give completer expression to the Life we preach. On behalf of these destitute masses, therefore, we earnestly plead with the men of wealth in the Home Churches that they will consider the claims of these suffering ones; and not only by their gifts and prayers will largely aid the reinforcement of the noble staff of medical missionaries already in the field, but will give themselves in larger numbers to benevolent enterprise abroad. The blind, the aged, the orphan and the destitute mutely plead for Christian compassion, and the LORD Himself has said, "Inasmuch as ye did it unto one of these my brethren, even these least, ye did it unto me."

We appeal then to our lay brethren of the Home Churches, to men of sterling piety, and of strong common sense, that they would lay to heart the needs of this vast empire—its spiritual destitution, its stunted education, its physical distress—and that they would solemnly ask themselves whether for the greater glory of God they are not called to meet this pressing need, and to devote themselves, their service and their wealth, to this missionary enterprise in China. We would offer to them a most hearty welcome to our ranks, and would assure them that whether they come out as ordained or as lay workers, this welcome will be equally cordial; and in conclusion, we would earnestly pray that this appeal may be brought home to the hearts of many by the power of the Divine Spirit.

(Signed) J. L. NEVIUS, } Chairmen.
DAVID HILL,

An Appeal for One Thousand Men.

To all Protestant Churches of Christian Lands.

DEAR BRETHREN IN CHRIST,

We, the General Conference of Protestant Missionaries in China, having just made a special appeal to you for a largely increased force of ordained Missionaries to preach the Gospel throughout the length and breadth of this great land,—to plant Churches, to educate native ministers and helpers, to create a Christian literature, and in general to engage in and direct the supreme work of Christian evangelization, and

Having also just made a special appeal to you for a largely increased force of unordained men, evangelists, teachers and physicians,—to travel far and wide distributing books and preaching to the masses, to lend a strong helping hand in the great work of Christian education, and to exhibit to China the benevolent side of Christianity in the work of healing the sick ;

Therefore, we do now appeal to you, the Protestant Churches of Christian lands, to send to China in response to these calls

ONE THOUSAND MEN
WITHIN FIVE YEARS FROM THIS TIME.

We make this appeal in behalf of three hundred millions of unevangelized heathen ; we make it with all the earnestness of our whole hearts, as men overwhelmed with the magnitude and responsibility of the work before us ; we make it with unwavering faith in the power of a risen SAVIOUR to call men into His vineyard, and to open the hearts of those who are His stewards to send out and support them, and we shall not cease to cry mightily to Him that He will do this thing, and that our eyes may see it.

On behalf of the Conference,

Chairmen { Rev. J. L. NEVIUS, D.D.
{ Rev. D. HILL.

Permanent Committee { Rev. J. HUDSON TAYLOR.
{ Rev. WM. ASHMORE, D.D.
{ Rev. H. CORBETT, D.D.
{ Rev. C. W. MATEER, D.D., LL.D.
{ Rev. C. F. REID.

Shanghai, May, 1890.

Items of Interest.

FROM REV. J. W. STEVENSON.

SHANGHAI, *April 18th* - I have heard since last writing of ten baptisms at T'ai-chau, CHEH-KIANG, on April 2nd. I hear that Mr. Horobin has come to Kwei-hwa-ch'eng to seek medical aid ; it appears that while riding a horse he met with an accident and dislocated his arm ; Mr. Belcher, who came with him as far as Pao-t'eo, has returned to Ning-hsia.

May 23rd.—I grieve to say that Miss Dunn entered into rest last Saturday, 17th inst., at Chin-kiang, and also that this morning Mr. Souter, one of the Canadian party, passed away. He died of consumption, and Miss Dunn of small-pox.

We are profoundly thankful that GOD has blessed the general Conference of Missionaries in Shanghai ; it has exceeded the expectations of the most sanguine, and we are expecting great results in the future. The united appeal for a thousand missionaries will surely meet with a generous response. Dear Mr. Taylor has laboured incessantly since his arrival, and the strain is beginning to tell somewhat upon him. On his birthday we had the honour of presenting him with an illuminated address, signed by all the members of the Mission in Shanghai.

May 31st.—Our own conference was a time of blessing, and now that our Council meetings are going on they are characterised by great cordiality and unanimity.

Mr. and Mrs. Orr-Ewing leave us to-day, *via* Japan and San Francisco.

GOD is trying our faith in a good many ways, but we are very conscious of His presence and help, and therefore we go forward with hope. I can truly say that there never was a time in the history of the Mission when there was more unanimity and whole-hearted loyalty to our principles. The friends who came for the Conference are now rapidly dispersing.

In Memoriam.

MISS DUNN.

ON June 24th the sad tidings reached us that Miss Dunn was ill at Chin-kiang with black small-pox ; and it was added Mr. Huntley, who was greatly supported, was with her, as also Miss M. Murray and Mr. McCarthy. The next mail brought word that on May 17th she had passed away. We have no details, but would ask prayer for her sorrowing family and that of Mr. Huntley. Miss Dunn, who was the daughter of one of Mr. Spurgeon's Deacons, only sailed for China last August. She wrought but one hour, but her reward is sure.

MR. WILLIAM SOUTER.

FROM MR. H. W. FROST.

TORONTO, ONTARIO, *June 23rd.*—It is with sorrowing hearts that we have to tell of the passing away of another of our devoted workers in China, Mr. W. M. Souter, formerly of Hamilton, Ont.

The death of this beloved brother took place at Shanghai, on the 25th May. Mr. Souter had been sick for a considerable time, and had been brought from KIANG-SI to Shanghai, in the hope that a change might prove helpful to him. But this means, and all that the best medical skill could do, proved inefficacious. Quick consumption had set in, and its course could not be stayed. Mr. Souter was lovingly told this, and accepted the message quietly and calmly, knowing Him whom he had believed. Still no one thought that the end was so close at hand. There was hope that he might remain many days. But shortly afterwards the final summons came. Upon the morning of his death, Mr. McCarthy had been having sweet fellowship with him in the LORD, and had left him, expecting to return in half an hour. After Mr. McCarthy had gone, Mr. Souter desired to lie down and rest, which the friends with him tenderly arranged for. But no sooner had his head been lowered than a change was noticed. The breathing became laboured, the eyes closed, and our beloved brother fell asleep. At the very last a beautiful smile broke over his face, and thus he went in to see the KING.

"One by one!" Three out of the fourteen who left us in 1888, now in heaven, beholding their SAVIOUR'S glory. And how few left for poor, dark, needy China. May their places soon be taken by those who will serve with equal self-renunciation, desiring that CHRIST shall be magnified in their bodies, whether it be by life or death. We would ask prayer in behalf of a sorrowing father and mother and brother.

Lines Written in the New Mission House.

BY MRS. ORR-EWING.

"*The name . . . from that day shall be* JEHOVAH SHAMMAH—*The Lord is there.*"

LORD, Thy children's hearts are longing
    To uplift to Thee a song,
Praise for all Thy loving-kindness,
    Hallelujahs loud and long.

"Hitherto the LORD hath help'd us,"
    Truly we can praise His Name
Who has never disappointed
    Those for aid to Him who came.

Now we praise "JEHOVAH JIREH,"
    For this House of peace and love ;
May His SPIRIT, ever brooding,
    Make it like the Home above.

There, they face to face behold Him,
    Serve unceasing night and day ;
Here, our mortal eyes are holden,
    Yet we have His sweet "alway."

Thus we pray, "JEHOVAH SHAMMAH,"
    Name this House shall ever bear ;
May it be our happy witness,
    That the LORD is always here.

As from Temple-courts of Sion
    Rose the incense cloud alway,
So from this, thy children's dwelling,
    Prayer and praise arise each day.

See we no Shekinah glory,
    And no cloudy pillar view ;
Yet we know the GOD of Israel
    Will give grace and glory too :

Grace to tread the heav'nly pathway,
    Guidance that we may not stray,
Faith and love for happy service,
    Glory at the Crowning Day.

China Inland Mission House, Shanghai, May, 1890.

Testimonies at the Shanghai Prayer Meeting.

(From The Messenger.)

THE weekly prayer meeting of the C.I.M. is always an interesting and helpful gathering, but last Saturday night's was especially so, owing to the influx of members from different provinces for the Conference. Our readers will appreciate our endeavour to give a brief outline of the addresses.

After Ps. xlvi. was read by REV. J. E. CARDWELL, the chairman, REV. J. W. STEVENSON, stated that he had a letter from REV. J. MEADOWS, of Shao-hing, stating that the six Chu-ki Christians who were imprisoned have been released as the result of the enquiry by the officials. Pastor Nying writes that the six brethren have no resentment towards any, but have returned to their families with grateful praise to GOD, and the native church in Harg-chau have resolved to set apart a day for thanksgiving to GOD for this settlement of the case after five years of anxiety.

After prayer the REV. W. D. RUDLAND, of Tai-chau, told how a time of trial had been followed by a time of blessing. Some time ago there were fifty candidates in the various stations, and fifteen have recently been baptised. The first one of the fifteen baptised was an old man of over seventy, for whom prayer has been offered for eighteen years. He went on to say that for some months they have had special prayer on two evenings of the week for the children of the native Christians. He believed the LORD wanted all their children. Among the recent converts were four children of native Christians, and this has been a great encouragement to the natives. The examination of one of the candidates, he thought, showed how a word can be used. A little girl came into the chapel on one Sunday afternoon and was noticed by no one, and went home after hearing the Gospel. She told her mother what she had heard—that there is one GOD, who must be worshipped, and that they must not worship idols any more. "Men may be saved," said the mother, "but how can women be saved?" "The preacher," replied her daughter, "said that even women can be saved." "If there is news like that, I will go to hear for myself," said she. She came and is a most intelligent enquirer, in fact he believes she is converted.

The speaker said he had been sceptical about people hearing the Gospel once and carrying away as much as that girl did ; but he trusted he should not be again. Cases like that were a great encouragement to sow beside all waters.

He was followed by MR. MARCUS WOOD, who spoke about the work of the Young Men's Training Home at Gan-k'ing. One of the greatest difficulties, he said, was the monotony of study, but he thanked GOD for grace given. He tells friends there that the learning of the language is only the secondary matter, the primary one being the men's own walk with GOD. In leaving for England he said his desire was to stir up the young men there.

The thoughts of the meeting were then carried off to the distant province of YUN-NAN, as the REV. S. T. THORNE rose to speak. The work in that province, he said, was very much seed sowing, not much reaping. Speaking of Chao-tung, he said it was a large prefecture of about twenty days' journey from one side to the other, including two or three hundred market towns, besides several smaller towns, and the missionaries there are itinerating through the district sowing the seed.

REV. W. W. CASSELS, from Pao-ning in SI-CHUEN, said there was very much to thank GOD for with regard to the work in that province. Three years ago the Ch'ung-k'ing work was shattered, but now the church there has been more than doubled, while Kia-ting, Sui-fu, Lu-cheo, Pao-ning, Pa-cheo, Wan Hien and Kwan Hien have been opened, and the LORD is giving them great encouragement in all directions. A great deal of itinerating work, he said, has been done by Mr. Beauchamp and others, who have visited markets constantly, and it is beginning to bear fruit. The speaker concluded by saying how very much yet remained to be done, and that there are vast districts almost untouched.

MR. M. BEAUCHAMP then gave an exceedingly interesting account of a convert in the Pao-ning district, whom he described as very influential. He bought a New Testament there and took it home, and at the close of last year returned to learn more. Quite apart from this, the speaker being led to take a journey through his district, he was met by him in a market town, and he told of GOD's dealing with him. Mr. Beauchamp asked him to visit Pao-ning again, which he did for twenty days, during which time he studied his Bible, and, though very proud, asked many questions. As he was leaving, he said, "When are you coming up to break these idols of mine?" but it was not possible for Mr. Beauchamp to go then. When Mr. Hughesdon took a journey in the direction of his home, he found that the mother stood in the way of his accepting CHRIST.

Later, the speaker paid him a visit, and was shown into the room where the idols were. After the evening meal the man said, "What about these idols? One of them is made of mud, and two of them are wood." Mr. Beauchamp said, "Why not turn them out?" and he forthwith proceeded to do so. The wooden idols were burnt that night, and the next morning the speaker heard some heavy thuds, and saw the man with a hatchet pounding the mud idol into pieces on the floor. The speaker concluded by asking prayer on his behalf, as he will most probably be greatly persecuted.

MR. ORR EWING addressed the meeting shortly on their labours in the Ping-yao district in SHAN-SI Province, which was begun two years ago. He said the work centred around the opium refuges. While in them men have to attend worship and learn to pray and sing; and on leaving they are visited in their homes. He has found that, as a rule, only those stand firm who are converted. He had the joy of baptising five converts just before leaving. He referred to the ordination as pastor of Elder Chang at Ta-ning, and he was glad to see how the Christians were willing to contribute to his support.

After some prayer the REV. J. L. NEVIUS, D.D., of SHANTUNG, who was present, was asked to address the meeting. In the course of his remarks he said that the last famine relief work had given a new impulse to the work, and in connection with their own mission (American Presbyterian) there are *fifteen hundred* enquirers, and probably not less in connection with the English Baptists. Several hundred converts have been baptised this spring. He concluded by referring to the earnest efforts of the Romanists to proselytise among their converts. Some of them have gone over for a time, but have been glad to come back again.

By this time it was getting late, and the meeting broke up, all feeling what a joy it had been to hear so many inspiring testimonies.

Tidings from Scattered Workers.

Kan-suh Province.

FROM MISS M. GRAHAM BROWN.

Lan-chau, January 23rd.—My brother has good audiences and attentive listeners, and many show considerable interest until they see what the choice for GOD will cost, and then, alas! they draw back. We find much the same among the women whom we visit; on the other hand our friends are increasing, and some of us are out every day visiting in some house or other: the invitation is generally to "see the sick," but we try to use every such visit as an opening for the Gospel.

Only one of our old almshouse friends will come near us in this house; they all say it is too far, though they have no difficulty in coming to beg at the City Temple just behind; the one who does come, old Suh Nai-nai, satisfies us all that she is really the LORD's. We also consider that two of our servants have grasped the truth. One of them, a SI-CH'UEN man, has asked for baptism.

FROM MR. LAUGHTON.

Liang-chau, January 27th.—Oh, when are we going to be joined by some fellow-workers! We have been over five years in China, and yet no one has come to help us with the work of the LORD. Since our return we have had interesting audiences, mostly men. Two old widows come every LORD's day, and on Thursdays; they both profess to believe, and one of them has put away all her idols, except the ancestral tablets; she says she is afraid of her son returning and wanting these. The other belongs to Si-gan, and has no idols or ancestral tablets to give up; we believe they are not far from the kingdom. Our cook, a Si-gan man, professes to believe.

We are altogether unable to do what requires to be done here. On the LORD's days we have quite a room full willing to listen, who have to leave before they seem inclined to, because I have not strength to preach for any length of time. With the women it is the same, only my dear wife to attend to them, and she far from strong, and with two little ones to care for. When will some one come? We pray and hope, yet the months and the years go by, and no one comes; still the same lonely life. We have not so much as a native Christian to help us in the great fight, and sometimes we get downhearted, and then the LORD raises us up as it were upon eagle's wings.

Shen-si Province.

FROM MR. REDFERN.

Feng-tsiang Fu, January 30th.—Mr. Bland and I leave to-morrow for Liu-liu-pu, and after working there for a week or so, we are hoping (D.V.) to itinerate to the north, taking Pin-chau as a centre, and visiting all the places small and great in the district.

FROM MR. BLAND.

January 25th.—GOD is blessing us, and our every need is fully supplied. Doors are wide open for the Gospel.

Chih-li Province.

FROM MR. BRIDGE.

Shun-teh Fu, Jan. 15th.—I have been greatly encouraged in the opium refuge work lately—this week had eleven patients in at a time. Most of them have a very intelligent grasp of the leading Gospel truths when they leave. One dear fellow called Mei-chen, returned to his home some forty *li* among the hills, and began preaching to his relatives and fellow-villagers, some of whom laughed at and reviled him. He returned in a few days, bringing a younger brother to break off opium; he seemed full to overflowing, and I could do nothing but wonder and say, "This verily is the LORD's doing." I found that truths, and especially Gospel stories, of which I had spoken to another man during Mei-chen's first days in the refuge, and when he used to sit about the yard apparently indifferent, had all been received into good ground and were springing up to the glory of GOD. The native Christian here, who has seen much blessing in the work of the Americans at Ning-tsin, says he has never seen such a wonderful change in such a short space of time. Mei-chen's brother is also a hopeful case. Two others who left last week, as far as I can judge, are not far from the Kingdom. I think the LORD would have me during the coming spring go round and visit these men, and spend some days in their villages, confirming and building them up in the faith. Some of them have made me promise to do so at the earliest opportunity.

Shan-tung Province.

FROM MISS HIBBERD.

Che-foo, April 28th.—The school work here is certainly progressing most favourably, and much thought is needed to be given to further development. It is a most important work, influencing missionary work both amongst natives and foreigners. A great door of usefulness seems to me to be opened here.

Si-ch'uen Province.

FROM MR. GRAY OWEN.

Chen-tu, Jan. 8th.—You will be glad to know that we have seen decided progress here during the year. Thirty-one converts were baptised, one excluded, a net increase of thirty souls. Three out-stations have been opened, viz., Kwan-hien, where Miss Fosbery and a native Christian live; 2. Hung-pai-leo, a first preaching station on the plain, in a hamlet where two Christians live; we send a local preacher out there every Sunday, and the names of two men desiring salvation were sent in on the first Sunday of this year; 3. Mei-chau, 200 *li* south, occupied since the second week in December by our old teacher Cheng and family. Some progress has also been made in developing local talents for the LORD's service.

We are not without our trials, but the blessings always preponderate. Though we are only gleaning before the harvest, yet it is gladening with joy.

Our hearts long to see something done for the poor Miao-tsi, and if the LORD will, we hope to go to Mao-cheng, 410 *li* to the north, to spend the coming summer as preliminary to more permanent work for them. We shall have plenty of opportunities for Chinese work; the Miao-tsi are living in the immediate vicinity.

Compared with what needs to be done, our stations in this district are only so many oases in a heathen Sahara. Oh, when will these millions hear the Gospel! When will the Church awaken to its duty? The unutterable woe and need of this land has never yet been fully realised. May the HOLY SPIRIT keep us daily filled with power!

FROM MISS RAMSAY.

Chung-K'ing, Feb. 18th.—The work here goes on hopefully. Last Sunday was exceptionally fine; we had large crowds of men and women at the services. The chapel could not hold them, so the women sat out in the court; we tried to speak to them individually or in small groups after the service was over. We have to thank God for our Chinese evangelist; he is a spiritually-minded man; and his thoughts often help and refresh me. Miss Hook and I are now occupying the old house where Mr. Nicoll was for so long. One dear woman who heard the truth in Mrs. Nicoll's time is, I believe, simply trusting JESUS. Many show an interest, but are kept back by Satan. Alas! he has so many devices for deceiving these poor people. His power is very real in China. In all possible ways he would discourage us workers, but there is a stronger than he. I do rejoice to think of the strength of our LORD JESUS. Their REDEEMER is strong. "He giveth power to the faint, and to them that have no might He increaseth strength."

Hu-peh Province.

FROM MISS MARY BLACK.

Fan-cheng, Feb. 7th.—I wish you could have looked in on me last Wednesday morning. My class consisted of forty women and thirty children, and the attention I had almost said the eagerness—with which they listened was something to praise GOD for. On Sunday, too, there was a large congregation; my dear blind friend repeated part of John iii., which I have taught him during the week, and preached with his usual unction.

Feb. 17th.—The Lord is helping here marvellously. I had upwards of a hundred women and children at my class on Wednesday, and on Sunday the large hall was quite full. At the morning service many of those who come profess to believe that there is but one living and true GOD, and say they know that their idols are false, and have no power to hurt or to save. Several are, I trust, not far from the Kingdom, and a few have asked for baptism. I go out visiting regularly every day in the week except Wednesday. I spent a day lately at a village fifteen *li* off, the home of one of the teachers. We were so inundated with visitors all day that my kind entertainers had difficulty in securing time for me to snatch a hasty meal. I talked almost incessantly for nearly six hours, and reached home at dusk, feeling very weary, but with a heart full of praise to GOD for all the help given during the day.

We are praying daily for the thousand evangelists. May the LORD send them speedily!

Kwei-chau Province.

FROM DR. PRUEN.

Kwei-yang Fu, March 25th.—We left Chung-k'ing at the end of February, and reached here safely on the 17th inst. We have had a very kind welcome from Mr. and Mrs. Sam. Clarke. Mr. Waters has returned, but we have not yet met Mr. Windsor. The second mission-house has been placed at our disposal, and seems splendidly adapted for a small medical work. We are delighted with the prospect, and hope to move in by the end of this week. My wife is particularly pleased with our surroundings.

Gan-hwuy Province.

FROM DR. HOWARD TAYLOR.

Gan-K'ing, April 22nd.—Such a pleasant time I have had here these last five weeks. I get more and more fond of the place every week. You will be glad, I know, to hear that I have finished the course of study in the primer, and am busy just now revising it for my primer examination.

Kiang-si Province.

FROM MISS MUNRO.

Kwei-k'i, Feb. 22nd.—You will rejoice to know that the boy that dear Miss Parker took an interest in, and who is known as Miss Parker's boy, has decided for the LORD. With the money he got at the new year he bought a New Testament, and he comes every forenoon to read with me. We have every reason to believe that the boy's father is a Christian too. His mother was baptised last December and is very bright. Miss Lucas and Miss Parker were out visiting one day and were led to her home. From the first the mother seemed interested, and I remember that when Miss Parker came home she said, "There was one woman who listened so attentively, I am sure she is going to be saved." It was a special joy to me to see this dear woman publicly confess Christ, and to know that our dear sister's brief stay in Kwei-k'i was so wonderfully owned of GOD.

I have been taking short journeys into the country with the Bible-woman, that I might get used to Chinese living. A fortnight since I went with the evangelist and a woman for a tour among the villages, returning at the end of eight days. The LORD, indeed, was with us, and four professed to accept JESUS as their SAVIOUR. Yesterday I returned from a five days' trip. We did not visit many places owing to rain, but we blessed the LORD for the opportunity of telling the story to individuals as well as to crowds. It is so good of Him to give me this definite work to do.

Arrivals from China.

On Saturday, July 5th, Mr. and Mrs. WOOD, Miss BROOMHALL, Miss SEED, Mr. HUGHESDON, and a young son of Mr. JUDD reached England, having travelled by P. and O. steamer as far as Marseilles.

Supplement for "China's Millions," August, 1890.

China Inland Mission.

Dr. GENERAL SUMMARY OF CASH ACCOUNT FOR 1889. Cr.

	£ s. d.	£ s. d.		£ s. d.	£ s. d.
To Balances from 1888		1,988 9 3	By Expenditure—		
,, Receipts acknowledged in CHINA'S MILLIONS		48,662 19 3	Per Home Accounts .. 30,860 3 1 Per China Accounts (see Contra) 2,821 2 5		33,681 5 6
		50,651 8 6	By Balances—		
Less, Famine Fund Contributions .. .. 9,188 9 6 Other Special Receipts 2,414 7 4		11,602 16 10	Outfits and Passages Acct. 62 5 0 Building Fund .. .. 4,025 4 9 Superannuated Missionaries' Account .. .. 4,046 1 3 General Account 54 17 7		8,188 8 7
		39,048 11 8			
,, Receipts per China Accounts— Contributions in China and Receipts from America .. .. 2,866 15 2 From Exchange and Interest Account .. 103 4 11					
	2,970 0 1				
Less, Famine Fund Contributions 148 17 8					
		2,821 2 5			
		£41,869 14 1			£41,869 14 1

ABSTRACT OF EXPENDITURE ON GENERAL ACCOUNT.

	£ s. d.	£ s. d.	£ s. d.
For China Account:—			
Cash remitted to China from London .. .. 32,837 12 3 Less on Famine Account 9,188 9 6		23,649 2 9	
Cash otherwise received in China (see General Summary above), accounted for in China Accounts .. .. 2,970 0 1 Less on Famine Account 148 17 8		2,821 2 5	
Payments to Missionaries on Furlough		1,391 17 0	
Expenses of Telegraphing Funds to China		15 4 8	
Freights on Goods to China		172 19 10	
Postages on Famine Fund Account, omitted from that Account ..		16 0 0	
			28,266 6 8
For Candidates' Account:—			
General Expenses—			
Share of Rents, Rates, Taxes, etc. 130 0 0			
Board of Candidates and others 289 19 7			
Allowances to Candidates for Personal Expenses 50 10 0			
Travelling Expenses of Candidates 11 11 6			
Medical Attendance and Dentist 15 7 6			
Printing, Schedules of Questions for Candidates and Referees, etc. 8 8 7			
Clerical Expenses (proportion) 50 0 0			
Postages 8 0 0			
Petty Cash 2 5 8			
		556 2 10	
Carried forward		556 2 10	28,266 6 8

ABSTRACT OF EXPENDITURE ON GENERAL ACCOUNT.—Continued.

	£ s. d.	£ s. d.	£ s. d.
Brought forward		556 2 10	28,266 6 8
For Candidates' Account—(continued)—			
Training Home Account—			
Rates, Taxes, Mortgage Interest, etc.	185 4 8		
Tutor	200 0 0		
Housekeeper	53 0 0		
Furniture and Household Requisites	26 17 11		
		465 2 7	
Cambridge Account (part of year)—			
Fees for Students' Terms and Examinations	151 19 0		
Current Expenses for Housekeeping, etc.	57 16 0		
Housekeeper	22 0 0		
Furniture, and Moving ditto	8 3 11		
	239 18 11		
Less Special Donation for Cambridge Account	1 0 0		
		238 18 11	
			1,260 4 4
For Outfits and Passages Account:—			
Outfits and Passages to China	1,825 18 6		
Travelling Expenses, Shipment of Baggage, etc.	6 2 8		
Unexpended Portions of Special Contributions (*see* Balances)	62 5 0		
		1,894 6 2	
Less Special Contributions		545 16 5	
			1,348 9 9
For Houses Account:—			
Rents, Rates, Taxes, Coal, Gas, Water, Mortgage Interest, Repairs, etc., 2, 4, 6, 8, and 10, Pyrland Road			266 16 9
For Office Expenses:—			
Secretaries and Clerks			981 6 3
For Publications Account:—			
Printing CHINA'S MILLIONS	630 5 5		
„ Books (Various)	79 3 6		
Binding CHINA'S MILLIONS	49 5 10		
„ Books	172 11 1		
Wrappers (Printed), Postages, Carriages, Advertising, and Sundries	294 13 4		
Maps, Electros, Photos, Diagrams, etc.	82 8 6		
		1,308 7 8	
Less Sales and Subscriptions	542 9 6		
„ Proportion for Supplying CHINA'S MILLIONS to Donors (as next entry)	390 0 0		
		932 9 6	
			375 18 2
CHINA'S MILLIONS sent free to Donors, and Postage of same			390 0 0
For Missionary Boxes and Photographs:—			
Missionary Boxes, and Printing New Covers	11 8 7		
Photographs of Missionaries—Single Portraits and Groups	97 17 9		
		109 6 4	
Less Sales of Photographs		83 7 10	
			25 18 6
For Stationery and Goods:—			
Stationery, Books, Outfit Requisites, etc., for Office use, and for Sale to or benefit of Missionaries going to, and in China		493 6 6	
Less Sales		166 10 7	
			326 15 11
For Postages, Telegrams, etc.:—			
Postages of Letters and Telegrams, excluding telegraphing Funds to China (as per China account above)	94 6 2		
Carriage of Parcels	33 7 1		
		127 13 3	
Less Refund for Telegram to China		2 9 7	
			125 3 8
Carried forward			33,367 0 0

ABSTRACT OF EXPENDITURE ON GENERAL ACCOUNT.—Continued.

	£ s. d.	£ s. d.	£ s. d.
Brought forward			33,367 0 0
For Expenses of Meetings:—			
Travelling, Printing Bills, Advertising, Reporting, Clerical Help, etc.	211 6 8		
Less Special Contributions towards Expenses	9 18 5		
		201 8 3	
For Sundry Accounts:—			
Petty Cash	19 16 11		
Bankers' Charges for Commission on Scotch and Irish Cheques, and Cheque Books	7 0 4		
Annuities in consideration of Donations to the Mission	86 0 0		
		112 17 3	
For Property Account (Building Fund):—			
Purchase of 44, Newington Green, and Sundry Expenses	1,125 0 0		
Balance carried forward (*see* Balances)	4,025 4 9		
		5,150 4 9	
Less, Balance from 1888	1,895 0 7		
„ Special Receipts and Interest	3,255 4 2		
		5,150 4 9	
For Superannuated Missionaries' Fund:—			
Special Donation to Open the Fund, on Capital Account	4,000 0 0		
Interest on same, £45 7s. 3d. Special Donation, 14s.	46 1 3		
		4,046 1 3	
Less Balance carried forward (*see* Balances)		4,046 1 3	
Total Expenditure on General Account			£33,681 5 6

We have examined the above Accounts, with the Books and Vouchers, and the Bank Pass Book, and find them correct.   (*Signed*)   ARTHUR J. HILL, VELLACOTT AND CO.,

1, Finsbury Circus, London, E.C.   *Chartered Accountants.*
16*th Sept.*, 1890.

LIST OF DONATIONS IN CHINA AND RECEIPTS FROM AMERICA.

As accounted for in " Abstract of China Accounts " on next page.

Rect. No.	Tls. cts.	Rect. No.	Tls. cts.	Rect. No.	Tls. cts.	Rect. No.	Tls. cts.	Rect. No.	Tls. cts.	Rect. No.	Tls. cts.
A 406	3 65	A 430	73 20	A 454	15 46	A 478	23 32	A 502	6 00	A 518	446 51
407	4 74	431	11 03	455*	100 00	479	15 00	503	5 84	519	208 60
408	19 80	432	9 26	456	72 60	480	343 68	504	154 41	520	43 20
409	232 86	433	4 63	457	289 44	481*	94 11	505	50 00	511	90 00
410	18 32	434	257 73	458	26 36	482	4 39	506	5 00	512	118 36
411	17 50	435	5 00	459	4 68	483	83 02	507	5 92	112	209 69
412	40 35	436	9 50	460	6 01	484	14 15	508	8 90	113	50 20
413	15 00	437*	9 50	461*	74 50	485	121 21	509	23 41	114	195 26
414	196 17	438	60 00	462	74 52	486	46 94	510	500 00	115	28 73
415	711 11	439	14 40	463*	2 38	487	29 00	511	55 85	116	146 03
416*	37 00	440	22 38	464	282 15	488	5 84	512	22 14	117	343 72
417	70 00	441*	7 46	465	114 95	489	10 29	513	5 17	118	61 26
418	3 65	442*	5 22	466*	66 18	490	26 13	514	368 50	119	24 14
419	40 00	443*	21 52	467	1872 40	491	148 55	515	7,384 61	120	23 14
420	36 50	444	24 55	468	43 80	492	6 36	516	100 00	121	170 56
421	9 71	445	20 00	469	25 70	493	5 35	517	7 40		
422	20 00	446	51 70	470	4 96	494	14 20			Tls. 13,739 13	
423	54 43	447	23 76	471	100 00	495	197 03				
424	87 48	448*	100 00	472*	61 78	496	129 51	Tls. 13,739 13 at 4s. 4d. =	£2,862 6 5		
425	9 55	449*	47 51	473	476 42	497	74 65	Profits on American Remittances at current rates ...			
426	5 00	450	96 00	474	131 22	498	233 87		4 8 9		
427	207 41	451	179 07	475	50 00	499	92 08				
428	1 48	452	50 00	476	35 00	500	20 00		£2,866 15 4		
429	2 40	453	73 01	477	20 00	501	156 72				

* For Famine Fund.

ABSTRACT OF CHINA ACCOUNTS.

Disposition of Funds Remitted from England and America and Donations received in China during 1889.

Dr.

	Tls. cts.	Tls. cts.
Balances :—		
General and Special	1,105 44	
Old Relief Fund	206 99	
		1,312 43
General and Special Accounts :—		
Remittances from England—		
£32,837 12s. 3d. produced at Current Rates of Exchange Tls. 155,718 43		
Less Famine Fund (£9,100 at Current Rates) ... 43,714 96		
	112,003 47	
Donations in China and Receipts from America* ... Tls. 13,739 13		
Less Famine Fund (at 4s. 2d. = £148 17s. 8 $\frac{1}{3}$d.) ... 714 64		
	13,024 49	
From Rents, Exchange and Interest Account (at 4s. 2d. = £103 4s. 11d.) ...	495 58	
		125,523 54
Transferred Donations from Famine Fund for other purposes, by request of Donors ...	8,305 48	
Unexpended Funds returned to Account ...	2,000 00	
Famine Fund :—		
Remittances from England, as above	43,714 96	
Donations in China, as above	714 64	
Unexpended Funds returned to Account from Honan ...	2,936 79	
From Rents, Exchange and Interest Account ...	271 94	
		47,638 33
* For List of these, see p iii.		
		Tls 184,779 78

Cr.

	Tls. cts.	Tls. cts.
General and Special Accounts :—		
Payments to Missionaries—		
For Personal use ...	77,559 32	
For the Support of Native Helpers, Rents, Repairs of Houses and Chapels, Travelling Expenses, and Sundry Outlays on account of Stations and Out-stations of the Mission ...	17,792 32	
For Expenses of Boarding and Day Schools (including Tls. 206.99 from Old Relief Fund) ...	1,481 98	
	96,833 62	
For Houses Accounts ...	30,551 84	
For Passages to England & America	1,804 21	
Medical Missionary Work, including Hospital, Dispensary, and Opium Refuge Expenses ...	2,003 30	
		131,192 97
Famine Fund :—		
Remittances to Famine Districts and Expenses ...	24,578 43	
Transferred by request of Donors, as *per contra* ...	8,305 48	
		32,883 91
Balances :—		
General and Special ...	5,948 48	
Famine Fund ...	14,754 42	
		20,702 90
		Tls. 184,779 78

We have examined the above Abstract with the Returns from China, and find it correct.

We have traced the Amounts charged in the "Home Accounts" as remitted to China, and find that they are all duly accounted for. (*Signed*) ARTHUR J. HILL, VELLACOTT & CO.,

1, Finsbury Circus, London, E.C., 16th *Sept.*, 1890. *Chartered Accountants.*

The auditing and publication of the above accounts has been delayed through the miscarriage of a portion of the China Accounts.

This sheet should be transferred to the *August* number of CHINA'S MILLIONS.

CHINA'S MILLIONS.

The Last Days of Miss Annie Dunn.

EXTRACTED FROM THE DIARY OF MR. G. A. HUNTLEY.

"*Whether we live, we live unto the* LORD; *and whether we die, we die unto the* LORD."

CHIN-KIANG, *May 12th.*—I arrived here this morning from Shanghai, accompanied by Mr. Hutton. The attack is a very severe one. Sent Annie a note, to which she sent the following verbal reply: "He hath loved me with an everlasting love." "He doeth all things well." Later in the day I told her through her nurse, who spoke to me from the window, that I was writing to her father and mother, and asked if I should send a message. She quickly sent the following reply: "Tell them that I am 'resting;' that 'underneath are the everlasting arms,' and that this is one of the 'all things'" (Rom. viii. 28).

Tuesday, 13th.—Dear Annie is much worse this morning, very serious symptoms having set in, indicative of confluent small-pox. I felt very sad, and, going to my room, put the whole matter into the hands of our loving heavenly FATHER, who "doeth all things well." I then read James v., and my faith was strengthened. *Later.*—Chilliness has set in—a very unfavourable symptom; but "*He is able.*" I do want to "trust, and not be afraid." Annie desired a hammock this morning. I hadn't mine with me, and we could not purchase one, but Captain Alsing, on one of the hulks, very kindly lent us a swinging cot, which gave our patient much comfort. How good of the LORD thus to provide; but it is just like Him, "He withholdeth no good thing." 5.30 *p.m.*—Have just sent a text to Annie, which I printed in large, black letters on red Chinese paper: "Thy GOD hath commanded thy strength." She heard me, and sent the following message in reply: "As thy days, so shall thy strength be," and then immediately went off into delirium. The up-river steamer came in, and Miss Murray was on board: it was exceedingly kind of her to leave the Conference in Shanghai, but she said, "I could not stay away when dear Annie was so ill." She brought with her a very large box of ice in response to our telegram yesterday. 9.30 *p.m.*—Annie finds the ice very refreshing, and her temperature has gone down to 102°. Praise GOD! He is answering prayer.

Wednesday, 14th.—Annie had a restless night, and I could not sleep at all. Fetched ice for her at 1.30 a.m. She complains this morning of pain over the region of the heart. She is only able to lie on the right side, which is very tiring. Sent Annie a message, "He is able"; to which she replied, "He leadeth me." I feel well-nigh crushed, and very sad at heart. Oh to *realize* "His strength *made perfect* in weakness." *Mid-day.*—The doctor pronounces the case "most serious," and says she is getting into a typhoid condition. Lam. iii. 31-33 very comforting. 5 *o'clock.*—Had a quiet sleep for an hour, and feel refreshed. Took some ice upstairs, and Annie heard me and sent me a message, which was very cheering, especially as she was unconscious earlier in the afternoon. Have just sent the following telegram to Shanghai: "Symptoms very grave—pray." Since then Annie has been much soothed, praise GOD. This afternoon it was evident more help would be needed in nursing. After prayer we decided to ask Miss Thomas to kindly assist, and she cheerfully consented. She has had small-pox, so the exposure will be no great risk.

Thursday 15th.—Annie has had a comfortable night, praise the LORD. She has been carefully watched all the time. The general symptoms are more favourable this morning, but the pocks have come out more. She has just sent me this message, "Rest in the LORD." We used the last of the ice this morning, but before more was required, a fresh boxful arrived from Shanghai.

SEPTEMBER, 1890.

The LORD arranges all things so beautifully for us in this time of trial. "My soul, wait thou only upon GOD." Had a cheering note of sympathy from Miss Jones, of Yangchau, this morning. The sisters there had a time of fasting and prayer for Annie yesterday.

12 o'clock.—The doctor has just called, and the worst conceivable symptom has now set in - hæmorrhage. The case is not only confluent, but *black*. Annie is indeed now beyond all human skill, but even yet *He is able* to raise her up. Directly we heard the doctor's verdict, we all went to prayer, but I asked Miss Murray to excuse my meeting with them, and went to my own room. It was difficult to pray, my heart was so sad. The dear LORD did help me through, and I asked Him, even yet, to spare Annie, *if it could be His will*. I also asked the LORD to guide very definitely about my going into the sick-room. I went and asked Miss Murray what she thought about my going in? She said she also had been praying about it ; and it was decided that I should go.

Miss Murray sent a message to Annie to ask if she would like to see me. With her wonted thoughtfulness, she said, "But won't he catch it?" I went in immediately after dinner, and took some flowers with me. She was asleep. I waited a few minutes, and she awoke. Her eyes were covered with lint ; this was taken off, and ice-water applied. I stood before her as her eyes opened slowly. "I can see a little of him," she said ; "keep bathing my eyes." "Now I see him," she said, as her eyes opened wide, and she smiled a little. "I'm going home, Arthur dear," she said, confidently. "Are you?" I said. "Yes ; do you want me to go home?" "No," I replied, "I would like you to stay with me." Then in a little while, she said, "I would like to stay for your sake." "Is not JESUS very *near* to you?" I said, presently. "Yes, very near, very dear—dear—dear." This last word was very low and faint, and I did not speak again for awhile, for fear of wearying her. I feel so glad I have come into the sick-room, it has not excited Annie in the least, but rather comforted her. I feel comforted myself, too. The strain of the last three days, knowing she was so ill, and not being allowed to help her, has tried me much. Though I know nothing short of a miracle could raise Annie up again, and though my sorrow is very, very great, yet there is much joy in being able to do some little thing for her, if it be only to apply iced-water to her eyes, or assist in moving her into an easier position. A great amount of prayer is being offered for us just now. The LORD is graciously giving to me the spirit of resignation, and it is so precious to *realise*, as I really do *now*—His grace is sufficient. "JESUS is with you, isn't He, Annie?" I said, after awhile. She said, "I don't think He is ; I am so wicked, so impatient." This was the only cloud she had, and it was very short-lived. Although in intense suffering, she continually expressed gratitude for all the good things GOD had given to her, and for kind nurses.

7 p.m.—Physician has just come, and thought the symptoms a little more favourable. I read several loving messages to Annie, from the sisters at Yangchau, and she seemed greatly comforted and calmed; it seemed to take her mind off her much suffering. I read to her promise after promise from these letters. She said "Yes," after many of them. It was only a word, but it meant a great deal, coming, as it did, amid much pain. I reminded her of a line I had often quoted to her ; "Child of my love, lean hard." Then she continued the piece herself :

" And let me feel the pressure of thy care,
" I know thy burden, child ; I shaped it,
" Poised it in my own hand ; made no proportion
" Of its weight to thine own unaided strength."

Here she paused ; the mental exertion seemed much for her, and she said, "Tell me the rest." I succeeded in getting a copy of the piece, and continued—

" For even as I laid it on, I said,
" I shall be ever near, and while she leans on Me
" This burden shall be Mine, not hers.
" So shall I keep My child within the circling arms
" Of Mine own love. Here lay it down, nor fear
" To impose it on a shoulder which upholds
" The government of worlds. Yet closer come ;
           "'Yes,' she whispered,]
" Thou art not near enough : I would embrace thy care,
" So I might feel My child reposing on My breast.
" Thou lovest Me? I know it. Doubt not, then ;
" But, loving me, *lean hard*."

Later. Mr. McCarthy has just come with another box of ice. When Annie heard of his arrival she was very delighted, and said, "How kind of him ! The friends are all too kind." She asked me to give her love to Mr. McCarthy, and the text—a great favourite of hers—"Certainly, I will be with thee." "Tell mother there is no mistake in my coming to China. It's all right ; if I had not come I should not have lived longer, and if I could have I should not have been happy." How similar are these words to those uttered by Mr. Spurgeon at the Tabernacle on June 27th, 1887, on the occasion of saying farewell to Mr. Brown before his departure to the Congo. Mr. Spurgeon said, "We cannot lengthen our lives by avoiding duty, and if we could it would be a wretched thing to do." Then she continued her message to her mother : "It's been a very happy time ; 'all the way long it has been JESUS.'"

I gave her a message which her native teacher at Yangchau sent to her. I knew she had prayed much for him. She said, "I do hope GOD will save him. I think He will."

I then offered a brief word of prayer, after which she said, "He is precious."

"I think perhaps JESUS wants to take you home," I said.

"I am not afraid," she answered. "I would rather stay and work in China though, but I am not afraid."

"GOD is not unkind in giving you so much suffering, is He?" I asked.

She replied, amid much pain, "Too wise to err ; too good to be unkind. Yes, JESUS, JESUS, dear JESUS."

Toward midnight I whispered to her, "You remember that favourite hymn of yours, 'Peace, perfect peace' ?" and she said, calmly, "With loved ones"—the remainder of the verse "far away. In JESUS' keeping we are safe, and they," was not spoken audibly, but was doubtless realised in spirit.

Midnight.—"JESUS had a fevered brow once," I said, as I bathed her eyes with ice-water, "but He had no one to cool His brow for Him." She seemed to forget her own pains, remembering His.

Friday, 16th, 5.25 a.m.—Still "perfect peace?" I asked. "Yes." "Give lots of love to Alice," she said, five minutes later. "Tell them I would like to see them all again once more, but if I cannot it is all right." She then complained of pain in the heart. "It's stopping beating," she said, and it seemed like a last struggle with the great enemy, death.

"Do you see me?" I said, as I once more removed the pad to bathe her eyes. "Just a little," she said.

"You see JESUS clearer?" I asked. "Yes." "And nearer?" I continued. "Yes."

She was in great pain, and longed to go home. "LORD JESUS," she cried, "save me now. I'm coming ; I'm coming. LORD JESUS, take me now. LORD, take me now. Quickly come."

"I think you are going home," I said, after a while. "I don't want to go," she said. "I would rather stay if JESUS has anything more for me to do down here."

"But it's all right," I continued. "He has higher service for you, so it's all right, is it not?" "Yes," she said, contentedly.

I repeated her favourite text, "Underneath are the everlasting arms," which seemed to comfort her much. She then sent the following message to Albert (my brother in Cheng-ku), "Be thou faithful unto death, and I will give thee a crown of life."

6 *o'clock a.m.*—The end seemed very near, so we told Miss Murray and Mr. McCarthy, who came into the room to accompany Annie to the riverside. She was perfectly conscious, and knew us each one. Miss Murray said, "Annie dear, you are going home." She said, "When?" Then she said, "I have a great deal to say to you, but cannot say it now." She requested us to sing her favourite hymn—"Be still, my soul," which she enjoyed very much. She asked for Florrie (Miss McCarthy), saying, "Tell her to keep looking up; she is a dear girl."

She next asked for Miss Murray, and thanked her for all her kindness. "I will be waiting for you," she continued to Miss Murray.

She then mentioned Miss Clare, Miss Broman, Miss Leggatt, Miss Bradfield, and "All," she said : "they are *all* so good."

We sang the hymn, "JESUS, lover of my soul."

"I hope this won't keep Alfred from coming out," she said, after a bit; "I would like him to do the work that I cannot do." She also said she would like Sarah to come to China.

"Tell Kao Sien-seng (her Chinese teacher) to come into the fold ; you know the way so well ; don't stand out any longer, you might be taken."

She then mentioned Albert and Nellie, Mrs. Hutton and Tommy. "Would like to have seen Mr. Taylor ; will see him again." She then spoke of "dear Mrs. Broomhall, Mr. Broomhall, and the Miss Broomhall at home, I like so much." She then gave the following texts :—

For Miss Lucas, "Work while it is called to-day."
For Arthur, "Though He slay me, yet will I trust Him."
Miss Thomas, "Be thou faithful unto death."

Miss Miller (her kind and patient nurse), "I will instruct thee and teach thee ; I will guide thee with mine eye." "Thank her for all her kindness."

9 *o'clock a.m.*—She cried fervently, "O LORD JESUS, how long? Take me soon."

"Tell dear grandpa I have prayed so much for him, and I hope I shall meet him soon in Heaven, though I did not expect I should go home first." "Lead me gently home, FATHER !"

She was suffering intensely, and longed to go. I prayed, "LORD JESUS, if it be Thy will to take dear Annie home, do so speedily." "Amen," she whispered fervently, "I want to go home." "I have not mentioned Mr. Hutton (our missionary stationed here), give him my love and thank him for his kindness."

To one she said, "Which way are you going?" She continued, earnestly, "this time last week I was well and about, and now I'm going *home*. This time next week you may be going——. Where will *you* go?"

She was wonderfully thoughtful for those who attended to her. She knew I had watched by her all night, and said, "Arthur, you had better go to bed, you must be so tired." And after a little she said, " Tell your dear mother I love her so much." My presence seems a means of continual comfort to her; it is so good of the LORD to arrange for me to be here.

Presently she repeated each name in her family, father, mother, Alice, Alfred, Jessie, Willie, and the darling little ones, Charlie, Lizzie, Alfred, and Sarah.

"I would like to work with you, Arthur, but you will give me up, won't you, dear? Don't cry. 'Praise Him for all that is past, and trust Him for all that's to come.' 'Better to have loved and lost than never to have loved at all.'" "Not lost," I answered. "No," she whispered. "I hope you will not take this [the disease]. LORD JESUS, come quickly. I wish He would come ; He's a long time coming."

She slept a little. "So nice," she said, gratefully, as Miss Murray fanned her, and as I applied ice to her fevered eyes.

"Are you in pain now?" I asked. "Yes, a great deal."
"But you are resting in the Lord?" I continued. "Yes, and *waiting*," she said.
"Are you sorry you ever came to China?" I asked.
"No, very glad ; it's just as near to heaven."
Then she repeated the verse—

"How sweet the name of JESUS sounds
In a believer's ear ;
It soothes his sorrows, heals his wounds,
And drives away his fear."

Presently she said, "Darling mother, darling father, you'll give me up for China and for JESUS, won't you ? Dear mother, dear father, don't cry." Her mind often reverted to her happy home, and the names, "father," "mother," often rested sacredly upon her lips.

"Don't fret, Arthur," she said. " I don't think I shall," I replied ; "you can trust me with JESUS, can you not?" "I can trust JESUS with you," she replied. Soon she said—

"JESUS, the very thought of Thee
With sweetness fills my breast ;
But sweeter far Thy face to see,
And in Thy presence rest."

"I gave My life for thee ;
What hast thou done for Me ?"

"I would like you to have my baby organ, it will be useful in the work."

I sat by her side at 10.10 p.m. "Go now," she said, in loving thoughtfulness, thinking I needed rest.

"Good-bye," I said. "Good-bye," she responded. I retired from the room for a short time, intending to rest. Miss Murray, Miss Miller, and Miss Thomas are with her now, and are singing, "Shall we gather at the river ? " Went in again and watched till 1 a.m.

Saturday, 17th.—The others then left the room and left me alone with Annie for a few minutes.

She is wonderfully patient and calm, though her illness is an intensely painful one. She does indeed glorify GOD in sickness.

"Grandma will be waiting for you," I said. She answered, "Yes, and aunt and dear little Ebenezer, and my dear little sister Miriam. I suppose I shall know her ; I didn't know her here."

She said she hoped some friends would come to China.
"Is JESUS very near you now?" I said. "Yes."
"Can you see Him?" I asked. "Yes, yes ; coming, coming, coming." I then repeated the verse :—

"Only good night, beloved, not farewell ;
A little while and all His saints shall dwell
In hallowed union, indivisible.
Good right, good night, good night."

"Good night," she whispered softly, and dozed off into a quiet, restful sleep.

"Annie, are you happy?" I said, as she awoke. "Yes." "Very happy?" I continued. "Yes."

"Go on ; rescue the perishing," she said, earnestly ; "the LORD won't let me, I'm not fitted." "Not because you are not fitted," I said, "but because He has higher work for you."

Then she *sang* through the verse she repeated a little while before, "How sweet the name of Jesus sounds."

We sang the hymn, 'Praise the SAVIOUR, ye who know Him" (Sankey's, 562). She was becoming very weak, but tried to lisp some of the words. "Nor could be," were the only words I could catch from her lips.

"You will soon be in the bright sunshine of His presence," I said. "Yes," she answered, triumphantly.

"Arthur, are you going away?" she asked as I stepped across the room. "No," I said, "I'm going to see you to the river-side, and then leave you for a little time."

"Am I going soon?" she said, yearningly. "I think soon," I replied. "Pray that I may," she responded.

5 a.m.—Great change this morning. It *looked* like a change for the better. But soon she complained of pain in the chest, and the respirations rose suddenly. The end seemed very near. She called me to her and said, "Good-bye, Arthur; good-bye, mother; good-bye, father; good-bye, all." She remained quiet for a while and then prayed earnestly, "Come, LORD JESUS, come, come quickly, come," at the same time lifting her hands towards heaven in a beseeching manner—"Come, come." She passed the morning in much pain.

She was now becoming very weak, and could not speak much, though her mind was perfectly clear. With wonderful deliberation she said, "I shall not die, but live."

"Arthur, good-bye; 'My peace I leave with you,'" she said presently. I left the room for a minute, to see her suffering was more than I could bear. Then she called me and gasped "Good-bye." We sang the hymn " JESUS, lover of my soul," which she enjoyed very much.

"How long?" she enquired, after a little. "Only a little longer, Annie," said her patient nurse, who, sitting by her side, held up her right hand to rest it. "Oh, come, come, come, come."

Then she said "Eight months, eight months," this being the time of her brief service for CHRIST in China.

Nothing more of moment was said. The pain seemed to diminish, and she remained very calm and conscious to the last, and at 6.30 p.m., without an effort, without a sigh, her gentle, loving spirit flitted from us, into the presence of her REDEEMER.

The funeral service took place the next day, Sunday, and was conducted by the Rev. John McCarthy at the British Cemetery, Chin-kiang. Many residents of the Port attended, and some showed respect by sending wreaths, etc., of flowers. Among those gathered at the graveyard were five children whom Annie had taught on Sunday afternoons during her brief stay at Chin-kiang. These children had met their new teacher only two Sundays, but in this short time had learned to love her, and one, who brought a beautiful wreath for the grave, was deeply moved and wept sorrowfully.

The following was written with gold paint, in Chinese characters upon the coffin. "Tao K'uen-ren (Annie's Chinese name). 'Thanks be unto GOD, who giveth us the victory through our LORD JESUS CHRIST.' 16th Year of the reign of Kuang-hsu, 3rd Moon, 29th day (May 17th, 1890)."

The service was very solemn, and we sang the following hymns around the grave :—
"We speak of the land of the blest " (Sankey's, 347).
" Only good-night, beloved " (Christian Choir).
" Be still, my soul " (Scottish Hymnal).

Mr. McCarthy delivered an impressive address on the LORD'S coming again, and at the close Mr. Hutton addressed a few words of earnest exhortation to the unsaved.

Annie is happy now. Hers is indeed *gain*, ours only the loss.

"If thou should'st call me to resign
What most I prize, it ne'er was mine;
I only yield Thee what is thine.
Thy will be done."

Her grave lies immediately in front of Miss Maggie McKee, who died from the same disease ; and next to that is the grave of Miss Theresa Dawson.

GOD grant that she being dead may yet speak, and that the earnest exhortation, "Go on ; rescue the perishing," which fell from her dying lips, may call many forth to work for CHRIST in this dark heathen land. May the LORD Himself comfort each of us who mourn this loss, and enable us to learn the lesson well He desires to teach.

A Persecutor Saved and Taken Home.

FROM REV. J. MEADOWS.

SHAO-HING, *March* 5, 1890.—Herewith a translation of a letter from Mr. Ling, of Dzing-yun, touching the death of a woman who once opposed, but afterwards became a believer ; and for her short Christian life did good work for her MASTER.

"DEAR MR. MEADOWS,—I send you a note about a woman who has gone to heaven, though she was not baptised, nor formally received into the church. She was of this city, and was the wife of Mr. S-fu. This man, although he is a tailor by trade, is fairly acquainted with the character, and is quite advanced in the knowledge of the leading truths of the Gospel, having been an attendant and an inquirer at the services for more than a year and a half. But the good woman who has just gone to heaven never lost an opportunity to hinder and persecute her husband, therefore the latter was far from being established and satisfactory, and we objected to his receiving baptism last year. He was at Yih-ko-cun when we were all assembled there, and he attended all the services. He went home resolving to exhort his wife more earnestly, whether she persecuted and opposed him or not. The result was more than he expected : the woman turned completely round, and believed up to the light that she had, and in the first month of this new year she actually came with her husband to the services ! The more she heard the more she was pleased. Not only so, but she soon turned to her female neighbours and told them of the change of feeling, etc., that had come over her, and exhorted them most earnestly to go with her to chapel and hear for themselves, and a whole company had set a day for going to chapel, when, before the time of the cock-crowing in the morning they were all to come, the LORD had taken our sister to heaven. I saw this woman working only an hour—the last hour of the day, it is true—but I believe she had the same wages as the man who was engaged all day in the vineyard. We all got together to help poor Mr. Mö, and the latter, instead of listening to his friends' clamouring for heathenish rites over the dead body, was exceedingly pleased to have a Christian burial, and earnestly testified to his neighbours and the dead woman's friends to make haste and delay not, but come to the point at once, as we don't know who will be the next. LING LAO-FONG writes this."

I have no doubt that there are many such souls now in heaven who were never received into our churches here. I knew a man who was an opium-smoker, and so was not received, because he had not at the time of his examination cut off entirely the habit ; but afterwards he died rejoicing in JESUS, and leaving a good testimony behind.

Items of Interest.

FROM REV. J. W. STEVENSON.

June 20th.—I have heard of the following baptisms since last writing:—

Kwei-yang,	KWEI-CHAU,	Feb. 22	...	1
P'ing yao,	SHAN-SI,	Mar. 21	...	5
T'ai-chau,	CHEH-KIANG,	Apr. 13	...	5
Fung-hwa,	,, ,,	,, 20	...	3
Wun-chau,	,, ,,	,, 20	...	2
Sin-ch'ang,	,, ,,	,, 30	...	2
Gan-ren,	KIANG-SI,	May 13	...	7
Kwei-k'i,	,, ,,	,, 17	...	6
Chung-k'ing,	SI-CH'UEN,	,, 24	...	3
Hz-k'eo,	KIANG SI	,, 25	...	6—40

I have encouraging accounts from Kwei-yang and the neighbourhood. Mr. Owen Stevenson reports five enquirers at K'üh-tsing Fu, the new station in YUN-NAN. Mr. Taylor left us on Saturday, 14th inst., to visit the River stations. We expect him back in a week or ten days. After visiting Che-foo it is his purpose to leave for Australia.

June 27th.—Miss Mackintosh reports eighteen baptisms at Yuh-shan.

Baptisms at T'ai-chau.

FROM MR. RUDLAND.

APRIL 29th.—As several of those recently baptised are cases of special interest, I now send you some account of them. On April 2nd I baptised ten persons, six males and four females, ages from seventy-three to fifteen.

The first was the father of Koh Yih-djün, who was formerly one of our native helpers, now a colporteur for the National Bible Society of Scotland. For eighteen years we have prayed for this man and often spoken to him about his soul, but he has put it off. We rejoice that now after all these years of praying and working the due season has come and that he has publicly confessed CHRIST.

Then followed three women from Sin-kyü, the station where we have had so much trial for years, and which *seemed* such a hopeless place, but is now one of our most hopeful stations. Here, too, the due season seems to have come at last. What is needed there *now* is a foreigner to encourage the native workers and instruct the converts and enquirers. There are now several enquirers, chiefly women, as the result of the work of Mrs. Soh, and we trust that they may soon learn to read the Word for themselves. Mrs. Rudland has just sent up one of the T'ai-chau Bible-women to teach them to read and to instruct them more than Mrs. Soh is able to do.

Another was the eldest son of Mr. Soh, aged 15. He gave his parents much trouble about two years ago, but has for some time shown a different spirit, and on examining him there seemed to be no doubt about his conversion. The day before these were baptised several others came forward asking for baptism, but as there was not time to bring their cases before the Church, they were asked to wait. The next Sunday we examined among others a woman who has been brought to the LORD at our West Gate Preaching Station (a native Christian's house) where the Sunday afternoon service is conducted by our printer. There are still several enquirers there.

Mr. Soh's second son, eleven years of age, has also been examined. On seeing his brother baptised he asked why he could not be baptised too. As he answered the questions put to him, he could not keep back a tear, and his answers were so clear and convincing that we could only thank GOD for calling in the little ones. When asked how he first began to think of becoming a Christian he said it was by seeing his grandmother kneel down and pray before she got into bed at night. Then he listened to what she said. After this he began to pray himself and asked JESUS to save him, and He did. Nothing could be more simple or more real. These were baptised with three others, two of whom came from Din-tsi on Sunday morning, 13th. After the baptism we had the communion service, when over forty partook of the memorials of the LORD's broken body and shed blood.

How good of Him to give us this encouragement after all the trials and troubles of the past two years! He is faithful. May we ever be faithful to Him in all things.

The Work of God in the Yung-k'ang District.

FROM MR. WRIGHT.

YUNG-K'ANG, *Feb. 21st.*—We commenced the past year in Yung-k'ang with but one mission hall, now we can preach in six; our communicants at the beginning of the year were eighteen, now we number thirty, and at each of our mission halls there are several hopeful enquirers. The individual offerings for the work of the LORD have increased threefold, and individual efforts to spread the Gospel have, if anything, been greater than in former years. Outwardly we have every reason to praise GOD, and I trust that this is but the fruit of what is in the heart. We have to think of and pray for one or two who, to all appearance, have grown colder in serving the LORD during the past year.

For some time a few of the younger Christians have had to bear persecution, and one of the older Christians urged them to press me to entreat the mandarin for a proclamation. I listened to them, and promised to pray about it, and to bring their request before the Church. I did so, and placed myself and the matter in their hands; each had his say, and what was said gave me much secret joy.

This was the drift of what was said:—"The mandarin, though he might help us, might do us much harm. GOD, who is our great Mandarin, is all-powerful and *loves* us, and when He is for us who can be against us? We therefore decide not to ask the mandarin for help, but to give all into GOD's hands and to trust Him."

I received this answer from them as a Church, and gave it to those desirous of help. Since then all has gone on fairly well, thank GOD, who takes all the affairs of His people into His own hands. I also thank Him for this testimony to their desire to look to GOD and not to man.

I have been enabled to get out into the villages several times lately. This month is a quiet time for the farmers. Oh, how open all this district is to the Gospel!

We are hoping to meet for conference here, or in Kin-hwa, in the middle of March. Our Christians are looking forward to it; we hope to take up simple, helpful subjects.

April 10th.—Well, we have had our native conference, and it has been a thorough success. We met at Kin-hwa; 30 Christians and enquirers went from Ch'u-chau, Tsin-yuin, and here, and all are determined that (D.V.) next year shall see a similar gathering in Yung-k'ang. The most marked feature was the ready willingness of all to take part, which made our meetings lively and helpful, and caused me to hope for yet greater things in the future. Our subjects for the four days were Forward, Soul-winning, Our Unity, Cheerful Giving, the Benefit of Scripture Study, Protestants and Roman Catholics, How ought we to Treat Outsiders who visit the Chapel? Women's Work, Mutual Help, What Name to use for GOD? How to Win Idol-worshippers, Next Year's Conference. The four days were well filled, and on Thursday morning the majority had dispersed to their homes.

I reached home last night from a visit to the out-stations, and the outlook in all gives me much joy. In Hu-chen and Tsin-yuin the number of enquirers continues to increase, and their willingness to speak or suffer for CHRIST fills one with hope. In Ch'u-chau the work goes but slowly, but I hope in May to baptize three or four earnest enquirers. I cannot speak so happily of Yung-k'ang as I should like; some give me much trouble and sorrow of heart, while, thank GOD, the wholeheartedness of the majority inspires me with hope. I am afraid that, in the case of a few, strong measures must be taken to preserve a good foundation church: the LORD will guide.

A Family Itineration in Si-ch'uen.

FROM MR. GRAY OWEN.

CHEN-TU, *March 20th.*—We started for another visit to the east; quite a party we were—my wife and little boys, Miss Webb and two native women (one of them as Biblewoman *pro tem.*) on wheelbarrows, an old man, the boy and myself tramping it. All enjoyed the fresh-looking country, the plain covered with brilliant patches of yellow sesame relieved by stretches of bright green wheat and fields of beans in flower.

On the third day, crossing hills about 1,500 feet high, we had a good wetting and bitterly cold wind. At noon we were no sooner installed in a good inn than we found that there was a case of small pox in the house, so, much to the landlady's chagrin, we lost no time in moving to the "Three Stars" Inn.

Sunday, March 23rd.—Women came trooping in soon after morning rice, who were all told the way of salvation. In the court a few men listened with evident interest; my voice was quite hoarse with yesterday's wetting. Taking little Hugh for an airing, we met a number of farmer-folk returning from the village, and stood by explaining, while an old man read aloud a simple gospel tract.

My wife and Miss Webb going out the back way into the country in the afternoon it was amusing to see the whole country-side roused to see the strangers. When they returned the inn was soon crowded, and while they spoke to the women I preached to the men.

Monday, 24th.—Market-day. I went out with books; the others went with Chang-ma, a Christian woman with us, to her home. My wife had been there over three years ago and found some who still knew of JESUS; some women here say that they have not worshipped idols since that time.

A TRAMP ROUND THE VILLAGES.

Tuesday, 25th.—Lao-yang shouldering the basket, we started in the forenoon for a village tramp, leaving the others in the inn. Fifteen *li* bringing us to Tu-shin-ch'ang, we stayed to rest, finding interested hearers, some of whom bought books and one a New Testament. An old gentleman, named Li, who had met me last December, was very friendly.

Continuing our tramp for twenty-five *li* we reached the teashop of last Christmas Day. I soon found out the old man of the Gospel of John; he was very pleased to see me again and I to see him. With him and a few others we had long talks about JESUS. The old man's name is Chen; he is over seventy-three years of age, tall, hale and hearty, a small shopman by trade. Long after dark I returned to the inn very praiseful for having once again met the old man.

Wednesday, 26th.—Spent the first part of the day with old Mr. Chen and some of his relatives, a younger brother buying a New Testament, and asking freely about the doctrine. When bidding the old man good-bye he said, much to my joy:

"NOW I HAVE FOUND THE DOOR."

Having found the door, may the LORD graciously grant to him and his family the requisite faith to enter while it is still open.

At San-ho-chang, twenty-five *li* further, we rested for dinner, preaching to a group of farmers and shopmen who had not heard the Gospel before; no missionary or colporteur had even passed through their village.

Later in the day we reached a large river port, on the outer side of the sandstone heights that form the east border of the Chen-tu plain.

Skirting the hills on the homeward tramp, thirty *li* brought us to a market village, where we preached to people who were very friendly and seemingly intelligent. Here again no colporteur or missionary had ever been. There is a marked readiness to listen to the truth in this part of the country. Another fifteen *li* and we were all together again at the "Three Stars" Inn.

SIGHTS AT A FAIR.

Mar. 27th—April 24th.—The rest of our stay I spent in dropping a seed here and a word there, my wife and Miss Webb spending some days in the country.

A great annual fair was held on the 30th and 31st, attracting great crowds of country folk. There was something to suit all ages; many of the younger folks, and some old ones, too, found great attraction in a show where a four-footed duck and a fowl with a like number of appendages were to be seen. Not far off a quack medicine vendor fondled a venomless serpent about five feet long, while eloquently dilating upon the healing virtues of powdered snake skin. Hard by another of the same persuasion as eloquently told of the tonic properties of ground-monkey bones, a row of skeletons alluringly displayed at the back of his tent. A chief elder came to see us one day, affording a good opportunity to witness to the leading men of the place.

April 5th saw us once more at home in Chen-tu.

PART OF THE NEW C.I.M. PREMISES AT SHANGHAI: A SOCIAL REUNION OF THE GENERAL CONFERENCE.

An Appeal.

AN APPEAL FROM MORE THAN TWO HUNDRED LADIES, MEMBERS OF THE MISSIONARY CONFERENCE, HELD IN SHANGHAI, IN MAY, 1890.

To the Christian Women of the British Empire, the United States, Germany, and all other Protestant Countries:— Greeting.

WE, the women of the Missionary Conference now assembled in Shanghai, come to you, our sisters in Christ with an urgent appeal in behalf of the one hundred millions of women and children of China who "sit in darkness and in the shadow of death."

The work of women in China has been prosecuted at the oldest stations for about fifty years, at first chiefly by the wives of missionaries, but in later years single ladies have largely augmented this working force. There are now ladies engaged in educational, medical and evangelistic work in China. Much has been done by them, many lives have been uplifted from the degradation of idolatry and sin, many sad hearts comforted, many darkened minds enlightened, and much solid good effected. But our hearts are burdened to-day with love and pity for the millions of women around us, our sisters, for whom CHRIST died, still unreached by the sound of the Gospel.

Beloved Sisters, if you could see their sordid misery, their hopeless, loveless lives, their ignorance and sinfulness, as we see them, more human pity would move you to do something for their uplifting. But there is a stronger motive that should impel you to stretch out a helping hand, and *that* we plead—the constraining love of CHRIST.

We who are in the midst of this darkness that can be felt, send our voices across the ocean to you, our Sisters, and beseech you, by the grace of CHRIST, our SAVIOUR, that you come at once to our help.

Four kinds of work are open to us.

1. There is school work in connection with our various Missions, which in many cases the men have handed over to the women, in order that they themselves may be free to engage more directly in evangelistic work.

2. There is a work to be done for the sick and suffering women of China ; in hospitals, dispensaries and homes, for which skilful physicians are needed. Most of this work can be better done by women than by men, and much of it can be done only by women.

3. There is work for us in the families of the Church. There are converted mothers and daughters who need to be taught the way of the LORD more perfectly, and to be trained in whatever is necessary for their full development into lively members of the great household of faith.

4. There is a work of evangelisation among women, similar to that being done by men among the people at large. It is not claimed that the evangelisation of women cannot be done at all by men—but that there is *more* of

it than men can do, there is *much* of it that will never be done unless women do it, and much that men cannot do as well as women can. There is nothing in this kind of work transcending the recognised scriptural sphere of women. Women received from the LORD Himself upon the very morning of the resurrection their commission to tell the blessed story of a risen SAVIOUR. What they did then we may continue to do now.

But you will ask, who are needed for this work? Knowing the conditions of life and work in China, we would answer that—

1. They should be women of sound health, of good ability, and good common sense, also well educated —though not necessarily of the highest education—apt to teach, kind and forbearing in disposition, so that they live and work harmoniously with their associates, and win the hearts of the Chinese. Above all, they should be women who have given themselves *wholly* to the LORD'S work, and are prepared to bear hardship and exercise constant self-denial for CHRIST's sake.

2. It is desirable that they should pursue a systematic course of Bible study before coming to China, and have some experience in Christian work at home.

Further, we would suggest that they should labour in connection with established missions, in order that the good results of their work may be preserved, and that they may have, when needed, the assistance and protection of their brother missionaries.

Open doors are all around us, and though idolatry lifts a hoary head, and ancestral worship binds the people as with chains of adamant, yet with GOD "All things are possible," and mountains of difficulty melt like snow-flakes before the rising of the Sun of Righteousness.

GOD is on the side of His own glorious life-giving word: we ask you to come in the power of consecration and faith, with sober expectations and readiness to endure hardness as good soldiers of JESUS, and take your share in the most glorious war that was ever waged on earth— the war against the powers of darkness and sin, assured that GOD will accomplish His own purposes of love and grace to China, and that will permit you, if you listen to this call, to be His fellow workers in "binding up the broken hearted, proclaiming liberty to the captives, and the opening of the prison to them that are bound."

That the Holy and loving SPIRIT of GOD may incline your hearts to respond to His call is our earnest prayer.

Yours in our LORD,

Signed on behalf of the two hundred and four ladies assembled in Conference at Shanghai.

Mrs. MARY LEES, London Mission Society.
 „   A. ELWIN, Church Mission Society.
Miss C. M. RICKETTS, English Presbyterian Mission.
Mrs. J. R. WATSON, English Baptist Mission.
Miss L. S. SUGDEN, M.D., Wesleyan Mission.
 „   I. NEWCOMBE, Church of England Zenana Mission.
Mrs. E. TOMALIN, China Inland Mission.
 „   JOHN ROSS, U.P. Church of Scotland.
 „   W. E. SOOTHILL, United Methodist Free Church.
 „   T. C. FULTON, Irish Presbyterian Church.
 „   ARTHUR H. SMITH, American Board.
 „   J. M. FOSTER, Baptist Missionary Union.
 „   C. W. MATEER, Amer. Pres. Mission (North).
Miss L. H. HOAG, M.D., Meth. Epis. Mission (North).
 „   E. F. SWINNEY, M.D., Seventh Day Bap. Mission.
Mrs. ELIZA M. YATES, Southern Baptist Mission.
Miss L. A. HAYGOOD, Meth. Epis. Mission (South).
 „   K. M. TALMAGE, American Reformed Mission.
 „   R. E. REIFSNYDER, M.D.,Woman's Union Mission.
Mrs. J. L. STUART, Amer. Pres. Mission (South).

A Heathen's Testimony to the Power of Prayer.

FROM MR. JAS. SIMPSON.

OUR teacher tells us that when this house was being mortgaged the old grandmother was much displeased with him about it, and said "These people are always praying to JESUS, always praying to JESUS, and you see what He has done. He has taken our good house from us and given it to them: this is what these people do by praying to JESUS." When I heard this I said, praise GOD for such an unconscious testimony from the lips of a heathen woman to the all-prevailing power of prayer in the name of JESUS.

The Story of Mr. Ts'u.

FROM MR. DONALD.

THE *Missionary Training Home, Gan-K'ing, 28th March.*—Most of us in the C.I.M. have heard a good deal about Mr. Ts'u, one of the most interesting and best native Christians in China, and the head of a clan of over 10,000, but few have had the privilege of meeting him. He is in this city on a visit just now, and of course makes the mission-house his dwelling-place and chief resort. Well, to-day, just before our usual noon prayer-meeting for the workers and work in China, one of our brothers remarked that he thought Mr. Wood should get Mr. Ts'u up to the prayer-meeting, as it might be the means of blessing to him and us, even if neither understood the other's words. No sooner said than done. Mr. Wood spoke to the old man, who was very willing to join us. Mr. Wood first of all explained (for the sake of those of our number who have only recently come out) who the Chinese gentleman was; and then he explained to Mr. Ts'u the meaning of our gathering, and also pointed out to him on the large wall-map the four provinces for which we always pray on the Friday (HU-NAN, KIANG-SI, KWANG-TUNG, FUH-KIEN), and told him about the various workers there. Then he explained to him that several of us would pray, and asked him to pray also. Oh what a blessed time we had! Dr. Howard Taylor led off in a chord of praise for the truth of the hymn we had sung, "Blest be the tie that binds," and for the blessed privilege of our thus, with our dear Chinese brother, meeting around the common mercy seat, and in the same almighty name of JESUS. Mr. Wood prayed in Chinese, and after several short pointed prayers, dear old Mr. Ts'u poured out his heart to GOD for his fellow-countrymen. Oh, I do wish some of those who speak about the impossibility of a Chinaman's conversion could have seen what we have seen to-day, and heard the words we heard. Would that GOD'S grace were received, and manifested in the hearts and lives of all His children, as it is in the case of dear old Mr. Ts'u. Mr. Wood sang the Doxology in Chinese, while we sang it in English, and afterwards invited our brother in to take dinner with us. By what some would call a coincidence, but which I call the LORD'S arrangement, we were having dinner in Chinese style to-day, and the thought of inviting him to dine with us struck Mr. Wood as he rose from his knees after our little prayer-meeting. Now we have cause to praise GOD for it.

After dinner, Mr. Wood asked our dear Chinese brother if he would tell us about his conversion, and some other interesting points in his remarkable life. You should have seen the dear old man's face as he spoke of "Shang-ti-tih en-tien"—the grace of GOD—it was worth coming to this heathen land to see the face of this old man, who used to be, as Mr. Wood told us before the story began,

ONE OF THE MOST TERRIBLE PERSECUTORS POSSIBLE

—a very *Saul:* now, thanks be to GOD, a *Paul* so far as is possible for him. I have heard the story of this old saint's life from his conversion more than once, but as I listened to him telling it himself to-day, my soul was stirred. As he went on from point to point, Mr. Wood interpreted for the sake of most of us who did not understand Chinese. I shall seek to give in as brief a way as possible the story we listened to, and may the LORD, who raised up this man and made him such a grand testimony to His saving and keeping power, bless it to the stirring up of all who read it to pray, and of some, if He will, to come out to this heathen land.

Before his conversion (some eight or nine years ago) Mr. Ts'u lived with his father, who was one of the principal men in the place—what is known in China as an "elder," and the owner of a good deal of property and land. On the father's death Mr. Ts'u took his place and became owner of all the land and head-man of the clan. The home is about 100 *li* from this city, and Mr Ts'u had a good deal of land in the hands of a number of men in his employ in the Ku-ch'en district to the south of this province. Through the visit of his nephew (who is now one of our colporteurs) to that district, several people were converted ; and, among others, several of the men in the employ of Mr. Ts'u. When he heard of this he wrote them a very strong letter, saying that if they did not stop believing this foreign doctrine, he would turn them all out. Shortly after this he went down to collect his rents and found that his *uncle* had been converted too. He was very wild and threatened with much reviling and cursing to turn all of them off his property, but his uncle spoke to him, and even entreated him with tears, to consider what he was saying, and offering him Gospel books, asked him to read for himself. He would have nothing to do with the books, however, and would not go near the "worship hall."

Some time before this, while in Nan-kin at one of the periodical examinations, a gentleman in foreign clothes had stopped him as he came out of the examination hall, saying he wanted to give him something precious, and thereupon had handed him a little packet, on opening which he found a tract. At the time he was now speaking of, while staying down in the Ku-ch'en district collecting his rents, he saw a book in one of the houses, "The Pilgrim's Progress," and in the reading of that book the light dawned upon him, and he was really convicted of sin. The fact that not only was he doing wrong to his kirsfolk and relations in persecuting them as he had been doing, but that he had also been sinning against GOD, so lay upon his heart that he wept for three *days*, and was utterly miserable. At last his strong prejudice was broken down, and soon after he went to worship with the others. When they were going to kneel down for prayer he was going to do the same, but one of the Christians asked him not to, saying, "Don't *you* kneel down, for we know very well *you* don't believe the doctrine." Mr. Ts'u answered that he wanted to worship GOD as well as the rest of them. While they were praying he could not restrain his feelings any longer, but burst out crying ; the glorious light of the Son of GOD had shone into his soul, and from that moment he says he was *really born again.*

Soon after he returned home, and of course created a great sensation among his people. He, once so terrible in his hatred of the Christians, was now a Christian himself ; and then began a most bitter persecution. But he had determined to be out and out for GOD, and so he was and has been ever since. His mother's brother, the only one in the clan who had any authority over him, threatened to bury him alive if, when the time came round for the annual ancestral worship of the clan, he would not join with the rest. However, the uncle *died* a little before the time came round, and the threat could not be carried out.

About this time, when he was passing through this city, Mr. Tomalin, who was then here, asked Mr. Ts'u to stay with him for a time, and this helped him to tide over the bitter persecution which was raging against him. Since then he has been employed in connection with the mission, and up till last year he was down in the south of the province doing good service for the LORD. He heard, however, that his son and one or two others in the family, not far from here, were not living very bright or consistent lives, and, having the needs of his own family and friends laid on his heart, he asked leave to give up his employment and go back to his home, so that he might work among his own people for the salvation of their souls. He was soon busy preaching among his relatives and friends, having gladly given up his post and his salary for the sake of conveying the glad news of GOD'S grace to them. The persecution has been severe, but the grace of GOD has been and still is triumphing.

HIS MOTHER'S CONVERSION.

He gave us also a very touching account of his old mother's last illness and death. He said that as soon as he received news of his mother's illness he returned home to attend to her, and of course preached and pleaded often, urging the old lady to repent and to trust in JESUS. Before this he had been praying for her for about two years, *fasting every Sabbath day.* And now every evening he called all the members of his own house into the mother's bedroom and had worship beside her, as she was unable to get up. Well, one evening there were no prayers. Some visitors had called on matters in which Mr. Ts'u was much interested, and when he went to call the family together for worship he found that they had all gone to bed. In the middle of the night the old mother called Mr. Ts'u and told him to call the family and get her carried out of the bedroom into the family ancestral hall, in the middle of the house. But no one would begin to remove her ; she then broke out into the most awful language, reviling them, and saying and doing things she had never done nor said before. She also threatened to kill herself, and tried to do so by knocking her head against the bed. She said she would believe the doctrine no more, would no longer believe GOD, for He was not going to save her, and such like. Next day, after breakfast, Mr. Ts'u called all the family together, and after singing a hymn and reading out of Matthew's Gospel about CHRIST casting out devils, he knelt down with them by the old woman's bedside, and prayed that GOD would cast out the devils that had taken possession of his mother and cure her. When they got up she was better, and quite sound in her mind again! Then she told them how it was that she had done and said such wicked things during the night. She said there was no worship in the evening, and five devils came to her and got her to do as they liked, things that were contrary to her own desires. These demons told her not to think of believing the doctrine, and to give up trusting to JESUS. Now, however, she said she was very sorry for all she had said and done.

Some time after this, when she was fast dying, and not able to speak, she gave them to understand by signs that she was quite happy, and free from any fear of death. And when, according to Chinese custom, they brought in the new clothes and the coffin, to be ready for her burial, she tried to sit up and watch them. Mr. Ts'u, thinking it would save his mother's feelings, put his arm before her eyes to hide the scene from her, but she put it down, and, making a great effort, managed to say almost with her last breath, "I am not afraid to die, for I am going home to be with JESUS. He has come to take me away." Almost immediately after she passed away, with a happy and peaceful smile on her face. It was a striking contrast between her death-bed and that of her brother, who threatened to kill Mr. Ts'u. Just before he died he said that the devils had come for him with their warrants to take him away to hell!

After the mother's death, poor Mr. Ts'u suffered a great deal of persecution, for of course he refused to call in the priests, or to burn incense, or to carry out any of the heathen rites which Chinese practise on a parent's death. When one of his younger relatives appealed to him that he would be persecuted if he did not do as the others wished, he replied, "I do not fear persecution. What I fear is lest GOD should not be able to trust us with persecution." However, GOD did trust them with it, and it is not all over yet. But the old man, now fifty-seven years old, holds on bravely (or, might we not say, *is held on*), and GOD is using him.

We do thank GOD that we have seen and heard him, and ask you to join with us in earnest prayer that the LORD may use him to the salvation of many. May there not be in this dark China many more like Mr. Ts'u to be won for CHRIST?

"*The angel of the LORD encampeth round about them that fear Him and delivereth them.*"

The platform from which the 420 missionaries attending the Conference were to have been photographed as it appeared after it had collapsed.

Visiting round the Po-yang Lake.

FROM MISS GILLHAM.

MARCH 31*st.* Miss Ord and I went by boat to visit in the neighbouring villages. We had two native Christian servants with us. Having a fair wind, an hour took us to the little bay where we intended anchoring. It was a lovely warm day. We dined early, then we four started off up the nearest hill to visit the marble quarries. There seemed to be quarries in all directions, and we met many coming and going. The Christian lad and Miss Ord were able to speak to them, and tell them the object of our visit. Many of them seemed hardened, but one man, an opium-smoker, lingered behind the others; he had never heard the Gospel before, and looked in earnest he wanted to break off opium.

The scenery was exquisite. We seemed to be right among the mountains, with the beautiful lake on one side, and on the other a valley carpeted with bright green rice, and wheatfields, and bright yellow flowers; away in the distance Li-shan and its waterfalls, and all around lovely azaleas, etc., and ferns of every kind. We were soon glad to return. As we came down we were greeted by quite a crowd of women and children; the news of our coming had spread, and they had come out to look at us. It was too late to stay then, but we promised to accept their many invitations next day. We had gone thirty or forty *li*, so were glad to see our "floating home," which, after tea, we soon made ready for the night. Miss Ord and I occupied the front division of the boat; we had just room to lie side by side in it; we were very cosy, and I was soon asleep. However, this quiet state of things did not last long; I soon woke, to hear heavy rain on our thin roof, and to feel it on my head. This had a rousing effect. Our roof was leaking in various places. Miss Ord suggested our umbrellas, which we found in the dark, and soon put them up, and, after a good laugh over our comical position, we tried to sleep.

April 1*st.*—Still heavy rain till late in the morning,

when it cleared up, and after an early dinner, having with me thick shoes, I started off with the woman and lad to visit the women we had promised to come to. We soon found their homes, and received a hearty welcome. The two natives preached, and we sold some Gospels. My part was to be looked at. How I longed to talk to these dear people. We went from house to house, crowds following. Then we returned, feeling so glad that more had heard the words of life.

April 2nd.—We now have beautiful weather again, our woman who was not well was sent home by chair. We three started early for a distant temple close to one of the waterfalls, visiting various hamlets on our way, and distributing many Gospels. Here again we found many had never heard the Gospel—it is such happy, glorious work going amongst these people. Having dined at the temple, we had a lovely climb to see the waterfall. This is a well-known spot. The water is supposed to be able to wash away sins, and they tell me mandarins, etc., come from round about to wash their sins away. There are characters cut in the stone by the side, calling on people to wash away their sins. It was a solemn thing to look on this spot where people come continually to seek cleansing. I am so glad I have come to this land to tell them the only way.

April 3rd.—This morning we started quite early in chairs for a far-off temple, we were nearly three hours going. We stopped to preach in several villages on the way; most had never seen a foreigner, some seemed afraid of us, but listened to our message. The temple is a wonderful one; it is hard to believe people can worship such images, some so hideous, and yet even whilst we were there one priest was bowing continually to the ground before them. We dined there, and Miss Ord spoke to one of the head priests who entertained us, and gave him a testament, many others listened too.

Coming home, in one of the houses a woman reminded Miss Ord that last year in another village she had met her, she was then suffering with very bad eyes. Miss Ord and a friend had put the Gospel before her and prayed with her just where she was in the road. Now she looked so glad to see Miss Ord, and told her how her eyes had been quite well ever since, and she said she did not worship idols now. She knows very little and cannot read: we can only pray for her.

April 4th.—We set out to visit the hamlets. Then, hardly knowing where we were going, our lad led us over a hill—it is a very long way—till we found ourselves under Li-shan, close to a very picturesque temple in the midst of lovely trees. It was a cool spot after our long hot walk, the mountain peaks towering majestically overhead.

April 5th.—We had our usual Saturday reading together on our little deck, and then tried to return home, but the wind being strong against us, we had to walk, and reached Nan-k'ang Fu rather tired, but rejoicing that the LORD had given us the privilege of telling of JESUS to so many who had never heard before. This is real joy. Hallelujah!

Praise Him all the Time.

FROM MISS J. MUNRO.

KWEI-K'I, *March 3rd.*—Yesterday had a very happy meeting in the morning. The spirit of prayer was manifest. Requests were brief, pointed, and from the heart. Early this morning Miss Say left for Shan-tsin, a town 70 *li* away. The chief Taoist priest of China lives there. I will relate an incident in connection with the present priest's father. A woman in this city had a dream that all the gods in Kwei-k'i came to her and told her to excuse them to the Taoist, as they were very busy and could not come to welcome him on the morrow when he came into the city. Next day the Taoist came to this woman's house, and told him her dream. Afterwards she became his wife, and is the mother of the present Taoist. Since then, written in large characters on the outside of his sedan chair is the following: "Don't trouble to do me reverence, ye gods, I excuse you." This priest is believed to govern all the gods. There were not many at the women's class this afternoon, but the LORD was with us as we looked at Mark xiv. 12-26—the guest-chamber—place of feasting, searching, cleansing, and communion with our MASTER. One thought seemed to impress me: "And when they had sung an hymn they went out;" with Gethsemane and Calvary in view and the hour of separation at hand "They sung"; blessed thought. "He giveth songs in the night." Let us in difficulties and trials sing praises. "Praise Him, praise Him, praise Him all the time." Yes to-night, alone in a Chinese city, I do praise Him. He has become to me a "little sanctuary."—Ezekiel xi. 16.

March 6th.—"Men Sino-tsi, come quick, my wife has taken opium!" This was the cry that greeted my ear late in the evening. I hurriedly got the medicine, and with my faithful Hong mo-mo, followed the man out into the dark streets, past the same opium dens, through the same alleys that three weeks ago I traversed on my way to the case I have previously referred to in my diary. Yes, it was the very same house and the same room; and oh, I shudder as I recall the sight. Not only had she taken opium, but she had attempted to choke herself. Her brother was cutting the cord that she had wound round her neck, just as we entered. We gave her the medicine, and then was the time of suspense. Would she too be added to the lists of daily suicides by opium? We could only wait and pray. Praise the LORD, she is now out of danger. I have since learned that she had no money to buy opium; but her brother is an opium smoker, and she stole some of his. Several of us have agreed to pray definitely that her soul may be saved. Will you please join us? "Is anything too hard for our LORD"? "There is nothing too hard for Thee," "The great and mighty GOD."

March 7th.—Out this afternoon for a walk on the city wall. On my way home, I noticed four women standing by the side of a large pool, burning paper. I stood and watched to see what it meant. It so happened that a sister of one of the women had that day caught cold while washing clothes in this pool. They believed that she dropped one of her spirits here (all people are supposed to have three souls or spirits), and they came to the water to call her spirit back, and appease the gods by burning paper and incense. This over, they bowed to the blackened ashes, and said: "Don't scold because we haven't brought you a better offering." Poor, poor women! O that they knew my SAVIOUR!

FIVE DAYS IN THE COUNTRY.

March 25th.—Rather cold when we started, and while crossing the river there was quite a stiff breeze blowing, the current was strong, and we were landed with difficulty some distance from our usual pier. The pier was crowded with barrows waiting to be taken to Kwei-k'i, and numbers of boats were loading lime and coal-dust.

Perhaps you wonder who the "we" are? Myself, two women, two barrow-men, and a Christian man. We only stayed at two halting places, hoping to reach an important market-town before dark. The country is lovely at this time of the year. It is very mountainous, and there are numerous small streams; consequently the soil in the valleys is very fertile. Here for the first time I saw sugar-cane. Tea is also grown, and the fields clothed in white, yellow, and red (the white is the oil plant, the yellow a vegetable used for food, and the red, clover; with here and there violets and many other pretty flowers, made one think that it was the middle of July, and not cold, bleak March. But I must hurry past these scenes; truly, "every prospect pleases and only man is vile." Just in time for evening rice we came to a little village and put up at the inn. We were very unceremoniously thrust into the guest apartment, which was eight feet square, and separated from the hall by a partition of matting. There was no window. The landlady brought me a lamp, and the people outside, hearing there were foreigners in the room, made little holes in the partition. I soon discovered I had a companion, a very funny old woman crouched up in a corner smoking her pipe. After supper we had prayers in the guest-hall, and this dear old lady stood by me, and when the people crowded around us she used her stick pretty freely. We could not get the attention of the people so I retired to my room, leaving the two women to tell the Gospel. One woman who had been a vegetarian, believed the truth, and that night broke her vow. Praise the LORD for this one!

March 26th.—Pouring rain. However, we were able to start about noon, and reached our destination when it was getting dark. Went to the inn, there was no room inside, but there were little out-buildings, one of which was placed at our disposal, which was fairly comfortable. The landlord kindly gave us a table, and it was thought advisable for me to stay in here till morning. The morning brought crowds. The landlord was afraid his house would be pulled down, so it was suggested that we should go to a place where the idols are kept, and where theatres are held. We walked through the streets, I in front, the women and man following, and then the crowd. When we reached the "Tang" the large platform was covered with incense drying, but the owner quite readily cleared the place, and for three hours the Gospel was preached, and books sold. The evangelist told me there were no fewer than 700 or 800. Many were interested and followed us back to the inn, and while dinner was being prepared I spoke to several personally. After dinner we proceeded to the north side of the town and had a repetition of the forenoon's work. On our way back called at a few houses; was glad to see a man in a shop reading from the Gospel of John to a few men. May the HOLY SPIRIT enlighten his mind, and may he accept JESUS as his own personal SAVIOUR. About 8,000 of the population are engaged in the manufacture of paper, chiefly used in idol worship. It is a very wicked place; it has numerous opium and gambling dens. The Roman Catholics have a chapel, a few miles from the city.

A Year's Work in Yun-nan.

FROM MR. VANSTONE.

DURING the past twelve months Mr. Pollard and I have each paid a visit to Tung-ch'uan and Chan-t'ung; 150 fortnightly visits have been made to twelve villages, and fourteen other villages have been visited at other times. Sixty-four open-air meetings have been held in the city, besides the usual marches on the streets on Sunday and week evenings; 125 afternoons have been spent in conversation, preaching, and bookselling at the hall on the main street. Three quarterly visits have been made to markets about 160 *li* distant; 30,000 cash worth of Gospels and tracts have been sold and given away.

Hardly a day has passed without several cases of sickness being attended to, and medicines have been given on 1,144 occasions; to our knowledge there have been many cures, and much relief has been given. Nineteen opium poisoning cases have been treated; in some cases we were called too late, in others life was saved. Twelve taels' worth of anti-opium medicine has been sold with what results we do not know, but we trust that in some cases the habit of opium-smoking has been broken off.

For some months a weekly instruction class has been held for Christians and enquirers. Two series of united evangelistic services have been held; one at the new year for sixteen days, and one in August for ten days. At each of these services large numbers of handbills were distributed from house to house. About an hour each day has been given to the boys in our day school, through which we trust they have learnt much about the SAVIOUR. A thousand Gospels and other good books were given to students from all parts of the province on their leaving the M.A. examination. Some who were for a time encouraging enquirers have dropped off on finding what it meant to join the Church of CHRIST and that there was no pecuniary advantage to be gained. Thank GOD, however, we are full of hope for the future; there is no doubt as to the final results if GOD'S servants are only found faithful in the time of toil and waiting.

Tidings from Scattered Workers.

Kan-suh Province.

FROM REV. H. W. HUNT.

T'in-chau, April 23rd.—Will you pray very much for a B.A. here who is converted, but who lacks courage to come right out and confess Christ; especially as his elder brothers, also literati, threaten him. His case is very difficult. We are praying that the brothers may be brought to CHRIST.

Shan-si Province.

FROM MR. SAUNDERS.

Hung-t'ung, April 28th.—An accusation was sent to the Yamen the other day against five Church members in a village ten *li* from here, because they would not pay the temple taxes. You will be glad to hear that the magistrate did not even bring the case up, as he said that, as followers of this religion, they had a perfect right not to pay. It will soon get to be known that native Christians do not pay the tax.

From Mr. Russell.

Ping-ying Fu, March 8th.—There is quite a little revival in the villages, and the enquirers are some tens of persons, both men and women. Among them are some who may become good workers, if only they keep s'raight with the LORD. It may be too early yet to speak with any degree of assurance, but I may say that, including members, there are some fifty or sixty persons coming regularly to worship on Sabbaths. The LORD has blessed the members out there very much. I go to them regularly every week. I am hoping that, when a suitable man can be found, we may have a Church out there with its own pastor and office-bearers.

I wish I had as good a report to give of the city Church. There is a general coldness, and some of those formerly baptized have caused a great deal of sorrow. There are some enquirers for whom we praise GOD. It is more and more a joy to serve Him.

Shen-si Province.
From Mr. Bland.

Feng-tsiang Fu, March 29th.—By GOD's grace we are keeping the main thing well to the front, *i.e.*, telling out the message of salvation to poor benighted heathen. We have splendid audiences as a rule, and some listen with evident interest. You will praise GOD for this, and more still for the fact that at least two are enquiring the way. We shall value your prayers at this time, for only the SPIRIT can cause these dry bones to live, and we need to plead, too, that those who are interested may not be hindered by the enemy from coming out brightly for JESUS.

We are happy in the work, and more than satisfied with our inn accommodation, especially as we see a great deal of Chinese life, and are in continual contact with the people more than we could be in our own hired house.

Si-ch'uen Province.
From Mr. Wellwood.

Sui-fu, Feb. 28th.—Since I last wrote I have been away in the country preaching and bookselling. I took the opportunity of going with Brother James as far as Kiang-gan Hien, visiting other cities on the way. It is the first time that I have itinerated with a foreigner, and I greatly enjoyed the little trip. Brother James' earnestness and persistency in preaching did me good, and I am not sorry that he is coming near Sui-fu. I pray that GOD may prosper him at Lu-chau. I was also accompanied by our native Brother Wang, and his help and companionship I found valuable and enjoyable. It is a great advantage to have a native, as many of the people suspect the foreigner, whereas they will open their hearts to the native. A good native filled with the SPIRIT can do splendid work for the MASTER.

On the morning of the 13th inst. we started from Kiang-gan, and walking 30 *li* came to a good-sized village; being market-day I lost no time in getting amongst the people, who were very nice and most eager to buy, but rather too excited to listen attentively; we had a very good time in scattering the seed of the Kingdom.

At the inn in the evening I had a visit from some students who had heard the Gospel during the examination last year.

Next morning started at daylight and arrived at a large village about eleven o'clock; it was market-day here also, and large numbers of people were gathered; the sales were very good, the people crushing to buy the books.

On Saturday had 80 or 90 *li* to walk, in order to get to Chang-lin Hien for the LORD's day, so only stopped at one little village, where we had a good time of preaching and selling. We had to climb hills a good part of the day.

On the LORD's day we made for a temple, where we soon had a very good audience, who understood splendidly and appreciated the tracts very much. In the afternoon had long talks with some students, who seemed very favourable. It was a very profitable day, and I trust some of those poor souls may be led to turn to the LORD.

On Monday took out my books, which were disposed of in a few minutes; as fast as I could give the books and tracts away so fast did the cash come in, and many were disappointed that they could not buy as my store was exhausted. I reached home after being only eight days away. I intend next week to go away again. The work here is going on. GOD grant that thousands may be converted.

From Rev. W. W. Cassels.

Pao-ning, March 17th.—Thank GOD, things here are looking much brighter than they did. All the women's classes have increased, our little school has doubled its numbers, and the teacher is satisfactory. We have a list of close upon thirty enquirers who are candidates for baptism, nearly all of whom have been coming for the best part of a year. I do not mean to receive any who do not show very clear signs of conversion.

A man whom we have now employed for some time is a real help in our quiet hall-work, and gives me great joy. My wife has a class at his home, and his whole family are seeking the LORD.

Last Saturday we buried a poor blind man, who seems to have trusted the LORD from the first time he heard of Him. He is the first ripe fruit gathered home from this district.

Besides this, the itinerating work which has been so diligently carried on by Mr. Beauchamp and Mr. Hugberdon is giving encouragement, and there are many interesting cases.

From Miss E. Culverwell.

Kwong-yuen, March 3rd.—The work here at present scarcely seems like sowing, it is more like clearing rank weeds out of the ground, these poor hearts are so intensely dark. This is such a wicked, needy city, we are very thankful to be the messengers of salvation to those who have been so long bound in Satan's chains.

It is not surprising that the enemy is at work, and that many strange stories are about, or that some who were friendly when we first came now shut their doors when they see us coming. We know that our blessed MASTER has brought us here that some may be saved, and our hearts are full of hope and praise. Our GOD is almighty, while the devil's power and time are limited. Will you join in praying that the LORD will give us a Bible-woman?

Kwei-chau Province.
From Mr. Windsor.

Kwei-yang Fu, April 1st.—You know already of my first visit to Tung-chau, and perhaps of the second about three months after, when a relative of Mr. Mao ceased idolatry. The beginning of this Chinese year Bro. Mao came to Kwei-yang Fu, and was baptised. Three other men came with him two to be cured of opium-smoking, one of whom is the man who destroyed his idols, and the third to hear and learn more of the Gospel. This latter man took down his "Heaven and Earth" tablet at the end of the last Chinese year, and Bro. Mao put up the Ten Commandments in its place. After the men were cured of opium-smoking I returned with the four to their homes, and on the day we arrived the remaining one of the four destroyed his tablet and decided to follow JESUS The meetings were as usual very well attended, and marked attention was apparently paid to the "old story." About three days after my arrival another man destroyed his tablet and opium-pipe, and a few days after another man did the same. Wu Ma's son invited me to his house to eat rice, when we likewise abolished everything pertaining to idolatry from his house. Then after a few more days I was invited to a village thirty *li* from T'ung-chau to the house of an aborigine. Upon entering the house I saw his tablet had also disappeared, and upon inquiry learned he had ceased worshipping idols and burning incense since my visit to the place last year. Besides these there are other persons whom I believe will ere long turn to the LORD. There are now eight families in T'ung-chau turned from idols.

I stayed there eighteen days in all. During this time five or six persons were cured of opium-smoking. Attending to these necessitated my staying so long a time. I could not therefore visit the city of Tu-shan, as I originally intended. I sent my servant along, however. He stayed there three days, and sold 2,000 cash worth of books, did some preaching, and had some encouraging experiences with Romanist converts. Some of them asked intelligent questions, others bought the four Gospels and Acts, while one or two asked for the New Testament.

I ate rice in eight different houses at T'ung-chau this time, one of them being the house of a Romanist.

Before Wu Ma's son gave up idolatry he was not willing to

go and see his mother, but afterwards he was pleased to see the old lady. Accordingly he accompanied me to Gan-shun Fu, and I had the joy of presenting him to his overjoyed mother, and telling her the good news of her sister and son. A cousin of his, who went with us, I left to be cured of opium-smoking.

FROM MR. ADAM.

Gan-shun, March 4th.—I am sure you will rejoice to hear that after such a long time of waiting we have been able to rent another and more suitable house. Since the beginning of the Chinese new year we have been called to twelve opium-poisoning cases, and all recovered save one. Seed time before harvest ; we are believing for a harvest of souls in this dark place.

Kiang-si Province.
FROM MISS MARCHBANK.

Yang-k'eo, March 30th.—We mean as far as we have strength to aim at telling *all* the people the Gospel—to preach the Gospel to every creature in Yang-k'eo and round about that we can reach. My woman is very real, and such a comfort and help to me. The teacher came with us from Yuh-shan ; both he and the evangelist are kept busy speaking to the men. Oh for more HOLY GHOST power as we work day after day among so many precious souls.

May 2nd.—Our two women are ever ready to preach the Gospel in season and out of season. The teacher next door still continues to come ; his friends have been making it hard for him, but he holds on and comes every night to prayers. I have visited a great number of houses, and have also spent days in the country, leaving in the morning and returning at night, and in this way many have heard about JESUS. We have felt the power of the enemy of souls to be strong indeed very often ; there is much to depress one all around if we take our eyes off JESUS ; but He is mighty. This is a very wicked place. The evangelist opens the chapel every afternoon : on market-day— every third day— many people come in from the country and listen. It is a great privilege to tell of His love in the regions beyond ; it is well worth leaving all our nets behind to follow Him and do such work.

Cheh-kiang Province.
FROM MISS BARDSLEY.

Wun-chau, May 23rd.—One has many lessons to learn here besides the language ; and my earnest desire is to be so yielded to the LORD that He may mould His own instrument into His own pattern. I was delighted and surprised to find such a large Church here, and shall never forget the first Lord's day morning. The chapel was full, and many were standing ; some were strangers, but the greater part were Christians, many of whom had walked long distances. It was a heart-stirring sight to see so many of GOD's children together in this dark land, and to remember what they were but a short time ago. How I longed that some dear home friends could witness it ! We can generally tell who are Christians by their faces.

After the morning service on Sunday, there is an interval for lunch ; and at 2 p.m. the bell rings for the different classes to meet. The pastor has all the men in the chapel ; Mrs. Stott the women, Miss Judd the school girls, and the cook's wife takes the little ones. Mrs. Stott has about 40, I believe, and more on Communion Sunday, when a good many come from the country. It is delightful to see their earnest attention, and to hear their bright intelligent answers, as they are questioned about last Sunday's lesson. After the classes are over all who have any distance to go leave. In the evening there is a short service for those who live near enough to attend.

Since coming back Mrs. Stott has organised a band of voluntary preachers. They go on Saturday generally into the villages, and return on Monday morning. As they are too poor to pay their boat fare, she does that ; and if there are Christians in the village, they give the preacher his rice, while he gives his time. It is nice to see them setting off on Saturday afternoon so bright and happy.

Mrs. Stott has also opened two homes since returning, one to serve the double purpose of a street chapel and a home for very poor old blind men, of whom there are quite a number in the Church. The other home is for poor Christian widows over 60 years of age. Miss Whitford and I have been quite alone for a month, as Mrs. Stott and Miss Judd are in Shanghai, at the Conference. It has been good for us as regards the language ; but we shall be very delighted to welcome them back in a few days.

I need hardly tell you that I am very happy here, and when I think of all the way the LORD has led me, my heart is full. It has indeed been goodness and mercy every hour. I expected much, but He has quite exceeded my expectations. The one thing that made it hard to tell the LORD I was willing to come to China was the thought of the loneliness ; and, blessed be His Name, He has never let me feel it once. Isn't it just like Him ?

AN EXTRACT FROM A PRIVATE LETTER.
"*Brethren, pray for us.*"

"I feel very weak spiritually, and sometimes think the devil is making advances upon me. I know my walk has not been such a close walk with CHRIST lately as formerly, and I am conscious of less spiritual power in my service. This has been a source of much sorrow to my mind. Sometimes I have had much, both outwardly and inwardly, to trouble me, and, had it not been for GOD's unceasing, sustaining, and preventing grace, I fear I should have utterly fallen."

Departures for China.

Parties will (D.V.) leave for China on September 4th and 18th, and on October 2nd and 30th.

The following articles, kindly sent for sale, are acknowledged with warm thanks :—*April 8th* (476), Miss McM., 1 lady's gold hunter watch, silver shawl pin set with imitation stone.—*April 9th* (477), Miss A., 4 silver bracelets, 1 silver chain and cross, 1 silver brooch, 2 gold rings, 1 gold coin ; (478) M. F., 1 gold ring.—*April 16th* (479), Y.W.C.A., F., 1 silver card case, 1 silver bracelet, 1 silver chain, 1 silver chain with bog oak pig, 1 pair acorn earrings, 1 gold ring, 1 gold locket, 1 gold brooch, 1 pair gold earrings.—*May 7th* (480), N. B. C , 2 silver watches, 1 silver chain, 1 silver fork, 2 gold rings, 2 pairs gold links, 1 coral pendant, 1 silver 1½d.-piece.—*May 8th* (481), Anon., 1 lady's silver watch chain.—*May 13th* (482), Miss L. M. C., 1 parcel crewel work (valued by donor at 15s.).—*May 16th* (483), Miss K. J., 1 album of autographs ; (484) K. T., 1 jet and gold brooch, 1 gilt silver, locket and chain, 2 chains (gilt only), 2 lockets (gilt only), 1 brooch and earrings (gilt only), sundry small white metal ornaments 1 pair " 2 annas " earrings, 2 bracelets.—*May 10th* (485), Miss J., 2 albums of autographs.—*May 22nd* (486), Mrs. A., 2 gold bracelets, 1 diamond and turquoise brooch, 1 pearl cluster ; (487) L. H. and J. M. W. B, 1 brooch (silver coin), 1 gold ring (diamond, etc.) ; (488) Miss G., 1 gold watch and chain.—*May 19th* (489), Miss G , 1 parcel of socks. *May 29th* (490), J. W. C., lady's gold chain.— *May 30th* (491), Miss S., parcel clothing (containing 15 garments).—*June 9th* (492), E. C. F., imitation gold locket.—*June 12th* (493), " For Jesu's sake", 1 gold brooch, 1 gold ring, 1 silver bracelet, 1 silver bangle, 1 silver brooch (pebbles), 1 silver ring.— *June 13th* (494), Miss K. J., 1 album of autographs.—*June 18th* (495), Miss P. D., 2 silver bracelets.—*June 28th* (496), Anon., 1 small gold brooch, 1 pair silver earrings, 1 pair imitation gold earrings, 2 pairs (stone) earrings, 1 small gold locket, 1 silver ring.

CHINA'S MILLIONS.

Opening Sermon of the Shanghai Missionary Conference.

BY REV. J. HUDSON TAYLOR.

"Whence should we have so much bread in the wilderness, as to fill so great a multitude?"
—See MATT. xv. 29-38.

HIS narrative will, I think, touch all our hearts in one respect; it brings before us at the very outset and keeps before us all through *the presence of our blessed Lord*. The 32nd verse, which speaks of the feeding of the multitude, brings before us JESUS. "JESUS called His disciples unto Him." JESUS opened their hearts to the sympathy and compassion of His own heart: "I have compassion on the multitude;" "I will not send them away fasting, lest they faint in the way." This is just what we all need: we want our dear MASTER to draw us near to Himself; to open His own heart to us and let us see the depths of His compassion, and the strength of His determination to feed the multitude. And oh! shall not we be as His disciples were, utterly at His disposal? Shall we not feel as they evidently felt?

Our LORD has compassion on the multitude and wishes them to be fed; then they *must* be fed, and one question only may arise, How is it to be done?

Our blessed LORD had fed a multitude previously; a larger multitude probably,—five thousand men, beside many women and children. The disciples knew, no doubt, the condition of this multitude, they knew how long they had been with our LORD, they knew their great need, but they had not learned the lesson which they should surely have learned from the previous miracle. It never appears to have entered into their minds to undertake the work of feeding this multitude before they were sent away; and when our blessed LORD reveals to them His own thought and feeling about the matter, the question is raised, as though they had never seen the previous miracle, "Whence should we have so much bread in the wilderness, as to fill so great a multitude?"

It seems very amazing that they should not have remembered the feeding of the five thousand and should not have seen the whole thing at once. But how like these disciples were to ourselves! How frequently GOD has helped us in some time of special trial or special difficulty, and we have rejoiced in His help; yet perhaps the very next time the LORD has brought us into the same circumstances, our faith has been *so* wavering and weak, and our expectations *so* low. We have had but a very poor sort of hope, perhaps, when we should have had strong confidence in Him. But is it not very blessed to see that our gracious LORD did not upbraid these disciples; did not say, "Really you are no use to Me; it is no use My using you; you do not learn the lessons you should learn; I will work this miracle independently of you." No; He deals so gently, so graciously, so lovingly with them. He leads them along, and uses them again and yet again in His blessed service. This same JESUS is with us now; and with the task before us of carrying the Gospel to the dark multitudes of this land, we have the same forbearing, loving, mighty LORD—not in His weakness, as JESUS was when on earth, but now ascended to His FATHER's throne, having received all power in heaven and on earth.

II.—Then this narrative is very helpful to us, in that *it brings before us the disciples of the* LORD JESUS *as the instruments through which He wrought His greatest work.*

Weak and poor as they were, our blessed LORD fully realised His oneness with His disciples and their oneness with Him. *He* would do nothing independently of them, and I think there is a lesson

OCTOBER, 1890.

for us to learn that we should not work independently of one another. If our LORD worked through His disciples and would not work independently, how closely should we be knit together, and with what practical co-operative oneness do the work He has given us to do! Our gracious MASTER has told us that *He* is the Vine and *we* are the branches, and if we forget our corporate unity, He does not forget.

He remembers His oneness with us, and never ignores His people. He does not work independently of them, but through them. He called His disciples to Him and opened His heart to them. He told them His desire and purpose, and He looked to them to carry out that desire. Those disciples were very weak in the faith; they had not yet received the outpouring of the SPIRIT in the plenitude with which they were blest at Pentecost; but they had one thing in their favour. They were *near* to JESUS, and they *heard* what He had to say, and however conscious they may have been of the difficulty of the situation, they were *prepared to do* what they were told. Oh, dear friends! are we living habitually in such nearness to the LORD JESUS that the gentlest intimation of His wish comes to us with the force of a command, and with the consciousness that some way or other it *is* possible to obey, and that we shall be carried through in any service to which He calls us?

III.—Then we have brought before us *the multitude.*

I am so glad it was a *great* multitude, and that the disciples evidently thought it was impossible to feed them. All their previous experience of the LORD's goodness had not wrought in them this faith, that it was possible to supply the requirements of all these people, or to do it at once. "Whence should we have so much bread in the wilderness," they say, "as to fill so great a multitude?" So much! We are too apt to be arithmetical in our thoughts; we want so much to do so much. They forgot with whom they had to do. In the presence of the LORD, it was no matter how much there was. The widow at Sarepta might have said, "How much flour shall I need if I am to support Elijah for many days?" It was no question of how much she had. It was *better* for her to have only a handful of meal and a little oil in the cruse than to have a dozen barrels of meal. I have often thought of that since the great famine in SHAN-SI, when we saw how dangerous it was to have much money or much food. I have often thought it was much better to have small resources, in the hand of GOD, who is able to multiply them, than it is to have much. If that poor widow had had a large store in her house, do you think she could have kept the house over her head? It would have been torn in pieces by the hungry multitude, impelled by the famine to take possession of anything that would appease their hunger. But who would rob the poor widow of a handful of meal and a little drop of oil in the cruse? Yet it was amply sufficient, for the LORD's blessing rested upon it.

GOD in His Word gives us illustration after illustration of the great truth that what He has given us is all that we need in order to glorify His own great Name: we require nothing more! When Moses on the Mount was wondering how his message could be authenticated, the LORD said, "What is that in your hand?" Why he had nothing but a staff! That was quite sufficient. "Cast it on the ground," and it became a serpent. Afterwards, when he had *nothing* in his hand, the LORD said, "Put thy *hand* in your bosom," and that healthy hand was at once made leprous. The LORD does not require anything outside of that which He has given to His people to accomplish His present purposes, whatever they may be!

So it was not a question of large supplies; it was just a question of the presence of the LORD, and of that willing obedience which put all that they had at His disposal.

IV.—*Let us look at our Lord's methods. How* were the people fed?

1. By the united action of CHRIST and His disciples. He claimed their all; they gladly gave up their all, and unhesitatingly obeyed all His directions. Our LORD said to them, "How many loaves have ye?" Now, if there had been some stingy arithmeticians there, they might have set to work to calculate. "The LORD has done a great miracle like this before; then there were five thousand men and a great number of women and children; He had five loaves, and after the multitude was fed, there was enough and to spare. Here are four thousand men; four loaves will suffice; we will keep three for ourselves and give Him as large a proportionate supply as He had before."

Do not we hear a good deal of that sort of thing, and is it not very mistaken and foolish?

The LORD asked them what they had; they told him they had seven loaves and a few small fishes; and He asked them to bring, and took possession of, *all* the seven loaves and *all* the fishes.

It was not a question whether four loaves might not suffice, or one loaf might not suffice; it was just the question of *entire consecration.* Now, for our Conference *we* need to be in this position of entire consecration, utterly and absolutely at the disposal of our LORD. We do not need a larger number than He has brought together; we do not need greater ability; we do not need wider experience, in order to have full blessing; but we do need to be near to our LORD, *very* near to Him, to have Him reigning in our hearts. We want that He should know, and to know ourselves, that all we have and all we are are in unreserved consecration given up to Him. And if this be so, as the multitude was fed, so our own needs and desires will be met, and the needs of this great people will be met, to an extent perhaps far beyond our highest thoughts and most sanguine expectations. Oh, let us every day seek to be all for JESUS; and being all for JESUS, we shall be all for one another, and all drawn together. Let us give up our work, our thoughts, our plans, ourselves, our lives, our loved ones, our influence, our *all*, right into His hand, and then, when we have given *all* over to Him, there will be nothing left for us to be troubled about or to make trouble about ; when all is in His hand all will be safe, all will be wisely dealt with, all will be done and well done. When the eye is single, when the heart is true to CHRIST, then and then alone the whole body will be full of light. And if the whole body be full of light, having no part dark, then the whole of the questions that come before us, the whole of our circumstances and relationships and surroundings, will be full of light too, as when the bright shining of a lamp illumines our path and sheds light all around. We step forward with confidence ; we see where we are going, we know what we are doing, because we are full of light. This fulness of light is just what we want for this Conference ; this is just the preparation we require. How shall we get it ? Simply by unreserved surrender, taking our LORD as King, and putting ourselves and all we have and all we are into His hands.

If He take some plan very different from what is in my mind, what matters it ? We want China blessed ; we do not want *our* plans carried out. What does it matter which brother or sister the LORD honours in His service, if only CHRIST is glorified and China is saved ? When our hearts are true to Him everything becomes simple, and there is no danger of difficulty from personal matters coming in and blinding our eyes. Oh, let us by His grace be brought so low before Him, and yet be so lifted up by Him above circumstances and surroundings, that the heart is just singing with joy all the time, JESUS, JESUS, JESUS ! listening for the MASTER's voice, wanting to know His will, asking, What would JESUS do in this matter ? What would be His pleasure in this enterprise ? What would be His joy in that undertaking and then all our heart will gladly go after Him. As our brother stated, "We do love Him, and we do serve Him, and we mean to love Him more and serve Him better every day of our lives."

I am sure that our LORD has brought us together for grand blessing. I expect a great outcome from this Conference, and you expect it too. We have asked it of the LORD in faith, and we know that the One who had compassion, when on earth, on the multitude who followed Him for three days is not going to leave *us* hungering and thirsting in the dark, who at His own command and for His own sake have left things most dear to us, and have come to spend our lives in this land, and given all our dearest ones into His charge.

But let us further consider the methods of the LORD JESUS in the feeding of this multitude.

It is delightful to realise that we have in CHRIST the wisdom of GOD as well as the power of GOD, and hence the way in which He accomplished every purpose was the wisest way. His methods were perfect methods. Being the Servant of His FATHER, he was guided in all things by His HOLY SPIRIT. He fully followed the One who sent Him.

2. In the next place then our LORD did not act unsystematically. *He used both method and order.*

His first requirement was that the multitude should sit down on the ground. It is highly probable that some similar plan was adopted to that which we are told was used in the case of the feeding of the 5,000 ; that they were divided into companies easy of access, so that there might be no confusion and no difficulty about the distribution, that none might be overlooked or neglected, that all might be methodically served with the bread and with the fish.

Now, here is a practical lesson of wisdom. I am so thankful that one subject to be discussed at this Conference is "The Division of the Field." Our present forces, if wisely divided, would be able to accomplish very much more than we are now accomplishing. I think we all feel this more or less ; and I do pray that the SPIRIT of GOD may throw light on this difficult question, which is so impossible for us to manage, but so easy for Him. If one or two of the disciples had taken these loaves, and one had kept five in his hand and another two, it might have been very difficult to get them properly distributed ; but they were all first handed over to JESUS, and then, having offered thanks to GOD, He broke and gave them to His disciples, and sent them to distribute to the multitude. We are not told that He said to Peter, You go to this company, and to James, You go to that. He assumed that the sound judgment and the spirit of obedience, with common sense, were quite sufficient to guide them in these matters.

And they acted, no doubt, in a rational way; four or five of them would not go to one company, hindering one another, and none to the next company; but undoubtedly they distributed themselves wisely over the work that was to be done. It was all done in a methodical way. It would take a good deal of time for twelve men to break off pieces of bread, and to give them with pieces of fish to 4,000 men and we know not how many women and children; but they did not raise any question as to the time it would take or the difficulty of accomplishing it. The LORD gave them the bread to distribute, and they began and went on until all had their portion, so that all were filled and all were satisfied. I have little doubt that very soon those who were receivers in the first instance became distributors. Perhaps some man broke a piece off his bread and gave it to his wife, and found that he had no less after he had divided the bread than before; and when he found that out he would be ready to distribute further.

Are we not looking for something like this, to a much larger extent than we have yet seen it? Thank GOD, many of those who have been turned from the service of idols to the Living GOD are now distributing the Word of Life which they have received, and are spreading the message which has been a blessing to themselves; but we want it to be true to a very much larger extent; and how is this to be brought about? (*To be continued.*)

Items of Interest.

FROM REV. J. W. STEVENSON.

SHANGHAI, *July 4th.*—As I mentioned, I heard of the baptism of eighteen persons in Yuh-shan, KIANG-SI, on June 17th. We have much cause to praise GOD for the way the work is extending, through the labours of our sisters on the Kwang-sin River. At all the stations on that river there is considerable encouragement, and, as far as one can see, with GOD'S blessing there is a prospect of a rapid extension of the work.

July 11th.—I received, on the 9th, a telegram from T'ai-yuen Fu, which announces the opening of the lines thus far. They will soon be opened from there to Si-gan and Lan-chau.

July 18th.—Since last writing I have heard of the following 49 baptisms:—

Bing-yae, CHEH-KIANG, May 11th	...	...	...	2
Yun-nan Fu, May 4th	...	...	...	2
P'ing-yang, SHAN-SI, May 16th	...	...	...	20
K'uh-wu, SHAN-SI, May 19th	...	...	...	11
Han-chung, SHEN-SI, June 1st	...	...	...	10
Ch'ung-k'ing, SI-CH'UEN, June 21st	...	...	...	2
Bing-yae, CHEH-KIANG, June 29th	...	...	...	2

Messrs. Langman and Wright have visited Ch'u-chau, and Mr. and Mrs. Langman expect to remove there before long. Very interesting reports reach me from K'uh-wu and P'ing-yang; Mr. and Mrs. Thos. King have arrived at P'ing-yang, and the work there has been handed over to them.

July 25th.—You will be exceedingly sorry to hear that our dear sister, Miss Boyd, has laid down her armour. I have just heard that she passed away at Wun-chau on July 14th. Oh, how my heart aches as I think of the sorrow that will fill the hearts of her family! It was beautiful the self-sacrifice exhibited by our sister in going down to Wun-chau immediately on arrival in Shanghai.

Aug. 1st.—I have to report eleven baptisms at Cheng-ku, SHEN-SI, on June 15th.

I hear of very destructive floods in Tien-tsin and neighbourhood. The country for miles round and the roads in the settlement are under water; this will cause great suffering.

In Memoriam.

MISS FANNY BOYD.

"FATHER, I will that they also whom Thou has given me be with me where I am, that they may behold my glory." The mail before last brought word that "Miss Boyd was ill with fever at Wun-chau." That of July 25th tells that our dear sister, Miss Boyd, has laid down her armour, having passed away at Wun-chau on July 14th. We append a letter from Miss Whitford, giving the particulars of her last days, and hope to give extracts from some of her latest letters in our next number. May the LORD send many to tread in her footsteps.

FROM MISS WHITFORD.

Wun-chau, July 21st.—Our letters this mail cannot but be sad, as all our hearts are sore at the removal of dear Miss Boyd from our midst.

It is only three weeks to-day since I started for Bing-yae; we having heard the day before that they were all suffering from fever, it was decided that I, being pretty strong, should go and send Miss Britton and little Olive here. I was struck with the change in dear Miss Boyd, and indeed in all of them; but when I had been there a day or two I did not wonder at it, for the heat in that small house was so intense and unbearable. I did thank the LORD for sending me there, though, for I was able to be of some little assistance to them, and in a small measure to alleviate Miss Boyd's sufferings. She had suffered so intensely with her head from the heat upstairs that the night after I got there, and all the rest of the time, except once, she slept downstairs in the chapel, with the result that she had ague and fever every day; but we scarcely knew which was the greater evil.

By the LORD's help I was able to tend her almost constantly night and day, getting an hour or two's sleep now and then when I could. She scarcely ever complained; her first thought was always for others, and I am sure her patience and gentleness taught us many a lesson. She would often ask me to pray that the LORD would give her strength and patience to bear all that He put upon her, adding a few words herself when able, generally asking for strength for me. Once she asked me to read her a few verses; but the fever had left her little power to think or talk. The last hymn we sang together she chose "A few more years shall roll;" how soon it was to be fulfilled for her we little thought then, though I believe she felt her days were numbered; she seemed particularly to dwell on Rev. ii. 10, feeling it a message to herself.

On Sunday, the 6th, we decided that it would be better for us all to risk the journey to Wun-chau than to remain any longer, seeing that Miss Boyd was daily growing weaker On Monday morning, having had a worse night than before, she felt very weak and low, and quite unequal to a fourteen hours' boat journey, so we had special prayer for her and for guidance, and by the afternoon the LORD had strengthened her sufficiently to undertake the journey. We started about 5.30 that afternoon, and reached Wun-chau at 7.30 on Tuesday morning, where Mrs. Stott and Miss Bardsley at once did all they could for the dear sufferer.

She had borne the journey well, and we all trusted that the cool, healthy house, and all the kind care and attention she was sure to receive, would restore her at least sufficiently to proceed to her sister at Che-foo; but the terrible fever had taken too deep a hold on her system. She continued more or less in fever all the week until Sunday, the 13th, when she seemed much better. That night she asked me to thank the LORD with her, and when I left her to Mrs. Stott and Miss Bardsley in the morning, as usual, I felt quite happy about her, and quite hoped for a speedy recovery; but the LORD had other purposes. About ten o'clock on the morning of Monday, the 14th, she sank into a state of semi-consciousness, apparently feeling no pain or discomfort, answering when spoken to, and several times saying she had had a nice sleep. When I went again, about six in the evening, she was quite unconscious, and remained so until 7.30, when she quietly passed away without a struggle; indeed, though watching closely, we knew not the exact moment when her spirit went home.

On Tuesday, the 15th, we laid her to rest in the little English cemetery. We all assembled here about 5 p.m., when a short service in Chinese was conducted by Mr. Grierson, there being about sixty of the native Christians present. The coffin was then borne by eight native Christians to the cemetery, where Mr. Soothill, of the United Methodist Free Church, read the service in English, afterwards addressing a few words in Chinese to the bystanders.

There were twelve foreigners present, nearly all the Wun-chau community, including the Consul, the Commissioners, Dr. McGowan, who attended her, and ourselves.

Though I only knew her such a short time, I feel as if I had lost a dear friend; that week's constant intercourse at Bing-yae was very sweet, it taught me many lessons, and she seemed to like having me with her.

It will indeed be a sad blow to Dr. and Mrs. Randle and the relatives at home.

MR. FREDERICK SHARP.

A TELEGRAM received on August 21st conveyed the sad news that Mr. Sharp, who only left for China last December, had died suddenly. As yet we have no further tidings.

Good Tidings from Han-chung.

FROM MISS JOHNSTON.

THURSDAY, *June 5th.*—To-day two of my old scholars have been here to spend the day—one is fifteen and the other sixteen—both unengaged. The youngest is a fine tall girl and very pretty, with sweet, engaging manners, but, best of all, a real, bright, happy Christian. Her mother is a most worldly woman, and *will not* permit Hwan-tsz to come to the services or openly confess CHRIST, but the child said to me to-day, "The LORD JESUS never leaves me. He is by my side always, and He knows how I am situated. He knows I can't openly confess Him; but I do love Him and serve Him in my heart, and read His word every day, and sing hymns out of my hymn-book. Why!" she exclaimed, "often when mother is out and I am all alone, I feel as though JESUS were a second person with me, and I am not lonely."

In the afternoon the two children came into my class, and oh! how they enjoyed the hymn-singing! I was astonished at the number of hymns she could sing by heart, although she has not read in school for three years, and she listened so eagerly to the explanations in between the singing, as though she was hungry and had not had a meal for a long while. I used the picture of the "broad and narrow way," which is a never-failing source of interest and enjoyment. The other girl seemed very interested and happy too, but she has not given her heart to JESUS like Hwan-tsz. GOD grant that she may do so soon.

On Sunday, June 1st, we had a most glorious day! Eight men, one dear boy, and one woman baptised! I do praise GOD! It was such a blessed time, and how the faces of those people shone with the glory of the LORD! It was a real "feast of fat things" to my soul.

Another wonderful thing—Fung-ing's mother has given in her name, and desires to confess JESUS as her MASTER! My heart just overflowed when she told me, and thanked me with a beaming smile for the day I put the piece of meat on the top of her rice, and she broke her vegetarian vow. Oh! how Fung-ing will rejoice. Also one woman from my Sunday-school class has given in her name, desiring baptism—she has he'd back for years. Two more of my girls have desired baptism, and one is now waiting to come before the church. Another cause for praise is that two young fellows, engaged to two of my girls, have given in their names, desiring to confess CHRIST openly! Oh! there *were* "showers of blessing" yesterday ! We all felt it ! and "Still there's more to follow !" Some women from Mrs. Wilson's class will be coming before the church soon. The LORD *is* in the midst ; He is working *mightily*. Among the boys in Mr. Easton's school there is more than one who has shown evidence of a real work of grace and requests baptism. It does rejoice my heart to see first one and then another among these dear little ones of the flock coming out on the LORD'S side. May He lead them every one into His fold !

Baptisms at Cheng-ku.

FROM MR. A. H. HUNTLEY.

MAY 25th, *Sunday.*—This day we examined thirteen candidates for baptism, and received eleven of them. Good services all day.

June 1st to 7th.—My Monday evening "preachers' class" continues very encouraging, and the addresses given by the brethren at that class and on Sunday afternoons show that they have benefited by teaching. Our Wednesday evening prayer-meeting and Friday evening Bible-class, together with my wife's Bible-class on Friday mornings, are fairly well sustained.

June 8th.—Examined three candidates for baptism and refused them all this time, thinking it better to defer a little than to receive those who were not fully satisfactory. We find a difficulty with our country catechumens—they live at a distance and very rarely come to town, and hence have very little instruction. We are praying very definitely for native workers.

June 15th.—We have had the great joy to-day of baptising and receiving into our church circle the eleven new converts. The baptism has been looked forward to for a long time, and we had hoped for a fine day and much blessing ; but, with respect to the former, the LORD saw it better to give us a trial to our faith and zeal by sending pouring rain. This, however, was not sufficient to damp the zeal of our converts, for, though many had to come from a distance, yet most of them turned up. The day previous an old man and two aged women, with small feet, walked in from Yang-hien (distance, seventeen English miles), having come all that way through mud and water in order to be present. On Sunday morning another man came thirteen English miles to worship, and other men and women trudged along the bad roads, some walking three and others four miles, and none of these seemed to think they had done more than they ought to have done. We commenced the services with a time of prayer, and then the six male candidates publicly confessed CHRIST before the congregation, each giving a simple testimony and account of their conversion. The five female candidates answered such questions as were put to them, and in this manner publicly testified to their faith in the only SAVIOUR. After an address from Rom. vi. 3, 4, we proceeded with the ordinance. Among the candidates my teacher came first. When I first engaged him, he was a proud Confucian, who constantly sought to justify himself by the fact that he read *good books*. He has been the subject of very many prayers, which GOD has graciously been pleased to answer, for now he is a *humble* follower of the much despised JESUS. Before entering the water he spoke simply and sincerely of the change that CHRIST had wrought. This man has for many months given his spare time to preaching in our street chapel.

Until recently I only paid him for a half day ; the other half he laboured for the LORD. Now he uses all the time in which we don't use him in preaching the Gospel. After him came Mr. Ch'en, who once was a very strict Buddhist. His wife and he sincerely believed in the idols, and she was, moreover, a vegetarian for twenty or more years. These give us much hope, and we praise GOD for them. My wife is especially pleased with the woman's simple faith. A little time ago we both spent a day at their house in the country, and found that they had indeed made a clean sweep of idolatry ; Christian tracts occupied the places where pictures of the idols once were ; and upon the family altar, where incense was once burned to false gods, we found the New Testament and Hymn-book, which, we understand, are used daily in family worship. Also there was a small heap of Christian tracts for distribution. And this was not all, for we also found that all around seemed to know of their Christianity, and were exhorted continually by this couple. After this Mr. Ch'en came Mr. Chang, who (with his little niece, baptised at the same time) makes the sixth member of one family who have been received into fellowship. Mr. Shi came next—the fruit of one of our older members, who was not only instrumental in getting him to decide for CHRIST, but got him to pull down his ancestral tablets and idols, and also brought them for us to publicly burn at one of our Sunday services about six months ago. The last of the men candidates was a blind beggar, who, on principle, has received only the slightest material help from us. I know the poor man does not want, but seems quite satisfied with what he gets through begging. He is rejoicing now in the SAVIOUR who has given sight to his blind heart. It is nice to see how all the other members receive this man among them, and do not despise him in the least.

I have already told you of some of the female candidates. Mrs. Nyien seems to show very distinct indications of the SPIRIT's work in her heart and life. She has much love for her SAVIOUR, and has received much blessing through a long period of waiting for baptism. Mr. Pearse did not receive her at his last baptism (before leaving for England) because there was one sin she had not given up. Being refused on account of this made a great impression upon her, and we believe her now to be one of the most consistent of our members, and certainly one of the most happy, for her face is always cheerful, and she is never unready for either praise or work. Two other women also evidenced much sincerity, and it gave me peculiar joy to baptise the little girl of twelve years who came in at the last.

After the baptisms we met together to remember the death of our LORD at His table. The new candidates were then received into fellowship, and each received a card of membership, bearing upon it a suitable text. A few words on these texts were addressed to each, and then they took their places among us. How happy our united communion with our common LORD ! Truly our fellowship was with the FATHER, and with His SON JESUS CHRIST ! After this service we held a short church meeting, and received four other country candidates for the next baptism (August 10th, D.V.), and also received four names as fresh inquirers, for whom we praise God. I am sure Mr. and Mrs. Pearse would have had great joy could they have been with us to-day, for most of the above found CHRIST when they were in this place.

THE TUNG-LING RAPID ON THE YANG-TSE.

Visiting a Fresh Village.

FROM MR. DUNCAN KAY.

K'UH-WU, *April 28th.*—We are still having large meetings here every Sunday, the hall being quite filled. Chang Chu-hwei attends regularly, and brings the people from his refuge to worship. There are not more than four in the refuge at a time, but it is never without a patient. His experience corroborates the natural conclusion that when there are few a larger proportion become enquirers.

I have been down at Kiang-chau since I last wrote, and have had a very good time. Two farmers 15 *li* from Kiang-chau broke off their opium two months ago; both could read, and from the beginning showed great interest in the Gospel, and studied the New Testament very carefully. They returned to their home cured, and immediately after four men and one woman came from the same village. These with one exception have been cured, and all come regularly to worship. The two farmers invited me to their home during my last visit, and I gladly accepted the opportunity to get an entrance into their village.

I daresay you know the villages here are all walled, and unless you go at the invitation of some resident you cannot stay, as there are no inns. Three of the enquirers from the village escorted me, and one had gone before to prepare a place to preach in. The refuge-keeper, a SHAN-TUNG Christian, and two city enquirers also went with us, making eight in all. We sang hymns all the way, mostly to Chinese tunes. We reached the village early in the evening, and our host who was the first to break off opium in his village had supper ready for us, the court and rooms swept clean, and the table and forms placed ready for worship.

In the evening from twenty to thirty gathered together, and after worship some of the villagers joined with the enquirers in singing the hymns they had become familiar with. A poor blind man who, with two brothers and an old mother, came here from North HU-PEH at a time of dearth, two years ago, enjoyed the singing exceedingly, and asked me when going away to let one of the enquirers teach him the hymns.

After worship, one of the enquirers gave his testimony, and told those present that there would be a meeting in his court on the morrow to worship the true GOD of heaven, and whoever would not bend the knee in prayer would be expelled from the court! This was strong language, but met with only one objector, and he was one who had broken off opium and gone back to the drug.

We had a meeting in his court in the forenoon, when from twenty to thirty bent the knee in prayer to GOD.

We are to have a large meeting here on the 30th of the third month, when some will be baptized. Thirteen have given in their names, most of whom have been waiting for over two years.

The Bright Side and the Dark.

FROM MISS GIBSON.

HO-K'EO, *April 1st.*—Ere this you will have heard of the arrival here of our sisters, Misses Ramsay and Cowley. They are delighted with their teacher, a Christian HO-NAN man, baptised a year last Christmas.

The Sunday services this last month have been very well attended; rainy weather does not seem to make much difference to the Christians. A few inquirers are giving us joy, while the steady growth in grace among the dear women is very manifest. I wish you could be present at some of the little meetings and hear these dear women pray; I am sure it would give you joy.

The woman-inquirer I mentioned in my last continues to come. The HOLY SPIRIT has wrought in her heart a work which we believe will never be erased: how precious is this one soul in His eyes! She has such an anxious look. I never met one in China who drew out my heart in pity so much: the soul's need was pictured in her face.

One man, an inquirer, has given up his trade, and is on the outlook for another situation, because he wants to obey GOD. He made crackers; will you pray for him? His face brightens up wonderfully at the meetings, and even now JESUS is a blessed reality to him. His former master's wife is now an inquirer, and is equally earnest.

I have given you the bright side first. I find it a good thing to look to see what there is to praise GOD for previous to dwelling on the trials. Wang Nai-nai and her son are still keeping away from the meetings; we believe they were truly converted. Lao-hu, who used to be called an opium devil in the streets, is still smoking opium, though he comes to the meetings, and, I am sorry to say, sometimes speaks to outsiders. His is a very sad case.

Mr. Wang, the first who believed in his family, has not been able to attend the Sunday services this last month. For some time he held out and would not engage himself to any one without the promise that he could keep the Sabbath; at last, seeing his family inconvenienced by want of money, he has taken work of a man who will not allow him to keep Sunday.

Baptisms at Ho-k'eo.

FROM MISS GRABHAM.

MAY 28*th.*—On Saturday last ten came forward for baptism; six were accepted, and it was thought better for the others to wait. About 7 o'clock on Sabbath morning the Christians began to come, and at 9.30 the hall was filled with people. I have never seen so many together in Ho-k'eo before. It was a splendid opportunity of telling them the Gospel. After the morning service Mr. Ts'ang baptised the six accepted ones. The first was Mr. Tang, who has been an inquirer for more than a year; he was an opium smoker. We believe that he has now given it up, and is very true and real, but he needs very much to be upheld in prayer. He has already brought two from a village who have given up idol-worship. The second was a village woman, who has suffered a great deal for CHRIST's sake; she needs very special prayer, as hers is not by any means an easy life. The third, a dear old lady of seventy-four, is very bright, and always ready to tell the Gospel. The fourth was a woman about thirty. The fifth was the wife of our teacher; when she first came here she was the most unlovable woman I have ever seen, but now she is quite changed. Praise GOD! The sixth was our cook's wife, a dear, bright girl of twenty-one. Please pray that each one may be kept faithful unto death.

How the City of I-yang was Opened to the Gospel.

BY MISS JESSIE GARDINER.
From "The Faithful Witness."

THIS City will probably not be found marked on any map of China. It is in the north-eastern part of the province of KIANG-SI, situated on the Kwang-sin river, half-way between the cities of Kwei-k'i and Ho-k'eo.

Four years ago, Mr. Hudson Taylor, together with four or five missionaries, passed down this river on their way to the coast. As their boat drew near to each city, and they thought of the thousands groping in darkness within the walls, they joined in prayer asking GOD to quickly send forth labourers for these cities. On nearing the city of I-yang, the crowds, attracted by the arrival of the foreigners, seemed particularly rough and boisterous. The lady missionary who gave me this information, and who was one of the party, remembers distinctly the specially earnest prayers that rose to GOD for this city, which prayers He has now answered.

About that time a house was rented and a native Christian sent to live there and sell books; but the people were so opposed to the foreigners' religion and the probability of a foreigner living in their city, that he was not allowed to remain; the house had to be given up at the end of a month. No further attempt was made to procure a house until last year. In the meantime several visits were made and books sold on the street.

In July last year, the native evangelist from Ho-k'eo, accompanied by a native Christian, made another attempt to get an entrance. They put up at an inn, and after spending about a week, at last found a man willing to rent his house to us. It was a little way outside the city wall, but that was no great disadvantage, and it was really getting a footing in the city. A few chairs, a bed, etc., were bought, and the Christian man took possession, the evangelist returning to Ho-k'eo. Two or three weeks after this, a lady missionary, who has been in China five years, and myself, with two native Christian men and one woman, made our first visit to the house, simply taking our bedding and a few extra chairs and tables. The boat reached the landing just outside the city about 8 p.m., but fearing false reports of our being afraid to land in the day time, we decided to remain on the boat all night. Between six and seven the next morning we went on shore and walked up to the house, which was only a few steps distant. In a little while women began to come in; they appeared frightened, never having seen a foreigner before;

but when they heard us speak, and saw that we were so little different from themselves, they became more friendly and soon were quite at home. We remained five days and then returned to Ho-k'eo. Quite a large number heard the Gospel, and all appeared friendly. The house, we saw, could be made comfortable with a little repairing, which we thought it best, however, not to begin just then.

Miss McKenzie and Miss Gibson went down in October to spend another few days; they found the people still friendly, but the landlord not so much so.

On Nov. 11th, Miss Gibson and I again went down, expecting to make final arrangements about necessary repairs, but the landlord, we found, was positively unwilling, having decided not to let us have the house longer than the end of the year. At first we thought it was a scheme to get more rent, but found it was really fear, as the students of the city had threatened to take away his degree (which he had just received) if he rented his house to a foreigner. We still hoped, however, that if this was the house the LORD wanted for His work, He would move him to let us have it. During this visit we thought it best to let the city people know we had arrived, and after praying for guidance decided to simply walk slowly through the principal street and back. We started out with a native Christian man, and our women as escorts. Entering at the east gate we passed through the main street to the west gate. We went out beyond this gate till we came to an open space, where we stood a few minutes and spoke to the crowd that quickly gathered round us. As we returned, the street was lined on both sides. We should have liked very much to stop and speak a few words to some of the women who looked so frightened of us, but dared not for fear of a crowd blocking the street. I must say one felt rather strange to be so gazed upon, but the people were very civil. We were favoured with a smile from two or three. We reached the house about twelve, just in time for dinner (native). This little outing brought us a great many visitors that afternoon and the next day, and more of the precious seed was sown. We returned to Ho-k'eo thinking the landlord's fears would wear away.

In December, Miss McKenzie and I came down. The main object of these visits was that the people should gradually get to know us and trust us. Their poor superstitious minds are so full of fears as to what the foreigner can do and does do, such as taking out hearts and eyes with which to concoct medicine, etc., etc., that only seeing will convince them; so we gave free access to any part of the house at first, and living before them day after day these reports were soon lived down. On this visit we remained two weeks, taking the good of the house while we had it. The landlord still remained firm in his refusal, and with the exception of one or two men, no one particularly cared that we should have another house. But we had committed the matter to the LORD and we left it with Him. The hearts of all men were in His hands.

We returned to Ho-k'eo, leaving the evangelist to look out for another house. Early in January he returned with the good news that one had been procured. We did not forget to praise GOD for this token of His mighty power. It was so entirely of the LORD that I think full particulars will be helpful to you. The evangelist tells it thus: He had spoken to many, but none were willing to let us have a house. One of the men I mentioned as favourable to us and our message had houses to let but they were all occupied. It came to the last day but one. In the evening after tea the two men (the evangelist and a native Christian) knelt down and asked the LORD again. They believed nothing was too hard for our GOD, and that at this late hour, if it were His will, He would give a house. As they rose from their knees there was a knock at the door—it was the man previously mentioned as favourable. He came to tell them of a house he had; it was very old and broken down, but could, perhaps, be made fit for foreigners to live in. The family living in it had been in it for generations, and he did not wish them to go, but if the house was at all suitable for us, he would put the matter before these tenants, and if they would move out he was quite willing that we should have the house. He went off to speak to the tenants, and the two men again knelt in prayer, asking GOD to make the people willing to move. In about half an hour he came back, saying they were quite willing, and had not raised one objection. He truly believes it was our GOD who had made them willing, and that it was GOD who had made Him think of offering this house to us. We should like your earnest prayers for this our landlord, that he may accept the Gospel for himself and come right out and follow JESUS.

By twelve o'clock that night the papers were made out and the house rented to us for five years for 20 dols. (£4) a year. The next week the repairs were started. The LORD, in answer to prayer, gave beautiful weather—something unusual at that time of the year—and with the outlay of about 50 dols. the house has been made most comfortable. It is just a few steps from the east gate of the city, so suitable for the work and beautifully situated, the back looking out on hills and the front overlooking the river. Miss McKenzie and I came to live here on the 25th March. In this last month thousands have heard the Gospel.

You may be sure the devil did not stand and look on and do nothing. No; he started false reports about us in the city, which roused the people, and we have been on the eve of a riot once or twice. It was wonderful to see the power of GOD quieting a crowd of heathen men. The LORD has turned the hearts of the officials, and yesterday the mayor of the city put out a proclamation in our favour. The people are very friendly. We feel the crisis is over and I-yang is opened to the glorious Gospel. The LORD has many chosen ones in this city, and we remember our MASTER'S words: "All that the FATHER giveth ME shall come to ME." Already three or four are earnestly inquiring. "Oh, magnify the LORD with me and let us exalt His Name together." Dear friends, pray that we may speak to this people, and live before them in the power of the HOLY GHOST.

The Joy of being on China's Soil.

FROM MISS GUEX.

YUH-SHAN, *April 22nd.*—I am just now alone here with dear Miss Mackintosh, who is a great help to me in every way and with whom I work very happily. The LORD deals tenderly with me, and since I put my feet upon China's soil my heart has been so full of joy and praise that it cannot contain it all, so I let the overflow go to the dear people around me. I have desired this my present happiness for fifteen long years, so it is no wonder that now "the desire accomplished is sweet to the soul."

I now take the praise-meeting on Sunday evening, and have the children of the Christians with some others twice a week. We have two Bible-women with us, and I go out to visit with one of them.

One day, in a house outside the city, there were five women, to whom San Nien-sao spoke very faithfully, I praying meanwhile; the place was solitary, so that we were not disturbed, and two of these dear women became very interested, and asked us many intelligent questions about how to worship the living GOD. They asked if they could not *now* ask the forgiveness of their sins and worship Him *now* and there. We, of course, complied, and we all knelt down before GOD; the HOLY GHOST was at work, and we had a blessed time. May the LORD complete what He has begun. One of the women was over seventy, the other was her daughter-in-law.

I went on a short tour with Miss Mackintosh at the end of March; we were absent seventeen days, and went first to Yang-k'eo, walking part of the way, and going through villages where nobody had yet been, but where the people were friendly and willing to listen. We reached Yang-k'eo on a Tuesday, and spent two Sundays there. We had crowded meetings, and Mr. Li spoke with much power; every day a great number of women came.

Leaving Yang-k'eo we went on foot to Kwang-feng, again having many to whom to speak on the way. The sisters there were very happy and well, and before we left we had the joy of seeing the landlord bringing his idols and beads, saying, he wanted to trust in GOD alone; a young man, a fortune-teller, also brought his books the next morning and the little bird he used, which is now with us and sings all the day long.

We returned to Yuh-shan very thankful for what we had seen, and with a deeper sense of how much workers are needed.

Making Friends.

FROM MISS CASSIE FITZSIMONS.

KWANG-FENG, *April 18th*.—The dear woman (Mrs. Chiu), whom I have had ever since I came here, has proved such a blessing and help to me. I see her daily growing in grace and in the knowledge of CHRIST JESUS. She is learning to read and getting on very nicely. The HOLY SPIRIT is also working in the hearts of her husband and sons, for they have all given up false businesses for the Gospel.

Women continue to come daily, but not in such numbers as at first. They are not so curious now, and listen more attentively to the Gospel. We are praying that soon many of them may come to the classes regularly; there are a few who do come regularly on Sunday and Wednesday afternoons, and we believe they are called and chosen ones; but they need much care and teaching, and it is very slow work. We need patience and real tender love for their souls. These poor women, before they heard the Gospel, knew nothing outside of their home or street, nothing beyond preparing rice, making shoes, or tending babies. Please remember our women when you pray for Kwang-feng.

The men are not so difficult to deal with, as they can read and are more intelligent. Tuesday and Thursday evenings I meet with the men who are interested, for the study of the Bible and prayer. We all enjoy this very much, and the LORD is blessing. We sit at His feet, and He has promised to teach, enlighten, and satisfy us. Praise Him!

You will be glad to hear we have been visiting a number of the villages around; some are so large and busy. It is often impossible in going to a place for the first time to speak so that the people will profit; for on all sides we are surrounded by hundreds of people, full of curiosity, and very often of fear, as many of them have never seen foreigners and only know us as a rather wild people, or sort of devil (as they call us), who have come to their peaceful flowery country to do all kinds of bad things, such as to kill and eat their little girls, take out their eyes, heart, etc., to make medicine, bewitch them with a mysterious foreign doctrine, and finally carry them off to our country, which a great many think is a tiny island just outside of Shanghai or Ning-po where we live in holes, not in houses, and wear very unsightly garments. Yet many bought that precious living Word, which GOD has promised "shall not return unto Him void!" We are often amused at the change in these people after we have talked to them a few minutes.

When they first catch sight of us coming into a place the shout "Foreign devils arrived" goes all around, and in a moment we are surrounded by men, women, children, and dogs, as if they, too, knew we were strangers. Then some one musters up the courage to ask if we have eaten our rice, and when we say "Yes" or "No," and ask if they had eaten their rice, they nearly all as with one voice exclaim, "Ah! they speak our native words." This makes a wonderfully good impression on them, and one after the other asks questions until all fear seems gone and they begin to make remarks to one another about us, such as, "Strange! their hair is not so red as I heard it was, but they have green eyes; how white their skin is; I wonder if they use powder?" (all Chinese ladies do); "If their feet were not so extremely large, they would not be so very different from us." Then six or eight in one breath would ask our ages. At last some dear mother puts her hand into ours, looks lovingly into our faces, saying, "Why, you are just the same as we are; come into my house and drink tea." Then everyone seems to want us to go to her house to tea, saying what the Chinese call "polite words," half of which they don't mean; however, we generally go into the nearest house, and speak to the women while the evangelist sells books and speaks to the men outside. It is with burning hearts we try to make known the story of salvation to these poor, dull-minded women. How we feel our great need of the HOLY SPIRIT at such a time as this to open the eyes of their understanding and reveal the deep and glorious truths to them. We generally leave these places feeling satisfied that the people have found out we are not such cannibals after all, and many are moved to think about the eternity we told them of, and so seek to know through the books they have bought, or else come to the hall to hear more.

Our house is entirely native, and we are just one with them and try to be as like them as possible in ourselves; so we think with much love, patience, and prayer, their prejudices will be lived down and many of the precious souls from these villages, and from our city will make a part of "the LAMB'S bride."

We feel more and more how weak, ignorant and helpless we are, how utterly unable we are to do anything except as He enables us. I am so glad that there are special promises for the weak things, and that we can do "all things through CHRIST." Our part is to trust and to lean hard on Him.

T'ai-yuen Converts.

FROM DR. EDWARDS.

THIS engraving represents two women, Tsun Ta-sao and U Ta-sao, who were baptised and joined the Church in T'ai-yuen Fu in 1887. The former (on the left) had been under Christian influence since 1883, when Mrs. Schofield took her as nurse, but her self-righteousness and conservatism long withheld her from yielding obedience to what she seems early to have recognised as the truth. She was of a respectable and well-to-do family, her husband being a cabinet-maker and her son a farmer; she prided herself much on her honesty, truthfulness, and thrift, and on the fact that she did not smoke opium, nor even tobacco. The only sin one could bring home to her conscience with any force was her violent temper, and then she would take refuge in it, as an unanswerable argument against being a Christian, for a Christian could not indulge in it and she must. She held, too, very strongly that while foreign customs might be best for foreigners, the Chinese certainly ought to follow their own. However, little by little, and almost imperceptibly, her prejudices gave way and her heart seems to have been finally softened by the death of the little boy to whom she was nurse and of whom she was very fond.

The home of the other woman is in the hills, about forty *li* east of the city, where her husband has a little land, on which he cultivates maize, millet, potatoes, opium, etc., working in a coal mine when there is nothing to be done in the fields. Both husband and wife smoked opium, and both broke off the habit in the T'ai-yuen Refuges, the latter in 1886, the former not till 1888, and then only for a very short time, his excuse for taking to it again being constant pain and ill-health. He never seemed to show any real interest in the Gospel, though his wife did from the time she first heard it, and is, we hope, a sincere, though faulty, believer.

As illustrating how superstition keeps its hold on the minds of the people, even after they become Christians, an incident may be mentioned, which occurred some time after the baptism of these women. The latter had been paying the former a visit, and had returned to her home some two or three weeks, when Tsun Ta-sao appeared, wringing her hands and weeping over the loss of a silver chain, which she declared U Ta-sao had stolen. "But," she was asked, "how do you know that? It is nearly a month since she left." "Oh," she answered, "I have not had it since she left, and the dust-pan says she is the thief." "The dust-pan? What do you mean?" "Don't you know our custom? When we want to discover a thief we consult the dust-pan, and it always gives a correct answer. There is no mistaking. Come and see." Three of them sat round on the middle of the k'ang, and on their six upraised forefingers placed a dust-pan, which one of them addressed to this effect: "O dust-pan, dust-pan, thou hast a spirit. Tell us truly, who stole the chain; did so-and-so? did so-and-so?" mentioning several persons, with a pause after each name. The dust-pan remained motionless until U Ta-sao's name was mentioned, when it slowly began to turn on the fingers. This was repeated once or twice, and the woman asked triumphantly, "Now is it not clear who stole the chain?" "By no means; your fingers moved." "Oh, no, we held them quite still." "And besides, the dust-pan is only wood and cane, and has no spirit, so cannot divine." "But it can and does." "But, above all, you displease GOD by consulting a dust-pan instead of Him. You are Christians, and this is no Christian method." "Truly, it is not a Christian method, but it is a Chinese method and a good method, and we know it always gives us Chinese a correct answer." Further argument was plainly hopeless, but the hour for the midday prayer-meeting was more than due, so the matter was confidently laid before Him who is able to bring hidden things to light and "who worketh for him that waiteth for Him." This time the waiting was short, for scarcely was the short meeting over, when Tsun Ta-sao appeared before the door, the chain aloft in her hand and crying, "Oh, come and pray with me! Let me confess my sin to GOD, truly it is great. Truly you are right. Our Chinese method is not to be trusted, and I will never appeal to a dust-pan again." The chain had been discovered under a box by Mao-tan, a mischievous little thief of a girl, in all probability the hider.

Tidings from Scattered Workers.

Kan-suh Province.
FROM MISS MUIR.

Lan-chau, April 15th.—There is such constant work that we can scarcely get through it. Of course it still mainly consists in medical cases, but during this winter so many doors have been opened by this means, and so many have heard the Gospel for the first time, that we cannot but praise GOD. The seed is being sown, and we are looking for the increase.

One woman here we are specially interested in, and we should like *to ask definite prayer* for her. Her name is Kwoh, and we were called to see her last November, when she was extremely ill, indeed at the point of death. The LORD in His goodness brought her round, she gave a feast in our honour, and showed much gratitude for the help given, and seemed to like listening to the Gospel. Recently we were hastily called to her, being told that she had taken mercury, not opium, to put an end to her life. Her husband had died a few weeks before and left her considerably in debt, with two children, no means of support, and scarcely a real friend. Her eyesight, too, has been too dim since her husband's death to allow of her doing needle-work, and her health is otherwise bad. So she thought to put an end to it all. We were with her for some hours, but had great difficulty in making her take any of the remedies. The next morning our hearts were full of praise to find her much better, and she has gone on improving. We are praying much for her, and have had one or two straight talks with her. She has now confessed that this was her third attempt at suicide, having twice taken opium, but recovered. Surely the LORD has some definite purpose in thus frustrating her efforts.

I am sorry to say that three out of the four women of whom we were so hopeful last year have gone back, my woman among the number. This has caused us much sorrow, but we are hoping in GOD. May He give a mighty blessing all through KAN-SUH very soon. We want to see His promise fulfilled, "I will be exalted among the heathen," in every station throughout this province and throughout China.

FROM MISS KINAHAN.

May 5th.—Left Si-ning on April 30th. We start very early, just as it gets light, so, though we go 90 or 100 *li*, we get in in good time. On the second day, at Kao-miao-ts, I had such a splendid time with women : I don't think I ever had anything like it before, certainly not while travelling. A few came in just after I arrived, at three o'clock, and I had a good beginning with them ; when my tea was brought in by my boy they said they would go and return. I was sorry that they should, as I was afraid they would not come back, though I was not sorry to get some food, as it was the first time I had drunk anything or had anything hot all day ; however, they did return, bringing others, and they kept coming in until it was quite dark, and I had to light the tiny oil-lamp. It was truly the SPIRIT'S power brought them, and gave the message ; they seemed to come in simply to hear, and asked none of the usual questions, but wanted to know about JESUS. I feel as if some will find the SAVIOUR in that place, though I may never know it in this world. Three times I was begged by different women to stay another day, as there were so many who had not heard the good news. I told them that if one or two of them really believed, it would soon spread. We had some prayer together. One woman came back to ask, Would I pray for her brother, who had been very ill? She said she wanted him to hear the Gospel too.

Lan-chau, May 6th.—Glad indeed to get into the city after fourteen hours' cart-journey, only stopping once for luncheon. It was very pleasant to be warmly welcomed by kind friends.

May 8th.—Soon after breakfast and Chinese prayers, we went out in a cart, as it was too wet after yesterday's rain to walk. We went to take medicine to a sick woman, and a good number listened to the Gospel. The house was on the bank of the bed of a river, so we had a pleasant drive outside the city, as the bed of the river was infinitely preferable to jolting over the uneven streets, when one's only chance of escaping being much knocked about is to hold on tightly. We then crossed the bridge of boats over the Yellow River, having patiently to wait for quite a long while, as carts cannot pass each other, so can only come from one side at a time.

The house we went to was a small inn, where a child of fourteen, whom they hoped trusted in JESUS, had recently died of consumption ; the parents were very grateful for all that had been done. The mother is in real sorrow at her loss; she is very delicate, and cannot come out, but the man and another little girl came to the Sunday service.

In the afternoon we went to Kwoh T'ai-t'ai's to dinner by invitation. She sent her cart for us, which is the remnant of her grander days ; she is very poor now. Her husband was in office here when she was first visited during illness. After her husband's sudden death she took mercury to poison herself, and would have succeeded, only Mr. and Mrs. Brown were sent for at once. We pray that she may yet know and love the GOD who has twice saved her life. Met another T'ai-t'ai, a Manchu, who was also a widow. Miss Muir had brought a picture and had an opportunity to talk about it before dinner. Miss Muir and I called again next day with medicine, and the other T'ai-t'ai asked to hear more about the Gospel, so we had a good time, and were so thankful. They took us to another lady who had seen us returning the day before, and had asked us in ; she and her daughter listened with interest.

In the afternoon Mrs. Brown took me to see Kao T'ai-t'ai, whom I knew at Ts'in-chau ; she was so friendly and glad to see me again. The other wives of this same mandarin (who is here waiting for office) were also cordial, but only the one loves to hear the Gospel ; she heard it first from an old nurse at Chung-k'ing. Mrs. Botham had marked and given her a Testament, as she could read. She would like to be a Christian, but her position is very difficult.

Saturday, 10th.—A man came early to invite us to a Mrs. Chco's, whose daughter was ill. It gave us an opportunity of letting them hear the Gospel for the first time ; then called at Mrs. Brown's woman's house, as she has been ill for some days.

In the afternoon went to visit Chang T'ai-t'ai who lives close to us ; it was not easy to speak of JESUS and His love, but, thank GOD, He did give a message.

Monday, 12th.—A man came for some one to visit his wife. I went with Miss Muir ; we found her in great pain ; some others came in, and we managed to tell them what we are here for, but it was not a nice compound and very hard to get a hearing ; we felt Satan's power. Those who read this do please pray for us who are working in this land, that we may ever give GOD's message in the power of the SPIRIT and be filled with love to the people, realizing that they are dead souls, lost, unless they hear of and believe in the SAVIOUR. The work in KAN-SUH has its own difficulties. The workers here are a happy party, and are kept very busy by the numerous calls to sick people. Mr. Brown does need help badly. Mrs. Brown visits a great deal, and has great joy in the work ; her baby is a great wonder to the natives.

FROM MR. C. POLHILL-TURNER.

Si-ning, May 8th.—Now we are looking forward to burying ourselves in some Tibetan village or monastery not far from here, that we may study that language preparatory to carrying the glad tidings to Tibetans—something in the way you suggest in CHINA'S MILLIONS, "as a witness," looking to the LORD to confirm the word with signs following, "every creature" being our one aim.

FROM MISS SMALLEY.

T'sin-chau, April 23rd.—In February I went to visit Mrs. Botham [at Feng-tsiang], and was away from home about a month. Mrs. Botham's donkey and Mr. Bland's servant were at my disposal for the journey, and Miss Ellis accompanied me for the first three days. One day we crossed a very difficult mountain, not so steep, but almost covered with great boulders, so that often one did not know where to put one's foot. Mrs. Botham came 20 *li* to meet me, and I had a very warm welcome when I arrived at their inn. I noticed that in the houses to which Mrs. Botham had access she seemed as welcome as in Ts'in-chau; she is making her way well. One Sunday we had relays of women all day long, and on other days they came too. Since my return I have felt much better, and have had much encouragement in the numbers coming to school, seventeen to twenty daily.

Shan-si Province.

FROM MRS. ELLISTON.

T'ai-yuen.—A poor woman, a confirmed invalid, whom I have visited regularly since Mrs. Edwards left, died recently, and I have no doubt she has changed her painful, lonely life here for a glorious home with the SAVIOUR whom she trusted. I believe she was a true Christian, though an unbaptised one.

My little Sunday school varies in numbers according as the congregation of women varies, but I always find it an interesting class, and some of the regular attendants are very intelligent little people and repeat texts, reply to questions, and sing hymns very well. My own little boys are able to join in this class.

FROM MR. LUTLEY.

Hiao-i, April 2nd.—The opium-refuge work at Yung-ning-chau is very encouraging as regards numbers. There were fourteen breaking off their opium when I was there about a fortnight ago, and a number of others waiting to be cured as soon as there was room to receive them.

Last Saturday we gave a feast to all our neighbours before commencing the repairs of the house here; there were thirteen guests, and they were all very friendly and expressed willingness for us to use their ground, adjoining our premises, in any way we wished during the alterations. The Christians having voted 11,500 cash of the Church funds towards repairing the house; we have taken them into partnership in the matter, and told them that some of them must always be about to help see that the work is done properly. They have taken the matter up heartily, so I hope to be saved a good deal of time and trouble.

FROM MISS JAKOBSEN.

Hoh-chau, March 4th.—A few days after the Chinese new year four families in one village took down their idols and they have been to the Sunday services very regularly since. The Sunday before last when they got home they were told that a wolf had been in the yard and taken a sheep. The next morning two of the men were ill with fever and a woman belonging to the family was also very ill. The cow, too, was shivering all over, and not able to take food. They sent for me to come and pray for them, but as I am alone just now I could not well go, so sent a Christian man named Wang. When he arrived at the place they sought GOD in prayer and singing. In the evening the two men were able to attend the meeting that Wang held. The woman was still very ill and not able to take food; Wang said, "I am not going to eat until she is able to eat." He prayed, laying hands on her; the next morning she was able to take a little food, and at dinner time her appetite was larger and she seemed much better. In the afternoon Wang took his food. During the night he heard the woman groaning as if she were in great pain, and early in the morning they found her aching very much in both arms. Wang said, "There must be something wrong; you must confess your sin." They said that some relative had been in the yard burning incense on the woman's behalf. Wang told them that it was no wonder that GOD did not answer prayer. They seemed very frightened, and asked what to do. Wang told them that there was nothing to do but to confess their sin; so they all knelt down and prayed again, after which the woman was much better. Wang came home full of joy to tell what GOD had done for that household.

It is indeed a real joy sometimes to live with these people and to see GOD's power manifested in their lives.

FROM MR. STANLEY SMITH.

Lu-ch'eng, June 9th.—There are some hopeful signs of the LORD's working here. The last month has been one of revival; some fifteen men have professed faith in the LORD. I have been going out with Mr. Cheng visiting a good deal during the week. This gives numerous opportunities for preaching the Word, and for looking after those who have heard the Gospel. On Saturday we have a field-day and turn out in all our available strength for the surrounding market towns, five in number. We sing all the way down the one long main street to announce our arrival, and then turn round and begin to pray and preach at about every hundred yards or so. We kneel on the ground, and GOD seems to use this to collect the people and to still them; then rising from our knees several speak in turn, the speaking being interspersed with easy hymns and choruses.

Chih-li Province.

FROM MR. SIMPSON.

Hwuy-luh, May 17th.—Since I last wrote our steps have again been guided to Hwuy-luh. All are kind and friendly here, and I cannot doubt but that in time there will be souls saved. When we left Ying-tseng, not a few were showing an interest in the Gospel. One is really a child of GOD; he is a quiet, unassuming young man, and the real, simple, fearless trust in CHRIST which he shows would do your heart good. Last week the Ying-tseng rent came due, so I went out for two days, and found our brother happy in the LORD.

There is a great deal that I might write in detail regarding the work, but as we meet with so many disappointing cases, I think it is much better to wait and see fruit than to praise a tree full of beautiful blossoms. Still, I do in my own soul feel that the work is full of hope.

Ho-nan Province.

FROM MR. H. H. TAYLOR.

She-k'i-tien.—The Christians are standing well, though they have been a good deal persecuted. We need to lay ourselves out to be a great deal to them, for apart from what we are able to do for them, they get no help, no love, no sympathy, but are despised, maltreated, and forsaken.

Si-ch'uen Province.

FROM REV. E. O. WILLIAMS.

Pao-ning, April 14th.—I trust that none on whose hearts the LORD has laid this enormous province, with its many millions of souls, and who are, perhaps, waiting for the LORD to lead them to this splendid field of labour, will be in any way kept back. We are continually praying for more labourers, and I believe, if the labourers come out at the LORD's bidding, in faith looking to Him to guide their steps, He *will* open a way before them, and lead them to the very people, be it in city or country, whom He wishes to bless. We are joining you in praying for 1,000 labourers for China. Oh, may the LORD send them *very soon*, for they will need some time after they arrive before they can make themselves understood, and the people are passing away into eternity at a terrible rate! Oh, let us plead with GOD for these labourers to be thrust forth, whether from Europe, America, or, best of all, from China itself as far as we can see; only in that case what a blessing Christian lands and Christians in those lands will miss if they refuse to give the labourers the LORD needs and He has to find them elsewhere. How solemn are the words of Judges v. 23: "Curse ye Meroz, said the angel of the LORD, curse ye bitterly the inhabitants thereof; because they came not to the help of the LORD, to the help of the LORD against the mighty."

One Sunday evening we decided to have a testimony meeting for the natives instead of the usual service. We had on the premises, in addition to Mr. Murray's four colporteurs, two young men from Ch'ung-k'ing, who had come to do a little business; they are nice, bright young fellows, and, thank GOD, have the true ring about them. One of the most interesting testimonies was given by Chen Ta-ko, the ladies' cook. He said some years ago his mother scalded her foot by upsetting some boiling water upon it. I should have said that she lived in Han-chung Fu, in the neighbouring province of SHEN-SI. She met a young man named Sei Da-ko, who is now assistant to Dr. Wilson, who advised her to go to Mr. Geo. King, who was then working in Han-chung, and get him to doctor her foot. This resulted in her conversion, and she was afterwards baptised. At this time her son was living at Kwang-yuen. His mother advised him to come to Han-chung, but he was deceived by Satan, and was displeased with his mother for believing the doctrine, and tried to persuade her to give it up. After some time he did go to Han-chung; he was then an impatient, quarrelsome man. Some of the Christians advised him to go to worship, and at last he went, and said, "If GOD will save and keep me, I will worship Him from now." He turned to GOD and was subsequently baptised. In speaking of the change in himself, he said, "Now I am *not that man*."

Another bright testimony was given by one of the two young men from Ch'ung-k'ing; he is only eighteen years old, and has been a Christian for six years. He has lost an arm; he thanked GOD for his diseased arm: it brought him in connection with foreigners, and thus led him to CHRIST. Mr. Nicoll took him to Shanghai and had the arm amputated. He and his companion are very fond of singing hymns; we often hear them singing in the evening.

The other young man lives near the mission premises at Ch'ung-k'ing; he used to go and hear the Gospel, and after hearing for two or three years he was convinced of the truth; he thought he would keep it to himself, but he had no peace until he was baptised, and thus confessed CHRIST openly. He told us how GOD answers his prayers, specially in providing for him an inn on the road: it is difficult to get a room for one man, but GOD had done this for him. I have few such trust in our FATHER as this young man has, who a few years ago knew nothing of Him. He had been advised to sell on Sunday, but he said the peace of his soul was more important than making money. Praise the LORD for these two young men! The LORD raise up multitudes of such in every province to spread the truth and extend our dear REDEEMER's kingdom.

Gan-hwuy Province.

FROM DR. HOWARD TAYLOR.

Gan-k'ing, April 6th.—You would be greatly encouraged if you could see the state of things here in Gan-k'ing. A more satisfactory or better conducted college it would be difficult to imagine. You know, from my former letters, how much we all appreciated Mr. Baller's help on the way out, and I have been pleased to find what a good teacher Mr. Wood is. You would be surprised, I think, if you could see how devoted the men are to him and Mrs. Wood; both of them will be missed immensely. I think the secret of it is that they make themselves so much at one with us all. Mrs. Wood is like a thoughtful elder sister to the men, looking after everything that concerns them; and Mr. Wood is much more like the "captain" of the school than the principal of the college. He joins in the exercises on the bars, and makes us all feel that he is one of ourselves. His manly, outspoken bearing, his earnest Bible-readings day after day, and his native tact with men combine to make him an ideal leader in all that is good. There is not one of the men, so far as I can see, but would do anything for him. And then both of them work like Trojans, and set a splendid example in that respect

As you know, this is a very busy place. We get through, most of us, about six hours a day of Chinese, three hours of prayer meetings and Bible study, and an hour of exercise a day. Some of the men do a good deal more Chinese than that.

Yun-nan Province.

FROM MR. TOMKINSON.

Yun-nan, Fu.—Thursday we spent in the villages again, taking four fresh ones and three that we had visited. We had a good time at each place, and for the villages sold quite a number of books. I find that I have visited fifty-seven villages this season (many several times, others only once), nearly all within two miles of the city, and yet there are many others not visited within the same radius. During the month have sold 2,603 cash worth of books.

April 12th.—Yesterday and again to-day we were visited by some aborigines from Lu-nan. They seemed interested. I gave them a book and some tracts, as one or two could read Chinese. There is a large field of labour among these people, for whom at present nothing is being done.

April 24th.—At the evening service, while I was appealing to some who have been to the service many times (and who acknowledge the truth of the doctrine we preach) to come to an immediate decision, our cook stood up and expressed before all the people his desire to be saved, and asked for prayer. He has before expressed the same desire at family prayers, and I believe he is sincere.

April 28th.—At the morning service our cook asked for baptism. In the afternoon I had a long talk with him, and find that he has a very intelligent grasp of the great truths of the Gospel.

May 5th.—Yesterday was indeed a glad day, as I had the joy of baptising two of our servants. It is more than six weeks since our cook first spoke to me about his soul's salvation; we believe that he has come into the light, and so were very pleased to receive him into the church. The other, Kiu Ta-ma, has been Mrs. Tomkinson's woman since we first came, and having been Mrs. Easton's woman, she has known the Gospel a long time; for many months she has professed to believe, and has been a great help in speaking to the women. When she heard that the cook was to be baptised she also applied, and we were very glad to receive her. We trust that these are the first droppings of the shower, as others are convinced of the truth, but are afraid to come out.

FROM MR. OWEN STEVENSON.

K'uh-tsing Fu, April 17th.—Our five enquirers are making progress in the Divine life: it is very rarely that they are absent on Sunday or Wednesday; if they do absent themselves, they send word.

Kiang-si Province.

FROM MISS MACKINTOSH.

Yuh-shan, May 17th.—I daresay you know that Miss Marchbank and Miss Buchan have been in Vang-k'eo, a market town about thirty *li* south of Kwang-sin Fu, for some time. The LORD is helping them very much, and many are daily hearing the Gospel.

You will be glad to hear that we have reopened Hsing-keng: the old man to whom the house belongs is drawing near the end of his earthly pilgrimage, and seems to be turning again to the LORD. He has given us the small house there for five years for nothing, so we have had it cleaned, supplied a few forms, etc., and on Sunday about twenty come to worship.

You are remembered, and loved, and prayed for by the natives; one dear man named Tong, nearly every time he carries my chair, treats me to the story of the creation, the flood, the ten commandments, and the time when he met "Lao T'ai Sien-seng" (Mr. Taylor) on the street, who asked him, "Can you tell me where a man named Tong lives?" "Yes, he is my elder brother," and then Mr. Taylor asked, "Do you believe in JESUS?" "Yes, I do." You should see his face as he tells how Mr. Taylor took him by the hand and said, "Then we are really brothers." The love of the dear people is refreshing.

Departures for China.

ON September 4th, per P. and O. s.s. *Bengal*, Mrs. PRUEN, returning to her son in China, accompanied by Misses C. GROVES, A. M. LANG, SARAH QUERRY, R. F. BASNETT, IDA W. ROBERTS, and JANE STEDMAN; also Misses FREDA PRYTZ, ANNA JANZON and EDDA LOWENADLER, from the Swedish Mission in China; and Misses J. HOL and PETREA NÆSS, from Norway.

CHINA'S MILLIONS.

Opening Sermon of the Shanghai Missionary Conference.
(Continued).

BY REV. J. HUDSON TAYLOR.

"*Whence should we have so much bread in the wilderness, as to fill so great a multitude?*"
—See MATT. xv. 29-38.

IT seems to me that we need to ask more seriously than I have done in bygone days, What *is* really the will and command of our blessed LORD? and to set about obeying Him, not merely attempting to obey. I do not know that we are told anywhere in the Bible to try to do anything. "We must try to do the best we can," is a very common expression; but I remember some years ago, after a remark of that kind, looking very carefully through the New Testament to see under what circumstances the disciples were told to *try* to do anything. I did not expect to find many instances, but I was surprised that I did not find any. Then I went through the Old Testament very carefully, and I could not find that the LORD had told any of the Old Testament believers to try to do anything; there were many commands apparently impossible to obey, but they were all definite commands; and I think we have all to set ourselves, not to try to obey our LORD as far as we can, but to obey Him.

If, as an organised Conference, we were to set ourselves to obey the command of our LORD to the full, we should have such an outpouring of the SPIRIT, such a Pentecost, as the world has not seen since the SPIRIT was poured out in Jerusalem. GOD gives His SPIRIT, *not* to those who long for Him, not to those who pray for Him, not to those who desire to be filled always; but He *does* give His HOLY SPIRIT to them that *obey* Him. And if as an act of obedience we were to determine that every district, every town, every village, every hamlet in this land should hear the Gospel, and that speedily, and we were to set about doing it, I believe that the SPIRIT would come down with such mighty power that we should find loaves and fishes springing up on every hand—we do not know where or how. We should find the fire spreading from missionary to flock; and the native Christians all on fire, setting their neighbours on fire; and our native fellow-workers and the entire Church of GOD would be blest. GOD gives His HOLY SPIRIT to them that obey Him. Let us look to it that we see really what the LORD'S commands are to us now in this day of our opportunity, in this day of the remarkable openness of the country, in this day when there are so many facilities, when GOD has put steam and telegraph at the command of His people, for the quick carrying out of His purposes.

As to wealth, there is no end to His resources. Poverty in His hands is the greatest possible wealth. A handful of meal blessed by the LORD is quite sufficient to accomplish any purpose He chooses to accomplish by it. It is not a question of resources at all to those who are following the MASTER, who are doing just what He has for them to do.

To return, the miracle was wrought methodically. The disciples were not told to act in any erratic or fanatical way, but the common sense that GOD had given them was to be used. Our SAVIOUR Himself methodised their arrangements, and gave them the work to do in a way in which it was possible speedily and satisfactorily to accomplish it. He took their all, and it was quite sufficient; and not only were the multitudes fed, but the disciples themselves were encouraged. When all had been satisfied, they gathered up seven baskets full of the fragments that remained. We cannot set ourselves to do the LORD'S work at *His* command, and in *His* way, without reaping a rich blessing ourselves.

NOVEMBER, 1890.

I am speaking to missionary brethren who are accustomed to preach the Word of Truth, and to sisters who are accustomed to read that Word and to speak to the women in their own homes and elsewhere ; and do we not all know and feel that *we* get the richest blessing? If those to whom we minister the Word of Life get a tenth part of the sweetness and preciousness that we ourselves get in ministering it, they will be well fed, and we shall be well satisfied. It is in giving that we receive. It is in holding back that we lose. The disciples themselves were enriched; and if we claim from the Church at home seven loaves for the LORD JESUS CHRIST—not three or four or five—and if we give to the LORD JESUS CHRIST all *our* seven loaves, oh, how *we* shall be enriched, while He multiplies and magnifies and blesses far beyond our highest thought!

IN CONCLUSION :—The great commission which our MASTER has given to us is expressed in several different ways. Our brother read it to us as given in the Gospels of Matthew and Luke. The different wordings in which our SAVIOUR gave His commission on the various occasions are all to be considered, and the plans of service that He leads us to adopt are to be diverse in their methods and kinds, and very inclusive.

I do not know of any kind of missionary work in China, and I have never heard of any, on which the LORD'S blessing has not rested, or cannot rest, and in which we may not hope to see great enlargement. But beyond all this, within the last few months there has come home to my own heart, with a power I have never realised before, the commission as expressed in the Gospel of Mark, to " preach the Gospel to every creature,"—to the whole creation. I do not think our present methods of work need to be materially modified, and certainly none of them should be weakened or abandoned —they should all be strengthened ; but it does seem to me that we want to take this additional command of rapid evangelisation to our hearts (for I think it is additional), and say, What did the LORD mean, nay, what *does* the LORD mean to-day, by saying in His Holy Word, " Preach the Gospel to every creature " ?

I confine my thought to this one empire at the present time ; but I am quite sure we cannot obey the command of GOD with regard to China, and yet any other country be left unblest. For the field is the whole world, and the heart of GOD is so large that no part of the world is outside His thought or outside His purpose. As the body of CHRIST is one, we cannot have any member or any limb of that body (if I may use the expression) in healthy active exercise without improving the health and increasing the vigour of the whole body. And if we can, in an increased measure of intelligent obedience, carry the evangelisation of China forward rapidly, the Church cannot reach the villages and hamlets of China, and leave those of India, or the masses of Africa, where they are. However, confining our attention to-day to China, the thought has been very much on my heart, Can nothing be done to present the Gospel speedily to this great nation ?

I would commend to your prayerful consideration the question, whether there ought not to go forth from this Conference a united appeal to the Christian Church to undertake the work of rapidly preaching the Gospel over this land. I do not say that going to a village and preaching the Gospel there for three or four days is *all* that is needed, but it is something that is needed. It is a beginning. Suppose the Apostle Paul had said, " My work is quite useless : I cannot stay very long in any place I go to ; I am driven away before I have had time to form a Church ; I will give it up." The glorious work that GOD did by him would not have been done. He went as his LORD led him, and the LORD prevented him from making the error of staying too long in one place by driving him away.

He scattered seeds of truth, which slowly permeated through the minds of many. Beside those who were led at once to receive the truth, and who perhaps, as Jewish proselytes or Jews, were acquainted with the Old Testament, the Gentiles had new thoughts brought into their midst. Many important truths were talked over and thought over ; and the truth was working when the worker was gone. And He who sent him to preach the Gospel in this town or that city, and then allowed him to be driven away, sent other workers to follow it up. Paul was not the only worker for GOD, or the only arrow in His quiver. When Paul had planted and passed on, the LORD found an Apollos to water, and He Himself gave the increase.

I do trust that we shall not separate without a strong appeal to the Churches. I believe the appeal that went forth from the Conference thirteen years ago did incalculable good, and has been greatly blessed ; but the Churches now are in a very different state to what they were then. There was never such a preparation of evangelists as there is now in the Church. There was never known such a thing as some four thousand college students in America pledged, if the LORD opens their way, to give their lives to missionary work. There was never that preparation in the hearts of Christian young men and women in Europe to give themselves to mission work. I believe that it need not take very long to get a thousand evangelists from Europe and America into the field ; and if these evangelists were associated with the established missions—so that there was wise direction and supervision—I am sure they would be a strength in every part of the field, and a blessing in every part of China. We have about forty societies represented here; it would only want twenty-five men to be associated with each society to give us a thousand additional workers for the special work of scattering the Gospel broadcast by word of mouth and printed page.

I have been in correspondence with a number of earnest workers, and among them a number of retired missionaries, both in America and on the continent of Europe. I am told that there are many hearts praying for something of this kind. A missionary formerly connected with the Basle Missionary Society wrote me from Germany, after reading a paper written by me asking for prayer that a thousand evangelists might be speedily sent to China, and he said, "We must have one hundred of them from Germany."

I am quite sure, from my visit to Scandinavia, that one hundred would be within the number of earnest men who might be expected from there within a very short time. Would it be a very hard thing to expect three hundred workers from Great Britain and Ireland, leaving out the rest of the Continent? As for five hundred from America, it seems so ridiculously small, compared with the greatness of that country, its missionary zeal, and its capacity, as to be almost absurd to propose so small a contingent.

I do most earnestly commend this thought to you for your prayerful consideration. Wiser men may have wiser suggestions to make, but in whatever *way* we do the thing, let us *do* it. The LORD JESUS CHRIST has been for sixty generations looking down on this land; and from the very earliest post-apostolic times there has never been in the Church that zeal and enterprise which has attempted the evangelisation of its own generation. I think we shall all agree with Dr. Pierson that the command of CHRIST really implies that each generation shall evangelise its own generation;—just as the multitude that we have had our attention turned to in the narrative had an immediate supply of an immediate need. It would have been of no use to say to them, "After two or three days you shall be fed." They were hungry, and they would faint by the way. So to-day, the multitudes are perishing; and while we are waiting, they are dying without the Gospel. But oh! shall not our blessed LORD have the joy of finding in this sixtieth generation after He agonised for us in Gethsemane,—in this sixtieth generation after He so lovingly *trusted* His Church to be faithful to Him and carry out His command,—shall He not have the joy of seeing us obey the command in this generation? Then the Gospel shall very speedily reach every hamlet, and no family in this country shall be without the *offer* of the Gospel, whether they receive it or no.

"Whatsoever."

"*Whatsoever ye shall ask in My name, that will I do.*"—John xiv. 13.

JESUS, we ask a thousand
For China's myriad race!
To tell the story, olden,
Of free and sovereign grace.

A thousand Christian warriors,
Loyal of heart, and brave,
To wrest from Satan's thraldom
Each sin-enfetter'd slave.

And patient hearts, and tender,
We need, dear LORD, to go
To tend the springtide blossoms,
And solace earthly woe.

And, oh! we ask a thousand
To wrestle hard in prayer,

One for each one who toileth
'Mid sin's gloom over there.

Oh! *who* will go *for* JESUS?
Christians, dare ye withhold
The costliest of your treasures,
Your loved ones, or your gold?

Dear MASTER, whisper, "Go ye,"
To every halting soul;
Watch o'er each one Thou choosest,
And point him to his goal.

Thy people shall be willing
In this Thy day of power;
REDEEMER, claim Thy thousand
In this the world's last hour.

Items of Interest.

FROM REV. J. W. STEVENSON.

SHANGHAI, *Aug.* 14*th.*—Mr. Adam, at Gan-shun (KWEI-CHAU), has had the joy of seeing three persons baptised on July 5th, the firstfruits of his labour.

Mr. McCarthy has started on a visit to the stations on the Kwang-sin river (KIANG-SI). Miss S. E. Jones and Miss Burt will start shortly for Chau-kia-k'eo (HO-NAN).

Mr. Russell has definitely taken up the work at Hiao-i (SHAN-SI). I hear from Ts'in-chau (KAN-SUH) that Miss Clara Ellis is ill. Dr. Wilson had gone up to see her and would probably bring her and her sister down to Han-ch'ung (SHEN-SI).

China is suffering from floods at present, both in the north and along the Yang-tse valley; this will mean much suffering and mortality in the autumn and winter.

Aug. 23rd.—There is a great deal of sickness, but our trust and our hope is in GOD.

In Memoriam.

WE briefly announced last month the tidings received by telegram of the loss of Mr. Sharp. It is with profound sorrow that we now have to record the further loss we have sustained in the removal on the same day of Mr. Randall, of the Canadian contingent, and also, on August 26th, of Mr. Carter, of the Bible Christian Mission, who left for China on January 23rd as an Associate of this Mission. The subjoined extracts will give fuller particulars. We feel assured of the sympathy and prayers of our friends on behalf of those who are thus called to mourn.

MR. R. RANDALL AND MR. F. SHARP.

MR. STEVENSON writes under date August 23rd from Shanghai:—

"I am very sorry to report two deaths at Gan-k'ing in one day. On Thursday last, August 14th, at five o'clock in the morning, our Brother Randall passed away. He arrived here from Toronto on March 19th of this year. Strange to say, at five o'clock the same evening, our Brother Frederick Sharp, who arrived from London on January 23rd, was also called home. Mr. Randall died of pernicious intermittent fever. Mr. Sharp had been suffering from dysentery for some days before and recovered, but the day before his death he became suddenly ill, and the doctor pronounced it pneumonia. You may imagine what grief and sorrow this has been to us all, and how we are crying earnestly to GOD to comfort the dear friends who are bereaved. I telegraphed yesterday announcing Mr. Sharp's departure, as it may alter the plans of his *fiancée*, who is in England."

FROM MR. A. EVANS.

GAN-K'ING, *Aug. 18th.* — You will receive many letters from the home here at this time concerning the trial through which we have been brought in the going home of our two brethren.

We all knew when we left London that we were more fully trusting our health and lives to our FATHER in heaven. We knew that diseases unknown at home, or almost unknown, might at any time be permitted to lay hold of us; but I think we scarcely expected to be made familiar with death so soon as this, or realised that our lives were so much in the hands of our GOD and FATHER as this trial has taught us.

Among us Randall was the youngest and the strongest; his frame seemed set for hard work and endurance. Yet after a few short days of illness we saw him pass away before our eyes. Sharp also seemed full of energy and life, looking forward to many years of happy work for his LORD in this land, and enjoying with the rest of us many tokens of the good hand of our LORD upon us. Only a little while, and he also has passed away, leaving us amazed at the frailty of man.

Poor dear brother Randall seemed distressed that he could not live to labour here. I remember his answer when I spoke of the far better portion waiting on the other side. He just gasped, "The work, the work." Then one felt led to speak of the many who, coming forth *to live* for some dark heathen place, have been called upon *to die* for it instead.

The following extracts are from letters sent to Mr. Sharp's mother:—

FROM MRS. GEO. HUNTER.

GAN-K'ING, *Monday, August 18th.*—I think Mr. Sharp told me he had written to you about being away on a boat for a change. We thought he was the worse for it; he came home looking ill, and some of the bad symptoms began after that.

On Tuesday afternoon, August 12th, the doctor said he might get downstairs to tea, but he did not remain long; he felt weak, and went up to his room again. He had a good night, and was able to be down to breakfast. In the forenoon of Wednesday he sat out on the verandah on his deck chair. He was in bed in the afternoon, and did not venture down to tea. I went up and saw him; there was a great change. The doctor said he had taken pneumonia. At two in the morning your son asked my husband to read and pray with him, which he did, reading to him the 116th and 34th Psalms. Your dear son seemed to enjoy the comfort of the words. We were all glad to hear in the morning that he had had a good night, for we were grieved that he had been taken worse, as we thought he was far on the way to recovery.

On Thursday, from two o'clock and onward, he got weaker; still, I had hopes of his recovery, and when a message came across a little after four o'clock to say he was worse I could not believe it was true. I was stunned, but went across, and found he was unconscious and sinking fast. He went home at a quarter to five o'clock on the 14th of August, to be with the LORD and to behold the KING in His beauty. I saw him after death, when he looked very peaceful and beautiful. The verse I thought of was, "At eventide it shall be light." It had been a windy day, with some rain, but in the evening it got bright and beautiful, and there was such a lovely sunset that I could not help feeling, when I left his room, that at eventide it *was* light for him, and that the peaceful, lovely sunset I saw was just a figure of our dear friend, gone to that bright, happy home after the storm and suffering, to be at rest for ever.

Truly we have been passing through sorrow upon sorrow. The same morning that your son died Mr. Randall, another of our number, went home to be with JESUS. Mr. Randall died at five in the morning of the same fever as your dear son. They were the two youngest in the home, with the exception of our little fellow. Mr. Randall was perfectly conscious all through his illness. His dying words were, "Beautiful! Beautiful!" He evidently had seen something of the glory and loveliness of heaven and of our SAVIOUR there.

Both were buried together in the little Christian cemetery here. The funeral was very early on Friday morning, and we had a short service before it started. At the graves Mr. Baller conducted a service in English. He told them of JESUS and also of the triumphant death of our two brethren. One of the teachers had a Chinese service. So they were left, quietly sleeping until the resurrection morning.

"Asleep in JESUS; far from thee
Thy kindred and their graves may be;
But thine is still a blessed sleep."

One of the friends here told me he always wakened the brethren in the morning at half-past five, but he never had to arouse Mr. Sharp, as he always found him up and at his Bible, or just about to begin reading it—a testimony of his beginning the day early with GOD.

Mr. Baller, also writing to Mrs. Sharp, says :—

He was a most diligent student, and gave fair promise of making good progress in the language. He was a good Bible student, too, and we had fondly hoped that years of useful service were before him; but GOD has ordered it otherwise, and we can only bow under the stroke.

Everything that could be done to minister to his comfort and alleviate his sufferings was done. Dr. Stewart attended him, and the brethren in the home gave themselves to the work of ministering to him night and day with devotion and tenderness.

The blow has been a heavy one to us all, and it has been the heavier in that it came so unexpectedly. We had hoped he had nearly recovered when the sudden change took place.

IN MEMORIAM SERVICE AT HAVERHILL.

A TOUCHING and impressive service was held at the Market Hill Chapel on Sunday evening last. . . . The Rev. George Cakebread, the pastor, took for his text the words of Hebrews xi. 4.—"He being dead yet speaketh." Mr. Cakebread, in his opening remarks, said the first intimation of Mr. Sharp's death came to him in the form of a letter from the offices of the China Inland Mission in London, dated August 22nd. . . . Speaking of Mr. Sharp's character, Mr. Cakebread said he was one of his (the preacher's) right-hand men, one whom he could trust. In his home he was greatly beloved, in his business much respected and honoured, in the church and Sunday-school useful and happy, and his letters fully revealed his whole-hearted devotion to CHRIST, his simple but sublime faith in his mission, his unbounded delight in the Word of GOD, his genuine unaffected goodness.—*From a Local Paper.*

A MEMORIAL PORTAL.

MR. JOHN CARTER.

A LETTER just received from Mr. Baller, dated August 26th, notifies the death of Mr. Carter :—

I write in the midst of much sorrow. This morning we have to mourn the loss of dear Brother Carter, of the Bible Christian Mission. He was taken ill with dysentery last Wednesday, the 20th, and in spite of all medical aid and constant nursing night and day, he steadily sank. He was weaker all day yesterday, but we still had hope. This morning at 7.30 he said, in reply to a question put to him by Mr. Anderson, that he was feeling better, and was quite comfortable. In an hour's time a great change had come over him, and when I then saw him he was just becoming unconscious. I said to him, "Do you know me?" A puzzled look passed over his face, and he made no reply. I then said, "You know JESUS, do you not?" to which he replied "Yes." This was his last word, and in half an hour he had passed away. We are to bury him this afternoon. In him China has lost a good man. He has won golden opinions all round, and both before and after his illness manifested in a marked degree the spirit of CHRIST. Quiet and unassuming, he was yet earnest and persevering, and steadily kept to his work ever as in the sight of GOD. No murmur passed his lips all through his illness; a cheery smile and a bright word were ready for all who went to see him during his illness. I loved him as a brother, and feel his loss most keenly. Death is very busy everywhere this summer, the natives are falling around us on every hand, and foreigners in many parts are passing away. In Moukden Mrs. Young (U.P. Mission) has gone; the C.M.S. has lost Mr. Harvey, of the Theological Hall, Ningpo; and in Shanghai Mr. Dalziel, formerly of our Mission, has just succumbed to dysentery.

To the foregoing we may add, with great regret, Rev. A. Williamson, LL.D., also of the U.P. Mission, at Chefoo, after thirty-five years' service. While weeping "with those who weep," we can but rejoice for those for whom "the warfare is accomplished, the victory won." But how these sudden summonses loudly call for earnest purpose and devotion day by day while we may! Who among us will be "baptised for the dead?"

A Good and Faithful Servant.

FROM MISS CARPENTER.

I HAVE been thinking so much about dear Miss Fanny Boyd since I heard of her home-going, and feel I must send you a few loving memoirs of her work and life in China, praying as I do so that others may realise, as I do now, that "she being dead yet speaketh."

One afternoon when we were together at Kiu-chau she was just starting to go out and visit the natives when I, seeing she looked tired, remonstrated with her, and asked if she would not rest that day and go on the morrow, to which she answered "No, I will go if only for one hour; we do not know how many more opportunities we may have." I was rather surprised at her answer, and could not help thinking, as she went down stairs, "Surely you will have many more!" As I think of her now it is as one who always "served the LORD with such gladness." We have often said, "Miss Boyd will cheer us up," and we could not but admire her love for the perishing and her zeal for her MASTER.

Whenever we heard of a worker in China being called home, dear Miss Boyd was always the first one to remind us how much their loved ones at home would need our prayers. I remember her saying to me one day (just as news of this nature arrived), "I think these are very solemn warnings from GOD to us; we should seek carefully to learn all He is teaching us by them."

At another time we had been reading 1 Peter ii. 9 together, when she remarked, "How much our lives *ought* to 'shew forth the praises of Him who hath called us out of darkness into His marvellous light?' He has done so much for us, surely it is the least we can do to 'show forth His praises.'" Exodus xxxiii. 14—"My presence shall go with thee"—was one of her favourite verses; she once told me it had been so much blessed to her. Now she has entered into her rest. This verse has also proved a source of blessing to me since she gave it to me.

Another day we were looking up the different "crowns" mentioned in the Bible, when she remarked that "they would only be given to the faithful ones." Now she has gone to receive the crown given to all who are "faithful unto death." One almost envies the dear ones who have already obtained their crown. Yet, on the other hand, surely the words of our dear sister will stimulate us to use every opportunity as if it were our last, in the "little while" of our service for the MASTER here below.

I cannot but rejoice with her that her joy is now so full, though I cannot forget the vacant place left in China. Is there anyone who would be willing to fill that place? I would plead for dear Miss Boyd's sake, and for His glory that another worker be sent to take up her work in Kiuchau. She said so many times, "If I can only make a beginning, it will be easier for another to work among the women at the villages." I am sure *she* would desire that her place may be filled. She has sown the seed, who will reap the fruit? GOD grant that one not less earnest and zealous for the MASTER'S glory than our dear sister may soon be sent!

FROM MISS FANNY BOYD'S LAST LETTERS.

A FRIEND allows us to make the following extract from a letter dated February 27th:—

"That tract on washing the disciples' feet I have read, and must read; but, oh dear, I find so little time for reading. Thank GOD, the Bible gets more and more delightful to me. Last month I went through Rotherham's New Testament, mostly before breakfast, and enjoyed it so much. It has been a real blessing to me, and helped me in not a few passages. I wish you would introduce it to any Bible students who do not know it and are unacquainted with the original. . . .

Surely, as you say, there issueth a thing for us 'privates' as being 'filled with the SPIRIT.' The command stands as a command, does it not? and while it is so I see nothing for it but to go in for obedience, relying on what GOD is and promises to us. Some time ago the sin of disobedience to this command was forcibly brought home to me, and I felt I dared not confess and ask forgiveness unless I meant by His grace to go in for obeying, as the one in honesty of heart implied the other.

You will say, Well, how has it been since—all bright? No, not all bright, but, blessed be His Name, I think a greater closeness to Himself, and a determination to go on to know increasingly the workings of His blessed SPIRIT. If there is one thing I have longed for for months it is a close walk with GOD. And that brings me to another point in your letter. 'Your position,' you say, 'far away from human ministry may not, after all, be one of disadvantage;' that is the very thought I have come to. We have sometimes thought and spoken as if the privileges at home were so much greater, but this year I entered with this conviction that *ours*, not *yours*, is the place of privilege, where we depend upon GOD alone, and only have Him for our Teacher.

"One other thought rather akin to this came to me a day or two ago—our *present precious time now*, as far as we know, is our only opportunity to follow an unseen SAVIOUR, to pray, to fast, to win souls. Shall we not then gladly seize the opportunity? I confess that, much as I believe I shall enjoy heaven when I get there, I don't want to go just yet with all this pressing need around me—more doors open by far than we can enter, even in this little city, only three miles round. My request is. The service of earth in the power of the HOLY GHOST, a close walk with GOD, and great power in prayer. Have I been betrayed into writing out too much of the deep things of my heart? If so, I blame you in part for touching springs that, to answer your letter frankly, seemed as if they must find vent.

"I came back here in autumn. Since then we have had an almost uninterrupted spell of fine weather, and I have been able to do a good deal of visiting in the afternoons with my dear old Biblewoman. . . I believe we have reached a good many new hearers since I came back. Often we speak for the first time to souls, and, solemn thought! I fear often also for the *only* time."

ANOTHER friend sends us the following extract from a private letter:

"One can't help being disappointed in one's happy feelings going away, but we must not care too much how they go and come. Let us aim at a steady advance in our love for the LORD JESUS and in our knowledge of Him. I have been led to consider that things are much more a matter of habit than perhaps we have been inclined to think, principally by reading about George Bowen who seems to have determined to cultivate the habit of realizing the presence of JESUS at all times. He seems to have so succeeded that it became a life power with him. I think it is a great help and blessing when with others definitely to look to JESUS as nearer than they are, and as the One who is to have at all times our hearts. I am speaking more of what I want to aim at than of anything I have attained to. May you who are so much younger be able to cultivate this habit so that it may be a great life power with you. I want to feel about Him (as He says of the Bride, I think) "Thou hast ravished my heart." I want it to be a passionate, intense love for Him, my Beloved.

THE following cuttings from Miss Boyd's last letters home, will be of interest:—

March 29th.—Miss Littler has been staying with me for a few days. We have been prevented getting out for about three weeks in consequence of the rains, but yesterday we were at two quiet little places. One woman asked so many questions about prayer and worship, that I felt greatly encouraged. The people that we have seen are often difficult to find when we go a second time. Pray that GOD may not lose sight of them. We often speak to a little crowd in a yard, or small street and we do not know where the people all come from. I had been asked to go to a certain place the other day and was wishing to do so. I was much touched by a little boy of six years old offering to take me there. He looked so small, so I looked down at him as Goliath at David, and wondered whether he knew anything. Off he went though, and when we got near the house out rushed three furious dogs barking horribly and knocked the little man down. He got up again, however, and did not budge an inch, but the woman we sought seemed to have gone away. I felt quite grateful to the little fellow for not being afraid of the "foreign devil" or the dogs.

On boat between Hang-chau and Shanghai, May 8th.—I went ashore at four different places on my way down the river, and had a talk with the people. I think, if I were a little stronger, I should have to take to itinerating! I seem at such a suitable age. I often hear the remark, "Yes, you see her hair is all white." When I take off my hat, the people seem less afraid of me than when I have it on.

I use my wordless book in preaching. Some one has said, What we *see* we never forget, though what we hear is often forgotten. Yesterday we got into Hang-chau early.

Bing-yae, May 20th.—You will see from this letter that, instead of staying in Shanghai for the C.I.M. Conference, it seemed right the day after I reached there to start off on my journey again. I took the steamer to Wun-chau; arrived there on Friday, spent the day with Miss Bardsley and Miss Whitford, and started at night by boat for this place.

I never had quite such a rough journey. The natives had taken our passages on a little boat, so my head was half out beyond the boat-covering, and I could gaze up at the sky. At 5 in the morning we arrived at a city, and had to turn out and cross a river in a ferry-boat, literally packed like sardines in a box.

The welcome here, by Mr. and Mrs. Grierson and Miss Britton, was a very cordial one. This place, Bing-yae, used to be one of Mr. Stott's outstations, but is now separa'e, and has two out-stations of its own, which they supply with preachers, I believe, two or three Sundays a month. Dongling, which is also under Mr. Grierson, has a pastor, and a membership getting on for a hundred. This Wun-chau work seems a wonderful one. The large chapel is quite full on communion Sundays; I think there are nearly 200 members. Mr. Grierson speaks so highly of Mr. Stott's plan of work, and, I think, means to follow it out; it seems to consist in giving the Christians a great deal of Bible teaching, and leaving the Chinese to do the preaching and bringing in outsiders.

June 20th.—Mr. Grierson has been having two days of prayer, Bible-study, and fasting with his helpers this week. We were at a good many of the meetings. They were held from 5 a.m. to 5 p.m. It is the first thing of the kind here with the native Christians, but I think we all agree it must not be the last. I felt some real blessing in the meetings myself.

There is an old man here I wish you would pray for. He entered one night, hearing me speak in Mandarin, and came upstairs and sat a little while. He knows the Gospel and prays daily, he says, but it seems as if something hinders his coming right out. He is, I think, the only one in his village who worships GOD. He came last Sunday, walking 50 *li* to get here, and stayed all day for the services.

At the Front.—Where are the Helpers?

FROM MR. LAUGHTON.

LIANG-CHAU FU, KAN-SUH, *May 26th.*— The spring is past, the summer well begun, and still no sign or news of reinforcements; truly "hope deferred maketh the heart sick." It is almost six years now since I came to China. After the first year I was quite alone until my marriage, four years a.o. Since then we have been in the fore-front, where we do not see a foreign face from January to December.

Lack of Christian fellowship tells hard on us both, and we can only pray, "LORD send labourers soon," truly "the harvest is plenteous." The people are willing to listen as long as we can preach, and to all appearance there is a deepening interest. Yesterday one man asked

MOST INTELLIGENT QUESTIONS,

such as "What country was JESUS born in?" "Where was He crucified?" "Upon what day did He rise again?" and many others very similar. Then he and three others said, "Well, we can do no better than believe in JESUS and have our sins forgiven." We do trust that we shall soon see some come out for the LORD.

The chapel where we are at present holding our meetings is far too small, and as the summer goes on the people are sure to come in greater numbers.

ANCESTRAL HALL OFFERED FOR A CHAPEL.

The "Ancestral Hall" is a splendid place. It would seat about two or three hundred, and would cost very little to put into proper order for a chapel. The landlord proposed the subject to me himself last year, and added, "I trust you may soon have a flourishing church." I asked him why he wished this, and he said, "Because by so doing you will increase your merit, and I, being the landlord, part of it must come to me!"

I am happy to say that there is a more friendly feeling towards us this year than there was last summer, but how we are going to get through the summer without help I do not know. There is all this vast district lying around us, and we long to take a journey round the Hien cities and preach, and sell scriptures and tracts, but until there is someone here to relieve us, we really cannot go.

Evangelising in the Si-gan Plain, Shen-si.

FROM MR. BOTHAM.

FENG-TSIANG, *Mar. 27th.*—On Monday last we returned from a journey in the Long-chau district. After a walk of ten miles over the hills from Hien-i-kwan, arrived at a large village on the main road to Long-chau, and preached on the street to a large number of people. One of the men was intensely interested when I told him that my mission was to tell them that the SON of GOD had come to earth and died for the sins of all men; but when he found it was more than a thousand years since JESUS died, he lost interest, and seemed to think the story of the Cross no more than other fables of the past.

A CANTONESE SOLDIER

came to see me in the evening. Like thousands of other Chinese, his fear of the future was not caused by the consciousness of sin, but by the fact that he had no children to burn incense for him after he was dead. What good that could do him I do not know, as he expected death to be the end of him; but if he had children he said it would be like living on, to die feeing that his name would still be remembered. I told him of the riches in glory, and of eternal life for all who believed in JESUS. He could not get his mind over the sad thought that he might not be buried deeply enough, and the wolves and dogs would carry his bones east and west. I urged the Gospel, but still he could not see it, and left, after visiting me three times, saying, "The Heavenly FATHER is very good, but suppose I am not buried properly."

Leaving Ku-kwan, we came very slowly, stopping at nearly all the little hamlets. To preach the Gospel "to every creature" is our motto, and we resolved to lose no opportunity of delivering our message. The women generally gathered round Mrs. Botham, while I had the men, and much seed was sown. One old woman took it as a matter of course that the Gospel was true, and was very eager to know how to pray to GOD.

Tsao-kia-wan.—We had a very cool reception at first, and afterwards nothing but ridicule. We stayed two days, and saw many people; but they all seemed of one mind, and gave us clearly to understand that they neither wanted us nor "our JESUS." The men were most rude and uncouth. They would burst out laughing, ridicule the name of JESUS, and make fun of sentences from the tracts.

We stayed a week in Long-chau. Though a very quiet city, it is busy early in the morning, and after noon the people have plenty of time to listen to the Gospel. A good crowd always collected, and were all very friendly, and listened with interest. They were rather

LIKE THE BEREANS:

they wanted to get to the bottom of the matter. In Tsie-yang I sold a good number of tracts, and had several good times of preaching. Then we came home, *i.e.*, to Feng-tsiang—home still means an inn, and I might almost say any inn, we are so accustomed to travelling.

FROM MR. BLAND.

FENG-TSIANG FU, *April 5th.*—On Tuesday morning, April 1st, in response to an invitation given to us, Bros. Botham and Redfern went over to Kwei Hien, a distance of forty li south, to preach and sell books. They returned here on the Saturday. Mrs. Botham was away at the same time, thus I was alone for most of the week.

On Wednesday evening two coolies arrived with books, tracts, etc. These latter are a splendid assortment. May GOD use them to the salvation of souls on this Plain! At any rate, we intend to sow diligently both by preaching and book selling. During the week I had some happy times in speaking on the main street of this city.

April 12th.—Mr. Redfern left us this morning for Si-gan. I hope to leave shortly for Pin-chau.

Monday, April 14th.—To-day I left Feng-tsiang for the north, with the idea of making known the Gospel in Pin-chau and district. Am taking with me a good stock of books and tracts, Mr. Redfern lending his pony for the purpose. I have no attendant, as I intend to look after myself, and so come in contact with the people the more.

MR. BLAND'S SKETCH-MAP SHOWING HIS ROUTE.

Am first making for Lin-in Hien, a town some 120 li northeast from Feng-tsiang. Mr. Botham came with me for a few miles, and as we made for the neighbouring hills we much admired the appearance of the plain with its beautiful carpet of green wheat, variegated with patches of the yellow flower of the oil plant. All seemed so bright and fresh, affording such a contrast to the sad state of the heathen around. Praise GOD for the privilege of telling them of the good news of Salvation. On setting out my motto is, "Preach the Gospel," and I trust to keep this before me as my aim and object each day of this journey.

After reaching the hills the scenery became very wild, and there was scarcely a house or man to be seen anywhere. The people seemed to hide away in their cave-homes, but now and then I came across a temple or an idol house on which I had the pleasure of pasting up a good-sized tract. It was difficult to keep on the right road, and as a consequence, when evening came I had only gone sixty li, and was obliged to stay for the night in

A CAVE HOUSE

by the roadside. The accommodation was not over luxurious, as may be noted by the fact of the horse, two cows and a calf sharing the room with my teacher and myself, whilst I had to eat my mien (macaroni) and the horse take his drink from the same basin. Such experiences as these come as a sort of recreation to the Missionary whose worst trials are rather mental than otherwise.

Soon after noon on the 15th I reached Lin-yiu, a very small town perched on the top of a hill. I preached from our large sheet tract—one written out on calico some seven feet by six feet. I always find this a great help.

Friday, April 18th.—Nearly the who'e day occupied in travelling from Lin-yiu to Yong-sheo, a distance of 100 li. Arrived at Yong-sheo towards evening, and after feeding myself and the horse, I surveyed the place. Was disappointed to find it no bigger than an ordinary sized village, for my expectations had been somewhat raised on noting that the town had a fine new wall. Its only importance lies in its being a halting place for travellers between Lan-chau and Si-gan.

Monday, April 21st.—A bright sunny day, quite a contrast to yesterday. Left Yong-sheo for P'in-chau, a city some seventy li ahead on the main road to Lan-chau. A cart road lies all the way from Si-gan to the latter city, and is noted, I believe, for its depth of dust, at any rate, it lay some few inches thick on the road to-day.

Towards evening I was out on the streets preaching and selling books. A good crowd of people gathered round, but one man rather

SPOILT MY PREACHING BY RIDICULE.

Food is amazingly cheap here. A basin of mien, with plenty of pork and gravy added, costs but eight cash, and one may make a good meal from two basins of it. Bread sells at twelve cash per catty (thirty cash equals 1d., and 1½ English pounds equals 1 catty). Good water is sold on the street at a few cash per bucketful.

Wednesday, April 23rd.—Yesterday I was congratulating myself on being able to flavour my mien with a little pork or fowl, for at this time of the year one has often to be satisfied with simple vegetarian diet in this district, but this morning an order was issued by the mandarin calling upon the people to abstain from eating flesh, and with devout hearts to pray for rain, which just now is much needed, so not an ounce of meat is procurable in the place.

Thursday, April 24th.—Still at P'in-chau, but expecting to go on further to-morrow. Spoke again for some time in front of the Yamen, but the interest was scarcely so good as yesterday. The shopkeepers appear to be friendly enough, and occasionally invite me to come in as I pass by. My teacher appears to be growing in grace, praise GOD! It is wonderful how much he knows of the New Testament. He is looking forward to going to his home, which is near to Feng-tsiang, to tell his friends of what the LORD has done for his soul.

(*To be continued.*)

Instant in Season.—Work in South Shan-si.

FROM MR. W. G. PEAT.

P'ING-IAO HIEN, *June 26th.*—We had a very busy and encouraging time of preaching here on the 14th and 15th of the 5th Moon (June 1st and 2nd). On the 14th there were theatricals, and on the 15th a fair also, in our west suburb, the theatrical stage being in close proximity to our premises. This is an annual affair, so we prepared for it. We selected about fifteen or sixteen pointed arrows from the Word of GOD, and had these written out on large yellow scrolls of paper, and pasted them on the four walls of our courtyard.

The 14th being Sunday, we had our regular service with the Christians in the forenoon; then in the afternoon we threw open the street doors and

LET THE CROWDS COME IN

to our courtyard. Here we had arranged several forms in a semi-circle, had placed a table for Bibles and Hymn-books, chairs for the speakers, and the large American organ to help in the singing. To enter the yard, the people had to pass through the chapel, and there we stationed two Christians to give tracts and speak to the people as they went out or came in. The sound of the organ and singing drew in crowds of people, who listened very quietly, while one and another and another preached the Gospel. This was kept up till dark, or rather till the sunlight gave place to moonlight. We then sat down together, after the crowds had all dispersed, and under the beautiful moonlight remembered our SAVIOUR'S dying love by partaking of the LORD'S supper.

The members and enquirers remained over night with us, in order to be present and help on the Monday. On that day from after morning worship right on till after dark at night, with the exception of an interval for dinner, we kept on witnessing to the crowds of people that came and went in an incessant stream. On this day also we had a table spread with Gospels and books in the outside portico, and sold nearly a thousand cash worth at prices ranging from four to twelve cash each.

Altogether we had very attentive and interested audiences. Mr. Hsi spoke with real power, handling the Word of GOD in a very convincing manner. I was very much struck with the attitude of the crowd while he spoke; they seemed just to hang on his words. The

TEXTS PASTED ON THE WALLS

proved very serviceable for reference. I saw one man go deliberately round the yard and read them. Good work was done by two of the brethren in the chapel. Great quantities of sheet tracts were given away, and many precious seeds of truth sown in the hearts of those who stayed to talk or ask questions. The chapel acted as an enquiry-room for those who heard the Gospel in the yard.

Even after darkness had set in, two or three little groups of people remained in the yard while one and another explained more fully to them the way of life and peace. Eternity alone will reveal the results of these two days of seed-sowing; and we *shall* come again with rejoicing bringing our sheaves with us.

Village Work in North Shan-si.

FROM MR. W. E. BURNETT.

DAO-T'EO, *July 2nd.*—You will probably be glad to hear of my third visit to Ta-tai (the home of the country Christian), and of the reception I received there, as well as of the work I was enabled to accomplish both in that village and the villages around the district.

Of course, I had Mr. Kung with me after I reached his home, and he acted splendidly as an introduction to all the places we visited, although on several occasions he was roughly criticised and held up to ridicule. But, throughout all, his testimony was clear and to the point, which to me was an evidence of his sincerity, as well as a witness to those around of his changed life. In his own village, amongst his own neighbours, I enjoyed many opportunities of preaching the Gospel, and found more willingness to listen than on former visits. In his home we held

COTTAGE MEETINGS,

which were well attended by all "those who loved to hear the doctrine," as Kung termed them. He would gather them together and sit in their midst with a bright smiling countenance, and after I had finished my discourse he would follow with an exhortation, calling upon them to repent and believe.

I was very happy to find two more who seemed interested, and were in the habit of paying frequent calls to his home in order to hear his expositions of the Scriptures. One man, a Mr. Li, was particularly noticeable as being influenced; and when I bear in mind that this man has always been remarkable for being slow and steady, and tardy in action, I could not help thinking that he had already made some headway, and that he would, in time, come out to be a Christian of no mean standing.

The people of Ta-tai are beginning to believe, and quietly say amongst themselves that, after all, the object of the foreign teacher is a good one, although when I arrived on the last occasion with a cart, the rumour went about that I had come to take the whole family away. Of course, this was said mostly by those who were careless and had no interest in better things. They will learn in course of time, and undoubtedly the day will come when all these things shall have passed away, and the pure light of the Gospel shine unhindered. For this I pray, and for this I work. May the LORD grant us our desires in as far as they accord with His mind and will!

In that village there are several who are breaking off the opium craving, and I am getting medicine to help others who wish to follow their example. At most of the places to which Mr. Kung and I paid our visits, I found a readiness to listen to the Gospel, and a willingness to buy books; but at one or two hamlets I received a cool reception, and no appreciation whatever.

After one visit to a certain village, poor Kung seemed particularly hurt at the coldness of the people, and, notwithstanding my explanation, he failed to see a sufficient reason why the treatment should be such. The day following, however, a man from that very village called upon us, asking me there again, and offering a kind of apology for their want of friendliness. I told him that I should probably call there again on some future occasion, but as there were other places where I wanted to go, I could not fall in with his proposal just now. He gave me an invitation to his home and then took leave, accepting some books I presented to him. I trust the LORD will enlighten his mind. I enjoyed a long conversation with him.

I could tell you much more of my meetings with some of the "country-folk"; all the cases were of more or less interest. They are a people who are undoubtedly seeking after a "something more satisfying," but who in their wanderings and gropings have become more entangled.

For the Young.

FROM MR. R. GRAY-OWEN.

"*How shall they believe in Him of whom they have not heard? and how shall they hear without a preacher?*"—ROM. x. 14.

CHEN-TU, SI-C'HUEN, *July 2nd.*—On a late visit to the out-station I travelled the first day in a passenger boat down stream. At the small river ports we were continually taking in and dropping off passengers. Late in the afternoon an aged dame, accompanied by a youthful grandson, came on board for a few miles, most of the passengers having gone ashore. I had a quiet, blessed opportunity of telling her the way of salvation. She was white-haired, deaf, and bent, already in her eightieth year. Alas! how dark, oh! so dark was her soul, and eternity drawing nigh! When questioned about GOD, heaven, salvation, of life beyond the grave in sorrow or joy, her sad answer, still ringing in my ears, was, "I never heard before." I thought of my own dear grandmother, now in her ninetieth year, eagerly expecting day by day the heavenly chariot to take her home! How sorrowful the contrast! Why is it so? Is it not just because we have neglected the SAVIOUR's command to "preach the Gospel to every creature"? I pray this story, told in simple verse, will stimulate some of you to follow the example of those lepers of old amidst the plenty of the Assyrian camp, who said one to the other, "We do not well, this is a day of good tidings, and we hold our peace; if we tarry till the morning light guilt will come upon us. Now therefore come that we may go and tell the king's household."

"I NEVER HEARD BEFORE."

Of GOD that heaven above did spread,
Made this fair earth whereon I tread,
Supplied my needs, my daily bread—
    I never heard before.

That from above a SAVIOUR came,
To save me from my sin and shame,
JESUS, His sweet and blessed name—
    I never heard before.

That JESUS died, e'en died for me,
Nailed hand and foot on cruel tree,
From guilt and fear my soul to free—
    I never heard before.

Of mansion fair prepared on high,
Through JESUS'S blood to me brought nigh,
No more to sin, no more to sigh—
    I never heard before.

Of peace that like a river flows,
On troubled heart sweet calm bestows,
A daily balm for daily woes—
    I never heard before.

You tell me how to GOD to pray,
To trust in CHRIST's salvation way,
This "blessed news" told me to-day—
    I never heard before.

Oh! why should China's millions lie
In heathen darkness, hopeless die?
How could this agèd sinner cry—
    I never heard before?

Alas! 'tis we who "do not well,"
Neglecting CHRIST's command, to tell
All creatures bound by Satan's spell—
    To look to Him for life.

A SICH'UENESE GRANDMOTHER AND GRANDSON.

Itinerant Work in Ho-nan.

FROM MR. D. J. MILLS.

CHAU-KIA-K'EO, *June 13th.*—Three separate districts have been visited since I last wrote to you. The first journey, taken with Mr. Gracie, was to Chenchau Fu, and from thence south-east to Hsiang-chen Hien. This occupied some ten days, during which we visited some smaller places as well.

The next journey was with Mr. Shearer, and did not take us far from Chau-kin-k'eo, our idea being to reach some of the many small market-towns near here. We first of all proceeded west, and then made a circuit, taking in a great number of places, and reaching Hsiangshui Hien, due south of here.

On the third journey Mr. Shearer again accompanied me, our destination being Kuei-teh Fu. On the way thither, beside we visited numerous large market-towns, and spent a considerable time in T'ai-kang Hien, Tsui-chau, and Ning-ling Hien. On the return journey we also passed through Kieh-chen Hien and Chen-chau Fu (visited on first journey). We had also purposed going to Lu-ih Hien, but our sale of books having already greatly exceeded our expectation, and our remaining stock being insufficient for the places in the immediate route, we determined to defer our visit there till some future time, it the LORD will.

We did our journeys on foot, and though often weary, were compensated by the extra opportunities afforded of talking to persons and groups by the way.

When travelling in HO-NAN, the reception one meets with is so uniformly good that it seems superfluous to say it was so in these several places. T'ai-kang, however, had been visited before by Mr. Johnston and myself the year before last; I therefore hardly expected to sell as many as 3,000 cash worth of books there on a return visit. Yet so it was, and in addition I had the most attentive and respectful audiences for hours together on the streets, praise GOD !

Such also was our experience almost always in all the other places visited. Surely HO-NAN is open to the Gospel, that is, to *itinerant* work. There are ninety-seven Hien districts in the province, each Hien, as far as I can gather and judge, has somewhere about thirty-five market-towns in its district. What a field for labour here! In addition there are the Fu cities, Chaus, and Marts, not a few. Please pray for us in HO-NAN.

Ploughing and Seed-sowing in Gan-hwuy.

FROM MR. H. N. LACHLAN.

GAN-K'ING, *April 28th.*—I enclose notes of a journey from which I have just returned. We sold over four dollars worth of tracts and Gospel portions, chiefly at Wang-hsiang Hien and the various places between there and Shih-p'ai and along the Pih-kia-lin road from Wang-hsiang to Suh-song. I hope it will not be long before I shall be able to revisit the different places, and by living at each for some weeks evangelise them more thoroughly than is possible in such flying visits as I have hitherto paid. All the places in Su-song, T'ai-hu, and Wang-hsiang Hien, which are marked on the native map (and several which are not marked), with the exception of the mountain villages lying north of the road between Ur-lang-ho and T'ai-hu, are well supplied with tracts and Gospel portions. May the LORD bless His Word and guide us in what way best to water the seed sown, and sow the ground ploughed, and plough up fresh soil.

April 3rd.—Weather threatening, and colporteur (Ch'en Lohtsüen) not very well; however, we set off toward Kiang-kia-tsui. The winter rain had already impracticable, so we went, as last autumn, over Long-hsu-lin to Hong-kia-p'u, selling a few books on the way and on arrival.

April 4th.—Breakfasted at Mei-lin. Several people came in, some wanting to "eat the religion," and had to be told that there was no such thing as "eating" *our* religion. Kiang-kia-tsui, sold a few books. While we were lunching a man tried to

PICK A QUARREL

with the colporteur for not giving him a tract for nothing, wrenched the hook away, and with oaths and abuse threatened to beat him if he continued to demand the price. At a hamlet named T'ong-kia-yao, on the Shih-p'ai road, I was taken in by a little boy to a teacher named Liu, who was busy teaching two boys. I had great difficulty in getting him to understand that he *could* understand me. The Gospel seemed quite new to him, and too good to be true. He bought a Gospel, and promised to come and see me at examination time.

April 5th.—Slept at Ur-li-t'ing on the front door (*sic*); fortunately it was a warm, still night. The opium-smoking landlord showed more interest in our preaching than on our former visits. Passed rapidly through Shih-p'ai toward Wang-hsiang Hien. At Lao-hua-t'ang people said they had never seen a foreigner before. The landlord of the inn we dined at pressed us to stay Sunday. The people listened attentively to our message. A vegetarian seemed specially interested. He bought a book and asked many questions, but was called on business, and did not come back as he said he would. People came in considerable numbers, especially in the evening, and on the Sunday evening. Sunday, the LORD gave us a quiet time, both for united worship and private meditation.

April 7th.—Off early toward Wang-hsiang Hien. At Liang Hien our road joined that from K'i-kia-k'iao to Wang-hsiang. Gambling very prevalent. People bought books freely. The road from Shih-p'ai to Wang-hsiang is well frequented.

April 8th.—Selling and preaching in Wang-hsiang. The city is larger and busier than I thought. There are two north gates, with shops and inns outside. The business centres along the street which leads from the east north gate and a street at right angles to it, in which the yamen is situated. An opium-smoker was very rude and abusive to me because I would not give him a tract. Had a very good time preaching in various shops.

April 9th.—Visited Hwa-yang-chen, but found book-selling hard work. Kiu-kiang people had been there last year. One old man bought a New Testament catechism and other tracts.

April 10th and 11th.—Book-selling (also difficult) at Kih-shui-si, a busy water-side town larger than Hwa-yang-cheng. Thence by sparsely-populated fen country, between the Yangtse River and the P'eh Lake to Pih-kia-lin, a small place with some ten houses and two inns. Afternoon and evening, people kept coming to the inn. One intelligent old man asked, among other questions, how the colporteur came to believe the doctrine.

The colporteur told how he was given a tract by two native preachers in a town in SHAN-TUNG, who, after being away a short time, returned to the place and gave him a New Testament, telling him, whenever he came to anything he did not understand, to kneel down and ask GOD to teach him. This he did for two years, and afterwards heard the Gospel, and became converted to this province. At the time when he first heard the doctrine he was an opium-smoker and gambler. At times he would endeavour to make amends by idol-worship and vegetarianism.

Three brothers named Wu, tailors by trade, and an o'der man of the same name heard the Gospel. The youngest of the three, said to be twenty, but looking quite a boy of fifteen, took a great fancy to me, and said he wanted to follow JESUS

April 12th.—Crossed three ferries in succession. At the ferry, the boy took a tract in payment, in spite of the sneers of some other passengers. Put up at Hong-kia-lin, a busy little place, where books were bought freely.

April 13th.—Sunday. Hard rain all day. The landlord's younger brother in our inn opium-smoking, feasting, and gambling till second cock-crow, a gentleman named Shi, also related to him, being with him. Shi throughout the day kept borrowing a Luke's Gospel and coming to me for explanation. It was pitiful to see how seared was his conscience, and how fast the devil had him bound.

April 14th.—At five *li* distant was a small place with some decent inns, and at ten *li* we came to Hsu-kia-lin, at both which we sold books. One shopkeeper named Li knew a good deal about the doctrine, and was thinking of joining the Romanists. The colporteur explained to him the difference. Gambling terribly prevalent. Stopped by rain at a small hamlet about five *li* further on. Several people came in, and bought books, and listened.

April 15 *and* 16*th.*—Selling and preaching on the streets of Suh-song ; very few purchasers, but some attentive listeners.

April 17th.—Set out for Ur-lang-ho, thirty *li* to north. Detained by heavy rain and thunderstorms for a day and a half at Shi-long-tsui, a little place just where the road to Hwang-mei Hien (HU-PEH) branches off westward and crosses the river. Had a very interesting time explaining the Gospel and reading the Scriptures with a young scholar named Hong. He put me in mind of the young man of whom it is said "JESUS, beholding him, loved him." He readily confessed that he was a sinner, and that to follow JESUS was right and good *for me;* but he could not see that it was for *him.*

I think he could not bear the thought that his skill in essay-writing, his store of maxims and quotations, accumulated with so much pains during so many years, and his upright life should be weighed in the balances of this foreign doctrine and be found wanting. I hope to see him at examination time.

April 19th to 26th.—From this point we returned home by way of Liang-t'ing-ho (where we spent a quiet, delightful Sunday), T'ai-hu, Hsing-ts'ang (which we did not enter, as a high wind and swollen river rendered the ferry-boat unmanageable), Hwang-li kiang, and T'ieo-shan. The colporteur's health gave me some anxiety, as he was weak and feverish and very deaf, and at times coughed a good deal. Heavy storms detained us at various places, while here and there we found bridges either carried away by the stream or under water, and we had to wade and pull the barrow. However, the LORD gave us needful strength and help all along the way, and when we arrived on Saturday last I was in excellent health, and the colporteur rather better than at the beginning of the week. He is

A DELIGHTFUL COMPANION,

always seeking to give me the most comfortable bed and the most palatable food, full of contrivances for getting over difficulties, always ready to preach, however weak he felt, and to take joyfully the chastening of the LORD, and eager for the lion's share of any rough work, such as barrow-pulling over flooded sand or uphill against a high wind. Poor fellow ! once before he returned from a journey to find his wife and child dead and buried during his absence, and this time he found his only child by his second wife dying, a little thing about forty days old. His wife is not a church-member, but he says that she believes the Gospel. The little one died a few hours after our return. They need our prayers.

Baptisms at Gan-shun (Kwei-chau).

FROM MR. ADAM.

GAN-SHUN, *June 3rd.*—You will be glad to hear that an open door is set before us in a country district ten English miles from this city. More than twenty men have been cured of opium-smoking by the help of our medicine, and one or two of them have given up dumb idols. Oh, may they soon find the LORD.

Last week I visited that district, and was very well received ; the people wanted me to stay a few days, but I could only stay one. The family with whom I lodged have really renounced idolatry, and seem to be truly seeking the LORD.

The work in the city is hopeful at present. Numbers of visitors every day and night come to see us and hear the story of GOD'S love with fair attention ; among them there are a few interesting and very hopeful cases.

Mr. Windsor has been here about a fortnight ; it is such a change from being alone to have his cheerful, happy presence with me ; the LORD is giving us good times together. Truly in the LORD'S presence there is fulness of joy, and we are finding that this joy of the LORD is our strength.

My heart is often heavy and sad at the thought of so many dying every day without the knowledge of CHRIST. Oh, may the merciful LORD soon raise up workers, foreign or Chinese, for this pressing, important work ! And oh for more Holy Ghost power to fill our own hearts !

July 5th.—Just a word to tell you of the LORD'S goodness to us in this far-away station. To-day we had the joy and privilege of seeing three believers confess their faith in Christ, two men and one woman. Brother Windsor conducted the service, and catechized them before administering the sacred ordinance. All three replied so nicely to the various questions put. Praise the LORD.

1. Mr. Tsu, a farmer, fifty-one years of age ; this man is the first fruit of the labours of our native brother Fan.

2. Mr. Ngao, a weaver of this city, who has been a real enquirer since last November. He gives evidence of the work of the HOLY GHOST in his soul, and is not ashamed to own JESUS as his LORD. Mr. Ngao is a good reader, and has already read most of our Christian books.

3. Mrs. Hsia, of some sixty odd summers. She destroyed her idols and incense pots, and gave up chanting prayers *twelve* months ago. Nine months ago the old lady had opposition from her relatives, who did all they could to keep her away from us. Her daughter has since broken off opium-smoking with us. Mrs. Hsia is one of two souls brought in by Mrs. Wu, our helper's mother-in-law. She went through the service right bravely this morning. Will you pray much that they may all be kept faithful to the confession made to-day, and that each of them may rapidly grow in grace and in the knowledge of our LORD JESUS CHRIST. The weaver may still have trouble about keeping holy the whole Sabbath.

Tidings from Scattered Workers.

Chih-li Province.
FROM MR. M. L. GRIFFITH.

Shun-teh, May 17th.—In looking over the past twelve months I can indeed say that GOD has supplied all my need, and that I have wanted no good thing. I spent eight very happy months at the Ganking Training Home, where I obtained a good deal of useful and practical knowledge from Mr. Wood, which will be helpful to me in future work.

At the end of last year I lived at the West Gate House, Ganking, for five weeks, with Mr. Hunt. During my last few weeks in this city I was able to give a little Bible explanation at morning and evening Chinese prayers, which I took when Mr. W. Cooper was away.

After leaving Ganking I spent three weeks at Wuhu with Mr. Hardman. We lived with Mr. Yang, the native evangelist, and very much enjoyed the time there. It was helpful to me in learning to speak Chinese, and also cheering to see how happy the Christians were in this place. We did a little tract selling and speaking on the streets, which brought encouragement. I get on very well with Mr. Bridge. He can understand the people very well. I understand almost nothing at present, but hope I shall soon be able to.

The past year has been the happiest of my life; truly the LORD has more than made up for those I have left in England. I have had very good health during the year.

Shan-tung Province.
FROM DR. RANDLE.

Chefoo, July 3oth.—Our medical work increases on our hands, there is much sickness among the Chinese. Large numbers come for treatment, and they hear the Gospel. Mr. Judd has been speaking to waiting patients.

Last Sunday morning we had some twenty-five or thirty outsiders in to our service.

Mr. McMullan is helping as he is able, but just now he is far from well.

Kiang-su Province.
FROM MISS THIRGOOD.

Yang-chau, June 3rd.—I feel I must write you a few lines to tell you how happy I am, and what great things the LORD has done for me. Is it not wonderful how He teaches us in China? We have all been drawn nearer to the MASTER and closer to each other through the death of dear Annie Dunn. Her sufferings were very great, but she glorified her SAVIOUR. I do pray that many more, led by the LORD, filled with the HOLY GHOST, may come out to fill up the gaps.

Oh! the darkness of this city; it is terrible. Misery and wretchedness on every side; so few to tell of His love! GOD is using the dear workers here; but what are we among so many? Last Sunday week I went with Miss Young to visit some women in the city. They gave us such a warm welcome. The room was a large one, and was soon quite full. GOD helped me to speak to them. We also sang two hymns. How pleased they are with the singing, dear women!

Our minister at home writes to say that the Church is being richly blessed. They have all been stirred to pray for China, praise the LORD.

Kiang-si Province.
FROM MISS SAV.

Kwei-ki, June 7th.—I am kept pretty busy, and do not write as often as I ought. I find it easier to *do* the work than to *write* about it.

On May 17th six more were added to us by baptism, five men and one woman. There are also many enquirers, who will, I trust, prove such as shall be saved.

We have been able to open an out-station, Shang-tsing, within our own Hien, about seventy li from here. I returned this morning from my third trip to this place. We have rented a house which is being repaired. Two rooms are already boarded, and Miss Munro is staying in them for a short time. The people begged us to come, and have made us very welcome.

There are a good few interested, and several from this place who have broken off opium in our refuge are now, I hope, trusting in JESUS to break every chain. Miss Horsburgh went with me the first time, and is very much interested in the place.

FROM MISS J. GARDINER.

I-yang, June 23rd.—We have now been nearly three months living in this city, and how glad I am to be able to tell you that all is now so peaceful and the people so friendly. For the first six or seven weeks large crowds came every day, and such evil reports had been spread about the city that we feared serious results. But we knew our GOD reigned, and that whatever might happen would be the very best that could happen.

The mandarin issued a proclamation in our favour, and ever since there has been a growing friendliness among the people, and the LORD's work is going on. The evil reports have really been the means of spreading the Gospel, and so the devil's plan to hinder has completely failed. Already a few are, we believe, really interested in the Gospel—not in the foreigner.

In one home the paper idols have been torn down, and the Ten Commandments hang in their place. What joy it gives to see the light dawning in these dark hearts! Truly, flesh and blood cannot reveal the truth to them; it must be the power of the HOLY GHOST. We have had many invitations, which we have accepted, promising to come ere long, and many opportunities of proving the LORD's faithfulness. "He is faithful."

Kwei-chau Province.
FROM MR. S. R. CLARKE.

Kwei-yang, May 16th.—We recently returned from T'ung-chau, about four days' journey from this. The road is narrow and hilly, and the coolies had no little difficulty in some places in dragging my wife's sedan-chair through the bushes. The whole region around T'ung-chau is very sparsely populated, yet it is the most considerable place for many miles around, containing about two hundred families. The people were all very friendly and willing to listen to the Gospel, and during our stay I suppose nearly all the women in the place came to visit my wife.

Two men have asked for baptism, but we thought it well to let them remain on probation some time longer. There are also others who profess to believe, some of whom I know have taken down their idols, and instead have put up the Ten Commandments. There are, I think, about eight women who reckon themselves Christians.

Departures for China.

ON September 18th, per P. and O. s.s. *Bengal*, Miss F. M. REID and Miss CUNDALL.

On October 2nd, per P. and O. s.s. *Shannon*, Messrs. MARSHALL BROOMHALL, B.A., J. G. CORMACK, THOMAS GOODALL, H. FRENCH RIDLEY, JOHN TALBOT, J. E. WILLIAMS, M.R.C.S., etc.; of the Swedish Mission in China, Messrs. A. BERG and A. HAHNE; from Norway, Mr. S. GJERDE. The last three are Associates.

To leave on October 30th, per P. and O. s.s. *Kaisar-i-Hind*, Mrs. HUDSON TAYLOR and Miss F. E. MARLER, Miss TANNER and Miss FOWLE.

What wilt thou?

Y faith the walls of Jericho fell down"—yet what more unlikely! " *We* walk by faith." Do we? What record is there on high of things that "by faith" we "have obtained"? Is each step each day an act of faith? Do we, as children of GOD, really believe the Bible? Are we ready to take the place of even a worm as our MASTER did—" But I am a worm and no man"? Or if we realise our powerlessness and our insignificance, do we believe that it is possible—that it is GOD's will for us—that we should thresh mountains? "Fear not," said the LORD by the prophet of old, "fear not, thou worm Jacob, . . . behold I will make thee a new sharp threshing instrument having teeth: thou shalt thresh the mountains, and beat them small, and shalt make the hills as chaff. Thou shalt fan them, and the wind shall carry them away, and the whirlwind shall scatter them: and thou shalt rejoice in the LORD, and shalt glory in the HOLY ONE of Israel."

How then, do we ask, are we to thresh mountains? Let us listen to the MASTER, "Have faith in GOD. For verily I say unto you, That whosoever shall say unto this mountain, Be thou removed, and be thou cast into the sea; and shall not doubt in his heart, but shall believe that those things which he saith shall come to pass, he shall have whatsoever he saith." Do we ask *when* this shall be? The LORD continues, "Therefore I say unto you, what things soever ye desire *when* ye *pray*, believe that ye receive them, and ye shall have them." Let us therefore "be careful for nothing; but in everything by prayer and supplication with thanksgiving, let our requests be made known unto GOD."

Now let us stop and ask ourselves, What do we "desire"? and then let us claim the promise at once. Have we loved ones unsaved? Have we difficulties to conquer? Have we mountains to be removed? Then let us "take it to the LORD in prayer." But let us remember that "Faith is . . . the evidence of things not seen," and so be satisfied to see in GOD's own time and way.

It is interesting and helpful to turn from Hebrews xi., with a clause of which we began our meditatation, to Psalm xxii., from which we have also quoted, and to ponder the darkness, the extremity the seeming utter failure of earth's grandest victory, and to "consider Him . . . lest we be wearied and faint in our minds." His experiences will interpret for us His promises, and teach us how to walk by faith.

When our LORD taught us to say, "Our FATHER which art in heaven, Hallowed be Thy Name, Thy kingdom come," He put into our lips the petitions that we should all most desire. We are told too, what He desires,—"Who will have all men to be saved, and to come unto the knowledge of the truth." "Go ye into all the world, and preach the Gospel to every creature." Shall we not by faith claim that the very thing that He most wishes to be done on earth *shall* be done? "Thy people shall be willing in the day of Thy power." "All power *is* given unto Me."

Has not the LORD been opening the lands to the Gospel, and making travel easy for the very purpose that all should hear of His love? "The harvest truly is plenteous, but the labourers are few; pray ye therefore the LORD of the harvest, that He will send forth labourers into His harvest."

Seeing that in days of old faith wrought such mighty wonders, and that we "on whom the ends of the world are come" have the same GOD—seeing that GOD has "provided some better thing for us, that they without us should not be made perfect," shall we not ask large things? Can we ask anything less than that the Gospel shall be given speedily "to every creature"? Nothing less will satisfy our MASTER. Believing prayer will lead to wholehearted action, and the LORD for our encouragement

DECEMBER, 1890.

says, "If two of you shall agree on earth as touching anything that they shall ask, it *shall* be done for them of My FATHER which is in heaven."

Another year is closing, how many of GOD's people will band themselves together afresh to claim in faith and to labour for the spread of the Gospel to "every creature" in this generation? Believing, we shall "rejoice in the LORD and glory in the HOLY ONE of Israel," and shall prove for ourselves and before the world that "there is nothing too hard for the LORD," and that "all things are possible to him that believeth."

Mr. Hudson Taylor's Visit to Australasia.

EXTRACTS FROM HIS PRIVATE LETTERS.

AUG. 6*th*.—Yesterday we passed very near the northern arm of Celebes; it was like all the islands here, wooded to the water's edge. To-day, at 1 p.m., we passed through the Kulla Isles. The way seemed land-locked, and the passage was, perhaps, a mile wide, so we saw the huts on each side and a few of the natives. We expect to land our Portuguese soldiers at Dehli, a town on the north of Timor, on Friday morning. It is thirty-six years and a half since I saw Timor. *Nothing yet done for the souls of its people.*

Aug. 8th.—Reached Dehli at 7 a.m., and landed with the captain and some passengers at 9.15. Had a short walk up the one street of this little town. All the shops are Chinese. It has a few foreign houses, roofed with corrugated iron, gardens of flowering trees, cocoa-nut and areka palms, bananas, pomegranates, etc. The natives seem improved Malays. There is one R.C. church. Our sixteen passengers were landed and left, and at 11 a.m. we threaded our way out of the reef-bound harbour and sailed for Port Darwin. On Sunday morning we expect to enter this our first Australian port.

Aug. 12th.—Landing at Port Darwin about 10 a.m., we found the Methodist Church, the only Protestant place of worship, and attended service there. The young minister and his wife, who had only been there since April, were very friendly. Mr. Beauchamp addressed the Sunday scholars in the afternoon, and read prayers in the evening, after which I preached. We also had a missionary meeting on Monday evening, our first in Australia.

On Monday we visited a small settlement of the natives; nothing is done for their spiritual good by Protestants. They are sunk very low, seem to have only two numbers, odd and even, and cannot count beyond five! Their spears are made of iron-wood, barbed on one side fearfully, and they throw them with great force and accuracy. A chief, or king, whom we saw, has five wives, one of whom comes daily and acts as servant to the minister's wife.

Thence we were driven by the magistrate to see the gaol, a beautiful clean place in a healthy position. We also saw the botanical gardens, which are full of interest. Eucalyptus trees abound, and so do the hills of the white ants, of which we saw dozens in the course of our drive.

Aug. 15th.—We passed Booby Island half-an hour ago, and shall soon finish this stage of our journey at Thursday Island, the first Queensland settlement. There are not many people on the island, I believe, so we are not likely to be able to do much, if any, missionary work. We were much prospered in Port Darwin, and as we shall have part of Sunday at Cooktown, GOD may give us openings there.

Aug. 20th.—I have been poorly; severe cold and headache, with neuralgia and strange faintness before breakfast for several mornings, with a feeling that one's heart was getting tired of beating and might stop. I am better this morning. I have had some sweet times of meditation. "GOD, my exceeding joy," is a beautiful expression, is it not? About midnight last night we entered a narrow passage with islands on each side, which by day must be very beautiful, called Whitsunday Passage, from a large island which probably Captain Cook discovered, or spent the day there, on Whitsunday. We are still inside the Great Barrier Reef, which begins at Thursday Island and forms a natural breakwater of 1,000 miles long.

Newcastle, Aug. 25th.—We reached here yesterday at 7 a.m. Went to a Presbyterian Church in the morning, and to a Chinese meeting at 7 p.m., at which I spoke. In the afternoon Mr. Beauchamp and I both spoke shortly at a Y.M.C.A. meeting in the theatre. We are to have a meeting (D.V.) to night at the Y.M.C.A., and go on at 11 p.m. to Sydney, but a strike, which has been going on for some time, stopped the men who were coaling our ship at midnight. It is uncertain whether they will resume at noon. Some think our ship may be stopped altogether at Sydney. We know nothing of the future, but we know our GOD.

Sydney, Aug. 28th.—We arrived here at 9 p.m. on the 26th, and were met on arrival by a member of the Y.M.C.A. Board, who asked us to be their guests at the Hotel Métropole. The Rev. W. G. Taylor, the Superintendent of the Central Methodist Mission, asked me to preach for him in the evening. Next morning the clerical and Lay Secretaries (local) of the C.M.S. waited on us asking us to take part in their anniversary meeting on Monday, and the Rev. Dr. Steel (First Presbyterian Church) has engaged me for Sunday morning. A reception by the Y.M.C.A. is arranged for Friday afternoon, and we speak in their hall on Saturday and Sunday nights.

Aug. 29th.—To-day we have been up the country to Newington, where I addressed the inmates of a home for destitute women. Then returning we had a very representative gathering of ministers and leading Christian workers of all denominations; the LORD gave and blessed the Word.

Melbourne, Sep. 6th.—We had a good meeting last night at Malvern, a suburban town, and to-day a good prayer meeting in the Y.M.C.A. rooms. To-morrow I preach (D.V.) at 11 a.m., in Dr. Bevan's Congregational Church, and in the evening at Mr. Chapman's Chapel (Baptist). Mr. Beauchamp and Mr. Whitehouse have each meetings elsewhere.

Sept. 8th.—I have been busy with candidates all this morning; it is nearly time now for the ministers' meeting, and we have a public meeting after that.

Sept. 9th.—We had two excellent meetings yesterday. In the afternoon the first to welcome me, was Mr. Paton of the New Hebrides. We go to Tasmania on Monday (D.V.) for a week.

Caulfield, Victoria, Sept. 11th.—We have had a busy week. On Tuesday a council meeting at 3 p.m.; tea with the Presbyterian minister and meeting in the Wesleyan church at Carlton, a suburb (of Melbourne). On Wednesday, council prayer-meeting at 2 p.m., tea at Dr. Warren's, and meeting at 7.30 in Kew (a suburb) Wesleyan church. Thursday morning, conference with Rev. A Bird, secretary of the council, and afternoon drawing-room meeting at the Deanery. The Dean, the father of my host, is ninety. He is a relation of Lord Macartney, whose embassy to China is historical. Thursday evening, had meeting in Cairns Memorial Presbyterian Church.

To-day we have our meeting in St. Mary's schoolroom, Caulfield; to-morrow, Saturday, a meeting in the Y.M.C.A. hall for young men only; and on Sunday I am to preach in the South Melbourne Wesleyan Church at 11 a.m., and in the North Melbourne Presbyterian Church in the evening.

In Tasmania we hope (D.V.) to hold meetings in Hobart and Launceston. Then we are to visit Geelong, Ballarat, Adelaide, Melbourne, Sydney, and perhaps Newcastle and Brisbane ere we sail for China.

Sept. 15*th*.—My cough is not better, and to-day breathing is labour. My arrangements are to leave to-day for Tasmania, returning on the 25th; Geelong, 26th; Ballarat, 27th till Oct. 1st; Adelaide, Oct. 1st to 13th; Melbourne, Oct. 15th to 28th; Sydney, 29th to Nov. 11th.

We may reach Hong-kong Dec. 2nd to 10th, but the strikes so paralyse trade that there is no certainty.

Items of Interest.

FROM REV. J. W. STEVENSON.

SHANGHAI, *Sept.* 11*th*.—I have not known such a time of sickness and death in China before. There have been many deaths among the foreign community generally, and a terrible mortality among the natives. The weather has become much cooler and healthier.

Mr. Baller reports all the brethren at Gank'ing as being now quite well, and I trust that we shall be spared any further serious trial, if it be GOD's will. Dr. Howard Taylor has recovered and has returned with Mr. Anderson to Gank'ing. Messrs. Lachlan, Dickie and Willett are here, and improving rapidly. Mr. Lachlan expects to start to-morrow for Chefoo.

Miss Munro and Miss Doggett are at Ta-ku-t'ang, and I am thankful to say are both convalescent. Miss Clara Ellis and her sister have safely reached Han-chung, and are staying with Dr. and Mrs. Wilson. Miss Esam is better, and has returned hence to Yang-chau.

Miss Judd, accompanied by Miss Britton, arrived here on Aug. 24th from Wunchau. She is seriously ill and confined to her room. Miss Ord has been laid up for some days, and Mr. Eyres has been very ill; both are here. Mr. and Mrs. Miller are also with us at present; he is far from strong. Their medical adviser recommends a short trip to Japan, and they leave us on the 13th.

I am sorry to hear that the friends at Lao-ho-k'eo—Mr. and Mrs. Geo. King and Miss Emily Black—are far from well. Mr. and Mrs. Burnett start for home by the next P. and O. boat, a fortnight hence.

Mr. Cooper is visiting the stations in NORTH GAN-HWUY, and I have just heard that Mr. Meadows is visiting the out-stations from Shao-hing, CHEH-KIANG. Mr. and Mrs. Nicoll have reached Hankow, and will probably before long go on to Ichang.

The Canadian brethren in SOUTH KIANG-SI are prosecuting their work, not without difficulty. Messrs. Horne and Meikle have had to leave Kan-chau Fu.

Messrs. Darroch and Duffy report favourably of the work in their district. They seem to have many open doors. Mr. Duffy had been ill and under medical care at Nan-king for a time. He is now better.

I left Shanghai on August 27th on a visit to Ta-ku-t'ang, and returned here on Sept. 5th with my daughter. I am thankful to say the change is evidently doing her good.

Miss Knight and Miss L. K. Ellis left Shanghai for Japan on Aug. 17th. [They have done a most valuable work in our girls' school at Chefoo.] They are hoping to be able to remain and work in Japan.

I have the following baptisms to report:—Five at Ts'in-chau, KAN-SUH, in June; and at Chen-tu, SI-CH'UEN, two on July 30th and two on August 8th.

The Floods in China.

IN the "Items of Interest" from Mr. Stevenson last month, reference was made to the floods with which parts of China are now visited. Some fuller idea may be formed from the subjoined extracts of the magnitude of the calamity, and the apparent hopelessness of dealing with matters under existing circumstances. We must not be understood, however, to endorse all that is therein expressed, but would yet urge all Christians to plead with GOD that much blessing may come out of these distressing circumstances, and that wisdom and energy may be given to the Government to grapple with the difficulty. That it is a difficulty, and a many-sided one, may be further gathered from the extracts we give (p. 162) from Professor Douglas, and calls for much patience and forbearance from us as Christians. Possibly corruption and mutual jealousy among officials (not unknown outside China!) may be at the bottom, as much as anything else.

FROM MR. STEVENSON.

I FEAR little can be done in the way of relief. These floods might be prevented if the Chinese adopted proper methods of dealing with the Yellow and other rivers. The consensus of opinion out here seems to be that these repeated disasters will force the Chinese Government to face the problem of how to prevent these calamities.

If there is any reasonable prospect of distributing money, be assured I shall lose no time in letting you know. I have already put myself in communication with missionaries on the spot, and if they are prepared to undertake the work of distribution we shall very gladly help them to the utmost of our ability.

FROM THE "TIMES."

THIS year, again, China is visited by disastrous inundations, especially in the northern provinces of SHAN-TUNG and CHIH-LI. The reports say that tens of thousands of square miles are covered with water from one to fifteen feet in depth, that whole villages have been swept away and many lives lost, while the survivors in many districts are face to face with famine during the coming winter. The foreign communities in China have been appealed to for aid, which has in some instances been given ; but there seems a general indisposition to make any organised effort to give relief.

The *North China Herald*, describing the attitude of foreigners, says they see nothing practical being done to prevent these constantly recurring floods ; they see how floods have actually been increased in western SHAN-TUNG by opening the canal locks to let the tribute rice boats to Peking go through, the flood pouring through at the same time. A lock on one river would have prevented vast destruction, but it is not made ; in another case numbers of cattle might have been saved if some official took the responsibility of driving them to the Government pastures a few days away. "It is all these and similar evidences of indifference and neglect which disgust us with the Chinese Government, and which cannot be outweighed by the fine words of sorrow and sympathy used in the reports and decrees published in the *Peking Gazette*."

A graver charge made against the officials is that they profit largely by the floods ; this, though perhaps incapable of strict proof, is believed by every one. These considerations prevent foreigners from again subscribing, but the Shanghai journal proposes the formation of a committee for the collection of information on these and other subjects connected with vast public calamities of this nature in China, and the distribution of relief in the past.

FROM THE "LONDON & CHINA TELEGRAPH."

IN a private letter from Tientsin, dated September 4th, the writer mentions that he goes out sailing every day, and that in every direction outside the Sankolinsin Folly there is nothing but water. There are two feet of water on the raised racecourse. The water positively swarms with whitebait, and men, women, and children are constantly at work taking them out by basketfuls, so that as one *mow* (acre) of fish may reasonably be considered worth at least twenty *mow* of *kaoliang* (millet), the flood is not, after all, such a calamity as it appears at first sight. [A later report says the water continues to fall steadily.]

Evangelising in the Si-gan Plain, Shen-si.
(Continued.—See Sketch Map.)

FROM MR. BLAND.

FRIDAY, *April 25th.*—Reached Ch'ang-wu this afternoon, after a walk of eighty *li* on one of the dustiest of roads, and, praise GOD, my health is such that after a wash and brush down I felt fresh enough for anything. I was soon out on the street with a box of books and had a splendid time with the people. I find selling books at once on arrival allays a good deal of suspicion and makes preaching the more acceptable afterwards ; the reason, perhaps, being that the people look on it as doing something towards a living. Book selling, too, affords good opportunities of conversation as to our business, our country, etc.

Food is cheaper here than at P'in-chau, but the amount of opium smoking and beggary is awful. The natives sometimes say that "eleven out of every ten smoke !" Even women may be seen and

YOUNG CHILDREN SMOKING

at times. This is sad, but is worse still to think of all the souls ruined for time and eternity through this evil. Avarice reigns, so also does apathy towards better and higher things, and it is difficult to make the people understand that they have a part and lot in the message we bring them.

April 28th.—For the last fortnight I have rarely been able to procure anything beyond bread, hard boiled eggs, and mien. The latter is simply thin strips of stiff dough boiled for a few seconds, and then eaten with the addition of hot water, vinegar, pepper, and sometimes a sprinkling of vegetables. Still my health is good.

Thursday, May 1st.—San-shui was my next halting place some 100 odd *li* away to the East, but instead of going by the ordinary road, *viâ* P'in-chau, I first made for a village called P'ch-kih, sixty *li* somewhere north-east. "Steering" was rather awkward as there was no sun to be seen, and the road was nothing more than a foot-path with a road here and there branching off, but by inquiring the way as often as possible, I reached the place in the afternoon. I recognised GOD's own hand in leading me here, for on arrival, although the place contained little more than half a dozen houses and a small temple dedicated to the "god of riches," there was a good number of country people busy marketing. I tied my horse to a post and ordered a basin of mien, but before I could have my breakfast scores of people gathered round, inquisitive as to the business of the foreigner. I started selling books and tracts, and in a very short time disposed of over 400 cash worth, all at two or four cash each. It is good to think of these books entering the homes of these people for miles around. An hour later nearly all had returned to their homes, so I arrived none too soon.

Later on I posted tracts, and spoke for a short time to a few people who gathered around. They appeared to understand all I said ; praise GOD, through His grace I have no difficulty in making myself understood wherever I go. Spent the night here ;

MYSELF, TEACHER AND HORSE

occupying a room, or rather a cave, together.

Friday, May 2nd.—Continued my journey in a southeasterly direction, and reached San-shui after a walk of eighty *li* through a most fertile district. The town lies in a valley, and is prettily situated. Peace and plenty seem to abound. Bread sells at ten cash per catty, and pork at thirty cash the same, but here, as at the other places I have visited, the general cry is for "opium medicine." My room was full of visitors until dark

Tuesday, May 6th.—By sunrise I was on my way to Ch'eng-hua, or Shen-hua, a Hien town 100 *li* distant from San-shui. The weather and country were alike lovely, the growing wheat reminding one so much of the green pasture lands of Old England. On the way a young wolf crossed our path a few yards ahead of us, the first I have seen out here, although I have heard them howling in the night when at Feng-tsiang. Within twenty *li* of Ch'eng-hua I reached a busy village, at which the annual fair was being held, and it was not very long before I found my way on to the fair ground, where all sorts of amusements, including a theatrical performance, were in full swing. Here I commenced book selling, but did not dispose of very much stock. Had a better time in the street, the people inviting me freely into their shops.

Next day towards noon I continued my journey to Ch'eng-hua, with a cloudy sky overhead. Before I had gone many *li* the rain came down, making the rest of my walk rather disagreeable. Upon arrival was disappointed with the town, it being smaller, if anything, than the village I had just left, but I am thankful to have the privilege of preaching the Gospel in these small,

OUT-OF-THE-WAY PLACES.

This is the twenty-fourth town ("hien," "chau," or "fu") that I have visited on this Si-gan Plain, including all but one of the towns to the west of Si-gan. At some I have stayed two or three times, as well as at a good many villages, large and small. I do praise GOD for the pleasure of staying at these places, and for using me in a little way to spread abroad the knowledge of His Gospel.

Thursday, May 8th.—I awoke in the morning with sore throat and cold, which prevented me from doing anything in the way of preaching to-day, but, of course, was able to sell books and post tracts. As for the former I disposed of scarcely any, there being very few people in the place.

Friday, May 9th.—It would have been little use to have stayed over another day at Ch'eng-hua on account of sore throat, hence I left for Feng-tsiang Fu this morning. I am not thinking of working the places on the way, for one should do this on another journey. Already I have been away from headquarters for nearly a month.

To-day I travelled no further than seventy *li*. On the way had to cross the K'ing river by boat—generally a difficult business, but to-day fared worse than ever before, having to wait three or four hours before the boatmen would start; for, instead of attending to their business they were all smoking opium.

Saturday, May 10th.—After a walk of forty *li*, I reached Li-ts'6en Hien, a town that Brother Redfern and I visited together a year ago. Here I got on to the main road to Lan-chau once again, at a point some eighty English miles south of where I left it ten days ago. Am still about sixty English miles from Feng-tsiang, and yet the district I have traversed this time is but a fraction of the Si-gan Plain.

Towards evening arrived at K'ien chau. These two days I have passed through some splendid villages for Gospel work, the markets every other day being crowded.

Sunday, May 11th.—A day of rest—especially so to me, for somehow I felt very wearied. Still, how much one has to praise GOD for! Have been thinking how graciously He has dealt with me since my last visit to this place twelve months ago.

Monday, May 12th.—Arose early, fresh and well after yesterday's rest. Nearly all day occupied in going to Yi-t'ien, a distance of 100 *li*. As usual, when travelling, posted tracts as I went along. Passed through two large villages on the way. I hope, GOD willing, to stay at all these places ere long, for it grieves one to pass them by. Still, one feels it desirable to make as long a stay as possible in the far away places, and to leave those nearer home for a future occasion.

Tuesday, May 13th.—After a pleasant ride of eighty *li* I reached Feng-tsiang in safety. It was good to have the society of Mr. and Mrs. Botham once again, but for all that one does not feel the loss of company when travelling alone, provided that you

MIX FREELY WITH THE CHINESE,

and aim at becoming as much like them as possible in their manners, etc. Altogether I have done some 900 odd *li*, and made a stay at six "Hiens," but as one looks at the map of this Plain, this seems very little.

I do praise GOD for His goodness to me, and look to Him to bless the seed, notwithstanding my unfaithfulness; of which, at times, I am so conscious. May the HOLY SPIRIT work mightily, and stir the dry bones? Thank GOD there are signs of blessing at Feng-tsiang, a teacher having professed a desire to know the truth whilst I have been away. Just now there is an annual idol festival being celebrated, and this man, together with two women, have refused to contribute towards it. Evidently they see the uselessness of idols. May they personally know the worth of Jesus!

There is a general feeling here in our favour, especially amongst the poorer classes. A nice number of people have been cured of opium smoking.

Two Terribly Sad Cases.

FROM MISS KOLKENBECK.

YANG-CHAU, KIANG-SU.—We had a terribly sad opium case last night A woman who had been very much tried for months at last gave way and took a dose of opium. Poor thing! one cannot wonder or think hardly of her. For months she has struggled to keep out of debt. She has a husband who is an opium smoker, and a mother who has been ill for a long time, besides children to keep. Her mother needed constant care and the poor woman did not get proper rest at night, while during the day she worked hard making shoes. She partly depended on the rent of a house that belongs to her.

Yesterday a whole year's rent was paid her, and a brother-in-law and cousin came and took all the money away. This, with other things, was too much for her. Oh, these poor Chinese women! how little we realize of their sorrows. I must add that the LORD has graciously spared this woman's life. We do not want to think lightly of the sin, but I trust it will draw out our love and sympathy for our down-trodden defenceless sisters.

To-day two women came asking for medicine. The mother of a five months old baby had given it opium for some trifling ailment in her ignorance. I knew there was no hope, but went with them to satisfy them. The child was still able to swallow, and at the mother's request I gave it a slight emetic, though I told her it was too late. Poor little creature! How my heart ached for the poor mother who had killed her child and had no hope of meeting it again. It was a real joy to be able to tell her of the GOD who loves the little ones, and to know that it was safe in His keeping. These people are utterly ignorant about illness and the care of little children; one does so long to help them, but, after all, how little one can do!

China and the Language of China.

FROM LECTURE BY PROFESSOR DOUGLAS.

FEELING that all information relative to China and its people will prove valuable and helpful to many of our readers, we have little hesitation in reprinting some extracts from a lecture by Professor Douglas at University College, on the 14th October, only regretting that exigencies of space compel us to omit much that is interesting. In connection with the existing floods a special interest attaches to what the Professor, speaking of the loess formation of North China, says concerning

CHINA'S SORROW.

Intersecting this "Garden of China," about half way between its northern and southern limits, runs the Yellow River eastward to the sea. This mighty stream has earned for itself, in consequence of the destructive floods caused by its overflowing, the melancholy title of "China's Sorrow." Its more common name is derived from the yellow colour which the loess, brought down in its current, gives to its waters.

This same loess is responsible also for the less happy title. Being light and friable, streams running through it become largely impregnated with its dust, and deposit it in great quantities in their course. The certain result of this process follows. The beds of the rivers silt up rapidly, unless by chance their streams are sufficiently strong to act as dredges. The stream of the Yellow River is not swift enough to rid itself of the evil, and the process of silting up has been undisturbed for centuries.

To meet this difficulty, the Chinese have been in the habit of doing exactly what the Italians have done in similar circumstances with the River Po, below Piacenza. Instead of dredging the bed, they have embanked its borders, and thus, as the process of silting up has gone on, the embankments have risen higher and higher, until, at the present time, the bed of the river is for a considerable part of its course above the level of the surrounding country.

The danger of this condition needs no commentary, but is illustrated with terrible frequency by the disastrous floods which periodically lay the whole of the neighbouring plain under water.

THE HIGHWAY TO SI-CH'UEN.—THE NIUKAN GORGE OF THE YANG-TSE-KIANG.

SI-CH'UEN AND YUN-NAN.

Separated from this plain on the westward by a series of mountain ranges lies SI-CH'UEN, the largest and richest province in the Empire. The position of this province is peculiar and unfortunate. On its northern, eastern, and western frontiers it is bounded by mountain ranges so lofty as to admit only of communication with the outer world by little more than bridle paths.

Happily the Yang-tse-kiang, on its southern boundary, affords a channel for conveyance of goods; but even by this means, the outer world is only to be reached by a voyage of four hundred miles over a series of foaming rapids and whirling eddies, which make the navigation a matter of infinite labour and difficulty.

To the south of SI-CH'UEN is the province of YUN-NAN, which is scarcely inferior to SI-CH'UEN in the natural products of the soil and the minerals beneath the surface. Together these provinces occupy an area as large as that of France and half of Germany added to it. They offer unusual advantages to trade, but by their geographical position they are at present isolated from the rest of the world.

For some years it has been the dream of English explorers to break through this isolation, by converting the old native trade route between Yun-nan Fu and Bhamo, in Upper Burmah, into a railroad. . . . Unfortunately for the scheme, the verdict of the late Mr. Baber and others is so conclusive as to its impracticability, except at the cost of "piercing half-a-dozen Mont Cenis tunnels and erecting a few Menai bridges," that it is now to all intents and purposes abandoned.

In lieu of it a route rather more to the south has been recently surveyed, and meanwhile Mr. Hallett has brought forward a scheme which at least presents no physical difficulties, and offers manifold mercantile advantages, by which he proposes to lead a railway from Maulmein, in Burmah, into Siam, and up the river valleys which connect Bangkok with the Shan States and the YUN-NAN frontier.

FERTILITY AND PROSPERITY OF CHINA.

From one end of the country to another the land blossoms as the rose, and yields to the diligent and careful tillage of the natives, enough and to spare of all that is necessary for the comfort and well being of man. Nor have these advantages become the recent possession of the people. For many centuries they have been in full enjoyment of them, and on every side the evidences of long-established wealth and commercial enterprise are observable.

From the great wall to the frontier of TONG-KING, and from THIBET to the China Sea the country is dotted over with rich and populous cities, which are connected one with another by well-trodden roads or water highways. In these busy centres of industry, merchants from all parts of the Empire are to be found who are as ready to deal in the fabrics of the native looms, porcelain, tea, and other native products, as in cottons, metals, and woollens of Europe.

The rivers and canals are crowded, the vessels bearing silks and satins from CHEH-KIANG and KIANG-SU, tea from GAN-HWUY and HO-NAN, and rice from the southern provinces to parts of the empire which give in exchange for such gifts the corn and other products which they are able to spare.

The Professor, remarking on their remissness in making themselves acquainted with the country, the people, and especially with the language, is pretty hard on the members of

THE BRITISH MERCANTILE COMMUNITIES.

Our merchants congregate at the ports, and trouble themselves very little about their environments. It would not be running any great risk to say that not more than one or two out of every hundred of our merchants in China would be able to name the eighteen provinces of the empire, and certainly the proportion is not larger of those who can speak intelligibly half a dozen sentences of the language.

It is deplorable to think that men should live ten, fifteen, and twenty years in a country without learning even enough of the language of the natives to converse with them. How should we regard the settlement on our shores of communities of foreign merchants, who lived apart, made no attempt to learn our language, and conversed only with those of their underlings who could talk a broken jargon vaguely related to the language of the settlers? No bond of union could exist between them and the people of the country. They would be regarded as outer strangers, and if in any outbreak of fanaticism they were attacked and their goods despoiled they would get little sympathy from the people at large.

It has always been their custom to depend on their "pidgin-English" speaking compradores and servants in their intercourse with the people, and they find it difficult to break through their habit. This was all very well when, practically, they had no competitors in the trade. But in the last quarter of a century a complete change has come over the commercial balance, and the result of our obstinate refusal to keep abreast of the times has resulted in the fact, that while the foreign trade with China has steadily increased, our share in it has diminished.

It is not easy for us in Western lands thoroughly to appreciate the difficulties which lie in the way of progress, in our sense of the term, in China—a land hoary with antiquity, rooted in habits and customs unchanged for many centuries, and conservative to the last degree, and whose contact with Western nations has not been of a nature to encourage unrestricted intercourse or a liberal foreign policy. Hence the jealousy with which the admission of every thin-edged wedge is guarded. Even in England, we, who boast ourselves as a progressive, civilised and civilising nation, can but smile at the crass ignorance of our own fathers and grandfathers. Hear what Professor Douglas says on

THE ATTITUDE OF THE CHINESE TOWARDS INNOVATIONS.

The attitude of the Chinese towards innovations of steamers and railways is exactly that taken up by the last generation of Englishmen when first the introduction of railways was discussed in this country. Speaking to the House of Commons on this point, Sir Isaac Coffin said:—

"What, I should like to know, was to be done with all those who have advanced money in making and repairing turnpike-roads? What with those who may still wish to travel in their own or hired carriages, after the fashion of their forefathers? What was to become of coach-makers and harness-makers, coach-masters and coachmen, inn-keepers, horse breeders, and horse dealers? Was the House aware of the smoke and the noise, the hiss and the whirl, which locomotive-engines passing at the rate of ten or twelve miles an hour would occasion? Neither the cattle ploughing in the fields or grazing in the meadows would behold them without dismay. Iron would be raised in price 100 per cent, or more probably exhausted altogether. It would be the greatest nuisance, the most complete disturbance of quiet and comfort in all parts of the kingdom, that the ingenuity of man could invent!"

These are, with some slight modifications, the arguments which are used at the present day in China by the opponents of steam. And it must be remembered that though nominally a despotism, there is a large democratic element in the government of the empire.

Finally, after tracing the probable origin and history of the language, the Professor passes on to consider it as it exists at the present day.

THE LANGUAGE OF CHINA.

In Chinese the subject precedes the verb, the adjective precedes the substantive it modifies, and when two substantives come together the first is in the possessive case. The written language is monosyllabic, but not so the colloquial, which has become diffuse in consequence of the necessity arising from the difficulty of making orally intelligible the single words which are sufficiently plain to the eye by aid of the ideographic characters.

Like many other languages, Chinese has suffered loss through phonetic decay, and it is poverty-stricken in a grammatical sense. It is uninflected and only shows slight signs of agglutination. There is very little therefore, to mark the grammatical value of a word except its position in a sentence, since very few words belong absolutely to any one part of speech. The result is that the same word is often capable of playing the part of a substantive, an adjective, a verb, or an adverb. But when this is so, it sometimes happens that the transition from one part of speech to another is indicated by a change of tone in the pronunciation.

The tones are not fixed quantities. They vary considerably in different parts of the empire, from sixteen in some of the southern dialects to five in the Mandarin; and words are further constantly being transferred from one tone to another in obedience to the laws of popular phoneticism. Whatever may have been the origin of these tones, they play a very important part in making Chinese colloquially intelligible. In the Mandarin dialect, which is the most generally spoken dialect in China, there are only about 532 syllables, which are represented by the 12,000 or 15,000 characters commonly found in the dictionaries.

It is obvious that with so small a number of sounds to express vocally so large a number of words confusion must inevitably arise. And so it often does, though the introduction of the tones has served to mitigate the evil by giving generally each syllable five different vocalisations. Being an uninflected language, the cases of nouns and the tenses of verbs are either indicated by position in the sentence or by the addition of prefixes or suffixes to the original words, which do not undergo any inherent change whatever. As in the Accadian, there is an absence of any distinction between the masculine and feminine genders, and the plural is commonly only indirectly pointed out.

On paper the language is represented by characters which may be classed as hieroglyphics, ideograms, and phonetics. The hieroglyphics are the primitive characters of the language, and were originally drawings of the objects which they were intended to represent, though now, through the changes which have taken place in the form of the characters, it is often difficult to recognise the originals. It will easily be understood that these hieroglyphic characters soon proved insufficient for the literary needs of the people, and hence the practice grew up of combining two or more hieroglyphics to express an idea. Thus, for example, the character representing the sun placed above a straight line stands for the dawn, and one representing the sun shining through a tree for the east. Again, the characters for "a man" and "words," associated together, represent the word meaning "sincere," and the sun and moon, placed side by side the word for "brightness." But by far the largest number of characters are phonetics—that is to say, certain characters, about 1,600 in all, are used as phonograms, with or without reference to their own particular meanings.

According to Chinese records, the original characters numbered about 540, the Accadians are said to have had about the same number of primitives. These characters would at first represent so many words, but as time went on it would become necessary to associate derived meanings with these words, and to indicate on paper the particular sense in which the writer intended them to be understood. This would be done by the addition of determinatives or classifiers as they are sometimes called.

By means of their three classes of characters, the hieroglyphics, ideograms, and phonetics, the Chinese have been able to express and preserve the thoughts and sayings of their greatest and wisest writers, through a series of centuries which dwarfs into insignificance all Western ideas of antiquity. For thirty centuries, Chinamen have been accumulating stores of literary wealth, which are of themselves sufficiently important to attract the attention of scholars, and to stir the literary ambition of students, and which do so in almost every country but England. But by the fresh discoveries of Messrs. de Lacouperie and Ball, not only is a new interest added to the language, but it is brought into close and intimate relation with the tongues spoken by the great civilising nations of the world.

An Eclipse.

FROM MISS JOHNSON.

HAN-CHUNG, SHEN-SI, *June 19th.*—Last Monday there was a grand eclipse of the sun. More than half the orb was obscured, leaving a brilliant crescent. There was great excitement among the natives; gongs and drums were beaten furiously, and bells rung incessantly; crackers were let off everywhere, and guns were fired in the direction of the phenomenon. The priests were busy in the temple burning incense and worshipping. Everywhere there was commotion and alarm, and all for what reason? The heavenly dog was eating the sun, and unless prevented by these means, he would soon finish it! In the meantime the shadow grew gradually less and less, and after the sun had sunk behind the glorious range of dark blue hills in the west, it had almost disappeared. The gongs, drums, guns and crackers ceased; the priests no longer chanted; all was quiet in the temples and nothing but a little black ash from the burnt paper here and there was left to tell the tale. The natives heaved a sigh of relief and went about their usual work; their efforts had been successful, the dog was beaten off, and the sun preserved to ripen the coming harvest!

Oh that the "Sun of Righteousness" would shine into these dark hearts and dispel the gloom of superstition and idolatry with His bright beams! These people seem to be wholly given up to idolatry except (bless the LORD for this glorious exception!) those upon whom the "Sun of Righteousness" has "arisen with healing in His wings" —now a goodly company.

Six Months' Work at Ts'in-chau.

FROM REV. H. W. HUNT.

TS'IN-CHAU, KAN-SUH.—Half-yearly letter to July.—We praise GOD for all the victory He has given us, and will continue to give. In January two men and three women were baptised, and in June three more men and two more women. But in January and in June, one man and three women were excluded or suspended by the Church for their inconsistent lives....

The second man received this year is Mr. Huang. He is the last converted of a family of five, one of whom has already gone to heaven. His wife was led to our services simply by an invitation given by Mrs. Hunt in passing through her village, some forty miles from our station. Being a woman of character it was not long before she influenced for good not only her home circle, but also others who have been subsequently received, among whom is the most valuable voluntary female worker we have now in the Church. Mr. Huang held out a long time against his wife's exhortations and prayers, especially as his only and much-loved son died shortly after being received into the Church, the neighbours saying it was because he had followed the strange doctrine of the foreigners. But now he has come out, he is bright and true, and shows no little discernment at both Bible and Church meetings....

We now have the blind, the deaf, and partially insane among those who have discovered riches in CHRIST, and presently shall probably have the lame, too. Verily "to the *poor* the Gospel is preached," and GOD does choose the foolish, the weak, the base, and the things that are despised, that He may get the greater glory thereby. We are favoured here by having one after another in several families getting converted, so that soon we may be able to point to about half-a-dozen entire families having turned unto the LORD. How much easier this makes it for them, and how much harder for the evil one! Praise be unto GOD for all His benefits!

May there be many more such converted families! The man who was excluded, was so for habitual Sabbath-breaking, having shown ever since his reception that he entered the church from unworthy motives. The three women who were suspended have since sincerely repented, and two have been restored; but one is to give longer evidence of true repentance before it may be considered safe for her again to come to the LORD'S Table. A man formerly suspended for poppy-growing and opium-smoking was restored on full proof of a true repentance after a severe sickness and chastening at GOD'S hands.

A decided forward movement in the Church here has been the freewill offerings of the converts for poor and expenses, these being dropped into a box placed in front of the platform for that purpose. They are taught that all members should give, if it be ever so little, and it is touching to see some of the poorest drop in their mite.

A Wednesday evening Bible-class for men has been started, and is bringing some of the converts along into greater light and knowledge. Would that the LORD would take hold of some of them mightily by His SPIRIT, and send them forth as voluntary and powerful witnesses for Him.

If we want anything in China it is unpaid native helpers who will preach the Word and live in accordance with its precepts. Let us pray continually for this, for nothing else can take its place.

In the Boys' and Girls' Schools the children are confined to the reading of Christian books, which they learn by heart. One of the ladies takes a Bible-class for the girls every day; while I enjoy an hour or more of Bible-teaching and geography, a hymn and prayer with the boys each day that I have opportunity. We are sure you will join us in prayer that these young hearts may be converted to JESUS now, and then how different from the surrounding heathen will their lives be hereafter.

Breaking New Ground.

FROM MR. W. S. HORNE.

KAN-CHAU FU, SOUTH KIANG-SI, *July 17th.*—The dear LORD JESUS is blessing us here. Our teacher named Chang, a man for whom I have asked your prayers, quite broke down this morning at worship, as he prayed for himself and family. The LORD is certainly answering prayer, and the work is growing. We might easily burden ourselves with it, but the work is all our MASTER'S and we burden Him with all its care, for "He careth for" us.

This afternoon we had a splendid time on the street. Preached in front of the Yamens of the Prefect and Tao-tai (intendant of circuit). Another gracious time at evening worship; truly "all the way 'long it is JESUS."

July 18th.—This morning Mr. Meikle and our boy set out to hunt up a man who had manifested an interest in the Gospel. But he and all the others of the village were most frightened. He was specially afraid of persecution. We have glorious times at our evening and morning meetings. The LORD led a man in to see us from HU-NAN. He was much surprised to hear that all his gods are false, and also the name O-mi-t'o Fuh (Amidha Buddha) he trusted in. The LORD helped me in telling him that JESUS is the sinner's Friend, and that there is "none other Name under heaven given among men, whereby we must be saved."

July 19th.—The man from the south gate, named Lin, is growing daily in grace and in the knowledge of GOD. He speaks of real fights with the enemy, when he either quotes GOD'S Word, or gets his Testament, and reads to him what he is, and thus puts the wicked one to flight.

July 20th.—A blessed happy day's service for the LORD, and His own day, too! At morning service we had quite a number who listened attentively. In the street we spoke just in front of a temple in which a play was going on for the pleasure of the gods. The people came out and crowded round us so much that it was difficult to make oneself heard; however, the LORD was with us to help.

July 21st.—Some who had heard us on the street called this morning, to our great joy, to make further enquiries. All our preaching efforts on the streets may not have much effect, but if we can only stir them up to come and see us we have the opportunity of speaking right to their hearts.

July 22nd.—For the past few days the talk of the city has been the changes among the officials. The Tao-tai (the highest official) has been carried off by death. The Hien (magistrate) has been requested to retire by reason of age. The late Tao-tai was not in favour of the foreigner, and the Hien got men, some years ago, to raze the Roman Catholic chapel. The coming Tao-tai wanted this old man to indemnify the Catholics, but he refused. The official who takes the place of the retiring magistrate is favourable. He comes to this city from Kih-gan Prefecture. We cannot tell what these changes may mean for us, but we do know that "all things work together for good." Spoke in front of an ancestral hall, but were stopped by rain. Sold a few books.

July 23rd.—While speaking on the east-gate street the rain seemed likely to stop us, but an old house, with two sides open and a good roof, provided a free chapel. The people crowded in and listened well. A number of country folk bought books.

July 24th.—The days go by all too quickly. The people we spoke to to-day were inclined to be rough and made so much noise that we had to leave. We need your prayers that we may be so filled with the HOLY SPIRIT that these men will be compelled to listen.

July 26th.—We had two fresh hearers this morning at worship. All listened attentively, and we had a happy time. No sooner had we finished than men sent by the officials poured in; and finally an official of low rank appeared

ON THE STREET.

in person to ask us to leave the city. They are exceedingly anxious for us to get away before the new officials come. Pray for us!

We have been tried in every way. Some want to follow us and "eat our rice," others want to be bought into the doctrine. Without, wild rumours are afloat. "There are over one hundred foreigners who are plotting insurrection in the city!" they say. How they do fear two little fellows! How little they understand our mission! If it please the LORD to give us an open door here, we shall need your prayers that we may be able to make the message clear.

July 28th.—The official runners were about early urging the landlord to get us out; fortunately, he does not fear them much. In the midst of all the uproar the LORD JESUS is giving us encouragement. A young man wants to know how to get to heaven. He sat a good part of the afternoon listening to the Gospel, and came to evening worship. He says his parents are willing for him to come here. We have had many more blessed opportunities of preaching JESUS. The Gospel never was, and never will be, preached in vain. This is our encouragement. During the past few days, and in the present trying time, I have realised, as never before, such joy and peace.

Blessed, happy service, "till He come!" [It will be seen from Mr. Stevenson's notes that our brethren have since had to leave this city.]

Tidings from Scattered Workers.

Shen-si Province.
FROM MISS E. M. JOHNSON.

Han-chung, June 12th.—We have gained permission to build a small house in Pah-ko-shan, a lovely mountainous place, about seventy *li* away. Here we hope to be able to go now and then to recruit.

I have heard some very cheering news. About the beginning of last year a poor, ragged, neglected child of thirteen was brought here by my teacher, rescued by the efforts of one of our Missionaries from a wretched home into which she had been sold by her parents. She lived here a few months, being washed, dressed and cared for, and taught from the Scriptures. She was very quick in learning characters, drank in the Gospel eagerly, and committed the whole of Matthew x. to memory.

After a while her father came and fetched her away to his own home in Si-ch'uen. She was so transformed from what she had been that one would scarcely have recognised her as the same child. Since then I have heard that she is a bright, happy Christian, and not only prays from a full heart herself, but has taught her little brothers and sisters to pray too. My heart is so full of thanksgiving, for I grew to be so fond of the dear child, and did so long that the Good Shepherd might find her and bring her into the safety of His happy fold.

Ho-nan Province.

FROM MR. D. J. MILLS.

Chau-kia-k'eo, Aug. 12th.—Mr. Hogg and I have sought to go out on the streets here each day, and we have at times been much encouraged by our experiences. I hope soon to resume my itinerant work in the more distant parts of the province.

Mr. Hogg and Mr. Gracie have arranged to take up the systematic visiting of places more in the immediate vicinity, and Mr. Shearer, I believe, is also ready to help in this most important work if needful, so it seems that I am free to visit "the Regions Beyond," and Mr. Coulthard seems to approve of this arrangement.

Mr. Slimmon and Mr. Shearer left this a week ago for Fanch'eng (HU-PEH), so I am now alone on the north side of the river.

The meetings here each evening are still very encouraging, Every day I get a large number of patients—simple cases, coming for medicine—each one, of course, an opportunity for showing kindly sympathy and for telling out something of the truth of the Gospel. Our responsibility to preach it far and wide is not lessened by the fact that there seems such determined opposition to keep us from opening fresh stations.

Si-ch'uen Province.

FROM DR. PARRY.

Chen-tu, July 30th.—I am very glad to be able, by GOD's goodness, to be writing you once more from our own home, good tidings of the work.

This evening we have had a service of baptism, in which two persons were received, one Hwo Ta-yie, a quiet elderly man who is a mandarin's servant; the other, Yang Ta-niang, the wife of Yang the cloth-seller who was received last year. We have good hope and confidence that these two are true and humble Christians; and I am glad to say that both are the fruits of the efforts of an old Christian man, Wa, and his late wife (the Bible-woman —now asleep in JESUS).

Mr. Wa's son was received early this year, and now both his younger son and son-in-law are, I believe, decided in the desire to be Christians. We do rejoice to see young life coming into the Church.

There are besides these some twenty persons whose names are before us as enquirers and candidates. We ask prayer for each of them that, though there is perhaps a good deal of rather unpromising raw material among them, yet the HOLY SPIRIT will graciously take hold of each for the kingdom and glorify our SAVIOUR. These, of course, are not inclusive of the outstation enquirers of whom Mei-chau, we hear, has enrolled four.

As you will have heard, the Owens and Miss Webb have gone to the mountains. We have not had time, as yet, to hear of their safe arrival at Mio-chau.

We are praying that they may find some opening for establishing communications with the Man-tsi.

Aug. 8th.—We have had the joy of gathering the first-fruits of the Mei-chau work in the baptism of a Hwang Ta-yie, a country doctor, who has been a steady enquirer for half a year, and shows a very clear grasp of the Truth and evident spiritual appreciation that cheered me much. He came up here with the evangelist and requested baptism.

With him we also had the pleasure of baptizing the younger son of Mr. Wu (before mentioned), so that now the father and two sons are all decided Christians. Again we can say Hallelujah!

FROM MISS E. CULVERWELL.

Kwang-yuen, July 30th.—I know you will be glad to hear of the LORD's goodness to us, and be joining us in praise to our Almighty GOD for keeping us in safety and letting us live in peace for one year in this place. It was with hearts full of thankfulness that we commenced our second year on Tuesday last, the 28th.

As we look back and see how kwans (officials), unprincipled landlords, and others, have all been quieted, and the fear of us removed, how can we but praise. Theo, for a friendly spirit on the part of the women, and, more, for a nice number that come to the Sunday class, we are deeply thankful. I feel sure that the LORD has among their number some of His chosen ones.

I have been to T'ao-ning, and had a very happy time there, Miss F. M. Williams came up with me for rest and change.

FROM MISS F. H. CULVERWELL.

Aug. 10th.—The work here is encouraging. There are many villages on the other side of the river, for which we have been praying much, and now my sister has had such a warm welcome. At first there was coldness, and the people seemed too busy or frightened to take any notice; but it was different the second time. We do praise the LORD for this answer to prayer.

There are no definite conversions to tell of yet, but we believe that some of the women who have been attending the class regularly are not far from the Kingdom. Some, too, who were very opposed at the beginning are now not only coming themselves, but seek to bring others.

We are still four here. Miss Bastone and Miss Martin had hoped to have gone to Chao-hwa in the autumn to live, but it will not be for more than a short stay in an inn, as no house has yet been obtained; we, too, are in no hurry to lose them. We are greatly privileged to be four friends together.

Kiang-si Province.

FROM MISS ORD.

Nan-Kang Fu, June 6th.—On May 13th Miss Gillham and I went itinerating by boat, returning on the 24th. We sailed slowly along the shores of the lake as far as Ta-ku-t'ang, stopping wherever we saw a house and then walking into the country. We spent five days in this way, and the LORD gave us much encouragement. In most houses they heard for the first time and listened well; on the edge of the lake many had heard before.

On the Saturday we reached Ta-ku-t'aug, intending to start on Monday for Hu-k'eo, but a strong north wind prevented our moving till Tuesday afternoon, and then the following morning we were literally blown across the lake, and had to anchor where we best could. We had a most delightful time going from house to house; none of these people had ever heard before. There were some very interesting cases.

The head man of a village, quite elderly, listened most attentively, bought a copy of each of the Gospels, besides tracts, asked how he was to pray, said he knew he had sin, and, being asked if he were willing to believe in JESUS, said, "Why should I not be willing? I never heard before; how could I believe?" We were there quite a long time.

A little further we had quite an open-air meeting—all women —under some trees; they could not understand me, but our boy preached beautifully to them. In another place we went into a school, and all the village came in to hear; the teacher would have nothing to say to us, but in the afternoon we met him again and he bought three books.

The same afternoon we went to see an old man, very poor and very ill. He listened so eagerly, and said he knew he had sin; he cried and was quite willing to be prayed with, asking to be taught a prayer. Our boy says he is sure we shall see that old man in heaven.

In another house there was such a dear woman, very ill; there was a student there, her brother-in-law, I think, who was up for examination in Nan-k'ang when our houses were destroyed, and had heard the Gospel in our hall, and had told her about GOD not requiring us to burn incense, etc., but to believe in our hearts. We prayed with her, and stayed some time; she was so affectionate, and begged us to come soon again.

I feel so strongly that unless we go to them, these poor women have no chance of hearing, as they rarely leave their homes. The opposite side of the lake is much laid on my heart; there seems to be no large towns along the coast between Hu-k'eo and Tu-chang, but innumerable villages and clusters of houses; the people, too, with a few exceptions, most friendly.

Gan-hwuy Province.

FROM MR. DRYSDALE.

Luh-gan, Aug. 4th.—The work here is delightful and refreshing, so different to Cheng-yang-kwan. We had large numbers yesterday, and good services forenoon and evening. This morning we opened the door at ten o'clock, and had many hearers, Bro. Reid and myself taking turns in speaking to them. All who come are most pleasant, and listen well.

This afternoon the teacher informed me that a young man wanted to converse with me. I went to his room, and found him really anxious; he desired me to pray with him. This is the only one amongst the Chinese that I have met with who is apparently concerned about his soul. May the LORD bless him!

"Other Sheep I Have."
(John x. 16.)

HARK! 'tis the LORD who calls;
  Saved one, He speaks to thee:—
I shed My precious blood
  That thou mightst rescued be;
And now, rejoicing in My love,
  Thou'rt journeying to the Home above.

But "other sheep I have,"
  Who're wandering from the fold;
And how to enter in
  They never have been told:
Oh, canst thou leave them still to roam?
Wilt *thou* not seek to lead them home?

Thousands of precious souls,
  In regions far away,
For want of what *thou* hast
  Are dying day by day.
Wilt thou not take the Living Bread,
And let these starving ones be fed?

'Neath Satan's galling yoke
  They struggle all in vain;
Oh! must they still in sin
  And ignorance remain?
Canst thou their silent plea withstand,
And not stretch out thy helping hand?

Think, think what it would be
  If thou wert in their place,
With none at hand to care
  Or undertake thy case.
What if without one pitying eye
Thy soul had thus been left to die!

What if thou ne'er hadst known
  Of My redeeming love,
And so no peace were thine,
  Nor hope of joys above!
Oh, think of what thou owest Me;
Then surely thou "constrained" wilt be.

—My SAVIOUR and my LORD,
  Before Thy feet I fall;
Unworthy is the gift,
  But, oh, accept *my all.*
Send me wherever Thou dost choose,
And deign *Thyself* my life to use.—C. P. C.

Departures and Arrivals.

AS anticipated in our last, Mrs. HUDSON TAYLOR sailed on the 30th October for Shanghai accompanied by three young sisters, Misses F. E. MARLER, E. TANNER, and F. T. FOWLE. Mrs. TAYLOR hopes to meet Mr. Taylor at Hong-kong as he returns to Shanghai from Australasia, and proceed with him. For all these, for those who have preceded them this autumn, as already announced, and for the following we ask the prayers of our friends; and that Mrs. Taylor's presence may be a strength, help, and comfort to her husband in his many claims and labours.

In October, by German mail steamer, Messrs. EM. OHLSEN, N. CARLSON, JOS. BENDER, and Misses BÄUMER and SCHNÜTGEN, of the German Alliance Mission, as Associates of the C.I.M.

On October 30th, per s.s. *Abyssinia*, from Vancouver (sent by Council for North America), Messrs. A. E. THOR, J. E. DUFF, A. W. LAGERQUIST, G. MARSHALL, and W. TAYLOR.

To leave on November 13th, per P. and O. s.s. *Coromandel*, Miss EMMELINE TURNER (returning) and Misses E. S. POOK, BERTHA PORTER, ELSIE A. MAY, SUSIE RAYER and F. R. SAUZE.

To leave on November 27th, per P. and O. s.s. *Chusan*, Messrs. H. E. FOUCAR, W. T. GILMER, and GEO. PRENTICE.

We omitted last month to notify the arrival in England of Mr. and Mrs. ORR EWING, on 27th Sept., *via* America. We hear that Mr. and Mrs. BURNETT left Shanghai per *Peshawur*, on 27th Sept., due in London 12th Nov.; also Mrs. CHENEY and Miss H. JUDD were to leave on 11th Oct., due on 26th Nov.

Missionaries of the China Inland Mission.

Date of Arrival.

1854.
J. HUDSON TAYLOR, Director.
Mrs. HUDSON TAYLOR (1866).

1862.
JAMES MEADOWS.
Mrs. MEADOWS (1866).

1866.
J. W. STEVENSON.
Mrs. STEVENSON.
 . WILLIAMSON.
Mrs. WILLIAMSON (1875).
W. D. RUDLAND.
Mrs. RUDLAND (1875).

1867.
JOHN MCCARTHY.
Mrs. MCCARTHY.

1868.
J. E. CARDWELL.
Mrs. CARDWELL.
CHARLES H. JUDD.
Mrs. JUDD.

1870.
Mrs. STOTT.

1872.
Miss E. TURNER.

1873.
FREDK. W. BALLER.
Mrs. BALLER (1866).
BENJ. BAGNALL.
Mrs. BAGNALL (1880).

1874.
A. W. DOUTHWAITE, M.D (U.S.A.)
Mrs. DOUTHWAITE (1887).

1875.
GEORGE KING.
Mrs. KING (1883).
J. CAMERON, M.D. (U.S.A.)
Mrs. CAMERON) 1883).
GEORGE NICOLL.
Mrs. NICOLL (1879).
G. W. CLARKE.

Mrs. G. W. CLARKE (1880).
J. F. BROUMTON.
Mrs. BROUMTON (1879).
G. F. EASTON.
Mrs. EASTON (1881).

1876.
EDWARD PEARSE.
Mrs. PEARSE (1875).
GEORGE PARKER.
Mrs. PARKER (1880).
HORACE A. RANDLE, M.D. (U.S.A.)
Mrs. RANDLE (1878).
Miss HORNE.

1878.
SAMUEL R. CLARKE.
Mrs. S. R. CLARKE.
FRANK TRENCH.

1879.
EDWARD TOMALIN.
Mrs. TOMALIN (1866).
JOHN J. COULTHARD.
Mrs. COULTHARD (1884).
HENRY W. HUNT.
Mrs. HUNT (1878).

1880.
W. L. PRUEN, L.R.C.P. & s.
Mrs. PRUEN (1876).
Mrs. SCHOFIELD.

1881.
WILLIAM COOPER.
Mrs. COOPER (1888).
DAVID THOMPSON.
Mrs. THOMPSON (1883).
ARTHUR EASON.
Mrs. EASON.
GEORGE ANDREW.
Mrs. ANDREW (1882).
H. HUDSON TAYLOR.
Mrs. H. H. TAYLOR (1884).

1882.
E. H. EDWARDS, M.B., C.M.
Mrs. EDWARDS.
W. WILSON, M.B., C.M.
Mrs. WILSON (1883).
Mrs. ELLISTON.

1883.
Miss S. CARPENTER.

FREDK. A. STEVEN.
Mrs. STEVEN (1886).
F. MARCUS WOOD.
Mrs. WOOD.
OWEN STEVENSON.
Miss J. BLACK.
W. E. BURNETT.
Mrs. BURNETT (1881).
Miss S. SEED.

1884.
A. LANGMAN.
Mrs. LANGMAN.
THOMAS H. KING.
Mrs. KING (1888).
WILLIAM KEY.
Mrs. W. KEY.
Miss WHITCHURCH.
Mrs. CHENEY.
THOMAS WINDSOR.
Miss EMILY BLACK.
Miss EMILY FOSBERY.
CHAS. F. HOGG.
Mrs. HOGG (1883).
J. MCMULLAN.
Mrs. MCMULLAN (1885).
J. A. SLIMMON.
Miss MARY BLACK.
Miss ANNIE R. TAYLOR.
H. PARRY, L.R.C.P., M.R.C.S.
Mrs. PARRY.
Miss A. G. BROOMHALL.
A. HUDSON BROOMHALL.
Mrs. A. H. BROOMHALL (1887).
Miss MARIA BYRON.
DUNCAN KAY.
Mrs. DUNCAN KAY.
GEORGE MILLER.
Mrs. MILLER (1887).
W. FYFE LAUGHTON.
Mrs. LAUGHTON (1885).
STEWART MCKEE.
Mrs. MCKEE (1887).
THOMAS HUTTON.
Mrs. HUTTON (1885).
CHARLES HORODIN.
JOHN REID.
ALBERT PHELPS.
Miss C. K. MURRAY.
Miss M. MURRAY.
Miss MACKINTOSH.
Miss AGNES GIBSON.
Miss MCFARLANE.
Miss ELIZABETH WEBB.

1885.
F. T. FOUCAR.

T. JAMES.
Mrs. JAMES (1882).
JOHN SMITH.
Mrs. JOHN SMITH (1887).
W. J. LEWIS.
Mrs. LEWIS (1886).
STANLEY P. SMITH, B.A.
Mrs. STANLEY P. SMITH (1886).
W. W. CASSELS, B.A.
Mrs. CASSELS (1886).
D. E. HOSTE.
M. BEAUCHAMP, B.A.
C. H. POLHILL-TURNER.
Mrs. C. H. POLHILL-TURNER (1884).
A.T.POLHILL-TURNER, B.A.
Mrs. A. T. POLHILL-TURNER (1884).
F. W. K. GULSTON.
Mrs. GULSTON (1882).
RICHARD GRAY-OWEN.
Mrs. GRAY-OWEN (1883).
T. E. S. BOTHAM.
Mrs. BOTHAM (1884).
W. T. BEYNON.
Mrs. BEYNON (1886).
Miss JENNIE WEBB.
Miss JANE STEVENS.
W. HOPE GILL.
D. M. ROBERTSON.
J. A. HEAL.
Mrs. HEAL (1883).
R. GRIERSON.
Mrs. GRIERSON.
M. HARRISON.
T. G. Vanstone.*
Mrs. Vanstone (1887).*
S. T. Thorne.*
Mrs Thorne (1883).*

1886.
Miss J. D. ROBERTSON.
Miss L. E. HIBBERD.
Miss S. E. JONES.
Miss C. P. CLARK.
Miss A. S. JAKOBSEN.
Miss F. R. KINAHAN.
Miss C. LITTLER.
Miss ANNIE SAY.
ARCH. ORR EWING.
Mrs. ORR EWING (1887).
GEO. GRAHAM BROWN.
Mrs. GRAHAM BROWN.
ANDREW WRIGHT.
J. C. STEWART, M.D. (U.S.A.)

1887.

FRANK MCCARTHY.
JOHN BROCK.
WM. RUSSELL.
JOHN DARROCH.
Miss G. M. MUIR.
Miss E. J. BURROUGHES.
Miss F. M. BRITTON.
Miss EMILY M. JOHNSON.
Miss ANNIE MCQUILLAN.
Miss CAROLINE GATES.
Miss J. A. MILLER.
Miss ELLA WEBBER.
ALEX. ARMSTRONG, F.E.I.S.
Mrs. ARMSTRONG.
Miss HARRIET A. JUDD.
Miss EMMA CULVERWELL.
Miss L. M. FORTH.
A. HODDLE.
J. O. CURNOW.
Mrs. CURNOW (1888).
A. H. FAERS.
I. F. DRYSDALE.
D. J. MILLS.
JAS. ADAM.
ARCH. GRACIE.
Mrs. GRACIE.
ED. TOMKINSON.
Mrs. TOMKINSON.
Miss E. MAUD HOLME.
Miss A. K. FERRIMAN.
Miss S. E. BASTONE.
Miss A. K. HOOK.
Miss EMMA FRYER.
H. N. MACGREGOR.
J. A. STOOKE.
Mrs. STOOKE.
A. EWING.
D. LAWSON.
Mrs. LAWSON (1888).
A. H. HUNTLEY.
Mrs. HUNTLEY (1888).
Miss FLORENCE ELLIS.
Miss CLARA ELLIS.
Miss WILLIAMSON.
Miss M. PALMER.
Miss E. HAINGE.
Miss E. MARCHBANK.
Miss I. W. RAMSAY.
Miss GERTRUDE ORD.
B. RIGE.
F. A. REDFERN.
E. WELLWOOD.
A. R. SAUNDERS.
A. BLAND.
C. S. L'ANSON.
A. LUTLEY.
JOS. VALE.

B. CURTIS WATERS.
Erik Folke.†
Mrs. Folke (1888).†
F. Dymond.*
S. Pollard.*

1888.

Miss M. GRAHAM BROWN.
Miss F. M. WILLIAMS.
Miss E. KENTFIELD.
W. G. PEAT.
W. M. BELCHER.
A. H. BRIDGE.
EDE MURRAY.
GEO. A. COX, L.R.C.P. & S.
Miss F. CAMPBELL.
Miss E. HANBURY.
J. T. REID.
Mrs. REID.
Miss ROBINA CREWDSON.
Miss J. SUTHERLAND.
W. E. SHEARER.
T. D. BEGG.
THOS. EYRES.
JAMES SIMPSON.
Mrs. SIMPSON.
Miss BAKER.
Miss R. L. SMALLEY.
Miss SANDERSON.
Miss M. G. GUINNESS.
Miss MARY REED.
Miss MALIN.
Miss LUCAS.
Miss GRACE IRVIN.
Miss CASSIE FITZSIMONS.
Miss JEANNIE MONRO.
Miss J. D. GARDINER.
Miss HATTIE TURNER.
Miss REBECCA MCKENZIE.
Miss HORSBURGH.
WM. S. HORNE.
JOHN MEIKLE.
GEO. H. DUFF.
JAS. LAWSON.
Miss THOMAS.
Miss J. BANGERT.
Miss C. L. WILLIAMS.
Miss E. E. BROOMHALL.
Miss M. J. UNDERWOOD.
Miss ELLEN BRADFIELD.
Miss SARAH YOAK.
Miss MAGGIE STEWART.
Miss BESSIE HARDING.

1889.

M. MCNAIR.
A. DUFFY.
C. A. EWBANK.

Miss H. MCKENZIE.
Miss E. A. GRABHAM.
Miss LILY S. OLDING.
J. N. HAYWARD.
E. HUNT.
H. N. LACHLAN, M.A.
THOS. SELKIRK.
E. J. COOPER.
THOS. MACOUN.
E. O. WILLIAMS, M.A.
Mrs. WILLIAMS.
Miss P. A. BARCLAY.
Miss FLORENCE BARCLAY.
Miss NELLIE MARTIN.
Miss JESSIE BUCHAN.
Miss R. E. OAKESHOTT.
Miss F. H. CULVERWELL.
Miss H. STEDMAN.
Miss MARIE GUEX.
M. HARDMAN.
J. S. ROUGH.
J. J. P. EGERTON.
G. A. HUNTLEY.
J. S. DONALD.
M. L. GRIFFITH.
Miss E. M. S. ANDERSON.
Miss E. E. CLARE.
Miss F. E. DOGGETT.
Miss ALICE GILLHAM.
Miss H. M. KOLKENBECK.
Miss I. A. YOUNG.
H. A. C. ALLEN.
H. J. ALTY.
JNO. ANDERSON.
FRANCIS DICKIE.
ADAM GRAINGER.
J. C. HALL.
JAMES STARK.
Miss L. COWLEY.
Miss A. M. ESAM.
Miss MAY LANE.
Miss ELIZA RAMSAY.
Miss A. BARDSLEY.
Miss R. G. BROMAN.
Miss J. F. HOSKYN.
Miss A. WHITFORD.
Miss I. A. SMITH.
Miss E. A. THIRGOOD.
C. H. Tjäder.†
Miss Halin.†
G. N. Hunter.
Miss L. Carlyle.

1890.

GEO. HUNTER.
Mrs. HUNTER.
A. E. EVANS.
T. G. WILLETT.

Miss MAUDE FAIRBANK.
Miss THERESA MILLER.
Miss ISABELLA ROSS.
Miss M. H. SCOTT.
Miss T. J. SCOTT.
Miss E. G. LEGERTON.
Miss BESSIE LEGGATT.
Miss M. J. BURT.
F. HOWARD TAYLOR, M.D.
JOHN GRAHAM. [etc.
GEO. MCCONNELL.
Miss ROSE A. POWER.
Miss L. J. KAY.
E. M. MCBRIER.
CHARLES PARSONS.
Miss ANNA M. LANG.
Miss R. F. BASSNETT.
Miss S. QUERRY.
Miss IDA W. ROBERTS.
Miss JANE STEDMAN.
Miss F. M. REID, L.L.A.
MARSHALL BROOMHALL.
J. G. CORMACK, [D.A.
T. W. M. GOODALL.
H. FRENCH RIDLEY.
JOHN TALBOT.
J. E. WILLIAMS, L.R.C.P.,
Miss F. E. MARLER. [etc.
Miss E. TANNER.
Miss F. T. FOWLE.
A. E. THOR.
J. E. DUFF.
A. W. LAGERQUIST.
G. MARSHALL.
WM. TAYLOR.
Miss E. S. POOK.
Miss BERTHA PORTER.
Miss ELSIE A. MAY.
Miss SUSIE RAYER.
Miss F. R. SAUZE.
Wm. Tremberth.*
Miss Hultrom.‡
Miss Janzon.†
Miss Prytz.†
Miss P. Nøss.‡
Miss Holt.‡
Miss L. Crandall.
A. Berg.†
A. Hahne.†
S. Gjerde.‡
Em. Ohlson.§
N. Carlson.§
Jos. Bender.§
Miss Bäumer.§
Miss Schnütgen.§

The Names of the Associates are printed in Italic type.   * *Bible Christian Mission.*
† *Swedish Mission in China.*   ‡ *Norwegian Missions.*   § *German Alliance Mission.*

Third Edition, making 20th Thousand. Cloth, 2s. 6d. Cloth gilt, gilt edges, 3s. 6d. Size 10½ by 8.

The Evangelisation of the World:
A RECORD OF CONSECRATION AND AN APPEAL.
By B. BROOMHALL.

"THIS is a most remarkable book. . . . . . It is one of the most powerful appeals for Foreign Missions issued in our time, and altogether perhaps the best handbook that exists for preachers and speakers in their behalf."—*The Church Missionary Intelligencer.*

"IT is one of the best books conceivable to put into the hands of young men and women. Its paragraphs are a history, a poem, a prophecy, all at once. Short, suggestive, on fire with God's Spirit."—DR. A. T. PIERSON, *of Philadelphia, in* "*The Missionary Review of the World.*"

"A NEW and enlarged edition has been issued of that wonderful collection of missionary literature, "The Evangelisation of the World," prepared and edited by Mr. Broomhall, of the China Inland Mission. It contains a new portrait of Rev. J. Hudson Taylor, and four additional portraits of well-known preachers, some of whose rousing words enrich its pages—Rev. C. H. Spurgeon, Rev. Dr. A. N. Somerville, Dean Vaughan, and Rev. W. Arthur. A new and more permanent preface is found in a strikingly coloured copy of the missionary diagram showing the proportion of Protestants and the adherents of other religious beliefs in comparison to the great mass of unevangelised heathen. We cannot too strongly commend this volume to those who do not possess a copy; if it were prayerfully perused and studied in the churches once every three months, the tide of missionary zeal would be kept at high-water mark."—*The Christian.*

"THAT God has blessed it, we know; that He will bless it, we are sure. It should be on every drawing-room table, be within reach in every clergyman's study, and be given as a present to every Christian young man."—*The Church Missionary Intelligencer (Notice of new edition).*

Cloth gilt, with Large Coloured Map, 2s. 6d. Paper Covers, 1s. Size 11 by 8¼.

China's Spiritual Need and Claims.
By REV. J. HUDSON TAYLOR, M.R.C.S., F.R.G.S.
WITH NUMEROUS ILLUSTRATIONS AND DIAGRAMS, CONSPECTUS OF PROTESTANT MISSIONS IN CHINA, ETC.

"THE array of facts and figures collated by Mr. Taylor, not to speak of the striking diagrams (which bring the vastness and spiritual destitution of China into strong relief) and the many artistic engravings illustrative of Chinese life and scenery, combine to make this a perfectly unique production."—*The Christian.*

"A MOST attractively got up and well-illustrated volume. But these are its least charms. The story of faith and work told in it should be read by every earnest Christian. It is a mine of wealth for the missionary speaker and deserves a prominent place in missionary literature."—*Wesleyan-Methodist Magazine.*

Cloth boards, price One Shilling.

Days of Blessing in Inland China.
BEING AN ACCOUNT OF MEETINGS HELD IN THE PROVINCE OF SHAN-SI.

With Addresses by Rev. J. HUDSON TAYLOR, Messrs. STANLEY SMITH, C. T. STUDD, BEAUCHAMP, ORR EWING, and others; also Testimonies of Native Pastors.

Price 1d.; by post, 1½d. 12 or more, carriage free.

Two Addresses by Rev. A. T. Pierson, D.D.,
ON THE EVANGELISATION OF THE WORLD.

These are the Addresses given at the Anniversary Meetings of the C.I.M. in May, 1890, reports of which appear in the present Volume of CHINA'S MILLIONS. They are reprinted in this convenient form for wide distribution.

Book form, cloth plain, 6d.; by post, 8d. Cloth gilt (on Linen), 1s.; by post, 1s. 2d.
On board, to hang, 1s.; by post, 1s. 4d.

Map of China, showing C.I.M. Stations.

A list of Missionaries and Stations of the C.I.M., uniform in size, with suggested list for daily prayer, accompanies each *book* map. It may be had separately at 1½d.; or, with small coloured map at 2½d.

LONDON: MORGAN & SCOTT, 12, PATERNOSTER BUILDINGS, E.C.
CHINA INLAND MISSION, 4, PYRLAND ROAD, LONDON, N.

The China Inland Mission.

Directors { J. HUDSON TAYLOR, 8, Pyrland Road, London, N.
{ THEODORE HOWARD, Westleigh, Bickley, Kent.

ROBERT SCOTT, *Treasurer.*   B. BROOMHALL, *Secretary.*   CHARLES T. FISHE, *Financial Secretary.*

Office of the Mission :—4, PYRLAND ROAD, MILDMAY, LONDON, N.

Honorary Auditors :—Messrs. ARTHUR J. HILL, VELLACOTT, & Co., 1, Finsbury Circus, London, E.C.

Bankers :—LONDON AND COUNTY BANK, Lombard Street, London.

All Donations to be addressed to the Secretary, at 4, PYRLAND ROAD, LONDON, N. Cheques and P.O. Orders (payable at G.P.O.) to be made payable to CHARLES T. FISHE, and crossed "London and County Bank." It is suggested that, for greater safety, Postal Orders should, when practicable, be used for small sums. Donors will greatly oblige by saying how they should be addressed, whether as Mrs., Miss, Rev., Esq., Mr., or otherwise.

In the case of a donation, or part of it, being intended as a contribution towards the support of a Missionary or native helper, or for any particular branch of the work, it is requested that this may be stated very clearly; and any sums of money sent for transmission to a Missionary, and not intended as a donation to the Mission towards the support of the receiver, should be *clearly indicated* as for *transmission* only.

WHY FORMED.—The China Inland Mission was formed in 1865, because of the overwhelming necessity for some further effort to spread the knowledge of the Gospel among the unevangelised millions of China, and with the definite and avowed purpose of commencing missionary labour in the interior provinces, eleven of which, with an aggregate population of about a hundred and fifty millions, were without a Protestant Missionary.

Deeply impressed by the spiritual destitution of China, which at that time had only ninety-seven Protestant Missionaries among its hundreds of millions of people, Mr. Hudson Taylor was led to attempt the formation of the China Inland Mission. Referring to this some ten years later, he said :—

"There was a little difficulty attending it. I was very anxious that what we did should not appear for a moment to conflict with the work of any older societies; and still more that it should not actually divert any help of any kind from channels already existing, because that would have been no gain to China or the cause of God; but that we should have such a method of working given to us as should draw out *fresh* labourers who, probably, would not go otherwise; and should open *fresh* channels of pecuniary aid which otherwise, perhaps, would not be touched."—*From Address delivered at Westminster Chapel, August 14th, 1876.*

ITS CHARACTER.—Like the British and Foreign Bible Society, and the Young Men's Christian Association, the China Inland Mission is Evangelical and unsectarian. This is clearly shown by the fact that duly qualified candidates for missionary labour are accepted without restriction as to denomination.

ITS AGENCY.—The present staff of the Mission numbers 397, viz.—Missionaries and their wives, 146; unmarried missionaries, 224; together with 27 associates. There are 144 native helpers whose whole time is given to Mission work, as Pastors, Evangelists, Colporteurs, Bible-women, etc.

Some of the Missionaries, having private property, have gone out at their own expense, and do not accept anything from the Mission funds. The others have gone out in dependence upon GOD for temporal supplies, with the clear understanding that the Mission does not guarantee any income whatever, and knowing that, as the Mission does not go into debt, it can only minister to those connected with it as the funds sent in from time to time may allow.

HOW SUPPORTED.—The Missionaries and Native Helpers are supported, and the rents and other expenses of mission premises, schools, etc., are met, by contributions sent to the offices of the Mission, without personal solicitation, by those who wish to aid in this effort to spread the knowledge of the Gospel throughout China. The income for 1889 was £35,881, with £2,414 for special purposes, and £4,000 for Superannuation Fund.

ITS PROGRESS.—Stations have been opened in *ten out of the eleven* provinces which were previously without Protestant Missionaries; from one of these, however, the Missionaries have had to retire, but continue itinerant work from over the border. The eleventh province has been visited several times, and it is hoped that in it permanent work may soon be begun.

More than a hundred and fifty stations and out-stations have been opened, in all of which there are either Missionaries or resident native labourers. Some four thousand converts have been baptized; and deaths, removals and discipline leave nearly three thousand now in fellowship.

CHINA'S PRESENT NEED.—China, at the present time, taken as a whole, has only one male Missionary to about half a million of its people; while some of its interior provinces have a still smaller supply.

"CHINA'S MILLIONS."—Reports of the work of the Mission, and much useful information concerning China, appear in "CHINA'S MILLIONS," published monthly by Messrs. Morgan and Scott, 12, Paternoster Buildings, London, price One Penny. It may be obtained through any Bookseller; or direct from the Offices of the China Inland Mission, post free, for one year, upon sending 1s. 6d. in postage stamps to the Secretary, 4, Pyrland Road, London, N.

Any further information desired will be gladly supplied upon application to the Secretary.

November 20th, 1890.

www.ingramcontent.com/pod-product-compliance
Lightning Source LLC
Chambersburg PA
CBHW032150160426
43197CB00008B/853